Concreteness and Specificity in Clinical Psychology

Luciano L'Abate

Concreteness and Specificity in Clinical Psychology

Evaluations and Interventions

Springer

Luciano L'Abate
Department of Psychology
Georgia State University
Atlanta
Georgia
USA

ISBN 978-3-319-13283-9 ISBN 978-3-319-13284-6 (eBook)
DOI 10.1007/978-3-319-13284-6

Library of Congress Control Number: 2015934144

Springer Cham Heidelberg New York Dordrecht London

Printed on acid-free paper

Springer is part of Springer Science+Business Media (www.springer.com)

To Sharon Panulla, Senior Psychology Editor at Springer-Science who has believed in my work for four decades and supported it no matter what.

Foreword

In 35 years of practicing psychotherapy in the private and public sectors, I have read countless books and attended many conferences addressing modalities in clinical psychology and psychotherapy. The book you are about to read is ground-breaking and provocative. It is written by an extraordinary author whose innovative thinking, clinical practice, and academic writing spans for more than four decades. Readers familiar with Dr. L'Abate's substantial international body of work will recognise the continued evolution of his observations and critiques on prevailing models of clinical practice in psychology and psychotherapy. As expected from L'Abate, the content of this book is controversial, thought provoking and beyond it's time.

In this book L'Abate observes that current clinical psychological and psychotherapeutic practices are predominantly based on "Talk" and that the outcomes rely largely on the nature of the relationship between patient and therapist. In this way, the therapeutic relationship is argued to be a tool in psychotherapy that is based on talk that is not replicable. This leads to what L'Abate calls the "Artisan" component of current psychotherapy as no "Talk" can be replicated exactly in the same way. Controversially, L'Abate's original research encourages clinical psychology and psychotherapy to break with the face-to face "Talk" approach in favor of more visible clinical practices based on distance writing that is internet based, overtly structured and founded on a scientific replicable approach.

Readers might initially feel shocked. How can clinical psychology and psychotherapy be conducted without face-to-face talk? L'Abate argues that psychological evaluations and interventions should consist of uniformly replicable standard operating procedures based on distant writing and that these procedures must be replicable within one professional, among professionals and, among different clinical venues. L'Abate's proposes that the process of psychological interventions should consist of assigning concern-targeted written homework assignments including interactive practice exercises thought work books with continuous and consistent feedback from the therapist and with repeated evaluations of progress from one series of exercises to another. In this way L'Abate argues that written standard operating procedures in pre and post evaluations and interventions provide homogeneity and uniformity. This, then leads to replicability of the written standard operating procedures, which in turn forms the basis for scientific validation of those observations and operations. L'Abate argues that this approach can be reliably used and replicated by any psychologist or psychotherapist.

Beyond these dynamics there is another, perhaps less obvious dimension to L'Abate's work: his approach reflects global concerns such as social justice, access and equity in mental health services. As social justice, access and equity become more predominant in twenty-first century living, peoples' judicious access to information and the use of web based technologies are increasingly relevant. L'Abate recognises these significant changes in day-to-day living and he incorporates them in to his therapeutic approach. Therefore, this book is not only about a ground breaking, visionary approach in psychotherapy: this book is also about global access and equitable mental health services. This book continues L'Abate's passion to provide the best possible mental health services to as many people as possible in a format that is measurable and replicable.

Arthur van Eigen
Psychotherapist/Psychologist
(Drs Psychotherapy, Reg. Psychologist, MAPS,
APSM, AARC, AHI, PBA, AHPRA), Darwin, NT. Australia

Foreword

The book includes evolutionary and revolutionary views about psychotherapy and what is needed to improve both research and clinical care. Two contexts might be used to frame the contributions of this book. First, advances in psychiatric epidemiology have revealed that mental illness is quite prevalent. In the US, for example, approximately 25% of the population at a given point in time meets criteria for a psychiatric disorder; the lifetime rate is approximately 50%. With this scope of dysfunction, our interventions are not reaching people very well. Approximately 70% of people in the US in need of psychological services receive no treatment at all. Second, it is not as if effective interventions are unavailable. Hundreds of psychosocial treatments with empirical support—over 330 by one government count in the US—are currently designated as evidence based. And yet, clinical practice does not routinely include these treatments. A major thrust of this book is that the very model of providing treatment—face-to-face in person therapy—might not have much impact even if it were evidence-based. Too few people have access to that model of care. Thus, the two contexts I have highlighted show an enormous need and yet a model of care not well suited to meet that need.

This book has a strong science base while at the same time elaborating strategies for clinical practice. Among the highlights of this book, Dr. L'Abate insists on evidence and systematic evaluation (assessment) as a basis for clinical practice. In addition, he draws heavily on theory and shows the interrelations of theory, evidence, and clinical practice. These features reflect clinical psychology at its best. Core psychological processes (e.g., learning, memory, perception, cognitive representation, decision making, social interaction and support) are discussed in relation to clinical dysfunction and treatment. We want to draw on the rich literature at our scientific base and translate these in concrete ways to improve patient care. This book is a model in that regard. Dr. L'Abate's own work and thinking have been guided by theory and models of how to proceed to conceptualize the enterprise of providing effective interventions—what treatments and how to deliver them.

Although the book encompasses theory and basic research, these are not at the expense of concrete clinical guidelines. Specific treatments (e.g., self-help, online treatment, writing-based therapies) are carefully detailed. Concrete guidelines encompass practice exercises, assessment methods for determining the clinical focus, and workbook materials. The unique coverage and format would make the book quite useful for a course in training therapists.

Clinical practice, whether from psychology, psychiatry, social work, and counseling, has been slow to change. Talk therapy and non-evidence based interventions appear to be the default treatment for those seeking and obtaining individual patient care. This book discusses reasons for inertia (e.g., professional associations, regulatory boards) and why we are moving so slowly to draw on the evidence in providing clinical care. Dr. L'Abate argues that we can do better in light of what we currently know. Not only is their evidence in behalf of treatments he proposes, he also notes many have other benefits such as increased accessibility and lower costs.

Dr. L'Abate is an innovative thinker and pioneer. He has taken the less traveled path toward writing about theory, the nature of psychological dysfunction, and clinical care. His writings, including this book but other books as well, extend the boundaries of current thinking and in ways that have direct and immediate implications. The book is a strong, needed, and well-supported statement and reflects a remarkable career that at once has advanced science and practice and has caused us to think about inertias that impede helping people more than we currently do. It is difficult to imagine any professional who has contributed more significantly to making the case for novel ways of providing services than has Dr. L'Abate. His work might be called provocative—but it could also be called caring. Services are not reaching people who are suffering. Can anything be done to help? Many of his books have exactly addressed this question. What more could one ask from a book or career?

Alan E. Kazdin, PhD., ABPP
John M. Musser of Psychology and Child Psychiatry
Yale University
New Haven, Connecticut
October 2014

Preface

The thesis of this proposal is that, as long as talk remains the major if not the sole medium of healing in clinical psychology practices, there cannot be any improvement in these practices because talk is not a replicable medium (L'Abate 1999, 2008a). Particularly, instead of face-to-face (F2F) talk, programmed distance writing, as in interactive practice exercises (PIPEs), or workbooks, will take its place. PIPEs are published in print and can be replicable ad infinitum as homework assignments (L'Abate 2011c, 2013b, 2013d).

To be replicable these clinical practices ideally should be determined by theory. One purpose of a theory is to make evident and integrate behaviors that heretofore were hidden and unintegrated from professional and scientific awareness or knowledge (L'Abate 2005). One purpose of clinical practice is to improve behaviors that heretofore have been refractory to change. The best outcome occurs when practice, consisting of homogeneously written, concrete and specific homework assignments, as administered by professionals or semiprofessionals at a distance from participants, derives from a validated theory (Smyth and L'Abate 2001).

Therefore, this proposal argues that for progress to occur in clinical psychology practices, evaluations and interventions, including especially psychotherapy, three requirements will need to be fulfilled: (1) abandonment of face-to-face (F2F), talk-based (TB) practices in favor of increasing reliance on homogeneity and uniformity of written Standard Operating Procedures (SOPs) in evaluations and interventions; (2) replicability of those SOPs; and (3) validation of those observations and operations in the laboratory, clinic, and office, online and offline (L'Abate, in press; L'Abate and Sweeney 2011).

The thesis of this proposal, therefore, consists of beliefs held about evaluations and interventions in clinical psychology and psychotherapy: beliefs that the best expression of caring for our participants is a responsible professional practice. Responsible professional practice consists of evaluating participants' concerns from the very outset in an objectively systematic manner, even before seeing participants. That evaluation should allow to set baselines to evaluate the nature (type, severity, frequency, duration, and context) of the referring concern and whether any progress has occurred with possibly targeted interventions through post-intervention reevaluations and follow-ups.

Psychological evaluations and interventions should consist of uniformly replicable SOPs based on distance writing online and offline. These procedures must be replicable within one professional, among professionals, and among different clinical venues. The process of psychological interventions should consist of assigning concern-targeted written homework assignments including interactive practice exercises, that is, work-books, with continuous and consistent feedback from the professional with repeated evaluations of progress from one series of exercises to another (L'Abate 2011c, 2013b).

To support those beliefs, one would argue that to progress in clinical psychology practices, such as sickness prevention, health promotion, crisis intervention, psychotherapy, and rehabilitation, one needs to follow replicable, uniformly targeted, homogeneously written, SOPs in evaluations and interventions. Without this requirement, many clinical psychologists will continue to rely on F2F, TB personal contacts derived from immediate creativity, arbitrary and capricious whims and wills, "intuition-driven," artistic practices, without pre- and post-evaluation and follow-up. These practices, even though helpful, are not cumulative and do not add to intersubjective information and knowledge. Those artistic practices do no permit replication, comparability, and accumulation of information for the common good of clinical psychology professionals and of their participants. Without replicability the fields of clinical psychology and mental health are destined to continue to produce chaotic Towers of Babel in theory and in practice (Gaudano 2013; L'Abate 2005, 2013b; Lilienfeld 2010, 2012; Resenski 2013).

To reach the level of a profession, clinical psychology practitioners will have to abandon artistic practices, without any evidence of positive outcome in each case, for pre–post-intervention evaluation and follow-up to demonstrate improvement or lack thereof for every single case they treat, whether individuals, couples, or families. Distance or remote writing is replicable provided it is administered in a structured rather then unstructured manner, as seen in expressive and programmed writing. It is even more important to link theory with practice by having concrete and specific practices in programmed, interactive practice exercises and prescriptions using distance writing that flow directly from models of a theory, such as *Relational Competence Theory*.

This last and final proposal is the natural outcome of decades of work in prevention (L'Abate 1986, 1990), health promotion (L'Abate 2007c), homework assignments (Kazantzis and L'Abate 2007), self-help (Harwood and L'Abate 2010), technology in mental health (L'Abate and Kaiser 2012) supporting the use of structured, programmed distance or remote writing instead of unstructured and uncontrolled F2F talk according to the laboratory method in clinical psychology (Hooper et al. 2014; L'Abate 1991, 1992, 2001a, 2002, 2004a, 2004b, 2004c, 2004d, 2004e, 2008c, 2011b, 2013b, 2013c, in press).

Decades of work in clinical psychology practices occurred in parallel with theory-construction and testing (Cusinato and L'Abate 2012a; L'Abate 1976, 1986, 1994, 1997b, 2005, 2013a; L'Abate et al. 2010). Both practical and theoretical aspects of this decades-long enterprise come together in most chapters of this proposal.

Chapter 1 explains the rationale with historical and research background for using concreteness and specificity in clinical psychology practices, both in evaluations and interventions. Chapter 2 continues to support online over offline evaluations and interventions where major issues are structure and costs. Chapter 3 argues that verifiability and accountability are the earmarks of a scientific profession. Without these two requirements, clinical psychology practices, especially in interventions, will continue to be non-replicable, and therefore, noncumulative, leading to profiously confusing artistic practices that cannot demonstrate their usefulness beyond the opinion of practitioners. Chapter 4 shows how evaluations are divided into those for individual personalities versus those for couples and families, continuing to propagate theoretical and practical divisions and fragmentations. An unifying Relational Competence Theory (RCT) evaluated with relational test instruments could provide a way to evaluate relationally both individuals as well couples and families. Chapter 5 aims at demonstrating how clinical psychological practices are still occurring without an overarching theory that would connect theory with practice illustrating how unstructured clinical psychology practices, both online and offline, will continue to proliferate without any regard to their replicability and evaluation of their usefulness. Chapter 6 aims at introducing a general, overarching framework to clarify four basic theoretical constructs: paradigms, theories, models, and dimensions. Chapter 7 demonstrates how RCT can cover a vast range of behaviors with accompanying replicable PIPEs. Chapter 8 presents how RCT can link research with evaluations and interventions through replicably written, structured distance interactive practice exercises PIPEs contained in the Appendices of this volume. Conclusive Chapter 9 deals with how theory and programmed distance writing imply changes in training and practices.

Readership

Preferably, this proposal should go in the hands (and eyes) of graduate students in clinical psychology and the mental health professions, including psychiatry, counseling, pastoral counseling, and social work. However, this potential audience will not be able to lay its eyes and hands on it unless their teachers become acquainted with it first and endorse it as textbook second.

Acknowledgment

I am very grateful to the following co-workers and friends: Karen Viars, over the years, has continued to do all the spade, technical work of helping find relevant references, and where necessary, helpful summaries. Flyah Roots has continued to help me with all the many formatting problems encountered during the writing of this volume, well above and beyond my limited technical expertise. Arthur von Eigen and Alan Kazdin have supported my work in spite of its being outside the mainstream of psycho-logical theorizing and practices. Laura G. Sweeney has been an important source of support before, during, and after the writing of the manuscript and a trusted friend and excellent collaborator over different publications for the last few years. Grace Ratliff worked side-by-side to help me translate the original (1987) verbally-administered enrichment programs into computer-administered Programmed Interactive Practice Exercises (PIPEs).

Contents

Chapter 1
Definitions of Terms

> A conception not reducible to the small change of daily experience is like a currency not exchangeable for articles of consumption; it is not a symbol, but a fraud. (George Santayana)

> …intellectual abstraction serves to distance the individual from events or objects. (Lewis 2014, p. 115)

The purpose of this chapter is to define the two major terms proffered in the title of this proposal and to expand in greater detail on an integrative model in its clinical and practical implications (Fig. 1.1), already presented in previous publications (L'Abate 2013a, b, d). For instance, VandenBos (2007) covered multiple definitions about abstract attitude, abstract intelligence, abstract conceptualization, abstract impresssionism, abstract idea, abstract intelligence, abstraction, abstraction experiment, abstract learning, abstract representation, and finally abstract thinking characterized by the use of abstraction and generalization. Abstraction means the formation of general ideas or concepts, such as "fish" or "hypocrisy" from particular instances. The precise cognitive processes by which this [process] occurs have been subjected to many investigations. Abstraction would also mean an intangible concept, such as "goodness" or "beauty." (p. 4).

VandenBos (2007) also covered many definitions about concrete images, concrete intelligence, concrete operations, concrete operational stage, concrete picture, and more specifically concrete thinking that:

> …focuses on an immediate experience on a specific object. It is characteristics of young children and may also be seen in people with schizophrenia and people who suffered a brain disorder, especially front lobe damage. (p. 212)

General thinking applies to a basic ability that underlies the performance of different varieties of intellectual tasks, in contrast to specific abilities that are alleged to be unique to a single task (VandenBos 2007, p. 403). Global intelligence is composed by verbal abilities and non-verbal performance tasks as measured, and synonymous for general intelligence (VandenBos 2007, p. 411). Closer to the focus of this volume, global perception means looking at the totality of an event or a situation rather than its parts, i.e., the forest rather than the trees. Specificity means the quality of being unique, of a particular kind, or limited to a single phenomenon, and in this case a single intervention, the tree in the forest (VandenBos 2007, p. 880). What

L. L'Abate, *Concreteness and Specificity in Clinical Psychology*,
DOI 10.1007/978-3-319-13284-6_1

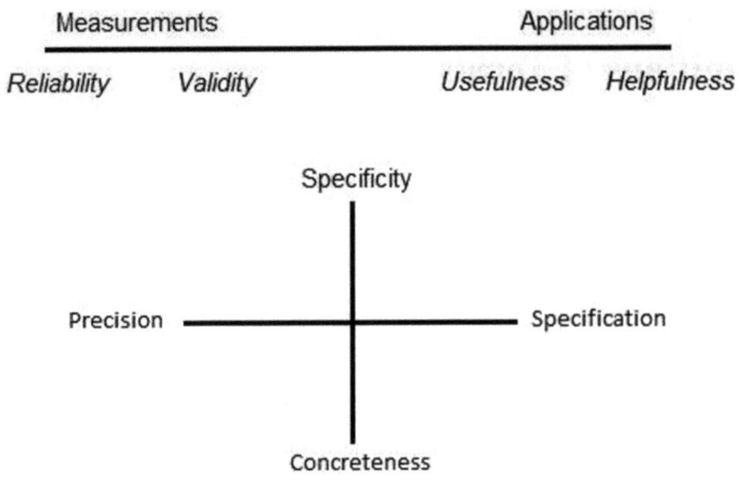

Fig. 1.1 Requirements for a science of clinical psychology and psychotherapy

started me thinking about specificity was the contribution of Ceccarelli (1996) that was expanded upon in previous writings (L'Abate 2008b, 2013d).

A Model for a Science of Clinical Psychology

The introductory Fig. 1.1 contains the larger conceptual context for concreteness and specificity. There is no need to explain already established, well-known criteria such as reliability and validity, while usefulness and helpfulness were already differentiated in previous writings as an act or object that may be momentarily useful but its becoming helpful depends on the long-range outcome of that act or an object's usefulness (L'Abate 2013b). Therefore, the purpose of this proposal is to expand on the vertical axis of Fig. 1.1 after clarifying that precision deals with numbers, such as an intelligence quotient (IQ) score or multiple scores on a test profile. Specification represents the qualification or explanation of the clinical and diagnostic meaning and nature of and IQ score or personality profile (L'Abate 2013a, b, d). Both horizontal and vertical axes, therefore, deal with evaluation even though the vertical axis deals more specifically with interventions.

Concreteness on the bottom of the vertical axis represents the developmental dimension over the whole life span, from childhood to seniority, the level at which participants are presently functioning or dysfunctioning, including psychiatric diagnoses or other objective criteria of functionality or dysfunctionality. Concreteness varies with age, physical status, educational, and socioeconomic level, presence or absence of dysfunctionality, including the presence or absence of a psychiatric diagnosis or physical illness.

Specificity at the top of the vertical axis applies to interventions designed particularly for an identified age group, concern, or diagnostic dimensions included above in the range and types of concreteness. The more specific the intervention, the easier it will be to replicate it. Generality cannot be replicated because, by its very nature, it is nonspecific. Specificity is achieved by performing uniform, standard operating procedures (SOPs) that by their very nature are replicable to match the level and type of concreteness. Without replicability, there is no way to check on the validity of any psychological evaluation or intervention (L'Abate 2004a, 2005, 2008c, 2013b, d).

Concreteness has already been introduced and considered within the context of seven psychological constructs (i.e., "orphans") in search of a theory (L'Abate 2013b, pp. 131–147). Constructs such as field dependence–independence and locus of control, for instance, reached an extreme level of professional and scientific interest a few decades ago, except to wane because of no connections to and with a larger theoretical framework. That is why they were called "orphans." On the other hand, there are various theoretical and empirical orphan constructs that were "rescued" or "recruited" by inclusion, assimilation, and support within the larger conceptual framework of randomized controlled trial (RCT; L'Abate et al. 2010; Cusinato and L'Abate 2012).

Constructs such as creativity, dependency, intimacy, happiness, positivity, subjective well-being, reactivity, self-esteem, and trust can be and are encompassed within and connected with specific models of RCT. In the case of ubiquitous, nonrelational "self-esteem," for instance, its relational counterpart, attribution, and bestowal of importance to self and intimate others, is linked to specific empirical evidence and to specific homework assignments, as expanded upon in Chap. 7 of this volume (L'Abate 2013b, pp. 138–147).

Specificity in interventions must be applied to a stepped-care model of evaluation, self-help, prevention, crisis intervention and psychotherapy, medication, hospitalization, or incarceration (L'Abate 2013b, p. 123; L'Abate 2013d; O'Donohue and Draper 2011). Additionally, progressively specific stages were included in psychotherapy (p. 124), writing therapy (p. 125), and an experimental, programmed, diagnostic–interventional homework assignments for couples (pp. 126–129).

A section devoted to specificity concluded that (L'Abate 2013b):

> The failure of the clinical psychology and psychotherapy professions to develop criteria and standards too designate, identify, and specify which disorder should receive which treatment, makes it mandatory to evaluate in vivo who will benefit by which approach following a stepped-care sequence. Perhaps, through stepped-care as a standard-operating procedure and programmed distance writing, we will be able to eventually identify who will be helped by which approach and at what cost. By the same token, a programmed [targeted] distance writing interactive approach using workbooks will allow such a match provided an objective evaluation is performed before intervening. (p. 129)

Further expansion of this model (see Fig. 1.1) will be presented in Chap. 6 of this volume. An impediment to progress in clinical psychology practices has been the search for matching psychotherapy with "persons" rather than with concrete and specific reasons for referrals, whatever concerns, issues, or symptoms brings people to seek psychological help (Norcross and Wampold 2011). That search leads to an impossible theoretical and practical outcome. We cannot match psychological treatments with people, no matter how successful such an approach may be (Norcross 2014). We can only match them with concrete and specific reasons for referral. Here is where both criteria of concreteness and specificity come into being. "Persons" or "people" are abstractions that cannot be treated in spite of the humanistic emphasis to do just that. Those abstract, generic persons or people suffer by concrete and specific reasons for seeking help. These persons or people are not interested in abstract generalities related indirectly to them. They want direct relief from pains and hurts, whatever hails them in the present.

If this approach means following the medical model (John Norcross, personal communication, July 25, 2014), so be it. Given one reason for referral, there are a finite number of targeted, programmed approaches that can match evaluation with treatment (L'Abate 1986, 1992, 2004a, b, c) to the point that psychotherapy and psychological interventions should consist of homework assignments based on the reason for referral, not the "whole person."

Two Different Origins: Same Conclusion

It is only by accident that I became aware of Michael D. Yapko's (2013) consistent insistence on using concreteness and specificity in psychotherapy, while perusing the program of the 2013 Evolution of Psychotherapy. After considering the importance of two dimensions of abstract–concrete and general–specific in theory construction, the two extremes of both dimensions, concreteness and specificity, were proffered as necessary to communicate and perhaps help in clinical psychological practices (L'Abate 2004a, b, d, 2009b, d, 2012, 2013a, b, d).

Independently from that trend, Yapko (2013) derived the very same requirements for psychotherapy. Arguing that global or overgeneral processes are at the base of disordered thinking, in his summary Yapko highlighted the importance of using concrete and specific skills "in making distinctions that lead to improved decisions and subsequently, better mental health." Yapko has emphasized that globality and overgenerality in thinking are present in psychopathology: "Global thinking is highly correlated with depression as well as PTSD." It was this source that energized this writer to expand on these two criteria and eventually write this proposal.

Let us consider in greater detail Yapko's distinguished contribution to the self-help literature before dealing with the origins of these two terms from the viewpoint of philosophy of science supported with relevant research and more recent contributions.

Clinical Experience

Yapko (1988, 1994, 1997, 1999a, b, 2009) has consistently focused on depression in its multifarious manifestations through an exhortatory style that was defined (L'Abate 2004a, p. 5) as: "if you learn this skill, you will be okay." His many contributions to explain depression to the general public form a wide-ranging encyclopedia second to none in the field. His self-help books contain very specific instructions on how to deal with depression in individuals as well as in children and families with administration of an incredible, really unbelievable, number of what I would call homework assignments based mostly on writing. For instance, in his earliest contribution (Yapko 1988), he provided uniquely concrete 91 "directives" to treat depression, ranging from "reframing from useless to useful" to "riversing roles." In another contribution (Yapko 1997), he provided the reader ("you") with 49 "pause and reflect" exercises and 73 "learn by doing" exercises plus 8 audiotapes ranging from self-hypnosis to "integrate preventive learnings."

More recently, Yapko (2009) has continued the same exhortatory style by providing the reader three "pause and reflect" and three "learn by doing" for each of nine chapters (except for the last chapter where only two learning by doing exercises were included). Multiply 6×9 and see how many exercises one gets. Furthermore, he provided (Appendix B) self-help materials to focus on feeling good in depression and for managing anxiety.

What is eventually more relevant to the topic presented in this section is how Yapko (2009, p. 125) dealt with "global thinking":

> Global thinking leads you to form overgeneralizations, beliefs and statements that are so broad in scope that they are overinclusive. If you find yourself using words such as "all" (as in "all men are bad news"), "never" (as in "you never think about anyone but yourself"), and "always" (as in "you always criticize me"), that's a good clue that you're engaging in global thinking in that moment. It helps counter global thinking to look for exceptions. Are there some times when your perceptions isn't true? If you get hurt in a relationship and conclude that "people can't be trusted," you're over-generalizing incorrectly because some people can be trusted. Global thinking also leads people to have poorly defined goals ("I just want to be married"), inadequate information before they make important decision ("Gee, how can this home loan be so cheap? Let's grab it!"), and a marked tendency toward overreacting to things ("My son doesn't like sports! Where did I go wrong?").

In another expansion about the dangers of global thinking in marriage, Yapko (2009, pp. 165–167) introduced one particular skill called "compartimentalization." He defined this skill as the "ability to set aside different compartments of some larger entity," as if they're in their own individual compartments separated by imaginary walls: what VandenBos (2007) called looking at the trees rather than the forest:

> The more global someone is in her style of thought the less able she will be to compartmentalize. If you can only see the forest and not the trees, compartmentalization isn't going to happen. If you habitually see only a global "all" or "none, " "perfect" or "lousy, and lose sight of the "gray" in between the black and white, then your very style of thought has most likely worked against you in relationships. It doesn't mean you're an "loser" or that "no one will ever love you" or that you must have some "unconscious fear of intimacy." (p. 167)

Essentially, Yapko dealt with what could be called "dichotomous thinking" as found also in cognitive distortions and errors emphasized by cognitive behavior therapy (Boyd-Franklin et al. 2013, pp. 132–134), such as: (1) all-or-none thinking; (2) catastrophizing; (3) disqualifying or discounting positives, emphasizing negatives; (4) labeling globally; and (5) mind reading.

Nonetheless, in spite of its many, undoubtedly creative condensations of Yapko's arguments into concrete and specific directives, it is indeed unfortunate that the nature of self-help books does not require writers to collect and evaluate participants' written homework assignments. Therefore, there is no way of knowing how and how many readers completed those assignments, and there is no way of finding how helpful those assignments were. One cannot help wonder why representative examples of completed homework were not included in those texts. Consequently, it is impossible to judge whether any possibly immediate and long-term outcomes were obtained either anecdotally or, heaven forefend, quantitatively.

Putting together all the incredible number of directives—pause and reflect—and learn by doing—available in all the three sources (Yapko 1988, 1997, 2009) would constitute a considerable contribution to the process and outcome of psychotherapy, especially if they were classified and administered online and offline to participants as interactive practice exercises for homework based on distance or remote writing, with a minimum of talk, as done for the last two decades (L'Abate 1977, 1991, 1992, 1996, 1997a, 1999, 2001a, 2002, 2004b, 2011b, 2013b, c; L'Abate et al. 1992, 2005; Hooper et al. 2014; Smyth and L'Abate 2001).

Consequently, both Yapko and I agree on the importance of written homework assignments, but we differ on the need to evaluate their therapeutic outcome. In spite of this difference, let us see how I arrived to the same conclusion about concreteness and specificity through a completely different intellectual origin than Yapko's clinical route.

Philosophy of Science

Even though I do not consider myself a philosopher of science, this field has been one of my interests—if not a hobby—since being introduced to that field as a minor during my graduate training (Kuhn 1970; L'Abate 2009f, 2012f, 2013a; L'Abate and Sweeney 2012; O'Donahue 2013; Rychlack 1969). One writer who had an enormous influence on my thinking and even practice was Alfred Korzybski (1949). Even though outside the mainstream of philosophers of science at the time, the 1950s and 1960s, nonetheless he was responsible for creating the field of general semantics. He influenced various thinkers on the borderline field between philosophy of science and what could be called applied philosophy of science for mature readers (Rapaport 1969).

Korzybski will be quoted as much as possible to show how ahead of his times his thinking was, lest he is forgotten and disappears from the relevant history. For instance, in regard to dichotomous thinking, this is what he wrote:

> In living, many issues are not so sharp, and therefore a system which posits the general sharpness of 'either-or' and so objectifies 'kind", is unduly limited; it must be revised and made more flexible in terms of 'degree'. This requires a physico-mathematical 'way of thinking' which a non-Aristotelian system supplies. (p. vii)

He insisted that "For maximum adjustment, and therefore sanity, needed neurological methods are to prevent and counteract these heretofore unavoidable old deceptions and self-deceptions" (p. xxi). He compared the old Aristotelian orientation to the new semantic non-Aristotelian orientation based on relational method and dynamic, ever-changing electronic orientation and dynamic relativism among many other comparisons (pp. xxv–xxvii). He emphasized the importance of the structure of language that up to his time was built on "fictitious animistic world" (p. xxxv). However, "for a revision of a system we must first get outside of the system" (p. xxxvii). Ahead of his time, Korzybski defined: "A system, in the present sense, represents a complex whole of co-ordinated doctrines resulting in methodological rules and principles of procedures which affect the orientation by which we act and live" (p. xiii). A theory, for instance, could be conceived as a system in its very structured nature.

His most important contribution consisted of insisting that "a word is not the object spoken about" (p. 10) or even more widely: "maps are not the actual territory," (p. 61), leading to a critical analysis of terminology and meaning as a "multiordinal term" (p. 22). His solution consisted of emphasizing mathematical thinking to measure objects and events. This thinking was applied to an arithmetical model of relational interactions (Cusinato and L'Abate 2012; L'Abate et al. 2010, pp. 153–161) recently validated by Colesso et al. (2013), and is reviewed in Chap. 7 of this volume.

In addition to the influence of early general systems thinking, that neglected Korzybski entirely, we now reach a crucial point, that let me to construct RCT according to a hierarchical structure (L'Abate, 2013a):

> Any student of science, or of the history of science, can hardly miss two very important tendencies which pervade the work of those who have accomplished most in this field. The first tendency is to base science more and more on experiments; the other is toward greater and more critical verbal rigour (p. 55)...any statement referring to anything objective in this world can always be analyzed into terms of relations and structure to know anything we must search for structure, or posit some structure (p. 63)...the main issues are found in the structure of language (p. 64).... Multi-ordinality is inherent in the structure of 'human knowledge (p. 74).... I accept relations, structure, and order as fundamental. (Korzybski p. 93)

After devoting whole chapters on function with a critical analysis of Freudian theory, and order with a critical analysis of structure, including evolution, Korzybski emphasized the importance of the cortex as having "a profound influence upon other parts of the brain" (p. 178).

What has been written thus far is just a brief and very abridged summary of Korzybski's thinking that eventually leads one to the relevant topic of abstraction (Chap. XXIV, pp. 371–385). His chapter on this topic starts with a quote by A. N. Whitehead (1936):

> ...to be an abstraction does not mean that an entity is nothing. It merely means that its existence is only one factor of a more concrete element of nature. (p. 5)

Korzybski followed up on such comment by attributing concreteness as being evolutionarily present in the past:

> When our primitive ancestors were building their language, quite naturally they started with the lowest orders of abstractions, which are the most imme-diatelly connected with the outside world (p. 372).....Again the organism works as a whole. All forms of human activities are interconnected. It is impossible to select a special characteristic and treat it in a delusional [elementary] 'isolation' as the most important. Science becomes an extra-neural extension of the human nervous system. (p. 377)

Even more specifically, Korzybski devoted two whole chapters "On Consciousness and Consciousness of Abstracting" (pp. 412–425) and higher-order abstractions (pp. 426–451). This differentiation about consciousness and consciousness of abstracting—which we would call awareness—predates theoretically what Cusinato (2012a, d) found after 10 years of research—that there are at least two type of awareness: awareness of awareness and awareness as a correcting recursive loop over emotionality, rationality, and activity. According to Korzybski:

> We can now define 'consciousness of abstracting' as awareness that in our process of abstracting we have left out characteristics as 'remembering that some characteristics have been left out (p. 417).... a well-adjusted, and, therefore, well-balanced individual should be neither of the extremes [in thinking and talking] but a balanced extroverted introvert" (p. 425)....I must stress once more the importance of the structure of language in which we analyze any given problem. (p. 449)

Korzybski's emphasis on abstractions leads one to conclude that the best solution to avoid abstractions is to approach the extreme of concreteness. Consequently, to reach a systematic understanding of how concreteness and specificity interact, we must include a model (Fig. 1.2) that views both continua of abstraction and generality orthogonally with their respective extremes of concreteness and specificity to distinguish among paradigms, theories, models, and dimensions, as discussed in greater detail in Chap. 6 of this volume. This model allows us to clarify systematically the relationships among the most basic four concepts in theory construction: paradigms, theories, models, and dimensions (L'Abate 2009f, 2012e; L'Abate and Sweeney 2012).

A few years ago (L'Abate 2009f), I criticized the standardly misguided, uncritically confusing equations of matching paradigms with theories or with models by distinguishing clearly among paradigms, as a way to view reality and theories as conceptual inventions or "speculative frameworks" that lend themselves to empirical evaluation through models. Models are defined by dimensions subjectable to empirical evaluation and verification. Models are considered the building blocks, the irreducible components of a theory. They are abstract summaries of more complex relationships. They represent the theory and include a few basic, directly observable dimensions classified according to their: (1) *discreteness,* such as roles; (2) *dimensionality,* from one to more dimensions; and (3) *directionality,* such as observational, mechanical, and measurable. Indirect models are those instruments

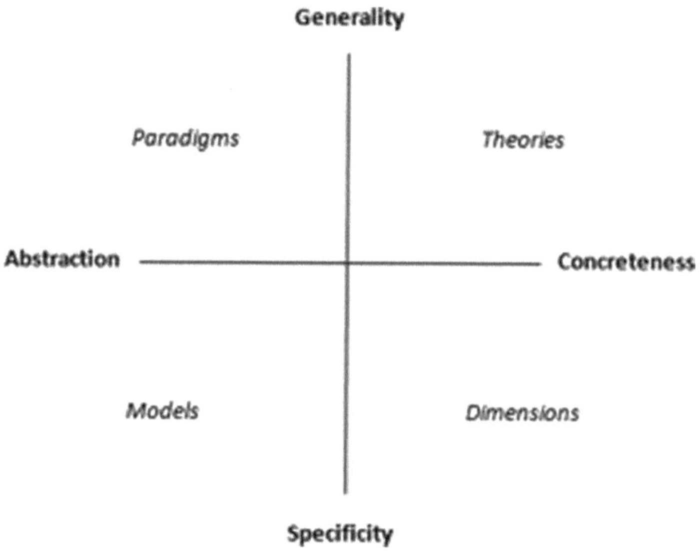

Fig. 1.2 Relationships among paradigms, theories, models, and dimensions according to two orthogonal continua of abstraction–concreteness and generality and specificity

measuring constructs or variables based on paper-and-pencil self-report questionnaires, as in intimacy, among others (L'Abate 2009f, 2012e).

In the same source, I presented a hierarchical framework to classify paradigms according to two major categories of metatheoretical versus operational paradigms (L'Abate 2009f, pp. 110–117, 2012c, d, e, 2013a). Metatheoretical paradigms were divided into general integrative, such as the biopsychosocial, ecological, interbehavioral, life span, and systems, and particular specific, such as behaviorism, cognitivism, contextualism, empiricism, existentialism, and rationalism. Operational paradigms were reductionism, emergent interactionism, spontaneous emergent interactionism, and synthetic integration. This classification was expanded in a more detailed exposition of paradigms (L'Abate 2013a).

Theories were classified (after Harkness 2007) into informal linear that would include intrapsychic, nonrelational personality theories, and interpersonal relational theories, such as attachment, versus formal hierarchical, such as relational competence theory (L'Abate et al. 2010; Cusinato and L'Abate 2012; L'Abate 2012a).

Eventually, L'Abate and Sweeney (2012, pp. 438–439) concluded that the two major continua that allow to distinguish among paradigms, theories, models, and dimensions were abstraction–concreteness and generality–specificity. Once these two continua were set orthogonally, Fig. 1.2 resulted. This figure could also be viewed as a hierarchy, with paradigms on top, theories second, models third, and dimensions fourth.

Furthermore, to achieve a greater degree of differentiation among these four major constructs, with the help of Walter Colesso, Mario Cusinato, and Eleonora Maino, as explained in greater detail in Chap. 6 of this volume, we expanded on requirements for paradigms, such as: (1) *comprehensiveness,* to the point that a paradigm should be as inclusive of as many relationships as possible, both intimate or communal (close, committed, interdependent, and lasting) as well as nonintimate or agentic relationships as in business transactions (possibly interdependent but not close, not committed, and not lasting; (2) *longevity,* as is the case of many paradigms (L'Abate 2012f).

Four requirements should be demanded of a psychological theory, and they are: (1) *relationality* emphasizing the importance of relationships rather than hypothetical and inferred internal states or traits; (2) *integrativity* representing the ability to put together disparate models into greater wholes; (3) *dismantability* means that components or parts of a theory can and should be evaluated empirically piecemeal, one by one; and (4) *productivity* represents that ability to create new instruments and research deriving from the theory.

The number of requirements for models increases to the point that they would help differentiate them from paradigms and theories: (1) *interrelatedness* among models, they need to "get along" with each other through correlations; (2) *applicability* to as many functional and dysfunctional relationships in individuals, couples, and families; and (3) *redundancy* applies especially to multidimensional constructs that cannot fit into a single model of the theory but that can be described by various models, such as love or control, as well as functionality and dysfunctionality. The two major requirements for a dimension lie in their being verifiable and measurable, to the extent that they vary in quality and quantity. (See Chap. 6 of this volume where these arguments will be replicated within a different conceptual context.)

An Example of Abstraction and Generality

In an exemplary inaugural editorial statement, Anchin et al. (2012) gave a shining illustration of combining abstraction with generality. Only the summary will be cited without copious references the authors may have used to buttress their proposal:

> We are pleased to offer the inaugural edition of this new journal. As elaborated in greater detail in the articles composing this first issue of the Journal of Unified Psychotherapy and Clinical Science (JUPCS), at a certain level of metaphorically speaking—visual resolution. We are witnessing the emergence of a major new phase of advancement in psychotherapy and in the clinical sciences more broadly. A shared theme coursing through diverse and developing realms of scientific and clinical research and activity is recognition of the multidimensional complexities of human development, functioning, dysfunction, and change. These views, reflective of a more holistic framework, move beyond the single domain perspective that dominated 20th century clinical science and together they suggest that, as our own field progresses through the first quarter of the 21st century, a shift in the intellectual zeitgeist toward unification is in the air. We believe that there is a need for this journal which will hopefully influence the development of clinical science from the pre-paradigmatic efforts of the last century to a truly unified clinical science from which unified psychotherapy will emerge. (p. 1)

First of all, given the high levels of abstraction and generality used in this summary, it remains completely unverified and unverifiable because it is based on talk as a medium of help and healing. Talk is not a replicable medium. Science is not based on talk. It is based on verifiable constructs in the laboratory and in the clinic. How is psychotherapy unified? By abstract and generic rhetoric or by actual operations? If there is a unified and unifying process, there will be empiricism and reliance on replicable operations rather than on empty, vague, and nondefinable constructs.

Second, how are the assumptions of this summary translatable into verifiable actions/practices? Put another way, how can one go back from practices to assumptions if the assumptions are so abstract that no connection between theory and practice can be made empirically? How does one go from multidimensional holism, for instance, to research in the laboratory or practices in the clinic?

Third, how can this summary be evaluated in its outcome? Through words or through pre–post, objective baseline evaluation and follow-up? What is this claimed emergence related to and what does it lead to in theory construction and clinical applications? (L'Abate 2011a)

Fourth, whatever proposal one makes, it must demonstrate that it is "better," i.e., more effective and more efficient than another proposal. No comparison is possible under these circumstances. How can abstractions and generalities be compared to what? Other abstractions and generalities? Discourse would remain at the rhetorical level leading to another confusing Tower of Babel. Therefore, no conceptual or even practical progress would be possible.

Fifth, the field of psychotherapy is chock-full of proposals, but ultimately the one that will survive will be the one that shows: (1) lesser costs, (2) more effective outcome, (3) complete replicability, and (4) competitive advantage over rival proposals. The summary proposal by Anchin et al. (2012) fails on all four counts.

Another egregious example of abstractions is found in Patterson and Sexton's attempt (2013) to integrate various conceptual frameworks through a "systemic heuristic" for understanding family diversity. While acknowledging new emerging family forms, these writers rely on shop-warned, magical "systems concepts" as if this ideology would solve all the problems faced by the American family. Basing their thesis on nonreplicable evidence-based intervention programs, relying mainly on face-to-face (F2F) talk, solution is found in vague, abstract, and generic "systems thinking" already reviewed and criticized as belonging to the last century. "Systems" is not an operational construct that can be reduced to concrete and specific operations (L'Abate 2013a). This argument is expanded upon in Chap. 3 of this volume.

Research to Support Concreteness and Specificity

A great deal of research supports the use of concreteness in clinical psychology and especially psychotherapy. Even though this research is highly technical, its major findings tend to support the use of concreteness over abstraction and of specificity over generality. For instance, in a pioneer study, 329 nouns from a frequency list were rated on a 7-point scale for concreteness, specificity, and pronunciability by 3 different groups of participants (Spreen and Schultz 1966). A fourth group was used to scale words by a 30-s production method. Means for each word were presented. The interrelationships among all parameters and the second-order partial correlations between M, C, S, and number of letters were discussed.

Associative reaction time (RT) data were obtained for 96 stimulus words, which varied in judged abstractness–concreteness and generality–specificity, under either a verbal associative set or a set to respond when a sensory image occurred to a word (Paivio 1966). Results indicated that RTS were faster under the verbal rather than under imagery set for concrete than for abstract words, and for specific than for general words.

Significant interactions indicated that the imaginal versus verbal difference in RT increases with stimulus abstractness and generality. These findings, and correlational analyses which included meaningfulness and rated imagery values for the words, were discussed in relation to hypothesized verbal and on nonverbal (imaginal) mediators of behavior.

Abstractness–concreteness and generality–specificity of words were simultaneously varied in a factorial design on the stimulus and response sides of paired-associate (PA) lists constructed from 96 nouns (Paivio 1967). The analysis of recall scores from the auditory presentation of two alternative study trials and recall trials revealed significant ($p<0.001$) effects of both variables on the stimulus side of pairs. A second experiment showed positive effects ($p<0.001$) of both concreteness and specificity on free recall. Mean scores were also available for the nouns on their rated capacity to evoke sensory images (I) and on the meaningfulness (M). A correlational analysis indicated that, of the attributes involved, I correlated most highly with learning scores. Consistent with the hypothesis that stimulus-evoked imagery can mediate response recall, the superiority of I was greatest when items served as stimulus terms in PA learning.

Data from groups of participants were used to scale 96 nouns on 30 variables, including scores on free recall and PA learning, and various semantic and associative attributes thought to be relevant in verbal learning situations (Paivio 1968). Correlations among word attributes and the resulting matrix were factor analyzed to yield six factors. Rotated factors were interpretable as concreteness–imagery, impressiveness, familiarity, specificity, associative variety, and learning factor I. Concreteness–imagery was of particular theoretical interest in the study. Loading highest on two measures of concreteness and on three indices of a word's capacity evoked sensory images. This factor represented a dimension of meaning not previously revealed in studies of semantic structure. Furthermore, only concreteness–imagery had appreciable loadings on the learning variables, the loading being highest for PA learning scores when the items served as stimulus (as opposed to response) member, as predicted from the hypothesis that stimulus-evoked imagery can mediate response recall.

When a noun is modified by two adjectives there is typically a preferred ordering of those adjectives (Lockhart and Martin 1969). Forty-two undergraduates were given 1 study trial with a list of 30 nouns, each modified by 2 adjectives which were strongly ordered. The order in which the adjective pairs were presented for study was counterbalanced. The test trial consisted of presenting one of the words from each triple and asking participants to recall the remaining two words. When cued with the adjective preferred close to the noun, recall was superior to when cued with the adjective preferred furthest from the noun. When cued with the noun, recall is superior to either condition of adjective cueing. *Results confirm a prediction based on the theory that adjective ordering is a function of the concreteness and specificity of adjective meaning* (italics mine).

Four experiments were conducted to investigate the effects of word concreteness (C), imagery (I), and specificity, and association value (AV) of nonsense syllables on stimulus–response (S–R) and R–S learning (Yarmey and O'Neill 1969). Results indicated that both S–R and R–S PA learning were highly facilitated by stimuli C and I with paired nouns and nouns-high AV nonsense syllables as stimulus materials. No differential effects were found for stimuli C and I with low AV syllable responses on either S–R or R–S learning. Stimulus specificity of concrete nouns, as opposed to abstract nouns, facilitated only S–R learning. These results were interpreted as supporting a theory in which high imagery stimulus items act as effective "conceptual pegs" for their associates for both S–R and R–S learning.

Johnson (1974) reported that the patterning of recall of linguistic subunits of textual prose by 58 undergraduates was strongly related to the semantic dimensions of abstractness–concreteness, specificity of denotation, comprehensibility, and interest. Attesting to the generality of the findings, the relationships between the textual dimensions and recall were evident with two textual passages, with two methods of measuring the semantic dimensions, and at immediate and delayed retention intervals. Remembering was characterized as being both a reconstructive and an abstractive process.

This study attempted to replicate an earlier finding that two process variables ("concreteness" of volunteers' verbal expressions and "motivation" of callers for receiving help) would predict whether callers to a suicide prevention and crisis service would show for appointments for face-to-face counseling (Slaikeu et al. 1975). The sample included all callers to a suicide prevention and crisis service during 1 month ($N = 1302$). An attempt was also made to operationalize R. R. Carkuff's concreteness construct by use of a new coding system for specificity focus of volunteer talk. In addition, a follow-up questionnaire was administered to shows, no shows, and cancellations. It was found that caller motivation (referral responsiveness) predicted referral outcome but that volunteer concreteness did not, and that the specificity–focus coding system did not correlate with concreteness. Callers' responses on the follow-up questionnaire challenged the assumption that not showing for an appointment is a sign of "failure" in telephone counseling. *This study is important in showing that concreteness and specificity did not correlate, supporting the orthogonal nature of Fig. 1.2* (italics mine).

Recent changes in pretheoretical orientation toward problems of human memory have brought with them a concern with retrieval processes, and a number of early versions of theories of retrieval have been constructed. This chapter described and evaluated explanations offered by these theories to account for the effect of extralist cueing, facilitation of recall of list items by nonlist items (Tulving and Thomson 1973), Experiments designed to test the currently most popular theory of retrieval, the generation-recognition theory, yielded results incompatible not only with generation-recognition models but most other theories as well: Under certain conditions, participants consistently failed to recognize many recallable list words. *Several tentative explanations of this phenomenon of recognition failure were subsumed under the encoding specificity principle according to which the memory trace of an event and hence the properties of effective retrieval cue are determined by the specific encoding operations performed by the system on the input stimuli* (italics mine).

Salzberg (1976) examined Tulving and Thomson's (1973) specificity effect as a function of grammatical class and concreteness of the cues in 2 experiments with approximately 150 undergraduates. Experiment I tested the hypothesis that a recognition cue of the same grammatical class as the input cue should produce better recognition performance than one that changed the grammatical class. This hypothesis was not supported. Experiment II showed that grammatical class and concreteness of the input cues affect the encoding specificity phenomenon. *The effect was observed only for concrete noun cues, and was mostly attributable to concreteness. Results suggested that concrete encoding cues produced a "specific" memory trace which can best be retrieved via the original encoding cue, while more abstract cues tended to produce a trace that is not cue dependent. The interpretation is that a cue-target word pair is encoded as a unit in memory and that the best access to the unit is provided by the more salient (concrete) member of the unit* (italics mine).

Czerwińska (1978) studied the vocational decisions of 521 students (ages 15–19 years) from 3 schools in the Warsaw area. Two scales derived from the work of D. E. Super were used to examine the nature of these decisions. *Significant differences were found between age groups in concreteness and specificity of vocational decisions, supporting the importance of both constructs on the response as well as on the intervention side* (italics mine).

One-hundred and forty American Indian and 226 White high school students were compared as they assessed counselors' empathy, warmth, genuineness, and *concreteness* as conveyed through 6 pairs of male and female counselor dress (Littrell and Littrell 1983). The two groups differed in their perceptions of each of the counseling conditions based on the counselors' attire. Participants' perceptions did not differ with the sex of the participant or, except for empathy, with the sex of the counselor. Results identified clothing dimensions useful for understanding cultural similarities and differences in nonverbal communication through dress. Further study of clothing dimensions of cultural *specificity,* regional uniqueness, and fashionability was recommended.

Pidgeon (1985), in another relevant study, reviewed the literature concerning the stages in concept development and in children's concepts of illness and illness causation. Findings indicated that children's concepts develop through different stages, from global to undifferentiated to concrete and abstract. In the concrete stage, perceptual and physical attributes of a concept are dominant. In the abstract stage, the essential mental and nonperceptual attributes of a concept are grasped. In general, children's concepts of illness shift with age from definitions based largely on feeling states to broader, more precise definitions that include specific diagnoses and psychosocial indicators of illness. *This study tends to support concreteness as a developmental variable* (editorial comment).

Children's concepts of illness causation also develop through different stages, with school-age children attributing illness causation to their own actions and to external causes as they grow older. Implications for the health teaching of well children and the education of chronically ill children about their illnesses were discussed, focusing on the importance of assessing the child's perception of illness, the child's readiness to learn, and the *concreteness and specificity* of school-age children's illness concepts (same as above).

Seginer (1988) examined sociocultural variations of gender differences reflected in the future orientation of Israeli Jews and Arabs as cases of modernity versus transition to modernity. Sixty-one male and 51 female Jewish adolescents and 67 male and 49 female Arab adolescents, all college-bound seniors, responded to a questionnaire and listed their hopes and fears for the future. Responses were categorized into eight life domains (school and matriculation, military service, higher education, work and career, marriage and family, self, others, and collective issues). Each domain was analyzed in terms of salience (importance and interest) and *specificity* (extent of detail and concreteness). Results supported the hypothesized instrumental—expressive division between Jewish males and females and the primacy of higher education for Arab females. *Note that, erroneously, concreteness was not considered as independent from specificity* (note of author).

Gibb and Wales (1990) examined figurative comparison statements in relation to relative preference for the metaphoric versus the simile format ("is" vs. "is like"), using a sentence-completion task in a preliminary study with 24 participants (aged 24–68 years) and in a main study with 20 university students. Variables identified as likely predictors of one form over the other were *concreteness* of vehicle, *specificity* of the tenor, and *concreteness* of the predicate adjective preceding the vehicle. The differential function of the two figurative forms is explained in terms of the kind of themes expressed within the ground of the comparisons. Data suggested that metaphor was associated with greater intensity of psychological effect than was simile.

Olson (1991) examined ways in which the experiences of support from within schools affected the professional growth and sense of satisfaction of four first-year elementary school teachers (aged 26–35 years). Data were based on the phenomenological analysis of interview transcripts from a larger study about the experiences of first-year teachers. The themes that emerged in the present study were: (1) support that allows a growth choice, (2) need for reciprocity, (3) need for appropriate levels of support, (4) need for *concreteness and specificity* (italics mine), (5) support through comparison with others, and (6) need for recognition. Appropriate support provided participants with nonjudgmental acceptance into the teaching subculture. Such support provided models of teaching behaviors and procedures and gave participants the courage to make growth choices.

Seginer and Halabi (1991) examined sociocultural variations of adolescents' subjective image of the future, or future orientation. Analysis of the responses of

152 Israeli Druze, Arab, and Jewish male adolescents to an open-ended, future orientation questionnaire partly supported the hypotheses that Druze adolescents expressed fewer concerns regarding the future (salience), described their concerns with less detail and *concreteness (specificity),* and that the importance of each future orientation domain relative to the other domains (density) is different for Druze than for Arab and Jewish adolescents. Results are interpreted in terms of modernity (Jews) versus early and advanced stages of transition to modernity and suggest that the intervening intrapersonal process explaining Druze future orientation involves alignment with powerful agents and related secondary control beliefs. *Please view critically the inconsistent and erroneous equation of concreteness with specificity in this chapter as well as in other publications reported in this section* (author's note).

Bucci et al. (1991) evaluated changes in contents and language style of dream reports during the menstrual cycle in seven women (aged 28–45 years) with premenstrual syndrome (PMS). Dream diaries were scored for referential activity (RA), and mean scores for overall RA and for the four individual RA scales (*specificity, concreteness,* imagery, and clarity) showed peaks in the early luteal phase (ELF), i.e., at the time of high gonadal hormone concentration. The dominant contents of dreams in the ELF reflected emotions directed toward other people, in contrast to the early follicular and late luteal phase themes of self-care. Results supported the interaction of physiological, emotional, and cognitive events as postulated by the multiple code theory, and they are consistent with other studies. Several questions were considered concerning the precise impact of hormonal fluctuation on emotional information process as reflected in dreams.

The purpose of this study was to investigate the interaction of defense and the communication of emotional experience in the context of psychodynamic inpatient treatment (Guiter-Mazer 1997). The concept of defense has been extensively discussed in the clinical literature and constitutes a clear focus of psychodynamic treatment, which is designed to address defensively affect through the verbalization of emotional experience. Thus, defense process and the symbolizing function of language are central to understanding treatment process and outcome. This study examined defensive functioning as reflected in the language samples of severely disturbed inpatients. It empirically examined the specific predictive value of defensive functioning to treatment outcome and its relation to the ability to symbolize affect verbally.

The Defense Mechanism Rating Scales (DMRS)—a hierarchical model of defenses reflecting a continuum of defensive functioning from least to most adaptive—was used together with the construct of RA—a measure which rates four dimensions of language style including *concreteness,* clarity, *specificity,* and imagery—to study outcome and change in the treatment of severely disturbed hospitalized patients. The relationship between language style and maturity of defenses was examined. Finally, both of these two dimensions of psychological functioning were related to the Global Assessment Scale (GAS), a measure of clinical change.

Findings indicated that among the severely disturbed inpatients studied in their sample, defenses did not change significantly during the course of treatment. A measure of general defensive functioning did not predict to clinical progress. However, when defenses were examined by maturity clusters, narcissistic and borderline defenses measured at admission predicted better clinical outcome and greater improvement. Results also showed an association between the use of language and maturity of defenses. Finally, the combination of higher RA levels together with higher levels of narcissistic and borderline defenses predicted to both the GAS level at termination of treatment and the degree of GAS improvement that patients achieved during the hospitalization. Interpretation of findings, suggestions for a model predicting to treatment outcome and, research problems were discussed. *RA needs further research to expand on its relevance to the level of concreteness of participants, as shown in the study below* (author's note).

This study utilized Bucci's multiple code theory and concept of RA to investigate the relationship of context and affect intensity to language style, as measured by RA linguistic features of clarity, *concreteness, specificity,* and imagery (Egan 2000). Context (violent or nonviolent) was measured by the Conflict Tactics Scale (CTS). Affect intensity was measured by (1) the depression (DEP) subscale of the Dietrich Object Relations and Representations Scale (DORRS) and (2) use of emotionally toned (ET), affect laden words. Language style was measured by computerized referential activity (CRA).

This study was situated within the context of current controversies in psychoanalytic theory and research. The significance of a language-based approach to psychoanalytic discourse was addressed. Subjectivist, hermeneutic, and postmodern perspectives were compared and contrasted with objectivist, empiricist, and modern perspectives. These competing perspectives, and the assumptions that underlie them, were explored with regard to investigating differences between people in forming interconnections between verbal and nonverbal systems of mental representation. One-hundred and sixty narratives from 40 psychological test protocols were obtained from archival data. Participants were divided into violent and nonviolent groups (Egan 2000).

As predicted, significant differences were found between participants' scores on depression with the violent group significantly more severely depressed. None of the measures differentiated the groups. Gender, affect intensity, and level of violence were not found to be significant predictors of CRA. Age was a predictor only when group membership was not considered. Overall findings were consistent with prior research that established RA as a construct that is highly sensitive to emotional, situational, and internal/external contextual factors. It was concluded that measures of nonverbal, subsymbolic processes (intonation, inflection, syncopation, pitch, tone, rhythm, gesture, sighs, crying, laughter, muscle tone, voice pressure, etc.) that frequently operate simultaneously with verbal speech, yet remained independent of formal language, constituted rich and essential areas for future research. The possibility is considered that quantitative methods currently available may not be able to adequately assess the human synergism of affect and its relationship to a language constantly contextualized by changing experiences and their meanings.

For instance, three experiments tested contrasting predictions of a dual-representation theory and a context availability model of concreteness effects in verbal processing (Schwanenflugel and Shoben 1983). Without context, reading times/ lexical decision times for abstract sentences/words were longer than for concrete sentences/words. Rated context availability was a good predictor of RT. *The importance of context could be represented by the interaction between levels of concreteness in participants and the specificity of the interventions* (author's note).

Four experiments used associated, unrelated, and neutral ({blank}–word) pairs that varied on prime and target concreteness (Bleasdale 1987). In experiment 1, associated targets were named faster than neutral targets when primes and targets were homogeneous for concreteness (i.e., concrete–concrete or abstract–abstract), but not when they were heterogeneous (i.e., concrete–abstract or abstract–concrete). Experiments 2 and 3, using lexical decision, showed priming for all pairs irrespective of prime and target concreteness. In experiment 4, the prime was presented for 16.7 ms, followed immediately by a 168-ms random letter mask. Lexical decision times showed priming similar to that in experiment 1. If priming in experiments 1 and 4 reflected lexical processes, whereas priming in experiments 2 and 3 entailed postlexical processes, then lexical processes may be functionally distinct for concrete versus abstract words. These findings seemed more consistent with dual-coding than common-coding explanations of concreteness.

Schwanenflugel et al. (1988) conducted 3 experiments with 281 undergraduates to examine contrasting predictions of dual-representation and *context availability* hypotheses for concreteness effects in lexical decision making. Equivalent lexical decision times were obtained for concrete and abstract words controlled for rated context availability, whereas longer lexical decision times were obtained for abstract words than for concrete words when the abstract words were rated lower in context availability. In the second experiment, rated context availability was a better predictor of lexical decision time than imagery and concreteness, familiarity, or age-of-acquisition ratings. In the third experiment, larger benefits of context were obtained for abstract words than for concrete words only when the abstract words were also rated low in context availability. Results supported the context availability hypothesis in concreteness effects.

Previous research has shown that abstract words are comprehended more slowly than concrete words (Schwanenflugel and Stowe 1989). In two experiments, the authors investigated the influence of a sentence context on the processing of abstract and concrete words. In the first experiment, 17 college students completed a word-naming task in which abstract and concrete words were presented in either a meaningful or a neutral sentence context. Abstract words took longer to name than concrete words when presented in a neutral context, suggesting that concreteness effects occur early in the processing of words.

In the second experiment, 21 college students judged whether abstract and concrete words were meaningful sentence completions; the words were presented in either a meaningful or a nonmeaningful context. Meaningfulness judgments were made more slowly for abstract than for concrete words when the words were presented in a nonmeaningful context. However, in both the naming and the meaningfulness judgment tasks, concreteness effects in processing were eliminated when the words were presented in supportive contexts. The authors discussed these results as supporting a context availability view—that abstract words are comprehended more slowly than concrete words when presented in nonsupportive contexts because it is more difficult to retrieve the associated contextual knowledge necessary for comprehension.

Schwanenflugel (1991), on the basis of research summarized above, was one of the first researchers to ask and answer why abstract concepts are hard to understand, suggesting that concrete concepts are comparatively easier to understand. More recently, basing their research on Schwanenflugel and his associates' work, Holcomb et al. (1999) recorded event-related potentials in two experiments while participants read sentences in a word-by-word congruency judgment task. Sentence final words were either congruent, semantically anomalous (experiments 1 and 2), or neutral (experiment 2) with respect to sentence context. Half of all final words referred to concrete and half to abstract concepts. A different scalp distribution of the N400 to concrete and abstract final words was found for anomalous and neutral, but not congruent sentences. Although the interaction of context and concreteness is consistent with the context availability model, the differential scalp distribution of effects for concrete and abstract words, as well as larger context effects for concrete words, was interpreted as being more consistent with an extended dual-code account of semantic processing.

Semantic reading errors are the central and defining feature of deep dyslexia (Gerhand and Barry 2000). This study compared the words that a deep dyslexic patient (aged 52 years) read correctly with those she omitted and those to which she produced semantic errors in terms of their concreteness, age of acquisition, frequency, and length. Semantic errors were made to less concrete, later-acquired, and shorter words than were read correctly; there was no reliable effect of word frequency. More importantly, the actual semantic errors produced were later acquired than the stimulus words, but they were not more concrete or reliably more frequent. These results implicate age of acquisition in the process that produces semantic errors. *It is proposed that concreteness determines the specificity of the semantic system to activate a set of candidate responses and that age-of-acquisition biases the ease with which certain words can be selected from this set to be produced as reading responses* (italics mine).

This dissertation examined short narratives written by 39 patient–therapist dyads about tension between them in brief relational therapy (BRT; Nikowitz 2001, January). Linguistic characteristics in the narratives were hypothesized to be predictive of session effectiveness, as rated by patients and by therapists, and overall treatment outcome. These characteristics were inspired by existing literature and by principles of meta-communication used in BRT. They were (1) variables reflecting the degree to which participants returned postsession questionnaires, and wrote narratives when they reported tension about the session, (2) levels of "concreteness" and "specificity" in the narratives, (3) attribution of blame, (4) use of the name of the other person in the dyad, (5) use of third person to refer the oneself, (6) use of "we" to express more inclusiveness, and (7) the ratio of "other referents" to "I referents."

Paired *t* tests examined differences between patients and therapists on the predictor variables regarding the participants' engagement in the therapy process. Regression analyses using a generalized estimating equations approach tested for relationships between the predictor and criterion variables. The main findings were that therapists reported tension and wrote about it more frequently than patients, and that several linguistic characteristics present in the narratives were significantly associated with session effectiveness ratings by therapists, by patients, or by both, and only one predictor variable, the level of blame patients attributed to their therapist for the tension in the session was associated with poorer overall treatment outcome. To be able to generalize from the present findings to the process in the actual sessions, narratives, including the predictor variables studied, could be used to examine the corresponding session transcripts.

This chapter reported results of comparing source and target text jabs (from Raymond Chandler's novels translated into Greek) involving allusive proper names, with a view to accounting for the contribution of this grammatical category to humorous effect (Antonopoulou 2004). The proper names discussed were socioculturally bound. Therefore, the difference in production dates, sociocultural environment, and audience design has resulted in different strategies being adopted for their intercultural transference. This has provided the opportunity to check the traditional strategies against respondents' reactions to humorous effect and compare source text and alternative target text jabs using the General Theory of Verbal Humor (GTVH) metric. Considering also the cognitive grammar account of the functions of proper names (PNs) has led to an interpretation of the unexpected finding that jabs with allusive PNs may well be humorously effective even if their referents are unknown to the audience. The following factors emerge as crucial in this respect: The brevity of the linguistic sign, the *specificity* and *concreteness* of the evoked scripts, and the immediacy with which mental contact is established. It was suggested that replacing socioculturally bound PNs in translating jab lines may jeopardize their humorous effect.

Icons were often considered as language free and therefore assumed to be especially suited for intercultural usage. This article examined if icons within the mobile context are interculturally comprehensible in Kerala, South India (Pappachan and Ziefle 2008). Fifty-eight participants of a wide age range (17–75 years) volunteered to take part in this study. Icons under study were representatives for common mobile phone functions and were partly taken from real interfaces and were partly self-created. Icons varied in their concreteness/abstractness and their visual complexity. A naming method was adopted: Participants had first to evaluate what a specific icon pictured (pictorial transparency) and, directly after, they had to indicate the icon's meaning in the context of mobile communication (semantic transparency and comprehensibility). Results showed that the comprehensibility of icons mainly depend on two major characteristics, which can be regarded as culture unspecific. *No matter which cultural background users have, the more details an icon contains and the more concrete an icon is, the more it is correctly interpreted* (italics mine). However, these researchers identified also cultural influences on the comprehensibility of specific icons, showing that icon design also should consider cultural specificity.

Past research has shown that concrete ad copies perform better than abstract ad copies in enhancing consumers' attitudes toward and purchase intentions of the product. These studies defined the abstractness–concreteness of an ad copy as the extent to which the ad copy activates visual imagery of the product information in consumers' minds. However, other researchers have proposed another definition of the abstractness–concreteness of an ad copy: generality versus specificity. That is, the more general (specific), the more (fewer) particular incidents an ad copy includes. Employing the alternative definition, this study reexamined the concreteness effect that has been reported (Ci 2009).

Specifically, based on regulatory focus theory and past studies on hedonic/utilitarian consumption, this study proposed that the impact of the abstractness–concreteness of an ad copy on consumers' attitudes toward or purchase intentions of the product would be moderated by their regulatory foci and types of product attributes (Ci 2009). Also, several propositions were set forth regarding the underlying process of the moderation effect. However, the online experiment this study conducted failed to support the propositions. Instead, the concreteness effect was observed. Based on the finding, this study discusses several issues that may advance our knowledge about the concreteness effect as well as about regulatory focus theory and consumers' hedonic/utilitarian consumption. Also, several suggestions are made for future studies in this regard.

Embodied accounts of language processing suggested that sensorimotor areas, generally dedicated to perception and action, are also involved in the processing and representation of word meaning (van Dam et al. 2010). Support for such accounts comes from studies showing that language about actions selectively modulates the execution of congruent and incongruent motor responses and from functional neuroimaging studies showing that understanding action-related language recruits sensorimotor brain areas. In the current experiment, these researchers explored the basis of the neural motor system's involvement in representing words denoting actions.

Specifically, the authors investigated whether the motor system's involvement is modulated by the specificity of the kinematics associated with a word. Previous research in the visual domain indicates that words denoting basic-level category members lacking a specific form (e.g., bird) are less richly encoded within visual areas than words denoting subordinate level members (e.g., pelican), for which the visual form is better specified. In the present study, van Dam et al. (2010) extended these findings to the motor domain. Modulation of the BOLD response elicited by verbs denoting a general motor program (e.g., to clean) was compared to modulation elicited by verbs denoting a more specific motor program (e.g., to wipe). Conforming with the authors' hypothesis, a region within the bilateral inferior parietal lobule, typically serving the representation of action plans and goals, was sensitive to the *specificity* of motor programs associated with the action verbs. These findings contribute to the growing body of research on embodied language representations by showing that the concreteness of an action-semantic feature is reflected in the neural response to action verbs.

It has been shown recently that a specific intervention designed to modify the overgeneralization bias (i.e., concreteness training (CNT)) can decrease depressive symptoms. The intervention, however, involves multiple components (e.g., relaxation, problem solving), so it is not clear if the increase in concrete processing is the crucial mechanism in ameliorating depressive symptoms. Using a dismantling design, this online study examined whether targeting only concrete processing in the absence of a therapeutic context reduces depressive symptoms (Mogoaşe et al. 2013). Forty-two stable dysphoric participants were randomly allocated to either a waiting list or a 7-day concreteness training condition. *Compared with the control group, concrete processing training resulted in a significant increase in the concreteness of thinking* (italics mine). No significant differences in autobiographical memory specificity, depressive symptoms, or rumination, however, were obtained post intervention between the two groups. These findings suggested that concrete processing can be trained, but training effects may not generalize to untrained cognitive contents. The effectiveness of CNT as a stand-alone treatment for depression may be limited.

A critical question for developmental psychologists concerns how representations in infancy are best characterized (Sommerville et al. 2012). Past and current research provides paradoxical evidence regarding the nature of early representations: In some ways, infants appear to build concrete and specific representations that guide their online perception and understanding of different events; in other ways, infants appear to possess abstract representations that support inferences regarding unseen event outcomes. Characterizing the nature of early representations across domains is a central charge for developmentalists because this task can provide important information regarding the underlying learning process or processes that drive development. Yet, little existing work has attempted to resolve this paradox by characterizing the ways in which *infants' representations may have both abstract and concrete elements* (italics mine).The goal of this chapter was to take a close look at infants' early representations of goal-directed action in order to describe the nature of these representations.

Sommerville et al. (2012) first discussed the nature of representations of action that infants build through acting on the world and argued that these representations possess both concrete and abstract elements. On the one hand, infants appeared to build representations of action that stress goal-relevant features of actions in an action- or event-specific fashion, suggesting specificity or concreteness. On the other hand, these representations are sufficiently abstract to not only drive action but also support infants' perception of others actions and to support inferences regarding unseen action outcomes. The authors next discussed evidence to suggest that by the end of the first year of life, infants possess increasingly abstract representations of the actions of others and use contextual cues, including linguistic statements accompanying action, to flexibly specify the level of representational specificity. Sommerville et al. (2012) further considered the possibility that language may play a role in infants' ability to build more abstract representations of goal-directed action.

One important deficit in many research studies cited above lies in their failure to differentiate more sharply concreteness from specificity. It seems that both constructs were used either synonymously or together as seemingly representing the same processes. Nothing could be more incorrect than such an equation, as discussed further in Chap. 6 of this volume.

Recent Contributions About the Role of Abstraction

Fujita et al. (2014) in reviewing the construct of control, defined abstraction as:

> ….the cognitive process of integrating inputs and extracting from them emergent commonalities that may not be evident in any one signal. Abstraction may promote control in two ways. First, it may facilitate the recognition of emerging patterns from lower-level inputs, which may help to determine what goals should be pursued. ……Abstraction may similarly promote a bottom-up, emergent organization of thought, feeling, and behavior toward a single end….The second way that abstraction may promote control is by promoting the ability to recognize discrepancies from coherent organization after thought, feelings, and behavior have been integrated and structured (p. 53)…….Thus, abstraction may have roles in both determining emergent patterns that form the consensual goal in a bottom-up construction process and imposing structure and order to promote and protect that in a top-down fashion. (p. 54)

These authors proceeded to review evidence that abstraction promotes control (pp. 58–59), arguing that effortful processing can impair control by differentiating between reactive versus proactive control (pp. 59–62). Fujita et al. concluded their chapter by suggesting that there are two meanings to the term *control:* The first meaning relates to its automaticity, without conscious intention, conscious awareness, not being disruptable, and being cognitively efficient, characteristics reviewed in Chaps. 6 and 7 of this volume. The second meaning "focuses on the degree to which a process sustains and promotes structured goal pursuit" (p. 62).

Furthermore, Semin et al. (2014) argued that concrete terms, such as *apple,* are grounded through direct, perceptual, sensorimotor experiences (touch, smell, sight, hearing), while abstract terms, such as morality, affect, valence, or power, are driven by semantic, representational processes, such as metaphors. Such a differentiation suggests that there may be "two processes driving the grounding of concepts" (p. 543). Concrete concepts may be grounded through the perceptual simulation hypothesis (pp. 544–545), via action (pp. 545–546), and, of course, through neuroscience.

There are conceptual and evidential problems concerning the evidence for concrete concepts, however, grounding abstract concepts is even more problematic because most abstract concepts are defined through metaphors as well as affect, spatial position, motor actions, interpersonal relationships, smell, temporal perspective, and ambient temperature. Abstract concepts, therefore, are as grounded on sensorimotor experiences as concrete concepts, suggesting "different degrees of proximity to sensorimotor processes. These degrees and types of proximity indicate that it difficult to summarize human experience into only two processes" (Amodio 2014).

Conclusion

The purpose of this chapter was to present a model that includes requirements for a science of clinical psychology based, among others, on the extremes of two continua in concreteness–abstraction and specificity–generality. These two continua set orthogonally allowed to distinguish paradigms from theories, theories from models, and models from dimensions. Additional requirements were given to differentiate these four components of the model in the chapters of this volume. Research on differences between abstract and concrete terms indicated the importance of including context availability as an important variable in the administration of concrete and specific terms. Perhaps, context might be the by-product of the interaction between concreteness level on the part of participants and the specificity of interventions on the part of clinicians administering them. Indirectly, this chapter started to make the case for the importance of homogeneously uniform concrete and specific standard operating practices in clinical psychology and psychotherapy. This case is expanded in the following chapters of this volume.

Chapter 2
The Future Is Now: Online Interventions Are Here to Stay and Grow

> Evidence is growing that several computer-aided psychotherapy (CP) systems can effectively improve a range of common mental health problems. Most clients find CP acceptable because of its convenience, confidentiality, and reduction of stigma. CP can be accessed in a clinic, but recently clients have used CP especially on the Internet at home, with brief support on a telephone helpline and/or by email. Brief and efficient screening and support greatly reduce attrition. CP's efficacy, and encouragement of its dissemination and implementation by some national funding bodies and government agencies [in the UK} has led to its spread as a regular care option and is increasing access to psychological therapies in some countries. (Marks and Cavanah 2009, p. 121)

> By 2025, when most of today's psychology undergraduates will be in their mid 30s, more than 5 billion people on our planet will be using ultra-broadband, sensor-rich smart-phones far beyond the abilities of today's iPhones, Androids, and Blackberries. Although smartphones were not designed for psychological research, they can collect vast amounts of ecologically valid data, easily and quickly, from large global samples. If participants download the right "psych apps," smartphones can record where they are, what they are doing, and what they can see and hear and can run interactive surveys, tests, and experiments through touch screens and wireless connections to nearby screens, headsets, biosensors, and other peripherals. This article reviews previous behavioral research using mobile electronic devices, outlines what smartphones can do now and will be able to do in the near future, explains how a smartphone study could work practically given current technology (e.g., in studying ovulatory cycle effects on women's sexuality), discusses some limitations and challenges of smart-phone research, and compares smart-phones to other research methods. Smartphone research will require new skills in app development and data analysis and will raise tough new ethical issues, but smart-phones could transform psychology even more profoundly than PCs and brain imaging did. (Miller 2012)

> The skepticism of many patients and professionals about CAP stems in part from a long-held belief that improvement with psychotherapies requires a relationship or other major involvement with a therapist. This may be true for some patients, but is not upheld in the thousands of people who improved when guided in CAP studies with only brief human contact… Just as patients may become overdependent in F2 F therapy, so they can get overattached to CAP." (Marks, Cavanah, & Gega, 2007, p. 215)…. As yet we lack conclusive information about the cost implications and impact of CAP on health service provision and utilization. Researchers and service providers need to identify what exactly they want to achieve by introducing CAP into health service and then explore the costs of different implementation models (Marks et al. 2007, p. 219).

L. L'Abate, *Concreteness and Specificity in Clinical Psychology*,
DOI 10.1007/978-3-319-13284-6_2

According to *Education Week*, the annual report by the Pew Internet and American Life project found that 95 % of teenagers in the USA are active online, and nearly three out of four children aged 12–17 access the Internet via mobile devices. The underlying implication is that virtual connection is an essential aspect of most students' lives. Where will these youngsters seek psychological help when they need it now and in the near future, when they become adults? How prepared will they be to speak face to face with a professional when most of their past interactions have occurred online? The same source found that 74 % of respondents in the USA preferred online writing to face-to-face (F2F) talking.

The growth of online interventions is inevitable and the sooner clinical psychology professionals understand the need to change, the better. *From an ears–mouth, auditory–verbal culture we are now changing to an eyes–fingers, visual–digital culture.* Whether we like it or not, we clinical psychology professionals will have to learn to work through remote writing and homework assignments, at a distance from participants, without ever seeing them F2F or talking with them. The challenge of the future lies in whether clinical psychology professionals want to continue practicing as artists, without any internal or external controls, or whether they want to change to practice as professionals, using replicably uniform standard operating procedures (SOPs) in evaluation and in practice (Olson and Olson 2003; Bargh and McKenna 2004; Kazantzis and L'Abate 2007; L'Abate 2007a, b, 2008a, c, 2011c, 2013a, b, c, 2015; Strecher 2007).

Online interventions mean e-counseling or e-therapy as a generic term referring to the delivery of mental health service to remote patients by using telecommunication technology (e.g., telephone, computer, video). This term has been referenced by many names: tele-health, online counseling, online therapy, tele-psychiatry, tele-psychology, tele-psych, tele-practice, behavioral tele-health, tele-medicine, online psycho-education, and mobile therapy (clinical psychology health) (L'Abate 2011a, 2013, 2015). The rise of the Coalition for Technology in Behavioral Science (CTiBC) is just one sign among many of the increased interest in online interventions, let alone new training programs to train professionals in Internet therapy. Internet-based clinical practice, such as e-counseling and online therapy, using distance communication and remote writing is already becoming an important component of physical and mental health promotion, prevention, and treatment of mental illnesses (L'Abate 2001a, 2002, 2003; L'Abate and Sweeney 2011; L'Abate and Kaiser 2012).

Finally, the American Psychological Association has released the guidelines for this admittedly, rapidly burgeoning innovation, compared by many different sources, to the revolutionary effects of the Gutenberg press:

> These guidelines are designed to address the developing area of psychological service provision commonly known as telepsychology. Telepsychology is defined for the purpose of these guidelines as the provision of psychological services using telecommunication technologies as expounded in the Definition of Telepsychology section of these guidelines. The expanding role of technology in the provision of psychological services and the continuous development of new technologies that may be useful in the practice of psychology present unique opportunities, considerations, and challenges to practice. With the advancement to technology and the increased number of psychologists using technology in their practices, these guidelines have been prepared to educe and guide them. (p. 791)

Historical Background

Since the early 1970s, my students and I have been involved in systematically written replicable enrichment programs for couples and families (L'Abate and Weistein 1987; L'Abate and Young 1987). Eventually, these programs would become "programmed writing," that is: administration in writing of questions, tasks, and homework assignments to participants remotely at a distance from psychotherapists and clinical psychology professionals (L'Abate 1977, 1983, 1986; 1992, 2001a, 2002, 2004a, 2004b; L'Abate and Rupp 1981). Rather than expensive and nonreplicable F2F, talk-based (TB) personal contacts, this approach values the objectivity of uniformly replicable, systematically written interactive practice exercises or workbooks as SOPs in psychological evaluation and interventions (Hooper et al. 2014; L'Abate 2013b). Consequently, these interactive practice exercises, administered and answered in writing, can and should be administered online as well as offline initially as structured interviews if desired for training purposes targeted to specific reasons for referral (concerns, issues, symptoms, syndromes (L'Abate 2015).

The validity and reliability of these homework assignments were evaluated from the very outset, suggesting that they are not only easily replicable but also potentially cost-effective. This conclusion was found to be untenable after a review of 25 years of private practice with individuals, couples, and families and showed that participants using interactive practice exercises attended significantly more F2F, TB sessions than participants who did not receive those exercises (L'Abate et al. 2005). Furthermore, a meta-analysis of 12 mental health workbooks compared to six physical health workbooks found a medium effect size ($d=0.44$) for the former and a lower effect size ($d=0.25$) for the latter (Smyth and L'Abate 2001). We can indeed help people who hurt without ever seeing them F2F and talking with them.

This approach emphasizes the importance of:

1. Objective pre–post-termination evaluation and follow-up for psychotherapists and clinical psychology professionals to practice proactively as serious professionals rather than reactively as creative artists. This point isexpanded in Chap. 3 of this volume
2. Unstructured and nonreplicable practices mimicking the unstructured nature of past-therapeutic interventions as art lead to chaotic Towers of Babel: every psychotherapist for him or herself without any internal or external controls. Under these conditions, therapists practice as artists controlled by "creative immediacy" and arbitrary whims and wills without evidence to support artistic practices except seemingly altruistic rationales to justify those practices (L'Abate 2013b). This point will be discussed in Chaps. 6 and 7 of this volume.
3. Structured, programmed, interactive practice exercises that allow for replicability of uniform practices within and among therapists: The therapist as professional evaluates objectively the outcome of interventions for each participant on a pre–post-basis with a follow-up. This point is expanded in Chap. 8 of this volume.

   a. Preferred and validated online programs (L'Abate 2013d) coupled with workbooks (PIPES) contained in the Appendices of this volume.

The Contribution of Hertlein and Blumer

This well-supported, important contribution to couple and family technology by Hertlein and Blumer is the book all couple and family therapists need to acquire if they want to enter and practice in the twenty-first century. Because of the importance and relevance of this contribution to the present and future of the profession of couple and family therapy, its contents will be reported in as much detail as possible.

Couple and family technology is an emerging new discipline because of the prevalence of technology in our daily lives, representing a revolution similar to the creation of the Guttenberg printing press. This revolution poses significant implications in the promotion of relationships at a distance between couple and family practitioners and their clients. This revolutionary change indicates that couple and family relationships need to be reconceptualized occurring according to the realities and needs of the now-digital twenty-first century.

Hertlein and Blumer compared and contrasted F2F and computer-mediated communications concluding that "relationship satisfaction in offline communications may also predict satisfaction with online relationships" (pp. 41). These writers compared and contrasted face to face with computer-mediated communication according to their similarities and differences and then added "…the characteristics attributed to people who prefer to participate in online dating, such as, shyness, social awkwardness, loneliness, difficulty with interpersonal interactions, primarily interested in sex rather than in a emotional relationship, and potentially deceitful" (p. 23). The bottom line for online dating, after one considers all possible various factors influencing it, is *convenience*. It is much easier to date from one's own computer than to dress up and go out to seek a possible or potential partner.

According to Hertline and Blumer: "One of the primary issues associated with technology in intimate relationships is the issue of accountability" (p. 54), being aware of one's online behavior in relationship to one's offline behavior. How congruent are they? This question is answered in a publication completely dedicated to answer it (L'Abate and Sweeney, in press). Within this context, one needs to consider the presence of suspicion and jealousy, cybersex, and Internet sex additions, and online infidelity. Gender differences play a large role in Internet dating as well.

Motivation plays an important role on whether participants will become involved in synchronous versus asynchronous communications. There are differences between those couples who will and will not participate in such communications as well as ecological influences on the couple system, such as (1) accountability, (2) anonymity, (3) accessibility, (4) affordability, (5) approximation, (6) accommodation, and (7) ambiguity.

The interactional nature of structure and function changes from online to offline interventions. The physical structure of online technology is different from the psychological structure of offline interventions. Relational roles and rules tend to produce different individual and relational roles, including intimacy development with and without technology. In spite of all these differences, relationship satisfaction in online relationships seems well established.

Hertlein and Blumer compared and contrasted F2F and computer-mediated communications concluding that "....relationship satisfaction in offline communications may also predict satisfaction with online relationships" (pp. 41). These writers compared and contrasted F2F with computer-mediated communication according to their similarities and differences and then added "...the characteristics attributed to people who prefer to participate in online dating, such as, shyness, social awkwardness, loneliness, difficulty with interpersonal interactions, primarily interested in sex rather than in a emotional relationship, and potentially deceitful' (p. 23). The bottom line for online dating, after one considers all possible various factors influencing it, is *convenience*. It is much easier to date from one's own computer than to dress up and go out to seek a possible or potential partner.

According to Hertline and Blumer: "One of the primary issues associated with technology in intimate relationships is the issue of accountability" (p. 54), being aware of one's online behavior in relationship to one's offline behavior. How congruent are they? This question is answered in a publication completely dedicated to answer it (L'Abate and Sweeney, in press; Resenski 2013). Within this context, one needs to consider the presence of suspicion and jealousy, cybersex, and Internet sex additions, and online infidelity. Gender differences play a large role in Internet dating as well.

Motivation plays an important role on whether participants will become involved in synchronous versus asynchronous communications. There are differences between those couples who will and will not participate in such communications as well as ecological influences on the couple system, such as (1) accountability, (2) anonymity, (3) accessibility, (4) affordability, (5) approximation, (6) accommodation, and (7) ambiguity.

The interactional nature of structure and function changes from online to offline interventions. The physical structure of online technology is different from the psychological structure of offline interventions. Relational roles and rules tend to produce different individual and relational roles, including intimacy development with and without technology. In spite of all these differences, relationship satisfaction in online relationships seems well established.

Very importantly, Hertlein and Blumer devoted a whole chapter to assessment, within their own couple and family technology (CFT) framework, consisting of specific ecological influences at the top, structure and process changes at a lower level, and at the bottom, redefinitions of rules, roles, boundaries, relationship initiation, maintenance, and dissolution. Relationship maintenance is defined by commitment and intimacy. The abstract and generic nature of this model makes impossible to actually operationalize it in practice. However, this topic is expanded in Chap. 4 of this volume.

These authors, therefore, consider treatment within the lenses of their CFT framework, including strategies, and two key issues in the treatment of technology problems: (1) evaluation of the therapist's stance on key therapeutic issues, including the self and (2) managing ecological elements with their structural and process issues included in their CFT.

What did I personally and professionally miss in this otherwise important and well-documented contribution? I missed the function that programmed, written homework assignments could play within the context of this technology (L'Abate 2007b, 2013d) as shown in the Appendices of this volume. Additionally, this shortcoming will be filled by comparing critically offline and online interventions in mental health (L'Abate, 2015).

Feedback in Psychotherapy

The importance of feedback was recognized since the publication of structured enrichment programs by administering a form to participants after each enrichment session (L'Abate and Weinstein 1987). A copy of this feedback form is available in the Appendices of this volume. The importance of online and offline feedback to therapy participants is the subject of different approaches that attempt to bridge the research–practice gap: art versus science.

Pinsof et al. (2012) presented the first online multisystemic and multidimensional client-report system specifically designed to assess and track system changes and the therapeutic alliance with individuals, couples, and families. The Systemic Therapy Inventory of Change (STIC) assessed and tracked reliably and validly changes in clients and their relationships to therapists. In this fashion, therapists are continuously aware of how their clients are doing outside the therapy room, enhancing collaborative assessment, treatment planning, progress evaluation, and termination. Treatment, however, is still offered verbally.

Arguing that usual care in the community is far from optimal, Bickman et al. (2012) argued that sufficient evidence exists that dropout rates are significant, and, therefore, treatment is effective for only a small portion of participants. Translation of evidence-based treatment in the real world is still problematic. Technology has been shown to be helpful in health care by improving the effectiveness of treatment. These authors introduced a relatively new technology used in their research called measurement feedback systems (MFSs). These systems are particularly applicable to couples and families because they provide information from multiple perspectives including the therapist (Bickman et al. 1999). An application of MFSs is found in the contextualized feedback systems (CFS) as an example of what can be accomplished with an MFS. The latter was applied by Sexton, Patterson, and Datchi (2012).

Relevant to the issue of feedback in F2F TB psychotherapy are the results of an important review article about expertise in psychotherapy as an elusive goal (Tracey et al. 2014). After examining the claim that psychotherapy is a profession without any expertise, these reviewers concluded that:

> There is no demonstration of accuracy and skill … associated with experience as a therapist… the absence of an expertise-experience relation is attributable to therapists' lack of access to quality outcome information regarding their interventions and an over-reliance on fallible information-processing strategies even when such outcome information is available

> ... although [outcome feedback] does relate to client improvement, it has not been shown to be associated with any gains in therapist skill or expertise. (p.218)

These authors' proposal of a model of "outcome information usage and specific a priory hypothesis testing" to develop expertise ignores completely that in the very near future, F2F TB psychotherapy will be supplanted by distance writing and remote online interventions, as argued in this chapter (L'Abate, 2015).

A randomized cluster-controlled trial tested the hypothesis that weekly feedback to clinicians would improve the effectiveness of home-based mental health treatment received by youths in community settings (Bickman et al. 2011). Youths, caregivers, and clinicians at 28 sites in 10 states completed assessments of the youths' symptoms and functioning every other week. Clinicians at 13 sites were provided with weekly feedback about the assessments, and clinicians at 15 sites received feedback every 90 days. Data were collected from June 1, 2006, through December 31, 2008. Intent-to-treat analyses were conducted with hierarchical linear modeling of data provided by youths, caregivers, and clinicians. Assessments by youths, caregivers, and clinicians indicated that youths (N= 173) treated at sites where clinicians could receive weekly feedback improved faster than youths (N= 167) treated at sites where clinicians did not receive weekly feedback. A dose–response analysis showed even stronger effects when clinicians viewed more feedback reports. In conclusion, this research shows that routine measurement and feedback can be used to improve outcomes for youths who receive typical home-based services in the community.

Additionally, Lei et al. (2011), argued that:

> Interventions often involve a sequence of decisions.... Altering the the intensity and type of intervention over time is crucial for many reasons, such as to obtain improvement if the individual is not responding or to reduce costs and burden when intentive treatment is no longer necessary.... The Sequential Multiple Assignment Randomized Trial (SMART) provides high-quality data that can be used to construct adaptive interventions. (p. 21)

By evaluating continuously whether change is occurred and occurring during psychotherapy, this approach deserves the attention of the clinical psychology community as illustrated by Whipple and Lambert (2010), who summarized the results of their meta-analytic review about outcome measures in psychotherapy:

> Using... patient feedback methodology... [that] suggests that measuring, monitoring, predicting treatment failure, and providing clinical support tools to clinicians enhance treatment outcome for patients who have an early negative treatment response.... Clinicians are encouraged to employ these methods in routine practice. (p. 87)

Finally, another promising approach is suggested by Shiffman et al. (2008) about ecological momentary assessment (EMA), consisting of studying particular events in participants' lives, periodically or randomly through written diaries, telephones, and physiological sensors. Among the many issues considered by these authors, they stressed the need for model applications of EMA methods in clinical assessment and intervention. Such a model can be found in an experimental checklist developed to measures contextual and ecological factors with individuals, couples, and families included in the Appendices of this volume (L'Abate 2008b).

Why Online Practice Can Be Harmful

Dr. Marlene M. Maheu (personal communication, December 16, 2013) argued that when connecting with online therapists, consumers don't expect to list the medications they take, report their current alcohol intake or provide a suicide history before asking a question about divorce. They don't typically want to undergo an intake process that includes informed consent or a depression inventory before they discuss how to improve their marital relationship. Have the last 20 years of unregulated, unmitigated, improperly licensed online psychotherapy ruined it for everyone, or created a new way of serving consumers? We may never know for sure, but it is clear that behavioral health care is being challenged by revolutionary online delivery models such as Google's Helpouts. See Google Steps into Mental Health with "Helpouts." [http://clicks.aweber.com/y/ct/?l=Lx8sR&m=3VwG5.JChs27Xrn&b=Veir02hMS0h16IMnU0sX9w] and How Might Licensed Professionals Think about Google's "Helpouts?") [http://clicks.aweber.com/y/ct/?l=Lx8sR&m=3VwG5.JChs27Xrn&b=RKtpjUbnDDKuax5fRhIG2g]. In light of these remarkable changes, how might responsible practitioners think about moving forward with tele-practice? This abstract is the first of three articles in which Dr. Maheu will outline the key controversies in online psychological practice.

In his second article, Dr. Maheu considered the differences between traditional and exclusively Internet-based practice, and the repercussions these differences might have for the professional. As we discussed in *Why Online Practice Can Be Dangerous—Part I*, working in traditional telehealth systems alleviates many of the risks inherent to telemental health and any other form of virtual practice. Client/patient intake, assessment, and history are often conducted by a team of professionals. Working online in a small group or independent practice is quite another story. We'll now look at the differences in more detail.

How tele-medical-health is now booming by leaps and bounds would take us away from our concerns with psychological tele-mental-health (L'Abate and Sweeney, in press).

Why Online Practice can be Harmful: —Part III

By: Marlene M. Maheu, Ph.D.

Posted on: December 30, 2013

In *Why Online Practice Can Be Harmful—Part I,* we examined the role of consumer protection in online practice. In *Why Online Practice Can Be Harmful—Part II,* we discussed the palpable differences between traditional telemental health and online psychotherapy. In this last segment, Why Online Practice Can Be Dangerous—Part III, we examine the role of regulatory boards and professional associations in assuring consumer safety with online practice.

Professionals, Their Professional Associations, and Regulatory Boards

Many licensed behavioral healthcare providers and researchers are unaware of the legal and ethical codes that govern their use of technology. In fact, a Google search for these or related terms will return more than 1.5 million websites:

- Online therapy
- Online psychotherapy
- Internet therapy
- E-therapy
- Online counseling (or online counseling) and
- A host of other related terms

Close examination of websites found by such a search will show that many professionals whose services are available online are operating without compliance with well-published mandates of their regulatory boards and professional associations. The current state of affairs has not improved dramatically since the year 2000, when an early study reporting such problems was published (Maheu and Gordon 2000).

Violations continue to include but are not limited to:

- Practicing over state lines without a license
- Lack of an informed consent process of any type
- Using technology that does not meet Health Insurance Portability and Accountability Act (HIPAA) requirements
- Failing to collect identifying information needed for mandated reporting
- Failing to collaborate with other treating professionals
- Failing to arrange for emergency backup, etc.

How Can So Many Professionals Ignore the Basics?

Most behavioral health providers are clearly operating with the best of intentions. They may not have realized their online practices need to be in line with their in-person services. It also has taken time for many of the regulatory boards and professional associations to devote significant time and attention to the complex and rapidly changing issues. Even more challenges to our governing bodies are just about to unfold….

Consumer adoption of technology and their demands that professionals do the same have forced the issue. Being accessible by e-mail is no longer a question for many professionals. The next big issue faced by many providers is whether or not it is acceptable to allow our clients/patients to reach us with their mobile device videoconferencing features, given their typical state of noncompliance with HIPAA standards for security and privacy.

The time has come for all professional groups to become more cognizant of the urgency with which behavioral health is becoming involved with technology, and the speed with which they must act. Many regulatory boards are quite clear that the use of technology does not represent a new service, but does pose many complex new training challenges. As outlined in *Why Online Practice Can Be Harmful—Part II,* outcome data need to be carefully considered. Generalization of outcome findings to all online practices can lead to faulty conclusions, particularly when online services are delivered without controlled settings or by using established protocols. Many parties are realizing the many ways in which existing rules have been rather lax. As professionals, then, we still need to perform basic functions, but now, through technology:

- Conduct full intakes
- Contact all involved professionals
- Keep secured notes
- Protect privacy and maintain confidentiality
- Conduct a fully informed consent process with added information about the use of technology
- Keep notes
- Document our work
- Know and be able to refer to local community resources
- Plan for and handle abuse reporting, homicide, suicide threats, etc.

Regulatory Boards

Many regulatory boards are currently bringing themselves up to speed and developing policies in harmony with that of other states, both within and across disciplines. The challenge is daunting. To date, boards have operated without much interference from outsiders. With many geographic limitations being eliminated by the Internet, these same regulatory boards are facing decisions about how to handle licensees and other professionals from around the world. Anyone claiming to be any type of professional can now suddenly deliver "professional services" to a state's citizens as they sit in the privacy of their own living rooms.

Some professionals are being censored and disciplined. Indirectly related regulatory boards are taking active stances on issues such as *supervision*. Their involvement is also likely to me aided by the Affordable Care Act, as depicted in the recent Forbes article, entitled, *Top Health Trend For 2014: Telehealth To Grow Over 50%. What Role For Regulation?*

Professional Associations

Professional associations are also taking more of a stand with respect to distance services. Several associations have issued *standards and guidelines* that provide varying levels of direction to their memberships. Furthermore, many are making it quite clear that providers have the responsibility of finding and obtaining adequate training before offering new services, including services that involve technologies that range from telephone to video teleconferencing. Their mandates extend to the delivery of services related that reach beyond telecommunication technologies, such as self-monitoring tools, robotics, haptics, virtual reality, biometrics, the newer forms of biofeedback, such as self-help tools that measure heart rate variability (HRT), and of course, all apps.

Leadership Possibilities

Continued leadership by ethical boards and professional associations has begun in all directions, and more now than ever. These efforts are applauded by many. Both regulatory boards and professional associations might also:

- Allocate resources to not only keep up, but set the bar for safe, high-quality use of all technologies
- Encourage professionals to obtain relevant and affordable training for the twenty-first century practice development (i.e., e-mail is commonly used by professionals, but most graduate or traditional training programs do not yet offer training in how to use e-mail for therapeutic contact; many professionals already use text-messaging services to contact their clients/patients)
- Formally and regularly educate decision makers about technology-related issues
- Become more visible centers of collaboration for technology-minded professionals
- Create entry points at all levels to acknowledge and invite change related to technology (i.e., create convention submission categories related to various types of technology, such as telepractice, mHealth, informatics, etc.
- Foster participation and leadership of graduate students and early career professionals in the adoption of technologies through speciality niches and new disciplines, such as informatics and other growing areas depicted in this volume.

Other Options

1. See the *TeleMental Health Institute's* convenient, affordable professional training options available 24/7 online.
2. Join the *Coalition for Technology in Behavioral Health*, a growing group of technology-minded professionals attempting to work toward developing a visible center of inter-professional collaboration. Their *LinkedIn* group is open to all interested parties.
3. If the reader knows of any other group(s) forming toward these goals, please mention them in the Comments section below. If possible, please provide links to their websites.

4. See *Why Online Practice Can Be Harmful—Part I* and *Why Online Practice Can Be Harmful—Part II* for more thoughts about how to protect those you serve by practicing legally and ethically with a wide variety of technologies (Maheu and Gordon 2000).

Conclusion

The major issue in the Internet practice of clinical psychological assessments and interventions is whether these practices will be left unstructured and, therefore, non-replicable, or structured and, therefore replicable. This issue will be discussed at greater length in the following chapters of this volume.

Chapter 3
Verifiability in Clinical Psychology Practices

> How do we educate each new generation of psychologists to successfully reach those goals of accountable, scientifically based quality care and beneficence? (Rezensky 2013, p. 704)

Up to the present time, clinical psychological practices have relied heavily on the face-to-face (F2F), talk-based (TB) paradigm as unfortunately professionally approved leftover remnants of undoubtedly useful clinical practices that began in the past century. As helpful and useful those practices may have been in the past, they are no longer appropriate to the ever-increasing mental health needs of our nation, including sickness prevention, health promotion, crisis intervention, psychotherapy, and rehabilitation. Technological advances in e-mental health interventions are growing by leaps and bounds every day, as discussed in Chap. 2 of this volume (L'Abate 1990, 1999, 2003, 2013b, 2013c, in press; L'Abate and Sweeney 2011).

As long as these practices continue to rely on the F2F, TB paradigm, little progress is going to occur in current clinical psychological practices because talk, by its very nature, is nonreplicable. Such practices do not follow uniform standard operating procedures (SOPs) that would allow replicability and compatibility within and among psychotherapists and clinical psychology professionals (L'Abate 1999, 2008a, b, c, c, 2013a, b). Most clinical psychology practitioners seemingly continue to rely on talk and unstructured, artistically creative immediacy without wondering on whether these practices produce the desired outcome for each single case, be it an individual, a couple, or a family (Barlow and Carl 2011; Boswell et al. 2011; Norcross 2011a, b, 2014; Spring and Neville 2011; Norcross and Karpiak 2012).

In an extremely important, critical paper, Lilienfeld (2012):

> ...delineated eight reasons why many laypersons are dubious of our field's scientific status [including the illusion of understanding, n/a]. (e. g., our field's reluctant embrace of evidence-based clinical practices) reflect professional psychology's failure to uphold rigorous scientific standards. (Lilienfeld 2012, p. 808)

The original paper was followed up by commentaries by Tryon (2012), who added three more reasons for public distrust of psychology, including the illusion of understanding seemingly obtained through description, explanation, and interpretation (Teo 2012).

L. L'Abate, *Concreteness and Specificity in Clinical Psychology*,
DOI 10.1007/978-3-319-13284-6_3

In addition to Lilienfeld (2010, 2012), Teo (2012), and Tryion (2012), Gaudiano (2013) commented on the status of psychotherapy being in decline due in part to the strong advertising of medications coming from Big Pharma. No matter how much psychotherapy may help in the long run, pill popping seems so much more convenient than going to see a professional F2F and talk:

> …psychotherapy has an image problem. Primary care physicians, insurers policy makers, the public and even many therapists are largely unaware of the high level of research support that psychotherapy has. The situation is exacerbated by an assumption of greater scientific rigor in the biologically based practices of the pharmaceutical industries-industries that, not incidentally, have the money to aggressively market and lobby for those practices, For the sake of patients and the health care system itself, psychotherapy needs to overall its image, more aggressively embracing, formalizing and promoting its empirically supported methods. (p. 1)

Unfortunately, as long as such empirically supported methods are trumpeted as the complete sinecure for psychotherapy based on F2F talk alone, they will continue to be nonreplicable within each professional and among different professionals, leading, as noted repeatedly ad nauseam, to a confusing Tower of Babel. Under those conditions, progress is difficult if not impossible to achieve. Were one to dispute such a conclusion, it would be sufficient to point to advertisements about 36 different types of therapy published in a brochure by the American Psychological Association. These Towers of Babel allow fake self-help gurus such as James Arthur Ray to advertise freely for miraculous cures for naïve and needy individuals seeking happiness and respite from suffering.

Another opinion article in *theguardian.com* (Bundlr 2/1/14) presented evidence that only articles with positive results and none with negative results were ever published in psychological journals. Therefore, there is now a movement to promote replications of positive findings for crucial studies:

> The best evidence for a genuine discovery is showing that independent scientists can replicate it using the same method. If it replicates repeatedly then we can use it to build better theories. If it doesn't then it belongs in the trash bin of history. This simple logic underscores all science—Without replication we'd still believe in phlogiston and faster-than-light neutrinos. (p. 1)

This statement applies also to clinical psychology practices—possibly no to objective evaluations before–after interventions or at follow-up—but definitely yes to most psychological interventions based on F2F talk. No wonder, therefore, if the American public does not trust our practices, and unfortunately, by this mistrust, extend it not only to the profession of clinical psychology but also, unfortunately, to the science of psychology (Lilienfeld 2010, 2012; Teo 2012; Tryon 2012; Guadiano 2013).

Structured or unstructured TB online and offline practices, without any uniformity of pre–post-evaluation and follow-up after termination, are bound to continue to produce Towers of Babel that impede progress. These practices are not comparable among themselves and are noncumulative within a single to another practitioner and from one clinical setting to another (L'Abate 2008b, 2013b; O'Donohue 2013).

By verifiability, therefore, is meant any replicable evaluation, testing, or intervention—used here synonymously—meaning any intersubjectively repeatable method that allows to study the empirical or experiential validity of a rhetorical or theoretical statement and intervention. This statement, for instance, must be evaluated by someone else who is extraneous to that statement.

The evidence-based movement proclaimed in the last generation (Chambliss and Holon 1998; Spring and Neville 2011), as based solely on F2F talk, remains an empty process since no replicability from one clinical psychology professional to another or from one clinic to another is possible. Millions of research funds have been applied to study various aspects of this movement in psychotherapy with or without any evidence that can be replicated from one professional to another or from one clinic to another (Norcross et al. 2006; Kazdin 2008; Norcross 2011a; Spring and Neville 2011; Boyd-Franklin et al. 2013).

To be sure, guidelines and protocols for clinicians were made available but no emphasis was given to ensure that pre–post-intervention evaluation and follow-up would be performed routinely, whenever such quasi- or full-therapeutic process occurred. The whole evidence-based process was applied to interventions with minimal importance given to: (1) written SOPs in pre–post evaluations and follow-up in online/offline interventions and (2) setting objective baselines before and after an intervention with a subsequent follow-up (Dimeff et al. 2011; L'Abate and Sweeney 2011; American Psychological Association 2013a, pp. 1–31, 2013b, p. 3014; L'Abate 2013a, b, 2014, in press).

For those readers who think such a conclusion about EBP might be too negative, this is a recent opinion given by reputable sources (Karlin and Cross 2014):

> Despite their established efficacy and recommendation—often as first-time treatments—in clinical practice guidelines, evidence-based psychotherapies (EBPs) have largely failed to make their way into mainstream clinical settings. Numerous attempts over the years to promote the translation of EBPs from science to practice, typically relying on one-dimensional Dissemination approaches, have yielded limited success. (p. 19)

Karlin and Cross (2014) went on to describe their efforts to disseminate and implement multidimensional models and specific strategies to deliver Evidence-Published Systems (EPS) to veterans. Unfortunately, no data were given to support their innovative approaches that seemed to still rely on F2F talk. Therefore, it will be difficult to prove that the approaches Karlin and Cross advocated will have a positive outcome on suicide rates and other disorders present in the US army forces and veterans.

The reason for the cautious questioning of such an innovative and courageous attempt lies in its not addressing the root problem of clinical practices still based on artistic rather than on empirical practices. This problem requires a complete overhaul of existing F2F TB practices based on replicable, programmed distance writing administered remotely by professionals without ever seeing and talking with their patients (L'Abate 2013b, c). For instance, Belar (2012) described a vision of psychology's future as a health profession. In broadening its focus from mental health to a range of health issues, the profession is faced with a number of challenges related to establishing its identity, ensuring public confidence, and participating in the health-care system. Specific imperatives included the need to articulate the core competencies of health service psychologists, assure quality in preparation and practice, and work collaboratively with other professions while participating actively in the redesign of the health-care system.

Before expanding on these requirements, we need to evaluate in greater detail how clinical psychological practices are occurring at the present time.

The Requirements of Verifiability in Clinical Psychological Practices

In the first place, in order to be verifiable, clinical psychology practices need to be replicable, this will occur only with there is an uniformity of SOPs in: (1) pre-intervention evaluation, (2) interventions proper, (3) post-therapy evaluation, and (4) follow-up some time after termination. In the second place, replicability is found in written, structured, programmed interactive interventions and not in verbal unstructured ones. This requirement is discussed at greater length in Chap. 8 of this volume. In the third place, validation of these practices must occur: (1) in each professional practitioner's office as well as (2) in the laboratory, to be replicable (3) from one professional to another, and (4) from one clinic to another (L'Abate 2008b, 2013b, c).

In addition to *verifiability,* however, clinical psychological practices should produce results in clinical practice, thus fulfilling a second criterion of *accountability*. Accountability and verifiability, however, are criteria independent of each other. We need verifiability in theory building as well as in therapy, but the criterion of accountability may be more relevant to therapeutic outcomes than to theory construction and testing whereas verifiability is the first and foremost requirement (L'Abate 2005, 2008b; Rezensky 2013).

Producing results, however, is no longer a sufficient criterion in clinical psychological practices. If a theory or a technique is useful to a practicing clinician, is that all that is necessary? For instance, some very appealing theories of therapy may produce impresssionistic results in spite of their inherent unverifiability, as it used to be (in part) the case with psychoanalysis and, more recently, with family therapy. At least in psychotherapy, a theory could conceivably account for a positive outcome but remain unverifiable otherwise. Apparently, many therapists work on the basis of this assumption (Norcross 2011a; Boyd-Franklin et al. 2013). Theories be dammed! What is important is to help people who need our help without evidence that we do indeed help one individual, couple, or family at a time.

Results as subjectively viewed by some professionals is all it matters (Norcross 2011b; Rezensky 2013). To take into account both criteria, verifiability and accountability, therefore, *a theory needs to be verifiable in the laboratory as well accountable in clinical practice.* Accountability may be necessary in therapy but insufficient in theory, just as verifiability may be necessary in theory but insufficient in therapy. Both criteria are necessary and sufficient to verify a theory in the laboratory if that theory is to be also applied in clinical or preventive settings (L'Abate et al. 2010; Cusinato and L'Abate 2012a; L'Abate 2013a, b, c, d; Hooper et al. 2014).

The Meaning of Evidence in Clinical Psychology: Concreteness and Specificity in Psychological Evaluation

Evidence means validated, written SOPs that are homogeneous and uniform enough to make them replicable from one clinician to another and from one clinic to another and verifiable in the laboratory and in a clinician's office as well. This definition includes apps, workbooks, and videos reproducible ad infinitum. If a procedure, in either evaluation or intervention, cannot be replicated, it is not evidence and should be unacceptable to responsible clinical psychology practices (Corcoran and Fischer 2013).

Except for projective techniques, psychological evaluations do follow a written and, therefore, replicable format. Therefore, the major issue with them is selection and cost. Which evaluation instrument offers the most reliable information with the least time for administration and scoring for which concern? In clinical psychology, we are flooded with so many validated test instruments (Corcoran and Fischer 2013; Hunsley and Mash 2011) that one can choose, especially if one wants to administer either one multidimensional test, such as the Minnesota Multiphasic Personality Inventory, or a battery of "quick-and-dirty" screening instruments. This problem of choosing and selecting an appropriate test or a battery of tests is much more difficult in selected test instruments for couples and families (Williams et al. 2011; Sperry 2012). This problem is compounded by the shifting nature and composition of the family as we knew it, as discussed in Chap. 4 of this volume (L'Abate 2013a).

After considering some current problems and scientific limitations in clinical assessment and some commonly used clinical instrument, Hunsley and Mash (2011) considered problems in instrument selection and interpretation with limited evidence for the clinical utility of commonly used instruments. First, they used the Bickman et al. (1999) criteria for rating outcome measures for use in child and adolescent mental health services. These criteria (Hunsley and Mash 2011, p. 84) were: cultural sensitivity, suitability (including cost), reliability, content and construct validity, norms, and developmental sensitivity. For adults, Hunsley and Mash (2011, pp. 86–87) used criteria of norms, internal consistency, inter-rater reliability, test–retest reliability, content and construct validity, validity generalization, treatment sensitivity, and clinical utility.

On the basis of their own criteria and those developed by Cohen et al. (2008), Hunsley and Mash (2011, p. 90) presented a list of the most useful instruments to evaluate psychopathology in youth. There is no reason to administer those very same instruments to adults provided norms for adults are available. However, in discussing the relation between evidence-based assessment (EBA) and evidence-based treatment (EBT), these authors concluded that: "Despite recognition of the critical synergy between EBA and EBT, EBT continues to generate considerable attention, EBA receives little to none.... Moreover, we know very little about how assessments and the data they generate are being used in the context of EBT" (p. 93).

This conclusion supports past and present contentions that while the process in EBT was emphasized, both pre- and post-evaluation were essentially neglected. The process was given more importance than the assumed outcome, rendering the whole EBT essentially meaningless if not transferable from one therapist to another, especially if relying on F2F, TB process (L'Abate 2013b). Unfortunately, many clinical psychology practitioners seem to routinely avoid tests to evaluate outcome, relying mainly on an unstructured interview without an initial baseline to evaluate progress or lack thereof for each single case, be it an individual, a couple, or a family without any evidence of positive outcome after interventions (Norcross 2011a, 2011b; Norcross et al. 2010; Spring and Neville 2011).

In spite of these shortcomings, reliance on the written rather than on F2F talk is the norm in evaluation because these measures are completely replicable from one practitioner to another, from one case to another, and from one clinic to another (Geisinger 2013). Therefore, the major issue about psychological interventions is the need to rely on distance, remote writing instead of F2F talk. As already argued in Chap. 2 of this volume, distance or remote writing on the Internet is rapidly becoming the new medium of communication online and hopefully healing for those who need and want behavioral or clinical psychological help (Dimeff et al. 2011; L'Abate and Sweeney 2011; L'Abate 2013d). Unfortunately, clinical psychology practitioners, counselors, and psychotherapists tend to repeat and mimic online what they had been doing heretofore offline, that is: continuing to practice like artists without pre–post-intervention evaluation and follow-up after termination (L'Abate in press).

For instance, Boyd-Franklin et al. (2013, pp. 22–35) covered extensively the whole field of evidence-based practice defined as: "…the integration of the best suitable research with clinical expertise in the context of patient characteristics, culture and preferences"(p. 22). Boyd-Franklin et al. (2013) quoted a great many sources related especially to psychotherapy. From evidence-based practice, authors went on to discuss evidence-informed practice to evidence-based relationships. However, the debate about evidence practices is bound to continue without realizing that the whole construction of this approach is built on two premises already noted above repeatedly, not covered by this approach, and that is: (1) the whole process of psychotherapy has been emphasized without any attention or thought on how such a process should be evaluated, no directions and links were given on how clinical psychological practitioners should evaluate their results, provided they just followed "evidence-based practices" and (2) the whole process of psychotherapy was assumed to occur within a context of F2F, verbally based relationships (Spring and Neville 2011). If that is the case, how can any individual clinical psychological practitioner ever be able to demonstrate that evidence-based practices were followed since talk is not a replicable medium? Consequently, attention should be given to tests to provide evidence on whether the claimed evidence-based process in psychotherapy or even clinical psychology has ever occurred.

Test Evidence

Psychological tests suffer from an embarrassment of riches (Hunsley and Mash 2011). In spite of most being well validated in order to be accepted by the clinical psychology community, we have such a plethora of tests that raises the problem of selection. Which test or battery of tests should one select? By their own very nature of being available in print, psychological tests are replicable. However, age group, concern or diagnosis, cost of administration and scoring, amount and nature of information received, and online availability should be the criteria for test selection.

Consequently, to achieve the same level of replicability as psychological tests, psychological interventions, to become replicable, must occur in writing because that medium assures that they can be printed ad infinitum within one professional and among professional helpers. However, a second requirement must be made of psychological tests. Besides being available on the Internet, they ideally should be theory derived, as is the case of paper-and-pencil, self-report tests developed to evaluate models of relational competence theory (RCT; L'Abate et al. 2010; Cusinato and L'Abate 2012).

Replicability does not belong only to the professional and scientific realm; it applies to behavior as well. We do not observe singly happening behaviors that may occur by happenstance or accident. We observe and try to change for the better toxic or maladaptive behaviors that repeat themselves in human relationships. Indeed, the very characteristic of repetitiveness applies to studying and trying to improve behaviors that are too embedded to make it difficult to change, such as: (1) duration, (2) frequency, (3) rate, (4) intensity, and (5) context. By their very nature, toxic and maladaptive behaviors occur repeatedly before we are able to become aware of their toxicity and maladaptiveness. We need new theoretical lenses to see and understand behaviors not otherwise visible without a theory (L'Abate 2013a, b; Hooper et al. 2014).

Fortunately, the major criterion for selecting a particular test at the present time lies in its being available online, considering the phenomenal rise of smartphones and applications (apps) covering an increasingly wide range of conditions that make it possible to communicate and perhaps heal individuals, couples, and families one by one (Dimeff et al. 2011; Proudfoot 2012; Maheu et al. 2013).

In spite of Norcross and Karpiak's (2012) survey of clinical psychological practices finding "…a relative decline in psychological assessment in general and projective testing in particular" (p. 1), Weiner (2012) argued instead that: "The majority of respondents are engaged in diagnosis/assessment, which dispels the impression that assessment is no longer of importance in the preparation of clinical psychologists. Psychological assessment is currently a thriving area of research and practice that is receiving less attention than it should in graduate programs" (p. 13). This is especially the case in working with children (Johnson 2012).

Within this context, it is important to quote what Gallo and Barlow (2012) emphasized about evidence-based interventions in mental health:

> With the development of empirically supported psychological treatments and the growing mandate for evidence-based practice, the dissemination and implementation of interventions with proven efficacy has assumed an growing sense of urgency, One barrier to the implementation of new procedures involves individual differences in the proclivity to adopt innovations, even in the context of supportive organizational structures (p. 93)." After "…a review of the literature on the characteristics of adopters and non-adopters and factors that facilitate adoption of evidence-based practice in the field of mental health, information about reasons for adoption and non-adoption of evidence-based practices in other areas of health-care delivery [was] reviewed to inform strategies for improving rates of adoption of evidence-based treatments by mental health providers. (p. 93)

Recently, there have been at least four serious attempts to deal with psychological evaluation in clinical psychology. First, Nordal (2012) produced a Medicare Physician Quality Reporting System (PQRS) that clinical psychologists need to know. This system is based on five steps:

Step 1. Determine which PQRS reporting method is appropriate for one's practice, including a registry-based qualified electronic health record (EHR) or a group practice reporting option (GPRO), A Centers for Medicare and Medicaid Services (CMS) website <go.cms.gov/Vk8V> is available to learn about the three options.

Step 2. Select a measure among the 13 available to psychologists to evaluate major depressive disorder, body mass index, pain assessment, screening for clinical depression, screening for elder mistreatment, tobacco use, and substance use.

Step 3. Check the measure worksheets in order to determine the required procedural codes available in the same webpage given above.

Step 4. Use the appropriate G-code to indicate whether the service was performed or why it was not performed.

Step 5. Record the information on the CMS 1500 Claim Form.

Second, Simons et al. (2013) argued that for both clinical practice and training purposes, reliable and valid measures of uniform therapist behaviors and practice elements are needed for the purpose of uniformity in interventions not only in cognitive behavioral therapy (CBT). Furthermore one would argue and add, for all psychotherapists who claim to practice as professionals: "Better ways to assess just what therapists are doing will also help research designed to identify mechanisms of change (p. 189), especially when dealing with children versus adult clients." These authors, therefore, conducted a comprehensive literature review to identify measures of declarative and procedural knowledge: two measures of therapist and one measure of client declarative knowledge, 22 measures of therapist and four measures of client procedural knowledge (pp. 187–188). This is another attempt to reduce psychotherapists' variability to SOPs.

Third, Sajatovic and Ramirez (2001) published an encyclopedia of rating scales that very likely should be updated by now. This source, together with the plethora of psychological test instruments available on the market, does produce a problem of selection: which therapist behavior should be used to improve therapist uniformity in practice? Which rating scale or equivalent test instrument(s) should be administered that yield the most reliable and valid information with the least cost of administration, scoring, and interpretation? This seemingly chaotic embarrassment of riches would require careful consideration in reaching a test battery that could serve as a baseline to assess the outcome of any intervention.

Fourth, another promising example of evaluation is found in the work of Pilkonis et al. (2011). They reported on: "...the development and calibration of item banks for depression, anxiety, and anger as part of the Patient-Reported Outcomes Measurement Information System (PROMIS®). Comprehensive literature searches yielded an initial bank of 1404 items from 305 instruments. After qualitative item analysis (including focus groups and cognitive interviewing), 168 items (56 for each construct) were written in a first person, past tense format with a 7-day time frame and five response options reflecting frequency. The calibration sample included nearly 15,000 respondents. Final banks of 28, 29, and 29 items were calibrated for depression, anxiety, and anger, respectively, using item response theory. Test information curves showed that the PROMIS item banks provided more information than conventional measures in a range of severity from approximately -1 to $+3$ standard deviations (with higher scores indicating greater distress). Short forms consisting of seven to eight items provided information comparable to legacy measures containing more items."

These authors confused different levels of analysis when they set depression at the same level with anxiety and anger. To speak at the same level as the latter two terms, the construct of sadness should have been used instead of depression. This differentiation was illustrated by a model that makes anger basic to the development of externalizing disorders, sadness basic to internalizing disorders, and fears basic to the development of psychopathology. Underneath the presence of these three states, there are unexpressed hurt feelings, that is, the unconscious (De Giacomo et al. 2010; L'Abate 2011a).

The Artist/Empiricist Distinction in Clinical Psychology: Counseling, Psychotherapy, and Psychoanalysis

This distinction is an important one because the artistic side of that distinction is how most clinical psychological, preventive, and psychotherapeutic practices are performed at the present time (Norcross 2011a). This distinction is summarized in Fig. 3.1.

This admittedly artificial distinction was introduced recently (L'Abate 2013b). Artists tend to work without internal or external controls and in clinical psychological practices do not account for their work except through a short interview but with no baseline, pre–post-objective evaluation to verify whether any progress has been made after an intervention and long-term follow-up. Furthermore, practitioners who work without internal or external controls seem to base their unstructured treatment on F2F talk which is a nonreproducible medium. However, many clinical psychological practitioners in growing numbers continue to practice online now by

The Artist/Empiricist Distinction in Clinical psychology: Counseling, Psychoanalysis, and Psychotherapy

Artist	Versus	Empiricist
	Evaluation	
	Consent Form Signed	
Questionable Administration		Routine Administration
Short Interview		Structured Interview
No objective tests		Battery of Tests or Multidimensional Tests (MMPI-2)
No baseline evaluation		Baseline set
No re-evaluation		Re-evaluation
No Follow-up		Follow-up
No-match between Evaluation & treatment		Match between evaluation & treatment
Overreliance on expensive & time consuming projective techniques (Rorschach & TAT) that rely on artistic interpretations and do not furnish a quantitative base-line. Emphasis on therapeutic Alliance. No homework Assignments.		Reliance on written home-work assignments Therapeutic alliance set online through objective evaluation. Stepped Care
	Theories or Models Underlying Interventions	
Either none or arbitrary and capricious mixture of various different models that are impossible to validate through face-to-face talk		Cognitive-behavioral RCT Mindfulness/Meditation Validation possible through replicable distance writing
	Interventions	
Insistence on Face-to-Face Non-replicable Talk or using unstructured, non-replicable procedures online		Insistence on Online Replicable SOPS such as Distance Interactive Practice Exercises (PIPEs)

Fig. 3.1 The artist/empiricist distinction in clinical psychology: counseling, psychoanalysis, and psychotherapy

mimicking at a distance the same unstructured, nonreplicable procedures they followed in the past verbally F2F offline (Norcross 2014).

The artistic position is best represented by Hamid Mirsalimi (2014), reprinted here with his permission (personal communication, November 1, 2013):

> Empiricism, in essence, is the only way to determine whether the artist/empiricist distinction is an artificial one. That is, utilizing double-blind, placebo controlled studies, is the only way the field can definitively judge the artificiality or accuracy of the artist/empiricist distinction. Until results of such research are available, the field is dependent on: 1. theories and common sense of those who believe more strongly in the art of psychotherapy versus those who believe more strongly in the empirical approach; and 2. what the field already knows about psychotherapy outcome research. Strict reliance on the type of empiricism that would recommend abandoning face-to-face talk therapy, and increasing the reliance on standard operating procedures (SOPs), would undermine the importance of relationship factors in psychotherapy and ultimately the effectiveness of patient care. This discussion

> is ultimately dependent on our philosophical views about the nature of human beings: Are humans robot-like creatures whose behaviors are strictly controllable, or are they beings whose motivations, struggles, hopes and behaviors are nuanced and individualistic? The essential question in psychotherapy is what works for whom, under what individual circumstances, within what contexts, and as delivered by whom? For example, a strictly empiricist approach toward a patient with trust issues is likely to have disastrous results. On the other hand, a strictly emotion-focused therapy with a patient who is too afraid of getting in touch with his or her feelings, can also be disastrous. The art of psychotherapy is in employing a savvy approach toward answering the above question, and can include a determination of the patient's readiness to engage in empirical approaches to psychotherapy. Additionally, an aspect of this debate is dependent on our definitions of what is art, what is empiricism, and how they are used; that is another reason why the distinction is an artificial one.

How are "trust issues" or "a patient who is too afraid of getting in touch with his or her feelings" to be evaluated? Apparently, a strictly impressionistic opinion of the therapist is necessary, nothing else. All of the above stands to show how practicing as artists reduces clinical psychologists and psychotherapists practicing as artists to the level of charlatans. No wonder the American public does not trust psychology as a profession (Lilienfield 2010, 2012; Teo 2012; Tryons 2012; Gaudagno 2013).

That artistic position leads directly to confusing Towers of Babel in evaluation and psychotherapy, as illustrated, among many others, by Boswell et al. (2011) and VandenBos et al. (2014), where no theory or techniques is superior in outcome in comparison to competing theories and techniques (L'Abate 2013b). These two sources do not include 21 types of psychotherapy included in the advertisements of a major publishing house. When one adds arbitrary, personally motivated, immediacy-oriented creativity, the outcome is a completely nonreplicable chaotic Tower of Babel, and, therefore, tends to produce the negative reactions from the American public, as reported by Gaudiano (2013) Lilienfeld (2010, 2012), Teo (2012), and Tryons (2012).

A middle-of-the road position was taken by Arthur Horne (Personal Communication, 02/11/2013) in response to this proposal (Fig. 3.1):

> …if I were working on this panel, my position would be in the middle—all artist with no science is corrupt and serendipitous whereas all science and no artistry is boring and inhuman. The consummate therapist would be one who embodied the humanistic appreciation for personhood in full, but who knows specific processes to use to address particular areas of concern, and can then evaluate the impact and influence. So, I would fall on neither side. Probably represents the culmination of my undergraduate and master's training in an existential/humanistic environment followed by a doctorate with rabid behaviorists, seasoned by a career of seeing extremes of both sides be harmful and ineffective. So, you know where I stand on this…In the middle. (Arthur M. Horne, personal communication, September 23, 2013)

Unfortunately, a middle, compromise position would lead to more problems than it tries to solve. Which middle? If there are no rules for taking such a position and clinical psychological practitioners were able to choose which part of the middle each of them would prefer and choose, would that middle refer to evaluation? Which tests to choose over others? Preferred theory or model? Which type of intervention should be administered? Consequently, such a compromise position would lead us back to the Tower of Babel already present in clinical psychological practices, arbitrary and capricious choices made on the basis of individually oriented, immediate creativity, intuitive whims, and idiosyncratic wills (L'Abate 2013b).

Empiricists, on the other hand, evaluate referring concerns objectively setting up a baseline to evaluate progress through a reevaluation and follow-up through replicable SOPs in writing, matching evaluation with intervention. Norcross, however, has taken a clear position against "eclecticism": (personal communication, 10/25/13):

> Much of what passes for eclecticism these days is, in fact, syncretism (unsystematic mishmash). By contrast, I favor evidence-based or prescriptive integration…. Gerry Koocher and I are working away on another Delphi poll (and eventually, a book) on what does NOT work—psycho-quackery. Here are articles related to that thrust.

It is important to identify what works and what does not work in evidence-based psychotherapy. As Norcross et al. (2010) demonstrated:

> Evidence-based practice promotes those research-supported treatments that have proven effective, but it rarely identifies discredited treatments that are to be avoided. Norcross et al. (2010) sought to establish a professional consensus on discredited addiction treatments using Delphi methodology. A panel of 75 experts participated in a 2-stage study, reporting familiarity with 65 treatments and rating these on a continuum from "not at all discredited" to "certainly discredited." We report their composite opinions and significant differences that occurred as a function of the panelists' theoretical orientation. These results require careful interpretation, but do offer a cogent first step in identifying a professional consensus of discredited treatments for addictions.

Furthermore, Norcross and Karpiak (2012) added more information about clinical psychological practices in the USA that are relevant to the artist/empiricist distinction:

> The American Psychological Association's Division of Clinical Psychology constitutes one of the oldest, largest, and most active organizations of clinical psychologists in the world. For 50 years, beginning with E. Lowell Kelly in 1960, researchers have chronicled the evolution of its membership and the transformation of clinical psychology in the United States. In this article, Norcross and Karpiak (2012) highlighted the continuity and change in clinical psychologists' demographics, educations, theories, employment, activities, and satisfactions over a 50-year span. Results from the most recent, 2010 study (N=588, 46 % return rate) are summarized in both contemporary and historical contexts. Among the prominent trends are steady increases in the proportion of female and ethnic minority psychologists, the rise of Psy.D. graduates, the domination of the cognitive orientation, a relative decline in psychological assessment in general and projective testing in particular (italics added), the ascendancy of independent practice, and a pattern of high career satisfaction.

Another article introduces the issue of the *Journal of Clinical Psychology: In Session* devoted to evidence-based means of adapting psychotherapy to the patient's (transdiagnostic) characteristics (Norcross and Wampold 2011):

> Practitioners have long realized that treatment should be tailored to the individuality of the patient and the singularity of his or her context, but only recently has sufficient empirical research emerged to reliably guide practice. This article reviews the work of an interdivisional task force and its dual aims of identifying elements of effective therapy relationships (what works in general) and identifying effective methods of adapting treatment to the individual patient (what works in particular). The task force judged four patient characteristics (reactance/resistance, preferences, culture, religion/spirituality) to be demonstrably

effective in adapting psychotherapy and another two (stages of change, coping style) as probably effective. Two more patient facets (expectations, attachment style) were related to psychotherapy outcome but possessed insufficient research as a means of adaptation. This special issue provides research-supported methods of individualizing psychotherapy to the person, in addition to his or her diagnosis.

According to John Norcross (Personal communication, 12/24/2013), at least one third ("percentage in the 25–35 range") claim eclecticism as their major theoretical orientation. However, further support for an empirical position is found in the article by Bobbitt et al. 2012). According to them, the US health-care system is in the process of rapid change that poses both opportunities and challenges for the discipline of professional psychology. Quality improvement processes and outcomes measurement are becoming key features of the evolving system. The current status of quality in health care and behavioral health care was reviewed, as is the growing use of patient-reported outcome measures in clinical practice. The authors articulated a vision in which quality processes and outcomes measurement are integrated into clinical practice within the discipline of professional psychology. Opportunities and challenges associated with that integration are reviewed, and recommendations are made for the American Psychological Association to assume leadership in ensuring that these concepts become central to training and practice in psychology. Unfortunately, such recommendations are too vague, too general, and not concrete and specific enough to allow implementation.

Some of the arguments and criticisms that Tee and Kazantzis (2011) leveled toward Beck's cognitive therapy could be leveled toward current clinical psychological practices. Despite the consensus regarding the importance of collaborative empiricism (CE) in Beck's cognitive therapy, absent are operational definitions, measures, or empirical investigations of the construct (Tee and Kazantzis 2011). CE bears significant similarities to the empiricist position taken earlier in this chapter (Fig. 3.1). Existing research has centered on constructs such as the working alliance and has produced inconsistent findings. It is unclear whether CE is related to treatment outcomes, or whether it mediates other cognitive change processes. This chapter argued that the core meaning of collaboration in CE, "sharing the work," is not captured by the most frequently used construct of the therapeutic alliance in cognitive therapy research. A theory of CE, based on self-determination theory, was developed that integrated the collaborative and empirical aspects of CE and addressed the motivational aspect of the construct.

As far as theory surrounding psychotherapy is concerned, Jurist (2013) challenged Norcross and Karpiak's (2012) conclusion that "…psychodynamic orientation is on the decline in clinical psychology" (p. 221). He argued: "…that there are psychodynamic researchers who have embraced evidence-based philosophy and practice" (p. 221), advocating a rapprochement between Division 12 (Society of Clinical Psychology) and 39 (Psychoanalysis), and proposing "…a defense of pluralism in which all clinical psychologists recognize the obligation to engage other orientations and points of view that differ from their own and to do so respectfully" (p. 221).

In line with Jurist's (2013) call for a respectful consideration of various theoretical viewpoints, Heatherington et al. (2012) noted: "…the increasingly narrow range of therapeutic orientations represented in clinical psychology training programs, particularly within the most research-oriented programs." Obtaining data from a variety of Ph.D. and Psy.D. training programs, these authors: "…reveal(ed) a strong predominance of faculty with cognitive-behavioral orientations at the more science-focused programs, and a narrower range of orientation than in the more practiced-focused programs."

To increase uniformity and, therefore, decrease the immense variability of psychotherapeutic practices, Goldstein et al. (2012) presented guidelines for adapting manualized interventions for new target populations using a step-wise approach (L'Abate 2005, 2013b; O'Donohue and Draper 2011). Unfortunately, as long as administration of such an approach relies on F2F, TB contacts, replicability will remain very difficult to implement (L'Abate 2005).

In line with the whole issue of replicability, various proposals were presented to guarantee "treatment integrity" (Carroll 2013; Garland and Schoenwald 2013; Houge et al. 2013; Landsverk 2013; McLeod et al. 2013; Regan et al. 2013; Southam-Gerow and McLeod 2013). Again, at the risk of sounding like a broken record, as long as all these attempts to safeguard the treatment integrity of psychotherapeutic approaches are based on the F2F, TB paradigm, these attempts are doomed to fail.

In a concluding article related to treatment integrity, Hoadwood (2013) noted that:

> The structure, organization, management, and design of the mental health system are changing profoundly as new health-care policies reshape its configuration. This special issue (Southam-Gerow & McLeod, 2013) is a call to action for the mental health services research field. The articles (cited above) represent an important attempt to identify specific concepts, constructs, and findings from psychosocial treatment research about fidelity and integrity of treatment and align them with healthcare quality. However, the current structure and processes for deriving quality indicators place other demands on the extant research base. These will challenge this migration unless changes are made in leadership around consistent measurement strategies, payment mechanisms to support quality, and attention to technological infrastructure development. The mental health services research field should be proactive. (p. 120)

What differentiates distance or remote writing from F2F, TB psychotherapy is the conviction (L'Abate1999, 2011b, 2013a, b, c) that, for psychotherapy to become a scientifically based treatment, interventions must be replicable, as in many homework assignments (Kazantzis and L'Abate 2007; L'Abate 2007b, 2012b; Harwood and L'Abate 2010). To be or become valid, any type of promotional, preventive, and psychotherapeutic intervention must rely on replicable writing. Words are not replicable (L'Abate 1999). As long as counseling, psychotherapy, or psychoanalysis are based on words, they will continue to be an artistic enterprise that, unfortunately, very likely will also attract charlatans (Lilienfeld 2010, 2012; Gaudiano 2013). Where can one draw the line between an artist and a charlatan?

Artists usually do not evaluate their works. They claim, declare, and proclaim that their works are art without any necessary evidence or external judgment. The distinguishing characteristic of empiricists/scientists from artists lies in the administration of an objective evaluation before, during, after termination of interventions, and on follow-up. This approach is necessary especially when there is a plethora of workbooks from which to choose to match individual concerns with concrete and specific treatments (L'Abate 1992, 2008a, 2008b, 2008c, 2011b, 2013c, in press), a level of specificity difficult if not impossible to achieve in F2F, TB psychotherapy.

Another recent version of an artistic position is shown by the following blog available online.

Will "User Experience-based" become the new "Evidenced-based" in Technology-Assisted Counseling? Please Support ACT! Sign the petition http://thewired-pro.com/ *Members here could get ACT to the 500*

Dr. Frank D. Hutchinson, Jr. Digital Media Psychology Consultant at HutchLux DesignTop Contributor

> User Experience (UX) based practice has the potential to replace "evidenced-based" practice as the new litmus test for quality delivery of technological innovations in healthcare and counseling. From a healthcare standpoint, it is obviously important that Technology-Assisted Counseling (TAC) applications do not provide users with experiences that are inferior to those traditionally provided in face to face settings. However, more than that, practitioners have a duty and responsibility to strive to craft ethical user experiences that are not only effective and efficient but compelling. From a Positive Psychology perspective the question must be "How do we build a GREAT User Experiences into TAC applications? User Experience is all about attuning with a target audience, applying human factors analysis to gather information and taking a user-centric approach to development. UX design aims to create practical yet intuitive end products while assuring the quality delivery of services to the user. While evidenced-based practice is about delivering quality, User Experience—based practice is about delivering quality services with a metaphorical "smile" of satisfaction—on the client's face.There are many human factors that come into play when designing the overall user experience for any TAC application. These may include factors such as visual, tactile, and/or cognitive aspects, training, and user expectations to name a few. In order to craft and build a compelling user experience, a multi-tiered approach should be taken:Define the Application's Goals
>
> - What are the goals and objectives (must be measureable)?
> - Why are you building this application? Who is the intended audience?
> - Why will people use this application?
>
> Establish the Application's Structure and Navigation
>
> - Identify how the TAC application content should be organized.
> - How will users use the application?
> - How will the application be mobilized if necessary?
> - How do you prevent them from getting lost?
>
> Define the User Experience
>
> - What are the intended user tasks?
> - Can a user complete the task quickly and efficiently?
> - How do your users feel after completing the intended tasks?
> - Will the application have extended use?

> Create the UX Design
>
> • Sketch the visual design of application's structure and mapping the layout.
> • Develop Prototype modeling and usability testing strategies.
>
> Prototype Modeling
> Prototype modeling is a highly valuable UX technique that helps to provide a clear vision of the design impact on user interactions—particularly when designing mobile medical applications. Some of the key benefits to prototyping are:
>
> - Effectively communicates functionality by demonstrating what the application is supposed to do by removing any ambiguity in user interpretation.
> - Quickly address any issue early, which allows the developers to iterate and make any adjustments before solidifying the final design.
> - Prototype modeling can be created and modified relatively quickly and inexpensively.
>
> Usability Testing
> Usability testing is another UX technique that is very effective at providing valuable insights into how a real user would use your applications, and helps to identify any areas of potential "use error" and user confusion. Testing can be performed both remotely, or in-person, where both options allow you to observe users and their overall user experience. By taking a user-centric approach when designing TAC applications, and utilizing the appropriate tools and techniques such as prototyping and usability testing, designers can lay down the necessary foundations to address and manage quality and positive delivery of client services.http://johnnyholland.org/2011/10/what-i-bring-to-ux-from-psychology/https://www.klick.com/health/news/blog/mhealth/user-experience-guidelines-for-creating-mobile-medical-apps/.

As long as these, seemingly unstructured "user experience based," practices are based on F2F TB contacts, it is doubtful whether they are going to be followed.

The Importance of an Initial Baseline to Evaluate Progress

The importance of an initial baseline to evaluate progress in clinical psychology interventions was not sufficiently or satisfactorily emphasized in a previous publication (L'Abate 2013b). Kazdin (2013) spent a great deal of time to emphasize the importance of baseline in its assessment of behavioral performance in its descriptive and predictive functions. Consequently, further support for this initial contention might be necessary. Kendall and Comer (2011), for instance, argued that:

> To evaluate the effects of treatment, it is essential to first evaluate the level of each client's functioning on the dependent variables before the intervention begins. Such pre-treatment (or "baseline") assessment provides key data to inform whether clients are comparable at the beginning of treatment (e.g., between groups comparisons) and whether clients' pre-treatment levels of functioning differ significantly from functioning assessed at subsequent assessment points (e.g., within groups comparisons). (p. 56)

Expensive (lengthy administration time, lengthy scoring time, lengthy qualitative and subjective interpretation), projective techniques, such as the Rorschach and the Thematic Apperception Tests, by their very nature, do not furnish a quantitative baseline. Therefore, tests of this kind become useless from a baseline viewpoint. Only tests that can be readministered either during treatment or at termination from treatment ("quick and dirty") can be included (Geisinger 2013). Indeed, I would recommend that, at least with adults, a battery of "quick and dirty" objective, paper-and-pencil, self-report tests should be administered routinely before participants meet with the clinical psychologist. This should give the professional or her/his assistant sufficient time to score those tests and arrive at a tentative evaluation even before seeing participants online or offline.

The Importance of Follow-Up in Clinical Psychology Practices

Until recently, as far as this writer knows, follow-up after termination of psychological interventions has not received the importance it deserves (Lebow 2006; Lilienfeld and O'Donohue 2007; Kazdin 2013). Insistence on the routine use of follow-up after termination of interventions was not coupled with a satisfactory rationale or even sufficient support (L'Abate 2013b). Kendall and Comer (2011), for instance, supported the importance of follow-up by commenting that: "it is highly recommended and increasingly expected that that treatment outcome studies include a follow-up assessment" (p. 56). One does not need to rely on "studies" to support the importance of follow-up with each and every client (individual, couples, and family) who asks for help. For instance, Foxx (2013) has furnished such a rationale, even though couched in behavioral terminology:

> Response maintenance is one of the three forms of generalized behavior change with the others being setting/situation generalization and response generalization. Long-term maintenance of treatment effects is an important issue after behavior change has taken place and is the goal of most programs. (p. 728)

Foxx also discussed including:

> …factors affecting the study of maintenance, technique for programming it, and analyzing and evaluating strategies for promoting it. (p. 728)

Fox presented a number of long-term follow-ups of programs to treat addictions, teach social skills, and language to autistic children, and decrease "severe maladaptive behaviors." He concluded his evidence-supported presentation with the following statement:

> The treatment and training of individuals with behavioral methods has evolved to the point where it is extremely important that lengthy follow-ups be conducted and disseminated so that maintenance and generalization strategies can be analyzed and evaluated. Changing journal publication standards may offer one way of ensuring this process, namely, by requiring a minimum follow-up period (e.g., 2 years or more) before a paper can be considered for publication. (p. 735)

This conclusion applies to individuals as well as couples and families. Without extensive and continuous follow-up, we are never going to find out whether our interventions are producing the long-term results necessary to demonstrate our competence as professionals (Lilienfeld 2010, 2012; Teo 2012; Tryon 2012; Foxx 2013; Gaudiano 2013; L'Abate 2013b).

In addition to standard requirements for SOPs in follow-ups, as concluded by Foxx, such requirement should become part of a code of ethics for the clinical psychology profession that heretofore has allowed artistic practices to flourish. Thus far, formal practice requirements focused on important ethical issues without requiring as SOPs initial baseline measures before and after termination of intervention and follow-up to occur without critical professional and scientific requirements, allowing a "...thousand flowers to bloom" (Rezensky 2013), akin and equivalent to the Towers of Babel present in clinical psychology practices (L'Abate 2013b).

Importance of Assigning Homework in Psychological Interventions

Psychological interventions should consist of programmed, written homework assignments at a distance from professionals with occasional control sessions over completed homework assignments and administration of new homework assignments (L'Abate 2011c, 2013b, c, in press; L'Abate and Sweeney 2011). Programmed homework has been presented by workbooks published decades ago (L'Abate 1986) on depression, negotiation, and intimacy. Since then, the crucial research by Kazantzis et al. (2005), Kazantzis and L'Abate (2007) has become part of the therapeutic armamentarium but not yet part of the mainstream clinical psychology practices.

Support for the cost-effectiveness of homework assignments, however, was questioned by the results of L'Abate et al. (2005) who found individuals, couples, and families with homework assignments produced significantly more therapy sessions than control individuals, couples, and families without homework assignments. In spite of these unpredictable results, L'Abate and Goldstein (2007) found that a problem-solving workbook reduced the number of hospital days for women who used it versus women who did not use one. Clearly, this is an area open to further research.

What is the rationale for using written, programmed homework assignments? There are two historical antecedents for this practice. One derived from the behavioral school (Kazdin 2013) and the other from the family therapy literature (Weeks and L'Abate 1982). The former justified its use on the basis of generalizing behavior from the office to the home. The latter justified its use on the basis of evaluating motivation for change, as supported by the results of L'Abate et al. (2005).

From these antecedents, a rationale was developed to consider psychotherapy and psychological interventions as consisting of programmed, written practice exercises monitored and given feedback online by continuous evaluation of progress (L'Abate 2004b, 2011b, 2012c, 2013a, c, 2015; Harwood and L'Abate 2010; Hooper et al. 2014). Whether cost-effectiveness is another reason for this practice can be found in L'Abate and Sweeney (2011). Recommended, replicable, symptom-related online computer-assisted treatments are available (L'Abate 2013c, in press).

Tompkins (2013, pp. 246–251) presented ten evidence-based recommendations to improve compliance with homework.

1. *Make the homework doable* by matching the specific nature of the homework to the level of concreteness of participants, specifying date, day, and time when to perform it.
2. *Consider the participants' level of functioning* already included in the level of concreteness necessary.
3. *Give a clear rationale for homework assignments:* cost, effectiveness, better outcome, greater involvement by participants in the process of change.
4. *Collaborate with participants in creating the homework.* For instance, given the plethora of workbooks available on the market (L'Abate 1986, 1992, 2011c, 2013a; Hooper et al. 2014), which one would be more appropriate and feasible to participants, individuals, couples, and families?
5. *Make up a homework backup plan.* Given the many choices available with workbooks, more than one workbook should be available to cover practically any concern or symptom may be the reason for referral. For instance, given the availability of quite a few workbooks on depression or acting out impulsivities, *one can change to another more appropriate workbook or to a Pre-para-post therapeutic activity more relevant to the case* (L'Abate, 2013c). (note of author).
6. *Uncover homework obstacles* by asking participants directly about whatever possible source may hinder their administration and completion.
7. *Make a set of written homework instructions.* This was originally the rationale for developing programmed workbooks, to make sure participants would not forget or distort what they need to do to complete an assignment.
8. *Practice homework assignments in session.* This requirement is based on the F2F TB model that is no longer applicable to online psychotherapy. Nonetheless, the professional helper should be aware and available to participants to explain reasons for whatever homework is administered.
9. *Be curious and consistent when setting up and reviewing homework.* This monitoring and corrective feedback after completed homework is at the very heart of the homework assignment process. It can be performed online just as well as offline. It is not a matter of curiosity but a matter of responsible professional practice.
10. *Reward participants' efforts and partial successes* through positive feedback. However, when dealing with acting out externalizing personality disorders, practitioners should be able to detect questionable answers and at times return the completed homework as being unsatisfactorily completed.

In this regard, participants' adherence to treatment could be enhanced by the recommendations proffered by DiMatteo (2013, pp. 182–185):

1. *Address adherence to treatment* by consistently reviewing, monitoring, and giving feedback on completed written assignments.

2. *Adopt an open and collaborative relationship* regarding the homework as the core of treatment and change online as well as offline.
3. *Do not equate adherence to outcome* because the two processes are not necessarily casually related. One could adhere to an inappropriately administered workbook and obtain no change in the results.
4. *Understand the prevalence of adherence and nonadherence* on the basis of the personalities involved in the treatment. For instance, internalizing participants (anxiety, depression) may adhere to treatment much more readily than externalizing ones (impulsivity, narcissism).
5. *Address participants' view of effectiveness* by raising reasons for changing and increasing effectiveness.
6. *Understand participants' practical reasons for nonadherence.*
7. *Use written communication.* This recommendation is consistent with a position proffered since three decades ago (L'Abate 1977, 1986, 1992, 2001, 2004a, 2004b).
8. *Encourage patient involvement* from the very beginning of a therapeutic relationship explained in an informed consent form signed by participants online or offline.
9. *Incorporate cultural beliefs* if and when necessary, including ethnic or racial background.
10. *Build in social support* by including as many significant persons in the life of participants.
11. *Screen for depression.* This should be a must even before participants are met either online or offline using a diagnostic battery consisting of "quick and dirty" self-report tests available online.
12. *Attend to risk factors for nonadherence* such as externalizing personality disorders in women as in men (L'Abate et al. 2010).

    What has been presented thus far deals mostly with individuals, even though many recommendations can be applied to couples and families as well (Jongsma 2013). A series of different stepped care lists were produced to help couples deal with their own concerns and issues using a systematic, programmed approach (L'Abate 2008).

Conclusion

One of the major issues facing any theory or intervention, but especially psychotherapy, is whether and how it can be evaluated, i.e., verified or tested. For instance, there are many theories of personality and psychotherapy as well as family theories and family therapy that vary in degrees of verifiability, ranging from verifiable and verified to unverifiable and unverified (L'Abate 2013a). Verifiability, therefore, as discussed in this chapter, means the condition of being evaluated, verified, or tested and implies an examiner external to the theory or intervention.

There is no question that unless traditional F2F TB clinical practices continue to be unstructured and not evaluated in their single outcome by most clinical psychology and mental health practitioners, these professions will continue to be perceived as artistic if not charlatanry pursuits. Unless professional organizations do include ethical and professional requirements for SOP evaluation of any type of intervention, confusing Towers of Babel will continue to proliferate without any progress and improvements in those practices.

Chapter 4
Present Status and Future Perspectives for Personality and Family Assessment

The personal and the social intertwine inextricably. In a 2011 paper published in the *European Journal of Personality,* a group of psychological scientists note that when we talk about an individual's personality, part of what we are talking about is how that individual interacts with others. Furthermore, the scientists write, "social relationships would not be such a challenging part of our lives if all people were equal in how they act, think, and feel"—that is, if all people were equal in their personalities (p. 90). Over time, social experiences play an important role in shaping personality, and personality shapes social experiences too.

Yet, according to lead author Mitja D. Back and his colleagues, scientists studying social interactions often fail to incorporate personality into their research, and scientists studying personality often fail to incorporate social factors. That is why Back et al. have proposed personal and social relationships (PERSOC), "an integrative and unified framework for analyzing the complex dynamics of personality and social relationships" (p. 90).

The PERSOC framework proposes principles and processes that can be applied to research on a variety of social relationships, such as friendships, working relationships, student–teacher interactions, and family relationships. Scientists interested in the PERSOC framework may visit the project online to connect with other researchers and learn about ongoing PERSOC studies (Back et al. 2011).

The above quote shows how both personality and social psychology continue to ignore the family as the best example of enduring relationships. Therefore, the purpose of this chapter is to argue that, at least in the USA, the construct of the intact *family qua family* in the sociological sense of a unit composed by two parents of the opposite gender and two children, is slowly disappearing. This conclusion is supported by evidence that shows how difficult it is to evaluate and to research the construct of "family" (Hofferth and Casper 2007; L'Abate 2005, 2013a; Patterson and Sexton 2013; Silverstein and Giarrusso 2013).

From the American viewpoint, the family, as originally thought, as an intact unit of two parents of the opposite gender and two children includes only 25 % of the population in the USA. Fifty percent of marriages end in divorce and people are marrying later in life. The rest is composed of singles, divorced couples of opposite genders, couples of same gender, couples or singles with grandchildren, and multi-

L. L'Abate, *Concreteness and Specificity in Clinical Psychology,*
DOI 10.1007/978-3-319-13284-6_4

generational families living together. When you add factors like education, ethnicity, and religion, we have a confusing amalgam of various combinations of people living together. Under these conditions, it is very difficult to evaluate families with existing tests because there are hundreds of tests for individuals independent from dozen tests for couples who are also independent of dozen of tests for families (L'Abate 2013a).

The issue of reaching a workable definition of the family was recognized by Pequegnat and Bray as early as 1997:

> The traditional two-parent family with children of the "Father Knows Best" generation is now the exception, rather than the norm, and accounts for fewer than 7% of the social relationships in the United States.... In recognition of this reality, the National Institute of Mental Health (NIMH) adopted the definition of a "network of mutual commitment" to connote the new structures that are the reality of families in the 1990s. Thus, people who fulfill the roles traditionally specified by genetic and legal relationships are acknowledged as family members. The members of these non-traditional families may be more similar than those of biological families because the former are developed around shared values and interests. (pp. 3–4)

The reason for this critical review of the construct of family lies in my convictions that: (1) we are flooded by so many, undoubtedly extremely well-validated, individually oriented tests that make it extremely difficult to choose among them, except to use the criterion of their being available online and, ideally, being derived from some theoretical framework (Hogan 2013; L'Abate 2013a, b; Nelson and O'Connor 2013); (2) by the same token, there are wide numbers of well-validated tests for couples and intact families (Sperry 2012; Williams et al. 2011); and (3) each of these three sources of test production originates from empirically derived sources or from some specific models (Quinn and Davidson 1984). If one were to examine individuals, it would be difficult, if not time-consuming, to evaluate them also with couple- or family-oriented tests. By the same token, it is just as difficult and time-consuming to administer individually oriented tests to couples and families evaluated with test instruments matching their composition (Bloom 1985; Fischer 1982).

How did this incredible outcome of separate tests instruments for individuals, couples, and families happen? It happened because lacking in a theory of human relationships produced a variety of models that were often well validated with matching instruments. Separate models for individuals, separate models for couples, and separate models for families produced separate tests for individuals, separate tests for couples, and separate tests for families. This is a chaotic state of theoretical fragmentation (L'Abate 2005, 2013b) that makes it impossible to demonstrate which model is better than others and whether there exists any overarching theory that may unify and integrate all these diverse models and instruments.

In spite of these changes, there are still contributions about couples and families that seem to ignore or overlook them (Sperry 2012; Williams et al. 2011): that is, evaluating couples and families without paying attention to the personalities composing them, while we have a plethora of measures to evaluate individual personalities without the immediate context of couple or family relationships. Therefore, there is a plethora of well-validated measures to evaluate individual personalities separate from couples, couples separate from families, and families without couples or personalities. Each discipline seems to operate separately from the other two, theoretically and practically (L'Abate 2005, 2012b, 2013a). This fragmentation has produced an incredible number of models, all separate from each other, without any overarching theory to integrate them.

How is one to choose among what tantamount to a Tower of Babel in evaluation? Once professional and scientific criteria have been satisfied, how does one chose which instruments to select? An answer to this question is proffered below. The issue lies on selecting *well-validated test instruments that evaluate human relationships, without regard to personalities, couples, or families.* We need to investigate how we behave in intimate (close, committed, interdependent, and lasting) and non-intimate relationships (not close, not committed, not interdependent, and short-lived).

Hence, *we need test instruments that apply to human relationships rather than having separate tests for individuals, separate tests for couples, and separate tests for families*. Therefore, relational competence theory (RCT) aims at producing test instruments that are devoted to evaluating individuals in a relational context, whether they are single, with a partner, or in a family (Cusinato and L'Abate 2012a; L'Abate 2005, 2008b, 2012; L'Abate et al. 2010).

However, one more requirement is requested from these tests, in addition to evaluate intimate relationships among individuals, and that is, these tests must link assessment to practice in prevention, promotion, psychotherapy, and rehabilitation. The connection between evaluation and intervention can only occur when interventions are programmed in writing, just like test instruments, psychological interventions need to be replicable from one clinician to another and from clinical setting to another (L'Abate 1991, 1992, 2004a, b, 2007b, 2008c, 2009b, 2011b, 2012b, c, 2013b, c, d, in press; L'Abate and Goldstein 2007; L'Abate and Sweeney 2011).

After 40 years of preparation, four different series of ca. 100-programmed interactive practice exercises (PIPEs) have been published to cover most imaginable or unimaginable possible clinical, preventive, promotional, psychotherapeutic, and rehabilitative concerns. Some PIPEs are theory free, some of them are loosely related to models of RCT, and some are directly derived from models of RCT (Cusinato and L'Abate 2012; Hooper et al. 2014; L'Abate 2008c, 2011b, 2013b, in press; L'Abate and Sweeney 2011).

Conclusion

Instead of personality considered independently from couples and from families, each field with its own well-validated tests, we need a taxonomy of human relationships that will go beyond personalities, couples, or families. This theory-derived taxonomy should address how individuals relate with other individuals, regardless of personality makeup or marital or family status. Furthermore, this taxonomy should produce relationally oriented tests that can be developed into PIPEs, matching evaluation with treatment in ways that would be impossible to achieve with face-to-face talk-based (F2F TB) interventions. This conclusion is expanded in Chaps. 6 and 7 of this volume.

Chapter 5
Practice Without Theory

Usual mental health care in the community is far from optimal. Sufficient evidence exists that dropout rates are significant, treatment is effective for only a small proportion of clients, and the translation of evidence-based treatments to the real world is problematic. Technology has been shown to be helpful in health care for improving the effectiveness of treatment. A relatively new technology being used in mental health is the measurement feedback system (MFS). MFSs are particularly applicable to couple and family psychology because of their ability to provide information on the multiple perspectives involved in treatment. The Contextualized Feedback Systems (CFS), developed at Vanderbilt University, is used as an example of what can be accomplished with an MFS. The advantages and limitations of this technology are described as well as the anticipated reimbursement requirements that mental health services will need (Bickman et al. 2012).

A theory could be verified in the laboratory but could be unverifiable in the clinic. Another theory could be evaluated clinically in terms of the results produced, but remains untestable in the laboratory. Another theory could be tested in primary prevention settings but not in therapy (tertiary prevention) or laboratory settings. Some theories are very appealing and seductive therapeutically but are either unverifiable and have not been verified as yet, as in the case with systems theory (L'Abate 2013b). For instance, many pioneering theories in family therapy are a prime example of a very influential theory that appears unverifiable. At least, as far as this writer knows, no one has as yet attempted to verify it. On the other hand, one needs to consider recent theoretical advances that are couched in ways that make them more amenable to verification (Alexander and Barton 1995).

Very appealing and seductive theories, like systems theory, may be very difficult or impossible to verify, because, as mentioned in the previous chapter, they are metatheories or paradigms that cannot be verified directly. Theories that are verifiable may not be very appealing to humanistically or dynamically oriented theorists or many therapists in general, as would be, for instance, the case with behavioral theory and practice. Many therapists seem to abhor empirical evidence to support their practices, creating a gulf between them and empirically oriented, mostly academic, psychologists (L'Abate 2013a, b).

L. L'Abate, *Concreteness and Specificity in Clinical Psychology*,
DOI 10.1007/978-3-319-13284-6_5

Some verifiable theories can be expanded to clinical applications and some cannot. For instance, attachment theory (Mikulincer and Shaver 2007), through its strange situation and structured, semistructured interviews, and rating scales, has been verified in laboratories around the globe but has failed to produce replicable procedures to evaluate the validity and applicability of its tenets to clinical populations (L'Abate 2013a).

In spite of its indirect therapeutic implications (Byng-Hall 1995; Cassidy and Shaver 1999), attachment theory has not produced, as far as this writer knows, any direct (i.e., theory derived) clinical application or therapeutic tasks that could be verifiable or that could be verified. The strange situation is applicable to early childhood, the Attachment Story Completion Task to older children, while its structured and semistructured interviews and rating scales are applicable to adults. However, these are all diagnostic tools and not therapeutic tasks.

Furthermore, what information would these procedures add to a clinical population? When people ask for professional help, it is assumed that they are "insecure," because if they were secure would they ask for help? Does being diagnosed as "insecure–dismissing" lead to different therapeutic practices than individuals diagnosed as "insecure–preoccupied"? If this is the case, what and where are these differential practices to be found? As far as this writer knows, this specificity has not been present in the vast attachment literature (L'Abate et al. 2010; Cusinato and L'Abate 2012; L'Abate 2013b).

In an excellent compendium of therapy in the real world, Boyd-Franklin et al. (2013) argued, I believed uncritically, that:

> Psychotherapy draws on many theories. These theories include behavioral, cognitive-behavioral, psychodynamic, family systems, humanistic, feminist integrative, and cultural competence orientations, among others. (pp. 23–24)

To be sure, Boyd-Franklin et al. (2013) reviewed in great detail the whole evidence-based practice controversy (pp. 24–35) in a way that deserves greater attention. These writers go on to support this possibility by arguing that "…most experienced clinicians ere integrationist…. Good clinicians borrow from each other and borrow what works" (p. 24). Boyd-Franklin et al. finally admit that: "Some psychotherapy-related theories contain constructs that are easy to isolate and measure; other do not." These authors contend that: "There are very few differences among bona fide therapies that have been practiced over time and that have a coherent theoretical structure and research underpinnings", citing Wampold's (2001) work as supporting their contention, going then to conclude that: "Good clinicians also become aware of new and emerging approaches such as cultural competence guidelines that evolve as society and practice change" (p. 24).

Their otherwise excellent review of evidence-based practice concluded with this statement:

> …value must be placed on clinical experience, relevant research, respected clinical publications from various orientations, the complexity and diversity of clinical populations, and the therapeutic relationship. (p. 35)

I would continue to argue, as done already in past writings (L'Abate 2013a, b, c), that the arguments and contentions held by Boyd-Franklin et al. are, with all due respect, sheer nonsense, if not leading toward absolute madness. First of all, how are "experienced" and "good" clinicians to be identified? By seniority? By disciplinary membership? Defining this type of clinicians is a difficult task to achieve unless one uses sheer therapeutic outcome as a way to measure clinical experience and goodness, a surefire criterion that needs further evidence.

Second, integrating various models does not allow to identify which model is more effective than others since no rules are given to "integrate" various theoretical viewpoints. Apparently, "integration" means mixing up arbitrarily and whimsically a chaotic-mishmash amalgam of theoretical orientations without any evidence on which orientation is more effective than others. This position leads again and again to a veritable Tower of Babel (L'Abate 2013a). Third, as long as psychological interventions and especially psychotherapy are administered face to face (F2F), verbally there is no way of knowing what which therapist did, said, or claimed to have said or done. This process is not replicable and, therefore, is useless except to produce researchers competing and supported for external support.

Fourth, that conclusion implies that clinical psychology professionals keep continuously and assiduously abreast of all the literature, are informed about what is going on in their discipline and in the field of psychotherapy, if not in the fields of sickness prevention, health promotion, and crisis intervention. This requirement, therefore, is unrealistic, difficult to follow, and even more difficult to demonstrate. The variability among various clinical psychology professionals would be so great that it would be absolutely impossible to find and identify what source was used and, if and when used, how it was used, since by occurring verbally, the whole process could not be accounted for.

How can we help individuals, couples, and families in crisis or at risk and in need of psychological interventions? The growth of online interventions is inevitable and the sooner the clinical psychology professionals understand the need to change, the better. From an ears–mouth auditory–verbal culture we are now changing to an eyes–fingers, visual–digital culture. Whether we like it or not, professionals will have to learn to work through remote writing and homework assignments, at a distance from participants, without ever seeing them F2F or talking with them. The challenge of the future lies in whether clinical psychology professionals want to continue practicing as artists, without any internal or external controls, or whether they want to change to practice as professionals, using replicably uniform standard operating procedures (SOPs) in evaluation and in practice.

According to Van Emmerik et al. (2013):

> …face-to-face psychological treatments have difficulty meeting today's growing mental health needs. For the highly prevalent posttraumatic stress (PTS) conditions, accumulating evidence suggests, for instance, that writing therapy may constitute an efficient treatment modality, especially when administered through the Internet.

Van Emmerik et al. (2013), therefore, conducted a meta-analysis to investigate the efficacy of writing therapies for PTS and comorbid depressive symptoms. The literature was searched using several structured and unstructured strategies, including keyword searches of the PubMed, Web of Science, PsycINFO, and PILOTS databases. Six studies met eligibility criteria and were included in the analyses. These studies included a total of 633 participants, of which 304 were assigned to writing therapy. Across five direct comparisons of writing therapy to waiting list control, writing therapy resulted in significant and substantial short-term reductions in PTS and comorbid depressive symptoms. There was no difference in efficacy between writing therapy and trauma-focused cognitive behavioral therapy, but the authors cautioned that this finding was based on only two direct comparisons. Writing therapy is an evidence-based treatment for PTS, and constitutes a useful treatment alternative for patients who do not respond to other evidence-based treatments. Internet adaptations of writing therapy for PTS may be especially useful for reaching trauma survivors in need of evidence-based mental health care who live in remote areas or who prefer to retain their anonymity.

Another example of practice without theory is represented by suggestions offered by Kazdin and Rabbitt (2013), who presented new models for the delivery of mental health services in the twenty-first century. These reviewers included task shifting, disruptive innovations, interventions in everyday settings, best-buy interventions, lifestyle changes, and social media. These innovations were selected on the basis of six criteria (p. 173): (1) reach to otherwise underserved populations, (2) scalability in the capacity for an approach to be applied on a large or larger scale than traditional services, (3) affordability, (4) expansion to a nonprofessional workforce, (5) expansion to settings where interventions are already provided, and (6) feasibility and flexibility of intervention delivery.

Among disruptive innovations, Kazdin and Rabbitt (2013) included smartphones and tablets to assess psychological states and provide continuity of treatment processes away from one's residence: "Multiple options are available online for the treatment of anxiety and depression" (Kazdin and Rabbitt 2013, p. 176; L'Abate 2011c, 2013b).

Homework assignments as well as any therapy-oriented interventions need continuous, consistent feedback from therapists, as shown by the following: "A randomized cluster controlled trial tested the hypothesis that weekly feedback to clinicians would improve the effectiveness of home-based mental health treatment received by youths in community settings" (Bickman 2011). Youths, caregivers, and clinicians at 28 sites in ten states completed assessments of the youths' symptoms and functioning every other week. Clinicians at 13 sites were provided with weekly feedback about the assessments, and clinicians at 15 sites received feedback every 90 days. Data were collected from June 1, 2006, through December 31, 2008. Intent-to-treat analyses were conducted with hierarchical linear modeling of data provided by youths, caregivers, and clinicians. Assessments by youths, caregivers, and clinicians indicated that youths (N=173) treated at sites where clinicians could receive weekly feedback improved faster than youths (N=167) treated at sites where clinicians did not receive weekly feedback. A dose–response analysis showed even stronger effects when clinicians viewed more feedback reports. In conclusion, this research shows that routine measurement and feedback can be used to improve outcomes for youths who receive typical home-based services in the community.

The Structured/Unstructured Continuum in Clinical Psychology Practices

The purpose of this section is to differentiate structured from unstructured interventions along a continuum of structure. Structured interventions usually may vary on their degree of replicability. Unstructured interventions are usually nonreplicable.

The distinction between structured and unstructured interventions in mental health was made years ago (L'Abate 1976, pp. 206–207) and became the basis for developing completely replicable structured enrichment programs (L'Abate and Weinstein 1987; L'Abate and Young 1987; L'Abate 1977; Haugvik 2012) leading to the laboratory method in psychological evaluations and interventions (L'Abate 2008b), play (L'Abate 2009i), technology (L'Abate and Kaiser 2012), to clinical psychology and psychotherapy as a science (L'Abate 2013b), and finally to research on pre-para-post-therapeutic activities in mental health (L'Abate 2013c).

This is what was written then (L'Abate 1976) about structured methods of intervention:

1. They can be used with a larger number of individuals, couples, and families than unstructured methods.
2. They can be used preventively (L'Abate 2007c).
3. The can be used propaedeutically (Harwood and L'Abate 2010).
4. They can be administered by subprofessional intermediaries (L'Abate 2001, 2013a).
5. They are cheaper than unstructured methods because a wider range of applications to larger numbers of participants, handling by subprofessionals whose time and availability are greater and less costly than those of professionals.

Furthermore, L'Abate (1976, p. 207) argued and asserted the following:

> Structured techniques, both evaluative and interventive, belong to the demonstrative realm, that is, they allow more direct control, and therefore, testing of theoretical expectations. Unstructured techniques, like interviewing and psychotherapy, dependent on the individual, are usually in the dialectical realm. (Rychlak 1968)

Let us see how these arguments and assertions fared over the past four decades. The clinical psychology and psychotherapy communities continue to rely on unstructured practices that do not allow replication within a practitioner or among practitioners, as already argued in Chap. 3 of this proposal (L'Abate 1999, 2013a, b, c). Furthermore, most clinical psychology practices failed to: (1) link theory with practice and (2) in practice, matching evaluations with interventions, as discussed in Chap. 6 of this volume.

Unstructured	versus	Structured
Immediacy		Delay
Indeterminate		Determinate
Dependent on therapist		Independent of therapist
Nonreplicable		Replicable
Relationship-oriented		Symptom-oriented
Subjective, global		Objective, detailed
Perhaps necessary to start a relationship		Necessary to produce changes
Impressionistic/anecdotal		Reductionistic/factual
Extremely variable		Variability reduced
Relatively unplanned		Completely planned
Reliance on office influence		Reliance on homework influence
Mainly reactive		Mainly proactive
Reliance of F2F talk		Reliance on distance writing
Overreliance on therapist Non-replicable		Reliance on method such as replicable sequential steps (stepped care)
Non-systematic		Systematic
Mainly idiographic		Mainly nomothetic but reducible To idiography
Mainly anti-empirical		Empirical

Fig. 5.1 Advantages and disadvantages of unstructured versus structured psychological interventions

Degrees of Structure

Structure needs to be defined and expanded because there are various criteria to define it according to: (1) preordained number of sessions, (2) prepayment for the program offered, (3) pre-post-intervention evaluations and follow-up, and (4) degree of replicability of program, varying from completely unstructured and, therefore, non-replicable, to somewhat replicable, to completely replicable when administered in writing. The pros and cons of unstructured and structured psychological interventions are summarized in Fig. 5.1.

The best example of structured interventions are programmed interactive practice exercises (PIPEs) or workbooks based on distance or remote writing (L'Abate 2011c, in press; L'Abate and Sweeney 2011). They will be discussed in Chap. 8 of this volume. Of course, there is no need to include unstructured interventions because the literature is littered with books and even manuals that continue to rely on unstructured F2F talk-based (TB) approaches. Instead, exemplary programs with a certain degree of structured will be included to indicate how even a modicum of structure does allow some degree of replicability.

Semistructured Programs

One of the earliest, semi-structured programs was developed by Kennedy (1992) who showed how to develop a master treatment plan based on an evaluation of the degree of psychological impairment, social skills present, dangerousness, occupational skills, substance abuse, medical problems, and ancillary problems. More importantly, this contribution contained blank forms to be completed by a professional to help them deal with a master treatment plan based on: (1) a problem list with a problem number, problem name, significant barriers to discharge, established status (active, inactive, inactive with treatment, or deferred), current status (resolved, cancelled, and revised), (2) patient strengths, (3) discharge planning, (4) psychiatric diagnosis, (5) problem description, (6) long-term goals, (7) short-term goals, and (8) treatment modalities, including patient participation in treatment planning.

Additionally, various questionnaires were made available to clinical psychology professionals, including criteria to evaluate the various components of a treatment plan listed above, including scoring them on a nine-point scale. Besides nurses' observation scale for inpatient evaluation, including a mini-mental state evaluation, the Brief Psychiatric Rating Scale was reproduced with detailed instructions on how to use and score it. An assessment of Tardive dyskinesia and extrapyramidal side effects closed this contribution.

Unfortunately, there is no way to know and to judge how often and by whom these structured fundaments were used. In spite of their decade-long printing, they may still remain remarkably useful for those mental health professionals in search of a semi-structured, somewhat replicable, program.

Another example of various semi-structured programs is found in the volume edited by Ford and Courtois (2013) where individual and systemic, research-based approaches to treat children and adolescents were reviewed following a certain degree of replicability, as for individuals: (1) integrative treatment of complex trauma (Lanktree and Briere 2013), (2) dissociation-focused therapy (Wieland and Silberg 2013), (3) trauma-focused cognitive-behavioral therapy (Kliethermes et al. 2013), (4) eye-movement desensitization and reprocessing (Wesselmann and Shapiro 2013), and (5) dialectical behavior therapy with adolescents (DeRosa and Rathus 2013).

Systemic approaches to treatment included: (1) the neurosequential model of therapeutics (Perry and Dobson 2013), (2) developmental trauma therapy models (Ford et al. 2013), (3) the Sanctuary Model (Bloom 2013), (4) child–parent psychotherapy and historical trauma (Klatzkin et al. 2013), (5) parent-child interaction therapy (Urquiza and Timmer 2013), and (6) trauma systems therapy (Navalta et al. 2013).

Functional family therapy (FFT) is an example of a replicable, semi-structured approach (Alexander and Barton 1995; Alexander and Robbins 2010; Alexander et al. 2013; Datchi and Sexton 2013). This is also a prime example of a therapy without any theoretical background except for tenuous links with behaviorism and family ideology. One cannot help wonder whether some disruptive behavior could be changed by workbooks directly related to that very behavior. Even though still based on F2F TB contacts between trainers and families, FFT does have a relative structure in terms of controlling what is discussed with a family of a rebellious youth and how to improve behavior of such youth (Alexander et al. 2013). Adolescents with disruptive behavior problems represent one of the most difficult and recalcitrant treatment populations. These youth and their parents often enter treatment unwilling or unable to try new behaviors. FFT is an empirically supported highly successful family intervention for delinquent and substance-using adolescents, by systematically, step-by-step altering important risk and protective factors associated with these behavior problems. The first step is to motivate family members to become increasingly involved in changing disruptive behaviors and attendant dysfunctional attributions about themselves and each other by replacing them with more positive self–other enhancing attributions. After changing dysfunctional behaviors, one must assure that these changes generalize out of the therapy office with new skills to use at home, school, and work settings.

More specifically, Kerig and Alexander (2012) described FFT as an innovative family systems approach to the treatment of posttraumatic stress disorder (PTSD) among traumatized youth involved with the juvenile justice system. Section 1 presented the rationale for taking a family systems approach to respond to this problem and describes the ways in which family processes and parent–child relationships reciprocally affect one another in the aftermath of traumatic events. Section 2 outlines the key features of FFT and makes the case for why this evidence-based intervention provides a firm bedrock upon which to build a targeted trauma-focused adaptation. Section 3 of the chapter outlines the FFT-trauma focused model and describes the methods of its flexible and individualized implementation with families of traumatized delinquent youth.

How to Make Exposure Therapy Work?

Exposure therapy is the most effective psychological treatment for anxiety, yet many clinicians lack confidence in their ability to implement it effectively while keeping clients engaged. In this free excerpt from *Exposure Therapy for Anxiety*, authors Jonathan S. Abramowitz, Brett J. Deacon, and Stephen P. H. Whiteside (2012) provide helpful advice to review with your patients before getting started with exposure therapy sessions.

These principles are an egregious example of concrete and specific instructions that are easily replicable.

1. *Prepare to feel anxious.*
   It is normal to feel uncomfortable when doing exposure therapy. In fact, if you become anxious it's a sign that you are doing exposure correctly. Your job is to remain in the situation until your anxiety subsides on its own.
2. *Don't fight the anxiety or fear.*
   If you try to resist or fight the anxiety, you'll only make things worse. Instead, let the anxious feelings just be there. Remember that they're temporary. The worst thing that will happen is temporary distress.
3. *Do not use safety behaviors before, during, or after exposure.*
   In order to work properly, exposure practices must be completed without safety behaviors, reassurance seeking, distraction, medications, alcohol, or other strategies that make you feel safer or that prevent you from becoming anxious. Even very small or brief safety behaviors will spoil exposure.

4. *Test out negative beliefs about the consequences of facing your fear.* Before starting an exposure practice, ask yourself what you're afraid might happen when you confront this situation. Then, like a scientist, test out whether your fearful prediction is true by doing the exposure. Afterward, consider what the experience taught you. What evidence did you gain? Have your thoughts about the situation changed?
5. *Keep track of your SUDS.* During exposure practices monitor how distressed you become using the SUDS scale from 0 (calm) to 100 (extremely anxious). Pay attention to whether your level of fearfulness changes as time goes by.
6. *Stay in the exposure situation until you feel a significant reduction in anxiety.* Remain exposed to the feared situation until your anxiety subsides, no matter how long this takes. If you leave the situation when you are still very anxious, you will only make your fear and anxiety stronger.
7. *Repeat exposures until they no longer make you very anxious.* The more you practice an exposure, the more your anxious feelings will decrease and the easier it will be to feel comfortable with the feared situation.
8. *Practice exposure in different settings.* Confronting your fears in new and different settings helps to solidify your improvement. Practice with your therapist, with family members (if applicable), on your own, and in different places that trigger your fear.

Conclusions

Most psychological practices, including interventions such as psychotherapy can be characterized as working without any concrete and specific links to a theory. More charitably, one could argue that theory is not necessary for clinical practice and that one could practice well without any theoretical background because up to now such a practice, performed mostly verbally and F2F, was difficult but impossible to link to any theory. Most structured interventions are replicable while unstructured interventions are not, especially if administered verbally F2F. How can one link theory with practice? This question will be answered in the next two chapters.

Chapter 6
Beyond Systems Thinking: Toward a Unifying Framework for Human Relationships

> There is always a tradeoff between the generality of a psychological theory and how well it can explain the details of specific behavioral effects. (Payne and Cameron 2014, p. 107)

This chapter describes the systematic classification of four basic terms necessary for the construction of psychological theory and a unified clinical psychology. Among these four terms—paradigms, theories, models, and dimensions—the first three lack substantive differentiation and have often been used synonymously or interchangeably (L'Abate 2009f, 2012a). In view of that specious interchangeability, this chapter seeks to define all four terms. In the absence of such distinction, the terms' synonymity will continue to cause confusion which, in turn, will impede the construction of psychological theory and frustrate ongoing attempts to unify clinical psychology.

The use of systemic thinking has influenced the practice of a great many individual and family therapists, including the writer of this chapter (Angyal 1941; Feiblemand and Friend 1945; Emery 1969; Carlson et al. 2012; Magnavita 2012a, b; Stanton and Welsh, 2012). The significant contributions made by Bakan (1966, 1968), von Bertalanffy (1950, 1968), and Korzyski (1949) added legitimacy to the advancement and acceptance of systemic thinking, particularly following the decline of behavioral and psychoanalytic thinking in the second half of the twentieth century and the ascendance of humanistic thinking as the third force beyond psychoanalysis and behaviorism (L'Abate 2013b).

While systemic thinking was habitually ignored by the more classical schools of thought, it deserved fresh consideration as the fourth force in the evolution of conceptual development in behavioral science, particularly since the value of systemic thinking has not yet been eclipsed by recent developments in attachment and relational competence theories (RCT; L'Abate 2005, 2009a, 2013a; Mikulincer and Shaver 2007).

Since then, a variety of personality (Canli 2006; Caprara and Cervone 2000; Corr and Matthews 2009; John et al. 2008) and family-oriented theories have been coined (Bentson et al. 2005; Williams et al. 2011; Sperry 2012; L'Abate 2013b). For

---

This chapter was written with the help of Walter Colesso, Mario Cusinato, and Eleonora Maino.

L. L'Abate, *Concreteness and Specificity in Clinical Psychology*,
DOI 10.1007/978-3-319-13284-6_6

instance, the same year that von Bertalanffy (1968) and Bakan (1968) offered their concrete proposal for agentic and communal relationships (an approach that remains relevant), L'Abate (2009a, p. 782), Cusinato et al. (2010), and others related to Leary's (1957) consideration of dual constructs of *affiliation* and *power.* McAdams (1988) promoted intimacy and power, while Harter et al. (1997) proposed autonomy and connectedness as a basic dichotomy. Recently, L'Abate (2013b) expanded on intimacy as being an evolutionary derivative of Bakan's original *community,* and identity as a derivative of Bakan's original *agency*.

Notably, the constructs of agency and community derive from two models essential to the development of models found in RCT. Community, affiliation, connectedness, intimacy, and other similar constructs were exhaustively reviewed by Cusinato and L'Abate (2012), L'Abate (2005, 2009a, 2013b), L'Abate and Cusinato (2007), and L'Abate et al. (2010). Community or intimacy derives from a model of space that is evaluated by the dimension of distance and defined by the extremes of approach and avoidance. In contrast, constructs such as agency, identity power, autonomy, and others derive from a model of time that is evaluated by the dimension of self-control, which equates generally to the speed with which one responds to the challenge of encountering or avoiding internal and external events.

Among others, von Bertalanffy (1950, 1968) differentiated between open and closed systems by introducing and defining a system by using the analogy of a river, the veins and capillaries of the body, or even roads. Evolution, of course, is a prime example of a system, as is a family tree.

What Is the Shape of a System?

What Is a Paradigm, a Theory, a Model, and a Dimension?

The pioneering definition of a system given by Angyal (1941, p. 243) went beyond a prescribed unit of relationships among different variables, as a holistic organization. To our knowledge, Angyal was the first to propose the connectedness of parts in a superordinate and therefore hierarchical whole. He described the three applicable criteria as identity, diversity, and similarity. In that vein, the arrangement of parts leads to the establishment of a system. Feibleman and Friend (1945, p. 20) added to Angyal's definition by proposing different levels of analysis as parts of a hierarchical perspective in organizations.

Despite the apparent progression of systems thinking evidenced by recent contributions (Carlson et al. 2012; Magnavita 2012a, b; Stanton and Welsh 2012), most contributions seem to have overlooked an important aspect of von Bertalanffy's analogies. Based on our assessment, most contributions do not appear to question the shape of a system, which is indeed a crucial question. While the question may initially appear somewhat banal, it has been neither raised nor answered in any of the systems-oriented writings cited thus far. Fortunately, the answer has been obvious since 1968: *The shape of a system is hierarchical*. As the original river segues into smaller tributaries or capillaries extend from veins and veins from arteries, all of these systems share the primary characteristic of being hierarchical, such that the system surpasses its origins to differentiate into smaller segments, parts, components, or fractals (Emery 1969).

Discussions regarding the ability to evaluate a system that has no specific shape appear to have been ignored in most of the recent writings cited above. Moreover, those writings demonstrate a particularly uncritical acceptance of rhetorical dogma associated with systems despite the absence of evidence (L'Abate and Colondier 1987). Furthermore, a specific practice cannot be traced to a specific part of the paradigm, since previous interventions were based largely on unverifiable conversations rather than replicable writing (L'Abate 2013a). L'Abate and Colondier (1987) criticized systems thinking as being too abstract to be reducible to empirical models or dimensions. Such an irreducible nature makes it impossible to evaluate any so-called conceptual system in any orderly or systematic fashion (Guerra and Capitelli 2009; Berntson and Cacioppo 2012).

Given this pyramidal characteristic, a theoretical framework has the same hierarchical, pyramidal characteristic as any human organization, be it charitable, commercial, educational, industrial, military, political, or religious. Additionally, Harkness (2007) differentiated between informal, linear theories, one component after another, as in attachment theory (Mikulincer and Shaver 2007), or formal, nonlinear, and hierarchical theories. A prime example of a formal theory is apparent in the RCT (L'Abate 2005, 2009a; L'Abate and Cusinato 2007; L'Abate et al. 2010; Cusinato and L'Abate 2012). This example demonstrates how a theory can be organized according to a pyramidal structure composed of various levels in organization and, therefore, analysis: (1) three metatheoretical assumptions necessary for any psychological theory and that, therefore, go beyond any theory; (2) five theoretical assumptions relevant to basic, developmental, and normative models; (3) three models that address dysfunction; and (4) a final model of the ability to negotiate, which requires a modicum of functionality. These major parts are elaborated in Chap. 7 in this volume.

As may be found in any organization, RCT has its own "organizational" chart that describes the function for which each component is responsible vis-à-vis the functioning of the entire structure. In systems thinking parlance, this characteristic has been called the interdependence of component parts to make a greater whole (Angyal 1941; Feibleman and Friend 1945).

A hierarchy, therefore, has a distinct shape in the sense that any unifying theory with empirical validity can be depicted in an organizational chart. Each component has specific functions that overlap and/or connect with other parts of the organization. Each component must cooperate with other parts of the organization, and each is held accountable for the overall functioning of the organization. If a given component fails to contribute to the overall functioning of the organization, it must be either overhauled or eliminated from the organization. Statistically, each component must correlate somehow with other components to be included in the hierarchy. If the measure of a model does or does not correlate with any other measure produced by any other theoretical structure, then that measure belongs to a different conceptual system (L'Abate and Cusinato 2007; L'Abate et al. 2010; Cusinato and L'Abate 2012; Colessoet al. 2013).

Typically, the terms paradigm, theory, model, and dimension are used interchangeably, such that a paradigm is defined as a model or equated to a theory (Kuhn 1970; Hillix and L'Abate 2012). Yet, since these important terms are indeed unique, it is crucial that each be defined clearly to ensure that each term is readily distinguishable (L'Abate 2009f). A paradigm, such as systems thinking, is a set of values on how to perceive reality. As Angyal (1941, p. 243) pioneered: "Our scientific thinking consists prevalently of the logical manipulation of relationships…the structure of wholes is perhaps amenable to logical treatment…it could be described in terms of some logical unit, representing an entirely different logical genus…. We propose to call it systems" (p. 243). Systemic thinking, therefore, became a new paradigm, the fourth force in our view, above and beyond psychoanalysis, behaviorism, and humanism, among many other paradigms (L'Abate 2013b).

In this regard, systems thinking is responsible for having elucidated the critical importance of attending to the interconnectedness of parts in a system, such as the importance of understanding our intimate relationships in a context as opposed to viewing them as discrete from a larger environment. However, as abstract and general notions, paradigms are not subject to direct empirical verification (L'Abate 2012a). In addition to their presence in the arts and social sciences (L'Abate 2012a, pp. 69–168), the sheer number of paradigms available to scholars makes it conceptually and practically impossible to link any of them to a specific theory, with the possible exception of the information processing paradigm (De Giacomo et al. 2012). L'Abate (2009a) originally classified paradigms in the two major categories of metatheoretical and operational. As described below, psychological paradigms in the metatheoretical category were ultimately divided into general-integrative and particular-specific paradigms.

Among the many definitions offered by Masterman (1970) regarding the nature of a paradigm, those presented by Hillix and L'Abate (2012, p. 7) and Overton (2012) seem preferable. Those definitions refer to paradigms as worldviews, or the way reality is perceived and validated by more than one individual or method and as an aggregate system of values that pertain to how one perceives reality (Kuhn 1970). Overton (2012, p. 58) defined "Scientific paradigms [as] coherent interlocking sets of principles that function in nested hierarchies, ranging from narrow concrete models to broad abstract views." Note that thus far the only dimension considered has been abstraction–concreteness. We need a second dimension of generality–specificity to complete an overarching framework.

Metatheoretical

The paradigms included in this section represent worldviews that go beyond theories and are very abstract and general in their perspectives. The list of paradigms that follows should not be considered complete. Indeed, many other paradigms were not included, such as contextualism, ecologism, or situationism (L'Abate 2012a).

General Integrative: The biopsychosocial paradigm (Woods 2012) interbehaviorism (Fryling and Hayes 2012), systems thinking (Cigoli and Scabini 2012; Magnavita 2012b), constructivism (Riegler 2012), and materialism (L'Abate 2012d) are included in this category.

Particular Specific: Paradigms that are more specific and concrete than others, such as empiricism and cognitivism (Loughlin and Alexander 2012), humanism and behaviorism (Ryback 2012), and existentialism (Cusinato 2012), are included in this category.

The continua of abstraction–concreteness and generality–specificity come into play at this point (L'Abate 2009b; L'Abate and Sweeney 2012) because the progression from general-integrative to particular-specific occurs because both abstractness and generality of a particular paradigm are necessary to complete a desirable framework. The biopsychosocial paradigm, interbehaviorism, systems thinking, constructivism, and materialism are more abstractly encompassing and generally nonspecific than paradigms of a more specific and concrete nature, such as behaviorism and existentialism. Another criterion for such a differentiation can be found in their clinical applications. Most behaviorism and existentialism paradigms ideally could lead directly to specific and concrete therapeutic operations while general-integrative paradigms do not. This latter criterion of generality = specificity is especially relevant to the next classification.

Operational

Paradigms included in this category are those where actual concrete and specific operations are performed, such as information processing (De Giacomo et al. 2012), reductionism (Guerra and Capitelli 2009; Berntson and Cacioppo 2012), produced and spontaneous emergent interactionism (Colesso 2012a), spontaneous emergence (Hillix et al. 2012), and essentialism (L'Abate 2012c). The information processing paradigm, for instance, was nominated as the reigning paradigm for this century because in addition to the pervasiveness of computers, smartphones, hybrids, and thousands of apps, it included an empirically verifiable model developed by De Giacomo and others (2012) and L'Abate and Sweeney (2012).

Theories

In contrast to a paradigm, a theory is a conceptual framework that does lend itself to empirical verification, particularly by investigating its underlying models. Like all hierarchical human organizations, theories are specific and concrete enough to be described by a chart that depicts their hierarchical structure. Theories are conceptual frameworks that permit empirical validation through their connections with models. For example, a unified theory of human relationships, such as RCT (L'Abate 2005; L'Abate and Cusinato 2007; L'Abate et al. 2010; Cusinato and L'Abate 2012), may be illustrated in a way similar to any other organizational chart. More specifically, psychological theories can be classified as being informally linear (and then being divided into intrapsychic, nonrelational categories vs. interpersonal and relational categories) and formally hierarchical (L'Abate 2009b, 2012a).

Informal Linear

Theories organized around a sequence of discrete topics may be classified as informal and linear. Such theories can be further categorized into intrapsychic and nonrelational or interpersonal and relational. Attachment theory, for instance, is a prime example of an informal linear theory (Mikulincer and Shaver 2007; L'Abate 2009b). Each component of the theory follows the preceding components logically and sequentially. However, no hierarchical organization is present. Moreover, there are no formal rules that link one component to another, and the sequence is linear, much like one chapter that follows the next. The notion of levels of organization, which is dear to systems thinking, is completely lacking, which explains its linear nature.

Intrapsychic Nonrelational

Most contemporary personality theories are essentially intrapsychic and nonrelational, usually with or without a passing acknowledgment or afterthought to family or parents (Hogan Johnson and Briggs 1997; John et al. 2008; Corr and Matthews 2009). The subject of these theories, for instance, consists of topics such as neuron-physiological processes that underlie feelings, emotions, and thinking. At best, group processes are included. Yet, except for psychoanalytic and behavioral theories, with the sole exception of attachment theory, no other relational theory is included, as if we were born and raised in a relational vacuum.

Interpersonal Relational

Thus far only one major theory, attachment (Mikulincer and Shaver 2007), has been formulated as linearly relational. As noted above, the attachment theory is constructed according to a rational sequence of chapters and topics, one chapter and topic after another; no overarching, formal pyramidal structure encompasses the entire theory. One could start with anxiety and avoidance, for instance, and then develop another level of topics (and chapters) that underlie both assumptions, such as arousal (which could reside on the same level as anxiety and avoidance). However, since such levels of organization are lacking, the attachment theory, despite being linear and informal, is indeed relational.

Formal Hierarchical

Only the RCT can be classified as formally hierarchical and relational, as it has been formulated according the flowchart of human organizations (L'Abate and Cusinato 2007; L'Abate 2008; L'Abate et al. 2010; Cusinato and L'Abate 2012). As noted above, this theory is built according to levels of organizations descending from seemingly abstract metatheoretical assumptions that descent toward the more concrete and specific models of functional–developmental–normative to dysfunctional relationships. Furthermore, each model of the theory is related to other models not only conceptually but also empirically.

All 16 models that pertain to the RCT are (or should be) amenable to empirical verification, either directly or indirectly. Direct verification took place using instruments developed from those models, and which were validated repeatedly. Indirect verification occurred by others not connected in any way to the theory but co-opted to become part of the theory. An example of such co-options will be found in Model[7] in Chap. 7 of this volume. It is derived from resource exchange theory (Foa and Foa 1974) according to the triangle of life composed of being or presence (love and intimacy), doing or performance (information and services), and having or production (money and possessions). Another example is Model[15]. That model incorporates the deadly drama triangle composed of a victim, a persecutor, and a rescuer (L'Abate et al. 2010; Colesso and L'Abate 2011; Colessoet al. 2012; Cusinato and L'Abate 2012; Hooper et al. 2014).

Models

Models are visual or verbal summaries of more complex constructs and are defined by specific, concrete dimensions that are directly and empirically verifiable (L'Abate 2009b, 2013a). The multitude of unrelated models in psychology, especially in family psychology (Liddle et al. 2002; Pinsof and Lebow 2005), attests to the need for an overarching theory capable of integrating such a theoretical Tower of Babel. Only related and intercorrelated models compose a theory, such as the RCT noted above.

Dimensions

A dimension is any behavior, factor, or parameter that varies according to space and time characteristics such as length, breadth, intensity, thickness, volume, or weight. Dimensions are psychological constructs that are amenable to operational definitions and empirical validations. Dimensions can be subdivided into two categories according to dimensionality and directionality.

Dimensionality

Just one dimension might be sufficient to produce a model, provided it is possible to include extremes in its definitions. For instance, distance in RCT is a dimension defined by extremes in approach (as in dependent personality disorders) and extremes in avoidance (as in avoidant personality disorders). Self-control is another model defined by a dimension of speed of reaction in extremes as in immediate discharge, visible in acting out, impulsive and externalizing personality disorders, and extremes in delay, as in procrastination and internalizing personality disorders. Further developments in expanding this dimension are found in the dual theories of the social mind, automaticity versus nonautomaticity (Gawronski et al. 2014): "…a process can be described as automatic if it is (1) unconscious, (2) unintentional, (3) efficient, or (4) uncontrollable" (p. 6). This dualistic view has been challenged by quite a few critics, far too many to review here among others (Baumeister and Bargh 2014; Fujita et al. 2014; Moors 2014).

Directionality

Directionality can be categorized according to the characteristics of direct and indirect.

Direct Dimensionality

This characteristic is present in operations that imply a concrete and visible observation and measurement of a behavior or a relationship between different behaviors. This behavior can be videotaped for later analysis.

Observations

For instance, as intimacy has been defined in numerous paper-and-pencil, self-report questionnaires, it has become an inferred construct (Prager 1995; Mashek and Aron 2004). However, L'Abate (2011a) defined intimacy from a behavioral perspective as the sharing of joys and hurts and the fear of being hurt, a process that can be observed directly and immediately without any intervening or interfering variables. Unexpressed and, therefore, nonshared hurts tend to fester in the organism and produce what has been called the unconscious (De Giacomo et al. 2010). These emergent, unconscious feelings can finally be expressed through distance writing approaches, nonverbal interventions, and face-to-face (F2F), talk-based (TB) psychotherapy. If these feelings are allowed to fester, they become responsible for three dysfunctional trajectories. When these hurt feelings are matched with hostility (as modeled by caretakers close to an infant), they tend to produce anger and acting out as visible in externalizing personality disorders. When such feelings are matched with sadness, they tend to produce anxieties, depression, and internalizing personality disorders. When hurt feelings are matched with fears, they tend to produce psychopathological conditions such as schizophrenia, bipolar disorders, and severe depression (L'Abate 2011a).

Mechanical Simulation

This process is present in the many attempts to reproduce "intelligent" robots (Pfeifer and Scheier 1999). The movements of robots toward or away from undesirable objects can be measured in terms of how much space they cover and how fast they move from one place to another. From these intelligent robots, we can learn how we humans approach or avoid objects and people.

Direct Measurement

Instead of trying to understand intimacy through self-reported, paper-and-pencil tests, it is possible to evaluate the sharing of joys, hurts, and fears of being hurt through a direct measurement of how often people cry or laugh when sharing those experiences (L'Abate 2011a). Frequency, however, is not the only measure that can be used to assess intimacy. Intensity and levels of authenticity versus manipulative laughing and crying must also be considered.

Indirect Dimensionality

The tendency to measure behavior through paper-and-pencil, self-report questionnaires shows the uncritical triumph of operationalism at its worst (L'Abate 2013a) because the same construct (e.g., intimacy) can produce an infinite number of paper-and-pencil self-report questionnaires purporting to measure the very same construct. Once intimacy is measured by a self-report questionnaire according to a conceptual or empirical model, then one can construct other questionnaires based on a different conceptual or empirical model. Consequently, myriad paper-and-pencil, self-report questionnaires are available to professionals and their clients (Prager 1995; Masheck and Aron 2004; L'Abate 2011a, 2013a).

Implications for Theory Construction

At this point, the hierarchy itself may be examined. It includes (1) paradigms at the highest supraordinate level; (2) informal theories at an intermediate level, as in most family or personality theories, or formal theories in which a hierarchy is clearly defined (Harkness 2007); and (3) models at a lower level defined by (4) empirically verifiable dimensions (L'Abate 2009b, 2013a; Hillix and L'Abate 2012). Models, therefore, and their underlying dimensions are the foot soldiers of a unified theory. On them rests the whole framework—assuming their dimensions are valid.

As in most human organizations, this hierarchy follows the two major dimensions of abstraction and generality mentioned previously (L'Abate and Sweeney 2012). Abstraction is present at the highest level of a paradigm, far away from lower levels, such that it cannot be accessed directly by the organization's lower levels. No rules or criteria govern the connection of one model to a theory or to another paradigm. The choice of any paradigm is arbitrary, even whimsical, according to the conceptual preferences of the theorist or therapist involved (L'Abate 2012a). As Bateson et al. (1956) suggested, there are "different levels of Abstraction" (p. 251) in communication. However, as we move down the hierarchy, abstraction becomes increasingly firm, such as in the empirically verifiable dimensions of a model.

While RCT may initially seem abstract, it becomes less so when broken down into models that are more concrete according to different levels of organization and, therefore, analysis.

Sartori (2009a) proposed a ladder of abstractions (pp. 21–36) that consists of three levels: (1) high-level categories composed of universal conceptualizations akin to paradigms, (2) medium-level categories that consist of general conceptualizations and taxonomies akin to theories, and (3) low-level categories that contain configurative conceptualizations akin to models. Fortunately, Sartori (2009b) defined a dimension "…as a characteristic that takes more than two values treated as a variable. Basically, a dimension is unidimensional when its values range across binary outmost opposites. A multidimensional dimension is ill-suited for its measurement" (p. 137). Unfortunately, Sartori seemed to confuse the abstraction ladder with that of generality (Goertz 2009), since he may have failed to recognize that a continuum of abstraction leads to concreteness and that a continuum of generality leads to specificity.

We move from both abstraction and generality—making decisions about lower levels such as theories—to concreteness and specificity, which are responsible for carrying out those decisions. Although RCT has a general connotation, when reduced to specific models and even more specific dimensions, it steadily becomes more concrete and specific, as shown in Fig. 6.1. For instance, while attachment or relational competence may seem abstract, they are responsible for determining at least four lower levels, such as metatheoretical and theoretical assumptions, dysfunctional relationships, and the ability to negotiate. Making decisions, therefore, means determining the nature of constructs at lower levels of organization. Models within each of the four higher levels are both concrete and specific, which facilitates empirical validation through direct and indirect measures developed or related to each model. Making decisions about lower-level models means that supraordinate models are responsible for the creation and development of lower models in the hierarchy.

It should be noted, however, that the relationship between paradigms and theories is tenuous if not entirely arbitrary, such that this relationship vacillates between being ill-defined and nonexistent. There are no rules that govern the choice of a paradigm, nor is there a taxonomy for deriving a theory from a paradigm (L'Abate and Sweeney 2012; L'Abate 2009b, 2012a). A unifying theory of human relationships can choose systems thinking as well as similar paradigms, such as interbehaviorism (Fryling and Hays 2012) or emergent interactionism (Colesso 2012a). Furthermore, such a unifying theory should provide a classificatory framework of dimensions for human relationships. Such a framework should apply to individuals, couples, and families, as discussed in Chap. 4 of this volume (L'Abate 2005; L'Abate and Cusinato 2007; L'Abate et al. 2010; Cusinato and L'Abate 2012).

Figure 6.1, therefore, integrates two major continua that pervade theory construction: abstraction to concreteness and generality to specificity (L'Abate 2009a, 2012c; Hillix and L'Abate 2012; L'Abate and Sweeney 2012; Overton 2012). Fig-

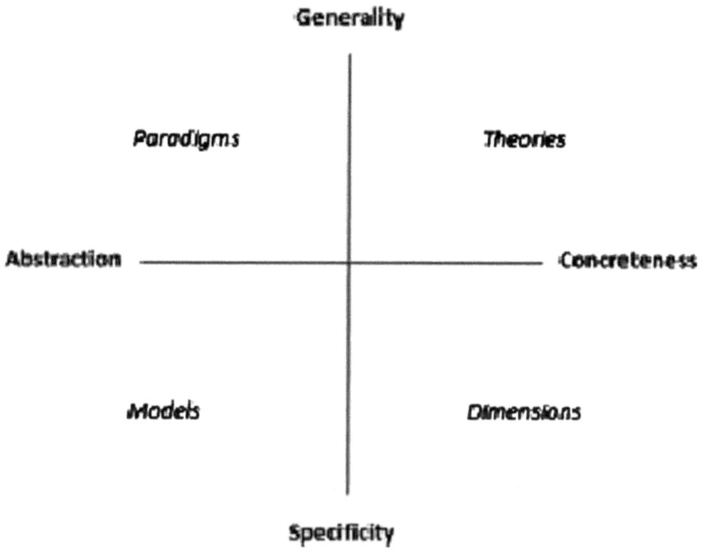

Fig. 6.1 Relationships among paradigms, theories, models, and dimensions according to two orthogonal continua of abstraction-concreteness and generality and specificity

ure 6.1 shows the classification intended here with concrete and specific definitions for each of the four terms, when the two continua of abstraction–concreteness and generality–specificity are constructed orthogonally.

According to Fig. 6.1, paradigms are separated from theories, models, and especially continua by being both abstract and general with few if any connections to the other three terms. Thus, the presence of numerous paradigms that have no clear or precise connections to theories, models, or dimensions is understandable (L'Abate 2009b, 2012a). In contrast, theories may be general in scope; however, they tend to become more concrete than paradigms. Models may initially seem abstract but tend to gain greater specificity than paradigms and theories. Dimensions tend to be concrete and specific, which enables their connection to theories and models, a characteristic that leads directly toward empirical validation. Dimensions are the most concrete and specific bases for the other three constructs, as they are close to theories in terms of generality and to models in abstraction. Alternatively, they are distant from paradigms to the point of explaining how paradigms remain independent conceptual constructions unless reduced to theories and models as the two necessary links between paradigms and dimensions.

Directionality, therefore, means moving from levels of abstraction and generality to levels of concreteness and specificity. This movement can be downward as well as upward, from concrete and specific dimensions to theories and models—and through them, eventually, to paradigms (L'Abate and Sweeney 2012).

Requirements for a Unifying Framework of Human Relationships

Requirements are needed to produce a greater differentiation among these four terms necessary for theory construction.

Requirements for a Paradigm

At the cost of seeming ambition, a unifying taxonomy of human relationships must meet numerous requirements to reach the goal of being both unifying and integrative. However, we must differentiate the requirements that apply to a paradigm, a theory, a model, and a dimension (Hillix and L'Abate 2012). These requirements vary along the very same continua of abstraction–concreteness and generality–specificity, which were discussed previously.

There are only two requirements that can be asked of a paradigm, and they are comprehensiveness and longevity.

Comprehensiveness: This requirement means that a paradigm should be as inclusive of as many relationships as possible. It should encompass relationships that are intimate or communal (close, committed, interdependent, and lasting) and nonintimate, such as in business transactions (not close, not committed, and not lasting), but clearly and temporarily interdependent as in many business transactions, i.e., each party to a business transaction plays a particular role (e.g., the seller and the consumer), and each such role depends on the other for its existence. Such interdependence, however, could be of limited duration because either party may cease to function or find a better deal elsewhere. In other words, a more adequate paradigm trumps a less adequate one (Kuhn 1970).

Longevity: Consider that a great many paradigms, including the systems paradigm, have persisted without being reduced to theories. At the same time, this point can be contended since cybernetics is one form of systems theory while chaos theory is yet another. Therefore, with no direct evidence regarding their validity, it is difficult to include this requirement except for a paradigm (L'Abate 2012a). Many so-called theories, such as behaviorism and psychoanalysis, have survived on the basis of having been applied and administered in therapeutic practices. Except for behavior-cognitive theory (Kazantzis and L'Abate 2007), no one could relate any specific intervention to any specific part of any theory as long as such practices are verbal F2F.

However, besides behavior-cognitive theory, the interpersonal psychotherapy of depression theorizes major depression as stemming from any of four types of problems (complicated bereavement, role conflicts, role disputes, interpersonal deficits) and presents specific interventions linked to each of these theoretically posited problem areas. However, when those therapeutic applications are performed verbally, they are not replicable. Given the idiographic nature of psychotherapy, even cognitive restructuring (a fundamental intervention in behavior-cognitive theory) linked to the theoretical postulate holds that cognitive distortions are central to psychopathology and cannot be replicated precisely when administered verbally.

Eclecticism is the psychotherapeutic buzzword used to hide the possibility of linking a theory, or parts of a theory, to any therapeutic intervention (L'Abate 2013a). Nonetheless, this remains an important requirement to include for a paradigm rather than a theory, despite the many exceptions to its usefulness. Its verbal application in psychotherapy makes it impossible to replicate the presence of the therapist and/or the power of the spoken word. Distance writing, and more specifically targeted programmed remote writing as represented by interactive practice exercises in workbooks, makes it possible to replicate any programmed intervention ad infinitum at a fraction of the cost of F2F, TB psychotherapy. That could be the major difference between intervening as artists versus intervening as professional scientists, especially when an objective evaluation is required on pre–post intervention and follow-up after termination, as argued in Chap. 5 of this volume (L'Abate 2011b, 2013a, b).

Requirements for a Theory

The four requirements that should be demanded of any psychological theory are relationality, integrativity, dismantability, and productivity.

Relationality: It should be clear that a unifying theory of human relationships must deal with relationships between and among individuals, the way we relate with each other communally and agentically according to prolonged processes (Bakan 1968; L'Abate 2013b). The ultimate outcomes of such relationship would not be based on brief, superficial, irrelevant, random, or accidental encounters (L'Abate 2009a). Rather, these relationships should be systematically replicable and, therefore, predictable and controllable using standard operating procedures. That premise explains why L'Abate (2011b, 2012a, 2013a) has insisted that psychological interventions in mental health (prevention, promotion, psychotherapy, and rehabilitation) must occur in writing and, more specifically, in programmed, targeted, and interactive distance or remote writing (L'Abate 2011b; 2013a).

Integrativity: The purpose of such a theory should be to unify as many seemingly disparate relationships that would form the component parts of the hierarchy. In this sense, integrativity is meant as a process of concatenating previously separate if not seemingly independent parts. For instance, a relational Selfhood Model[11] (among others) based on how we attribute and bestow importance to ourselves and others leads to four possible proclivities. These are (1) selffulness—attributing and bestowing importance positively toward self and others; (2) selfishness—attributing and bestowing importance positively toward ourselves and negatively toward others; (3) selflessness—attributing and bestowing importance negatively toward ourselves and positively toward others; and (4) no-self—attributing importance negatively toward ourselves and others. These four dimensions are linked directly to psychiatric categories (L'Abate 1997b, 2005, 2006; Cusinato and L'Abate 2012).

Dismantability: Once an entire structure is organized and unified theoretically, the process of stripping the structure and evaluating the empirical validity of its component parts individually can begin. The validity of the whole theory, therefore, rests on the outcome of the overall validity of its component parts—as with many human organizations. Each component part accounts for the functioning of the whole from the top down and from the bottom up. Whether the whole is the sum total of its parts remains to be seen but possible.

Productivity: A theory must produce effectively a sufficient number of studies that replicate and support the validity of its models. A sterile paradigm or theory that fails to meet this requirement will ultimately be discarded.

Requirements for a Model

The number of requirements continues to increase to ensure their utility in helping to distinguish them from paradigms and theories.

Interrelatedness: Already discussed qualitatively and quantitatively, each component part of this requirement is related to as many other components of the theory as possible, though not necessarily in linear fashion, such as correlations, regression analyses, and more contemporary statistical methods. For instance, Colesso (2012b) and others (L'Abate et al. 2010) have validated with individuals, couples, and families an instrument called EcoMap. That instrument estimates four different models of RCT, Model^{3} about settings, the ability to love and to control self (Models$^{4\text{ and }5}$ respectively), and Model^{7} about the triangle of life explained above.

Applicability: To actualize and justify its ambitious goal and scope, a unifying theory of human relationships should apply to as many functional and dysfunctional relationships as possible, such as criminality and psychopathology in individuals (children, youth, and/or adults), couples, and families. To establish a unifying theory, one must consider this requirement an end result, as with all other requirements that pertain to a given theory. RCT, for example, is isomorphic in its relational dimensions with static, psychiatric DSM (Diagnostic and Statistical Manual of Mental Disorders) categories (L'Abate 2006). As noted above, Model^{4} (which relates to the ability to love according to a dimension of space as defined by extremes in approach–avoidance) describes dependent personalities at the extreme of approach and avoidant personalities at the extreme of avoidance. Model^{5} relates to the ability to control and regulate the self according to a dimension of speed as defined by extremes in discharge accounts for externalizing disorders. Alternatively, extremes in delay account for internalizing disorders (Klauer 2014).

Redundancy: This requirement relates especially to multidimensional constructs that cannot fit into any single model of the theory. Examples of multidimensional constructs that require more than one model to describe their intent include love in its multi-splendored qualities, self-control and self-regulation, and relational creativity (L'Abate 2009c; Colesso and L'Abate 2011). For instance, psychiatric categories are viewed as dimensions according to Models$^{4\text{ and }5}$. They are also described by the Selfhood Model^{10} presented briefly above. Another model (Model^{8}) that relates the continuum of likeness or resemblance accounts redundantly for psychiatric categories from a developmental, dimensional, and relational viewpoint. Model^{8} serves as the basis for Model^{9}, which applies to the styles of intimate relationships. These are (1) abusive/apathetic or neglectful, as in criminality and psychopathology; (2) reactive/repetitive, as in most personality disorders; and (3) creative/conductive, as in most nondiagnosable relationships. Model^{8} also influences Model^{10}, which applies to interactions in intimate relationships according to an arithmetical/logarithm classification: (1) multiplicative, (2) additive, (3) positive static, (4) negative static, (5) subtractive, and (6) divisive. The validity of Model^{9} was supported in part by Colesso, Cusinato, and L'Abate (2012).

Requirements for a Dimension

The two major requirements for a dimension must be verifiable and measurable, despite their quality and quantity variances.

Verifiability: Within this context, verifiability means empirical, rather than anecdotal verifiability. It cannot be impressionistic, nor can it be influenced by authority or faith. If a component part cannot be evaluated empirically along one or more dimensions, it cannot be considered a member of the structure. As noted previously, all component parts of the structure are accountable for the overall verifiability of the whole. However, validity can vary from being different and interdependent evidence, or according to its face validity, construct, concurrent, and predictive validity. An additional type of validity, prescriptive validity, is the prescription of a specific type of treatment through programmed, targeted writing derived from a particular test instrument (L'Abate 1990, 2011b). Significant concurrent, predictive, and construct validities have been obtained via statistical analyses of most models of the RCT (Colesso et al. 2012; Cusinato and L'Abate 2012; L'Abate et al. 2010).

Evidence can vary by degree from being *independent* from theory, *related* to theory, or *derived* from theory. In one case, it can be similar to but independent from other theories or models. This is shown in the bibliography of secondary sources related in similarity (face validity) to RCT (L'Abate 2009a) as well as via some models of RCT that have not been as yet verified directly but certainly provide overwhelming, indirect evidence that supports the validity of the model. In another case, it can be related, such that the validity is derived indirectly from another model proposed and studied empirically by others. This would be the case for Models$^{7 \text{ and } 14}$, which relate to self-identity and intimacy, respectively, and have already been mentioned (concurrent and criterion validity). The final case shows that evidence can be derived directly from the empirical investigation of models of RCT (construct and predictive validity).

Measurability: Any ordinal, qualitative, quantitative, subjective, and objective dimension that allows quantitative scaling and ranking is measurable. As noted previously, intimacy can be inferred from self-report, paper-and-pencil questionnaires.

Under those conditions, intimacy is no more than a hypothetical or inferred construct similar to others such as ego, superego, or even self-esteem (L'Abate 2011a). Here, participant responses are subjective, which contrasts with direct observations of behavioral intimacy. Like any other directly observable behavior, intimacy defined behaviorally by the sharing of joys and hurts and fears of being hurt can be video-recorded, evaluated, and measured according to the criteria of (1) frequency, (2) duration, (3) rate, (4) intensity, and (5) authenticity.

Although the terms used in this chapter have different definitions and requirements, any unifying taxonomy of human relationships should certainly be reflective of all such requirements. That condition exists since it needs to be linked upward to paradigm requirements and downward to the requirements for models and dimensions.

Applications of Extremes in Specificity and Concreteness

As already shown in Fig. 1.1 (L'Abate 2013a), evaluation and psychological interventions, in addition to the traditional statistical criteria of reliability and validity, must follow the requirements associated with concreteness and specificity to be considered applied extensions of a conceptual classification. Psychological evaluations and interventions are composed of dimensions ostensibly related to each other. Although evaluations are intended to produce dimensional diagnoses rather than categories, the psychological evaluations designed to determine DSM-based diagnoses which are concretely and specifically provided as they occur through replicable, programmed, targeted, and interactive writing rather than through unstructured talk that cannot be reproduced (L'Abate 2011b).

As discussed already in more detail in Chap. 1 of this volume, both dimensions are orthogonal to the requirements for precision and specification, which must be included in psychological evaluations and interventions (L'Abate 2013a, b). In addition to the previous albeit relevant criteria for reliability and validity, clinical applications must be concrete and sufficiently specific to allow an understanding by other professionals and participants. While the continua of abstraction and generality are relevant to theory construction (L'Abate and Sweeney 2012), specificity and concreteness are required in clinical applications, both for evaluations and interventions. However, as long as psychological interventions are verbal, it remains challenging to replicate them in mainstream applications. Precision is found in intelligence quotient (IQ) scores, test profiles, and, supposedly, in psychiatric diagnoses. However, such precision is not sufficient. Once an IQ score is obtained, its meaning must be explained relative to the client's overall functioning and the score's relation to the context of the original referral. An IQ score or test profile means nothing without an explanation of its relationship to other contextual factors (L'Abate 2013a).

Conclusion

In the absence of clear definitions and classifications for these terms—paradigm, theory, model, and dimension—the process of psychological theory construction will be impeded by confusion and conflict related to the meanings and referents of each. Thus, benefitting from concrete and specific definitions, these terms can be distinguished and allocated according to their individual, concrete, and specific requirements. Moreover, while paradigms remain empirically unverifiable, models lend themselves well to such verifiability and represent the building blocks for the theories embedded in other overarching paradigms. Thus, theories formally based on empirically verifiable models will abrogate confusion and conflict.

Chapter 7
Combining Theory with Practice

> To have any predictive value, mathematical models must be rigorously specified and shown to accurately reflect reality. (Brown et al. 2014)

The purpose of this chapter is to elaborate and update, with recent and relevant research, a contextual and developmental relational competence theory (RCT) in intimate/non-intimate relationships (Cusinato and L'Abate 2012a; L'Abate 1976, 1994, 1997, 2002, 2005, 2006, 2008a, b, c in press; L'Abate and Cusinato 2007; L'Abate et al. 2010; L'Abate and De Giacomo 2003). RCT focuses on how effectively we deal with each other, with intimates and non-intimates, in close/distant, committed/uncommitted, dependent/interdependent/independent, and short/prolonged relationships. Relational means bidirectional rather than unidirectional interactions with intimates and non-intimates in a continuous interdependent and reciprocal exchange of resources available to us. Effectiveness is evaluated by how we feel, how we think, how we act, how we are aware, and how we evaluate proximal and distal subjective contexts as perceived by us. Theory means a hierarchical framework akin to the table of organization of any human enterprise with various levels expanding downward from generality to specificity and from abstract to concrete, going from overall general assumptions, normative models proper, models clinically relevant to dysfunctional conditions, improvement of competence, and conclusion.

However, not all models of RCT have been evaluated empirically. Hence, this chapter represents research in progress, because only a limited number of models have been evaluated while others have been ignored for at least two reasons. First, the literature on "ignored" or "bypassed" models is so extensive that it is questionable whether anything additional can be added empirically. However, that is not an excuse. Second, certain models were selectively evaluated more frequently than others because they were easier to evaluate than others, and/or they seem to be more relevant than others. Consequently, there are considerable gaps in the theory that have not been plugged but which are in the process of being plugged (Cusinato and L'Abate 2012a).

The field of intimate relationships is a vast and exciting one (Brehm et al. 2002; De Genova and Rice 2005), that perhaps no single theory or theoretical framework can encompass it. The theory updated here is an attempt to develop such an

L. L'Abate, *Concreteness and Specificity in Clinical Psychology*,
DOI 10.1007/978-3-319-13284-6_7

encompassing framework, even though it may fall short of its admittedly grandiose and ambitious goal. The field of relational competence (RC) and intimate relationships is so complex that to reduce it to a few models may be an exercise in futility. Nonetheless, the complexity of intimate relationships is a challenge that cannot be ignored. Will it be possible to reduce such complexity to a given number of theoretical models that are verifiable in the laboratory as well as applicable in the clinic? Not only should such models be verifiable in the laboratory but they should also be verifiable in their applications to primary, secondary, and tertiary prevention approaches, prevention, promotion, and psychotherapy. Hence, this theory attempts to fulfill a tall order to make sense of a complex field that, thus far, and to this writer's knowledge, lacks of an adequately integrative, verifiably unifying theory or encompassing theoretical framework (Klein 2014c).

A theory can and should be verified through models that are defined by concrete, specific dimensions derived from instruments or interventions, task assignments, or interactive practice exercises or workbooks (L'Abate et al. 2010; Cusinato and L'Abate 2012; L'Abate 2013a). Thus, a theory is as valid as the instruments or interventions developed to test its models. How is RCT linked with workbooks? First, we need to see whether the theory or models derived from the theory are valid in the laboratory and mental health interventions, as defined above. Then, we can see whether and how this theory is linked with workbooks, connecting theoretical models with research and practice (L'Abate 2013a, b, c).

RCT was originally created decades ago to relate the individual with the family (L'Abate 1976). This theory saw successive modifications over decades (L'Abate 1986, 1994, 1997b, 2005, 2006, 2009a, b, c, 2012a, 2013a). Its interrelated models can be evaluated either with static, single or multifunction, self-report paper-and-pencil tests (Cusinato and L'Abate 2005a, b, 2012a; L'Abate et al. 2010), and dynamic, written programmed interactive practice exercises (PIPEs) or workbooks administered as homework (L'Abate 2011b, 2013b, c). Consequently, this chapter assumes that readers will be familiar with the 16 models of RCT already summarized in previous publications. Nonetheless, a summary of RCT is presented in Fig. 7.1 and selected models will be highlighted to link PIPEs to models of the theory.

Over the years, with the help of his students and collaborators (Cusinato et al. 1998; Cusinato and L'Abate 2012; L'Abate 1997c, 1998a; L'Abate and Wagner 1985, 1988, Stevens and L'Abate 1979; L'Abate et al. 2010), this writer, has developed a series of self-report, paper-and-pencil tests derived directly from models of the theory. Not all tests have been validated as yet. For instance, a self-report questionnaire to evaluate one's perceptions of the immediate, familiar context is still at an experimental stage and is contained in the Appendices of this volume (L'Abate 2009).

The rest of this chapter: (1) shows how models of RCT are interrelated with each other, (2) summarizes methods and means used to evaluate and validate models with specifically constructed instruments, and (3) names workbooks or systematically written interactive practice exercises derived directly from models of RCT. This theory has already been applied to play (L'Abate 2009f), resilience (L'Abate 2009e), self-help (Harwood and L'Abate 2010), hurt feelings (Cusinato and L'Abate

Summary of a Theory of Relational Competence in Intimate Relationships					
		Requirements			
Verifiability		Applicability	Redundancy		Fruitfulness
		Meta-theoretical Assumptions about Relationships			
		Width[1]	Depth[2]		Settings[3]
Models		ERAAwC[1]	Levels of Interpretation[2]		Settings[3]
		Emotionality	Description		Home
		Rationality	Presentation		School/work
		Activity	Phenotype		Transit
		Awareness	Explanation		Transitory
		Context	Genotype		
			Generational-developmental		
		Theoretical Assumptions about Relationships			
Models	Ability to Love[4]	Ability to Control Self[5]	Both Abilities[6]		Contents[7]
Dimensions	Distance	Control	Functionality		Modalities
	Approach/Avoidance	Discharge/Delay	High/Middle/Low		Being/Doing/Having
DSM-IV	Axis II, Cluster C	Axis II, Cluster B	GAF* (100 to 0)*		Sexual deviations Driven Personalities
		Normative Models of the Theory			
Models	Self-differen-tiation[8]	Relational Styles[9]	Interactions[10]	Selfhood[11]	Priorities[12]
Dimensions	Likeness Continuum	AA/RR/CC	Functionality	Importance	Survival/En-joyment
a.	Symbiosis/Alienation	Abusive/Apathetic	Divisive	No-self	Vertical: Self/intimates
b.	Sameness/Oppositeness	Reactive/Repetitive	Subtractive/Static	Selfless/Selfish	Horizontal: Settings
c.	c. Similarity/	Conductive/	Additive/Mul	Selfull	
c.	c. Similarity/Differentness	Conductive/Creative	Additive/Multiplicative	Selfull	
DSM-IV	a. Axis I b. Axis II, Cluster B c. No diagnosis	a. Co-dependencies/addictions b. Conflict high c. Conflict low	a. Below 39 on GAF* b. 69 to 40 on GAF c. 100 to 70 on GAF		
		Clinical Applications of the Theory			
Models	Distance Regulation[13]	Drama Triangle[14]	Intimacy[15]		Negotiation[16]
Dimensions	Pursuer/Distancer/	Victim/Persecutor/	Sharing Joys, Hurts, & Fears		Structure/Process

* GAF= Global Assessment of Functioning

Fig. 7.1 Summary of relational competence theory

2012b; L'Abate 2011a), and four models of psychopathology derived from Model[14] about the drama triangle discussed below (Hooper et al. 2014).

Three areas of RCT will be covered. First, an attempt will be made to show how models of RCT relate with each other, as found in any human and theoretical hierarchal and pyramidal enterprise (L'Abate 2013a). Second, evidence gathered from the very outset by developing methods to evaluate RCT statically through self-report, paper-and-pencil tests, and dynamically through PIPES (L'Abate 1976; L'Abate et al. 2010). Most objective tests developed to evaluate RCT models are based on writing, either through self-report by participants themselves or through an examiner, as in the EcoMap and the likeness task (Cusinato and Colesso 2008). However, information and evidence to support the validity of most models of RCT is available (Cusinato and L'Abate 2012a; L'Abate et al. 2010). Interested readers, clinicians, and researchers, will find in those references original copies of model-derived test instruments. Third, model-derived and model-related workbooks are available to professionals in various publications (L'Abate 1986, 1992, 2011b, 2013b, in press; Hooper et al. 2014).

Meta-theoretical Assumptions

Model[1], as a horizontal information processing model, is basic to almost all the other 15 models, is composed by five distinct parts: *E*motionality, *R*ationality, *A*ctivity, *Aw*areness, and *C*ontext (ERAAwC). It can be evaluated objectively with a validated relational answers questionnaire (RAQ) available in L'Abate et al. (2010) and validated with different populations by Colesso (2012a, b), Cusinato (2012a, c), Gianesini (2012), and Maino (2012a, b). The intercorrelation of component parts in a single, horizontal model is shown in Fig. 7.2 about the first, information processing Model[1] ERAAwC as measured and validated repeatedly (Colesso 2012a, b; Cusinato 2012a, c; L'Abate et al. 2010, pp. 33–42; Gianesini 2012; Maino 2012a, b).

The most important component of Model[1], is *Aw*areness, which Cusinato (2012b) researched over a decade period, finding that there are at least two kinds of *Aw:* (1) awareness of awareness and (2) awareness as a critical feedback loop to correct errors or inadequacies in *E*, *R*, *A*, and *C*. The importance of Aw has been highlighted by the many contributions to dual-process theories of the social mind (Sherman et al. 2014) that will be discussed below in dealing with Model[5] on self-control. Some authors in that excellent treatise considered only a dichotomy of conscious versus unconscious (Baumeister and Bargh 2014; Custers and Aarts 2014; Hassin and Sklar 2014; Moskowitz 2014) while a continuum of conscious–unconscious should be considered in greater detail (De Giacomo et al. 2010; L'Abate 2011a). For instance, there could be: (1) a *total-general* unconscious versus a *partial-specific* unconscious, one could avoid dealing with a past, painful, and traumatic series of experiences versus a specifically limited painful experience, (2) one could be con-

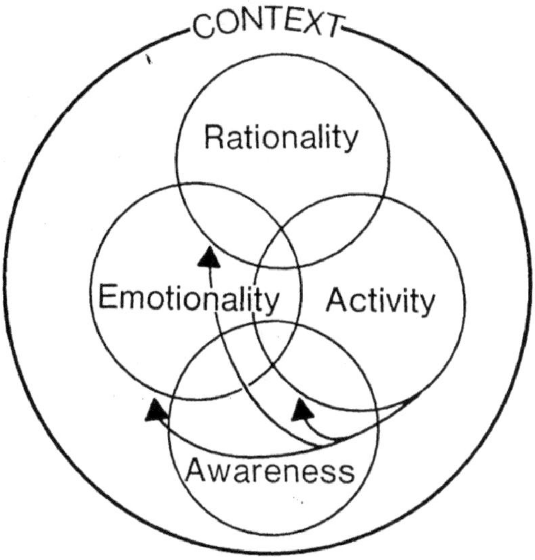

Fig. 7.2 A horizontal model of information processing (L'Abate 1986)

scious of all these experiences or some of them but chooses not to speak about them, and (3) if there are no past, painful, or traumatic experiences or if positive, pleasant or joyful experiences may trump painful ones, and, therefore, the unconscious may lose its grip on one's behavior. By the same token, too many painful experiences may trump joyful ones, as discussed below (L'Abate 2011a).

Interestingly, Lacewing (2014), in emphasizing the importance of "insight" in psychodynamic psychotherapy, drew some similarities between this construct and the two functions of awareness expanded according to Cusinato's (2012b) research. For instance:

> Psychodynamic insight is concerned with understanding the dynamics of one's mental states and processes. It involved grasping the *connections* between one's emotions, motivations, thoughts, and behaviors past and present, including one's interpretations of and relations with others.... [Psychodynamic] Insight comprises two elements. The first relates to specific insights: understanding the (often unconscious) dynamics under-lying particular conscious thoughts, feelings, choices, and behavioural reactions, especially those with maladaptive patterns. The second, which we may call "insighfulness," relates to a general capacity or ability for self-understanding in this sense. Insight aims at recognizing one's mental states and their interconnections (again, extending to one's interpretation of others as well. (pp. 154–155)

Model[2] (Fig. 7.2) can be evaluated with a recently developed measure related to impression formation and other vertical three levels of description and explanation (Cusinato 2012b). Model[3] can be measured objectively by how much time one spends in one setting over the other settings (home, school/work, transit, and transitory) as well as the theory-derived, multimodel EcoMap (Colesso 2012d; Colesso and Garrido 2012).

Interrelatedness of Relational Competence Theory Models

RCT models are not independent from each other. As in any human hierarchy (commercial, educational, industrial, military, and religious), one part of the whole needs to relate well, i.e., needs to get along with, i.e., correlate well with other parts of the hierarchy. Therefore, RCT models must be intercorrelated, conceptually first and empirically second. They do not function as isolated, independent parts. Each model, in one way or another, is related with other models, according to the requirement of redundancy (Fig. 7.1) enunciated in previous publications (L'Abate 2009b, c, 2013a) and Chap. 6 in this volume.

Theoretical Assumptions

Model[4] about the ability to love, can be assessed by a variety of measures developed by authors extraneous to RCT (L'Abate et al. 2010, pp. 97–101) as well as by observable alliances, favouritisms, preferences among parents and their children: who approaches or avoids whom more often than others (Hooper et al. 2014). In many cases, this favouritism is completely outside the awareness of family members. Love can be shown by how we chose to approach selected others for a lifetime ("… until death does us part") or strangers just for a few moments. These extremes define a dimension of space measured by distance, how close or how far we move toward or away from others. Higgins (2014) has promoted a well-validated and highly creative model (even though he called it a "theory"), based on the old principle that we approach pleasure and avoid pain (L'Abate 2011a). His research supported the argument that approach leads to positive promotional processes while avoidance of painful, negative experiences leads to preventive self-regulation. The implications of this model are wide-ranging and relevant to human relationships.

Model[5] about the ability to control and regulate self can be measured by reaction time, or speed of reaction: how fast or how slow one approaches or avoids someone else, a task, or an object, as well as by measures of temporal perspective (L'Abate et al. 2010, pp. 103–108). Recently, dual-process models have suggested a differentiation between automatic and nonautomatic processes. "…a process can be described as automatic if it is: (1) unconscious; (2) unintentional; (3) efficient, or (4) uncontrollable" (Gawronski et al. 2014, p. 6). A great deal of our behavior is automatic, with control becoming relegated to a small percentage of our behavior (Moors et al. 2014; Payne and Cameron 2014). In spite of its controversial status, this model has spawn quite a few dual-systems models, including one on reflectivity versus impulsivity that considers speed as one of its major characteristics, supporting the definition of control given above (Strack and Deutsch 2014). Nonetheless, dual processes can be applied to attitudes and evaluation, social perception, thinking and reasoning, habits, goals, and motivation, as well as self-regulation and control proper. Another example of duality in identity can be found in a recent

Two Factors Models of Intimate Relationships" Models [4 & 5] respectively*

Space ⟵		⟶ Time
Distance	Source	Self-control
Affiliation	Leary (1958)	Power
Communion	Bakan (1967)	Agency
Communal	Clark & Mills (1979)	Exchange
Intimacy	McAdams (1988)	Power
Affiliation	Wiggins & Trobst (1999)	Control
Cohesion	Olson (1996)	Adaptability
Intimacy	Canary et al., 1997	Control & Power
Connectedness	Harter et al., 1997)	Autonomy
Nurturance	Fehr & Broughton (2001)	Dominance
Support	Franks et al., (2004)	Control
Warmth	Grolnick & Gurland (2002)	Control
Communion	Horowitz (2004)	Agency
Intimacy	Segrin & Flora (2005)	Power
Distance	L'Abate (1986, 1994, 1997,	Speed
Being	2005, 2009; L'Abate &	Doing & Having
Presence	Cusinato, 2007; L'Abate &	Power
Love	De Giacomo, 2003	Negotiation
Proximity	Mikulincer & Shaver, 2007	Activation

*Adapted and adopted from L'Abate, 2009??

Fig. 7.3 Two-factor models of intimate relationships Models[4 and 5], respectively. (Adapted and adopted from L'Abate, 2009)

expansion of Bakan's (1966) community versus agency dichotomy expanded into communal presence versus agentic power (L'Abate 2013a). These two dimensions can be integrated into one model by Figs. 7.10 and 7.11.

Model[6] can be evaluated by any measure of functionality/dysfunctionality available on the market (L'Abate 2009c; L'Abate et al. 2010, pp. 109–114). Model[6] in Fig. 7.3 integrates most dichotomous models of relationships over the past few decades according to space and time dimensions combined.

Developmental and Normative Models

Model[7] could be measured by instruments developed by the original authors of resource exchange theory (Foa and Foa 1974), as well as with the classification of sex and sexuality (L'Abate et al. 2010, p. 119). It is composed by three modalities defined by resources: (1) being present, importance, and intimacy, (2) performance or doing, information, and services, and (3) production or having, money, and possessions.

Model[8] (Colesso 2012c; Cusinato and L'Abate 2008; L'Abate et al. 2010, pp. 122–146) can be evaluated with the likeness task developed and validated by Cusinato and Colesso (2008), L'Abate (1976, p. 79), L'Abate et al. and (2010, pp. 147–152). In another instance, Model[8], as presented in Fig. 7.4, shows how a simple dichotomy of similar/dissimilar is basic to a contextual, developmental,

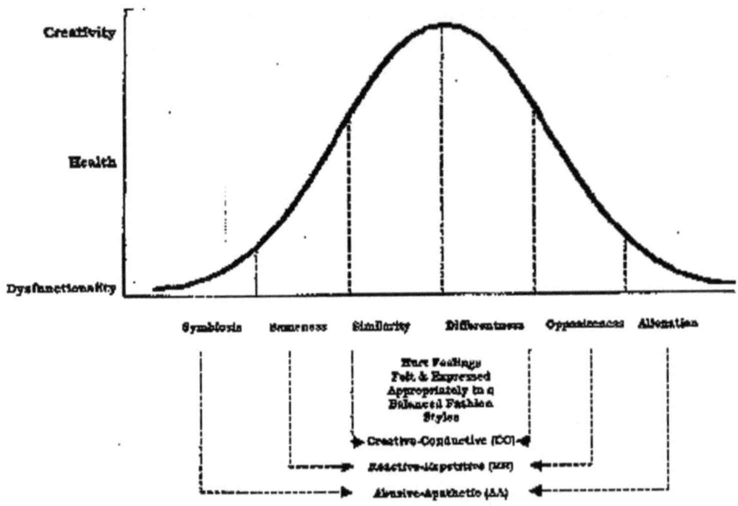

Fig. 7.4 A curvilinear, developmental model of identity differentiation (Model^{8}) integrated with hurt feelings (Model^{15}). (L'Abate 1976, p. 79)

and dialectical continuum of likeness or resemblance differentiated into six ranges: symbiosis, sameness, similarity, differentness, oppositeness, and alienation (Klein 2012, 2014a; Mussweiler 2014).

Model^{9} derives from Model^{8} by combining symbiosis with alienation to produce an abusive-apathetic, neglectful (AAN) dysfunctional style. Combining sameness with oppositeness produces a reactive–repetitive (RR) borderline style. Combining similarity with differentness produces a creative–conductive (CC) functional style.

Styles in intimate relationships as shown by Model^{9} should be visible concretely and directly by examination of dysfunctional individuals, couples, and families. However, this model was validated by Cusinato and Colesso (2008) through a new paper-and-pencil, self-report test.

Model^{10} is produced by an expansion from Models$^{8 \text{ and } 9}$ into an arithmetical model composed by multiplicative, additive, static positive, static negative, subtractive, and divisive interactions. The simple arithmetical model^{10} in Table 7.1 was proposed on the basis of four criteria: objective observations, assessment of context, psychiatric diagnosis, and psychometric testing (L'Abate et al. 2010, pp. 153–161). It was validated by Colesso et al. (2013) and results are reported in Table 7.1, comparing theoretical predictions with empirical results. Interactions in Model^{10} can be assessed according to a still-experimental ecologically oriented questionnaire (L'Abate 2008b) as well as four different criteria to evaluate them (L'Abate et al. 2010, pp. 153–161) according to a simple arithmetic model evaluated through log logarithmic analysis.

Model^{11}, composed by selfulness, selfishness, selflessness, and no-self, is related to all the previous models, as shown in Fig. 7.5. This Model^{11} is the most validated of all RCT models (L'Abate et al. 2010, pp. 163–188) through a visual–verbal

Table 7.1 Predicted theoretical simple arithmetical model distribution and obtained log Logarith-Mic percentages with a small sample of university students ($N = 130$)[a]

SAM categories for interactions	Theoretical percentages of SAM categories predicted in a large population (L'Abate et al. 2010, p. 159)	LM categories for socialization	Obtained LM percentages ($N = 130$)
1. Divisive	5.00	1. Very poor	5.08
2. Subtractive	20.00	2. Insufficient	15.25
4. Negative static	25.00	3. Mixed	26.27
4. Positive static	25.00	3. Passable	30.51
5. Additive	20.00	5. Adequate	20.34
6. Multiplicative	5.00	6. Excellent	2.54
Total	100.00		100.00

[a] Adapted from Colesso et al. (2013) SAM *simple arithmetic model,* LM *LogarthMic*

Fig. 7.5 Expansion of Model[11] to include functional and dysfunctional dimensions including and integrating psychiatric categories into one comprehensive framework

<table>
<tr><th>Setting</th><th>Relationships</th><th>Context</th><th colspan="2">Relationship Contents</th></tr>
<tr><td>Objective
(Model[3] & Model[12])</td><td>Elements of each intimate relationship</td><td>Participative
(Model[3] & Model[12])</td><td>**Resources**
(Model[7])</td><td>**Modalities**
(Model[7])</td></tr>
<tr><td>Home</td><td>Frequency</td><td>Home</td><td>Money</td><td rowspan="2">Having</td></tr>
<tr><td>Work</td><td>Self-importance
(Model[11])</td><td>Work</td><td>Goods</td></tr>
<tr><td>Survival</td><td></td><td>Survival</td><td>Services</td><td rowspan="2">Doing</td></tr>
<tr><td>Enjoyment</td><td>Perceived other-importance
(Model[11])</td><td>Enjoyment</td><td>Information</td></tr>
<tr><td></td><td></td><td></td><td>Importance
(Model[11])</td><td rowspan="2">Being</td></tr>
<tr><td></td><td></td><td></td><td>Intimacy
(Model[15])</td></tr>
</table>

Fig. 7.6 Elements for a relational competence ecological map

picture test, the Dyadic Relationships Test (Cusinato and L'Abate 2005a, b), and the Self–Other Profile Chart (SOPC). Model[11], as shown in Fig. 7.5, integrates discrete, nondimensional psychiatric categories with dimensions of superior functioning related to multiplicative and additive as well as to externalizing, internalizing, and pathological interactions (Model[10]), styles in intimate relationships (Model[9]), and the six ranges of likeness (Model[8]).

Model[12] can be evaluated with General and Personal Priorities Scales that are still experimental (L'Abate et al. 2010, pp. 189–201). Various other models already cited above can be evaluated with the EcoMap. Figure 7.6 shows how Models[3, 7, 9, 11, 12, and 15] overlap, that is, are interrelated with four types of settings (Model[3]), modalities (Model[7]), styles (Model[9]), priorities (Model[12]), and intimacy (Model[15]).

Figure 7.7 shows how the EcoMap, a multifunction, multiple-purpose instrument, evaluates how participants perceive their connections with intimates in various settings and contexts. Settings (Model[3)]) are objective and can be photographed and recorded. Contexts (component of Model[1]) are subjectively perceived and can be elicited through instruments, like the EcoMap (Fig. 7.8).

Figure 7.9 integrates the relational dimensions of Models[8, 9, 10, and 11] with standard psychiatric categories, offering for the first time different dimensions applicable to human relationships rather than just to individuals, couples, or families.

Figure 7.10 integrates Models[7, 11, and15].

Constructs	Modalities	Resources	Examples of Resources exchanged by Settings			
			Home	Work/School	Survival	Enjoyment
Communal Presence	Being	Importance	Valuing oneself, feelings valued, recognition's of one's goodness and value, feeling as a person who matters	Status related to Job or Profession, Level of education; titles, ranks, & honors	Positive attribu-tion of Importantce to self and in-timates	Free expression of plea-sure to see and welcome friends and intimates
		Intimacy	Sharing of confidences, joys, hurts, and fears of being hurt, affection, forgiveness of transgressions, emotional closeness	Not included or considered irrelevant or secondary to work/school performance; Avoided as much as possible	Ability to share hurt feelings with self and intimates, forgiving trans-gressions in self and intimates	Reflecting on one's own positive behavior, sharing confidences with intimates & friends without Doing or Having
Agentic Power	Doing	Information	Books, internet, magazines, newspaper, radio, telephone, TV	Knowledge relevant to job, occupational, or professional performance	Keeping up with news and with happenings within one's world & community	Crossword puzzles, brain teasers, virtual pursuit; computer and word games
	Having	Goods/posses-sions	Car(s), food, furniture, TV, radio, house, second home &/or land, clothing, jewelers, etc.	Work station, size and style of cubicle or office size	Avoiding debts by not buying extra-vagantly	Hobbies requiring manipulation of objects; play, collecting
		Money	Bank account, cash at hand, credit card, salary, other income, possessions	Salary plus bonus, insurance, perks, benefits	Savings, con-trolled use of credit cards;	Having fun, movies, travel, theater.

Adapted from L'Abate et al., 2010.

Fig. 7.7 A model for EcoMap administration.

Clinically Relevant Models

There are no instruments developed for Models[13 and14] because distance regulation and the deadly drama triangle should be observable to most experienced professionals, as in parentification, and the so-called Stockholm and parental alienation syndromes and bullying (Hooper et al. 2014). Model[15] can be evaluated with the Sharing of Hurts Scale as well as a workbook about hurt feelings (L'Abate 2011a, b).

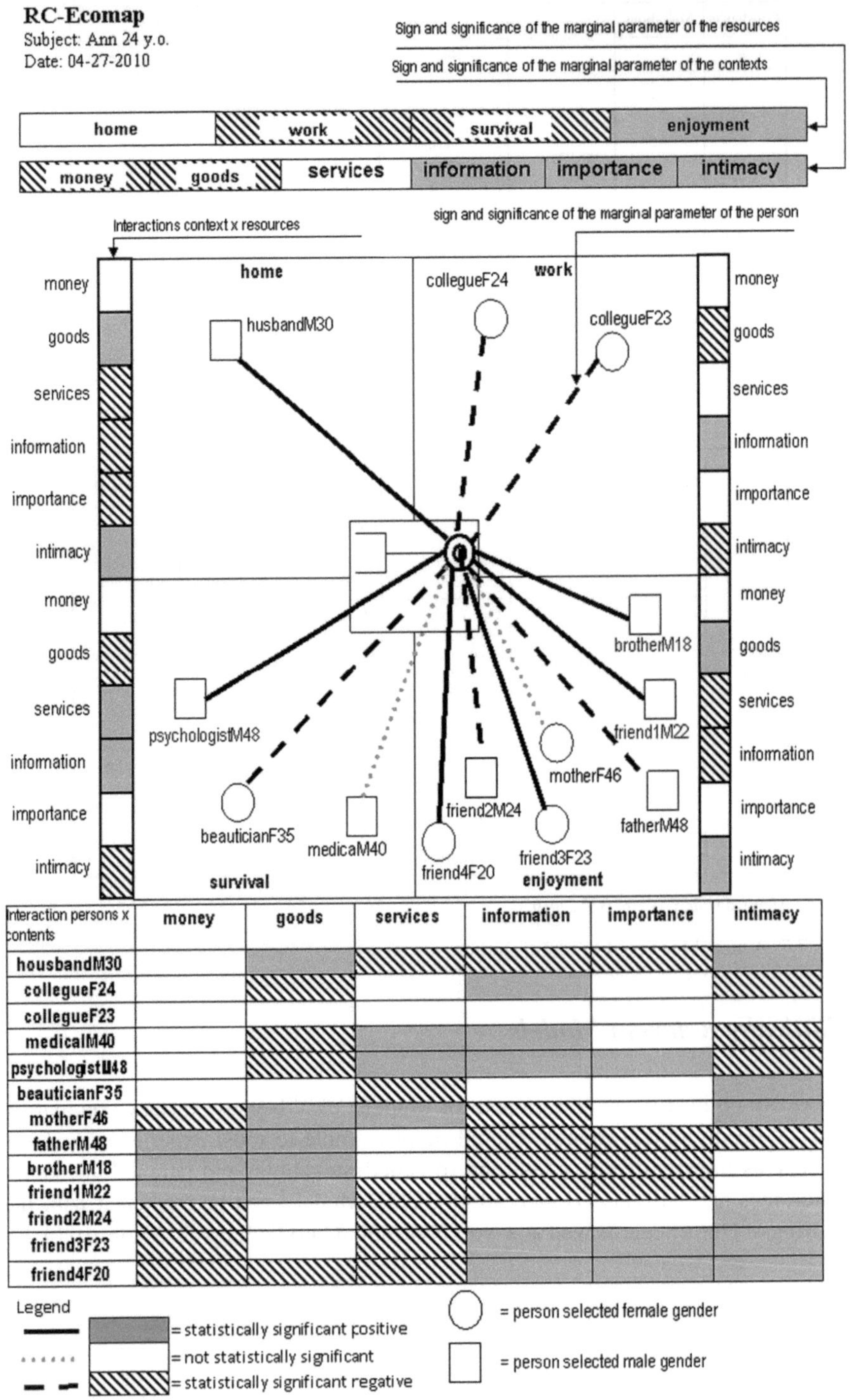

Fig. 7.8 Example of EcoMap

Relationships among four Models of Identity Differentiation[8], Styles[9], Interactions[10], Selfhood[11], and Psychiatric Classification

		Model[8]: Continuum of Likeness		
Symbiosis	Sameness	Similarity/Differentness	Oppositeness	Alienation
		Model[9]: Styles in Intimate Relationships		
Abusive Apathetic	Reactive Repetitive	Conductive Creative	Reactive Repetitive	Abusive Apathetic
		Model[10]: Interactions		
Divisive/ Subtractive	Static/ Positive	Multiplicative/ Additive	Static/ Negative	Divisive/ Subtractive
		Model[11]: Selfhood		
No-self	Selfless	Self-full	Selfish	No-self
		Psychiatric Categories (DSM-IV)		
Axis I & Axis II/ Cluster A	*Axis II Cluster C*	*No diagnoses*	*Axis II Cluster B*	*Axis I & Axis II/ Cluster A*

Fig. 7.9 Relationships among four models of identity differentiation[8], styles[9], interactions[10], selfhood[11], and psychiatric classification

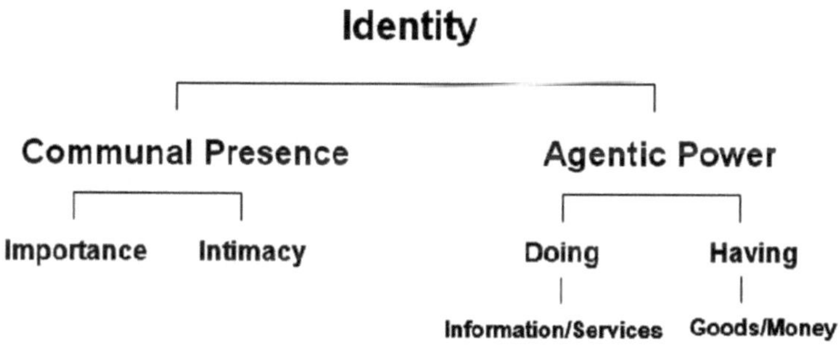

Fig. 7.10 Summary of emerging constructs of identity and intimacy in RCT. *RCT* relational competence theory

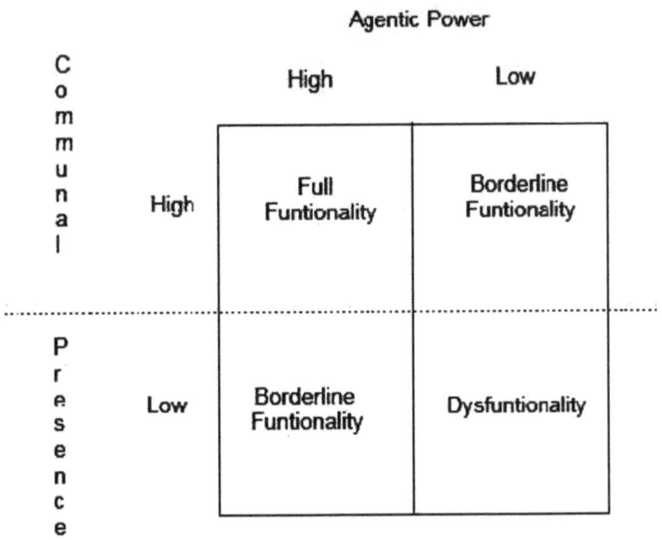

Fig. 7.11 Functional and dysfunctional outcomes of high and low communal presence and agentic power

Conclusion

RCT theory can be evaluated through writing, statically through model-derived test instruments and dynamically through interactive practice exercises or workbooks. In this fashion, it is possible to link evaluation with treatment in ways that would be difficult if not impossible to achieve verbally F2F through talk. The relationship between RCT and workbooks is considered in Chap. 8 of this volume.

Chapter 8
Workbooks: Programmed Interactive Practice Exercises and Prescriptions

Psychological interventions in health promotion, sickness prevention, psychotherapy, and rehabilitation consist of targeted programmed interactive practice exercises (PIPEs) or workbooks administered interactively as homework assignments (L'Abate 2004b, 2011c, in press; L'Abate and Sweeney 2011). To qualify as workbooks, they must be systematically programmed, specifically targeted, and continuously interactive.

This approach indicates a drastic, radical, and sharp change from traditional face-to-face (F2F) talk-based (TB) mental health interventions (L'Abate 1991, 1992, 1999). It is based on the conviction that people in need of help can and should be helped first without ever seeing them F2F through the administration of programmed, targeted, and interactive distance writing (DW; L'Abate 1992, 1997, 1999, 2001, 2002, 2004a, 2007a, b, 2008a, b, c, 2009a, 2012c, 2013a, b, c), and, second, seeing participants F2F only when TB interventions are necessary to control the effects of homework assignments and identify causes of resistance or inability to write at a distance (L'Abate 2012a). Regular control visits, online or off-line, therefore, serve to check and give feedback on completed homework assignments and, if appropriate, administer another series of homework assignments.

As long as talk remains the only medium of communication, as in F2F TB psychotherapy and preaching, it will be practically impossible to obtain cumulative (measurable/replicable) records and progress on the basis of data that can be obtained only through writing not talk (L'Abate 1999, 2011b). Given these definitions, workbooks or PIPEs qualify eminently as a mental health technology that has emerged and surfaced during the last generation (L'Abate 1986, 1990, 1991, 1992, 1997, 2001, 2002, 2004a, 2004b, 2007c, 2008a, 2008c, 2011c, 2013b; L'Abate and De Giacomo 2003; L'Abate and Goldstein 2007; L'Abate and Kern 2002; Hooper et al. 2014).

Together with recent advances in computer technology, the emergence of the Internet, the growing importance of homework assignments (Kazantzis et al. 2005; Kazantzis and L'Abate 2007), the growth of self-help (Harwood and L'Abate 2010; L'Abate 2013c), and emergence of low-cost approaches to promote physical and

L. L'Abate, *Concreteness and Specificity in Clinical Psychology*,
DOI 10.1007/978-3-319-13284-6_8

mental health in their delivery (L'Abate 2007d), there are now plenty of choices available to both professionals and participants in the mental health field, in promotion of health, and in the prevention and psychotherapy of mental illness.

The issue remains in finding ways to evaluate participants to help them find which approach will be more helpful and less costly to them than other approaches (L'Abate 2011a). These approaches would suggest targeted or step-by-step treatment, starting from the least expensive of professional help first and then moving on to the most expensive treatment, that is; F2F TB contacts with professionals, especially if least expensive approaches are not working. For instance, depression in its least severe forms (determined by scores on the Beck depression inventory) could be dealt with first by using much less expensive activities such as running, physical therapy, yoga, or meditation (L'Abate 2013c). Somewhere in between least and most expensive, F2F TB approaches PIPEs could be used either on their own, or in conjunction with most expensive approaches (L'Abate 2011c; Hooper et al. 2014)

Workbooks essentially perform as standardized *recipes,* furnishing professionals with specific ways of helping and intervening that can be replicated from one participant to another and from professional to another. There are no limits on how many times these workbooks can be reproduced and administered to as many participants as possible (L'Abate 2011c), just like recipes from a cookbook. If one particular workbook does not work for a specific condition, let us say depression, one would have to (1) question the initial reason for referral; (2) evaluate historical and developmental background for the referral; (3) evaluate results from a test battery administered even before seeing (or not seeing) the participant; (4) see whether another, different workbook for depression may be more appropriate than the one originally administered; or (5) administer a completely different, not depression-related workbook. That approach—stepwise—may be more appropriate for the context of the referral, such as one related to overall functioning rather than a specific workbook related to a diagnosis or to the reason for the referral, as would be the case with planned parenting or negotiation workbooks.

The use of workbooks in no way eliminates the important functions of professionals. On the contrary, a DW approach requires that more attention be given to an objective evaluation for the referral reason, concern, or symptom. An objective evaluation is an aspect that may differentiate between professionals who chose to practice as artists from professionals who chose to practice as scientists, evaluating participants from the very outset of a professional relationship, after termination of that relationship, and on follow-up (L'Abate 2011a, 20113b). In addition to an evaluative function, the professional/scientist needs to evaluate responses to each single workbook and feedback appropriate and specific information about the nature of those responses to participants. This function is implicit in the interactive nature of the process. Consequently, this conviction (L'Abate 2011a, 2013b) would not allow a professional to administer a entire series of workbooks without breaking them down into one assignment after another, one assignment at one time, with corrective feedback on completion of each assignment, after an informed consent form (ICF) about the importance of pre–post and follow-up evaluation is emphasized from the outset of the professional relationship (L'Abate 2013b).

Here is where theory and theory testing become relevant in linking both with applied and clinical practice. The same three-level criteria to evaluate a theory, presented in Chap. 6, can be used to evaluate the effectiveness of workbooks. For instance, *independent evidence* about the overall use of distance or remote writing, and especially focused DW, is represented by the research summarized by Esterling et al. (1999) and Smyth (1998). *Indirect evidence* about the use of workbooks and homework assignments in general is represented by meta-analyses presented by Kazantzis (2000), Kazantizis et al. (2000), and Smyth and L'Abate (2001). *Direct evidence* about workbooks specifically developed by this writer was summarized in L'Abate (2011c). Preliminary direct evidence is available in L'Abate et al. (1992), McMahan and L'Abate (2000), and Reed et al. (2000). Of course, more evidence will be necessary to evaluate the latter. The term "preliminary" is used in the sense that any evidence presented by the proponent of any method is suspicious at best. Consequently, no matter how much evidence this writer and his collaborators were to accumulate, it would never be enough. It is much more important for such evidence to be developed by researchers independently of this approach.

Workbooks, of course, are used primarily to help people, secondarily to test competing theories or models. In regard to both uses, the criterion becomes "Which workbook (representing which theory or model) will produce the best results in the shortest number of assignments?" This is a new rephrasing of the old psychotherapy dictum: "Who will be helped by which intervention and by which helper (at what price)?" For instance, given two different workbooks to deal with the two dimensions of the selfhood model, self and other, is it possible to compare each workbook with workbooks designed to deal with the same two dimensions based on different theoretical viewpoints? Both workbooks could be compared with the two workbooks about self–other concerns developed on the basis of two-factor model of depression, self-criticism, and overdependency. How well does the selfhood model compare with workbooks derived from other models about the same two dimensions of self and other? If no competing workbooks are available, it is possible to compare either the negotiation or intimacy workbooks (both derived from the theory) with workbooks on the same topic. In another instance, two assignments idiographic with two subsidiary models of depression (L'Abate 1986), the drama and distance triangles, are found in two respective assignments found in the workbook by the same name (Fig. 8.8). Through workbooks a wide range of nonclinical, semiclinical, and clinical populations can be helped, at the same time testing different theoretical models from which these workbooks were derived.

Theory-Derived Workbooks

Interactive practice exercises or workbooks administered as homework assignments indicate a drastic, radical, and sharp change from traditional face-to-face (F2F) talk-based (TB) psychotherapy (L'Abate 1991, 1992, 1999). This approach is based on the conviction that people in need of help can and should be helped first without ever seeing them F2F through the use of distance writing (DW; L'Abate 1992, 1997, 1999, 2001, 2002, 2004a, 204b, 2007a, 2007b, 2008a, 2008b, 2008c, 2009a, 2012c, 2013a, 2013b, 2013c, in press; L'Abate and Sweeney 2011), and, second, seeing participants F2F only when TB interventions are necessary to control the effects of homework assignments and identify causes of resistance or inability to write at a distance (L'Abate 2012a).

Workbooks (L'Abate 1992, 1996, 2010) can be divided into being (1) *independent* from relational competence theory (RCT) when produced from another theory or model; (2) loosely *related* to RCT, as in externalizations and internalizations (Fig. 8.5); and (3) directly *derived* from specific models of RCT. Three original workbooks about depression, negotiation, and intimacy were published in L'Abate (1986). One workbook, Planned Parenting (L'Abate 2010), includes all the models of RCT using concrete questions just as much as a concrete, simple interview (L'Abate 2009) has been reduced to workbook format. Models[1, 4, 5, 9, and 12] can be administered through structured enrichment programs for couples and families (L'Abate and Weinstein 1987). Intimacy (Model[15]) can be evaluated with a Sharing of Hurts workbook (L'Abate 2011a). Model[11] can be used to connect it with a classification of workbooks connecting a model of the theory with replicable interactive practice exercises.

The Nature of Workbooks

Workbooks as PIPEs are composed by four characteristics: (1) administered in writing as homework at a distance from professionals, with (2) participants in continuous interactions with professionals who (3) request consistent, reliable practice exercises, such as homework assignments, and who (4) try to match a specific workbook with the specific referral question, concern, diagnosis, or symptom.

Programmed

Workbooks are written according to systematic procedures to be administered at a distance between mental health professionals and participants, be participants composed of individuals, couples, or families. In the past, this distance may have been covered though regular mail. Nowadays, distance is covered through computers and the Internet. Being written means that these exercises are completely replicable and extremely specific for determined situations or disorders, as explained in Fig. 8.1. There is no need to repeat what has been already written in previous and present publications by this author as cited above (Fig. 8.2; L'Abate in press; L'Abate and Sweeney 2011).

By this, qualification means that these exercises cannot and should not be administered without continuous corrective feedback between a professional and a

1. *Structured-Unstructured* can vary from *open*, as in diaries or *closed*, as in answering specific questions in writing on pre-established topic, either positive, happy or unhappy memories. Closed writing can be guided or programmed.
2. *Goals* could be *prescriptive* to produce specific outcomes or *cathartic* to produce discharge of and release from tensions or traumas.
3. *Content* can be painful, traumatic, neutral, banal, or joyous, emotional, rational, problem-solving, individual, or relational/
5. *Level of abstraction* ranging from very concrete, i.e., "Write what you ate for breakfast, to very abstract, i.e., "Write about the meaning of life."
6. *Specificity*, ranging from general, as in an autobiography or: "Write about the meaning of life," to extremely specific, concrete, and restricted, such as: "Write about all the clothes you have in your closet."

Fig. 8.1 Toward a classification of distance writing dimensions. (Adapted from L'Abate 2004a)

A. *Automatic* was of questionable usefulness as a fad and in need of more controlled research before considering its use.
B. *Dictionary-aided* basic to many self-help practice exercises (L'Abate, 2007a).
C. *Expressive* , as in "Pennebaker's Paradigm" writing about hurts and traumas heretofore not shared with others for 15 minutes a day for four consecutive days. The literature on this approach is extensive and available in many old (Esterling, L'Abate, Murray, & Pennebaker, 1999) and new references (Kacewicz, Slatcher, & Pennebaker, 2007; Lepore & Smyth, 2002).
D. *Focused*, as in autobiographies to be mailed or sent online (L'Abate, 2007c)
E. *Guided* , as in answering written questions in writing, after completion, for instance, of an autobiography, journal, or other homework assignments.
F. *Open-ended*, as in personal information gathered through diaries or journals.
G. *Programmed* as in Workbooksfor non-targeted conditions and life-long learning and at risk populations (Figure 7.4) targeted and psychiatrically diagnosed children and youth, single individuals,couples, and families (Figure 7.5), single-or multiple-score tests (Figure 7.6).

Fig. 8.2 A classification of distance writing. Adapted from L'Abate (2004b); see also L'Abate and Sweeney (2011)

participant. Interactive means that workbooks are or should be administered after a thorough, objective evaluation of the referring concern, question, or referral reason (L'Abate 2013b). Furthermore, workbooks should be administered after an ICF has been read and signed by all participants. Participants should know what possible consequences or unpredictable side effects may occur in many instances, especially when dealing with hurt feelings (L'Abate 2011b) and how important evaluation is in finding which approach is more appropriate for which condition.

Therefore, the ICF should be administered to protect both professionals and participants, since one cannot predict whether (1) the reason for referral is a real and accurate one and (2) whether the evaluation uncovered contextual aspects of the referral reason that may have not been considered through a subjective interview. For instance, a participant may want help to deal with self-diagnosed anxiety, but without an evaluation, the professional may accept uncritically the participant's opinion and administer an anxiety-related workbook. When anxiety does not decrease on termination of the entire workbook, the patient may complain about the professional's incompetence and may threaten legal action. On the basis of this reaction, the professional may discover that there may exist a whole delusional, paranoid system that could have been detected from the outset with a thorough objective evaluation. An ICF represents the contract between professionals and participants about the use of workbooks.

Copies of such ICFs are available in L'Abate (2011c), including also a control workbook with seemingly neutral items to be used for research purposes (L'Abate 2011c). Whoever professionals choose to administer workbooks without a thorough, objective evaluation, a signed ICF, and continuous, exercise-by-exercise professional feedback, they should be considered artists/charlatans and should receive appropriate retribution from professional organizations in which they belong (L'Abate 2011a, in press).

Practice

Professionals should be careful to specify how, when, how often, and where workbooks should take place (L'Abate 1986), making sure that participants record place and time of occurrence and checking on complete homework before accepting it as given and administering the next assignment. For instance, in my experience with acting-out inmates, some of them tried to get away with as little work as possible. Consequently, they were required to repeat writing the same exercise until it showed that responsibility was taken to complete the assignment in the best possible manner. Incomplete or irrelevant answers are unacceptable and participants should not be allowed to get away with minimal performance. More instructions about this issue are available in L'Abate (2011c).

In a way, in addition to pre-intervention objective evaluation, workbooks, in and of themselves, allow professionals to evaluate whether there is motivation for change in participants or whether they expect the professional to produce change miraculously without their active participation (L'Abate et al. 2005). In stepped treatment, one could make homework assignments and completion of workbooks as a precondition for seeing the professional F2F through talk (O'Donohue and Draper 2911; Omer 1985). The expensive presence of a professional should also be contingent on the completion of the least expensive treatment. This approach is especially useful to evaluate motivation to change in cluster B participants, who may use professional help as a way to avoid criminal or legal persecution (L'Abate et al. 2011).

Exercises

Figure 8.3 includes a self-explanatory classification of workbooks. As in the previous paragraphs, the interested reader can find expanded explanations of this and the two previous figures in references already cited. One important aspect of

1. *Composition* of Participants: singles (adults, children, youth), couples, families, groups.
2. *Reason for Referral,* i. e., concern(s), diagnosis(es), single versus dual or multiple, problem(s), symptom(s),
3. *Level and Type of Functionality*: DSM-IV, Reason for Referral, or both
    a. Functional: No diagnosis
    b. Externalizations: Axis II. Cluster B (e. g., Aboujaoude & Koran, 2010).
    c. Internalizations : AxisII. Cluster C (e.,g. Millon, Blaney, & Davis,1999)
    d. Bor derline: Axis II. Cluster A (e.g.,Millon, Blaney, & Davis, 1999)
    e. Severe: Axis I. (e. g., e.g.,Millon, Blaney, & Davis, 1999)
4. Practice exercises for *specific symptoms* versus general conditions
5. *Symptom-free* versus symptom-related & diagnosis -linked
6. *Theory-derived* , theory -related, theory -independent (Cusinato & L'Abate, in press; L'Abate, 2005; L'Abate & Cusinato, 2007; L'Abate, Cusinato, Maino, Colesso, & Scilletta, 2010).
7. *Format*: (1) fixed (nomothetic); (2) flexible (idiographic); & (3) mixed (nomothetic and idiographic)
8. *Style*: Linear versus circular (paradoxical, i.e., Weeks & L'Abate (1982)
9. *Derivation*: Single versus multiple score tests, i. e., BDI vs. MMPI -2.
10. *Content*: clinical (addictions, affective disorders, Axis I and Axis II: Clusters A, B, & C etc. and non-clinical, life-long learning for individuals, couples, and families

Fig. 8.3 Classification of workbooks in mental health. (Adapted from L'Abate 2004b)

workbooks contained in Fig. 8.3 lies in their being produced from existing, validated test instruments, verified factor analyses, or symptom lists available in the DSM-IV (Diagnostic and Statistical Manual of Mental Disorders, Fourth Edition; American Psychiatric Association 1994). This is another way to indicate that PIPEs are isomorphic with their underlying composition based on validated measures. Hence, the gap between evaluation and intervention using PIPEs is greatly diminished, allowing professionals to match treatment with evaluation in ways that would be difficult, expensive, or even impossible to accomplish in F2F TB psychotherapy.

Transforming inert, passive test or factor analyses items or psychiatric symptoms into dynamic workbooks is a very simple process that apparently has not been thought of until recently (L'Abate 2011c). This process occurs in three easy steps (Fig. 8.4): (1) asking participants to define items of single-score tests, or dimensions of multiple-score tests, factor analyses, and DSM-IV symptoms lists with the help of a dictionary (L'Abate 2007a), and give two, possibly concrete, examples of the item just defined, a nomothetic task; (2) rank-order items just defined according to how those items refer to oneself in order of importance and relevance, an idiographic task that individualizes immediately the sequence to follow in treatment, starting with the item that has been rank-ordered first, moving then to the item rank-ordered second, and so on, until most of the top items (no more than five or six in my experience) have been administered one by one; and (3) administer a standard practice exercise (L'Abate 2011c) where the top item becomes the subject of an intense scrutiny, that is, asking participants to answer queries about the overall nature of that item, its developmental origins, duration, frequency, rate, and functional and dysfunctional outcomes to self and to Fig. 8.4 loved ones.

A. Establish Baseline through objective evaluation.
B. Nomothetic Introduction
1. Standard List of Multiple Items from Tests, Factor Analyses, Test Scores, or DSM Symptom Definitions relevant to the reason for referral
2. Definitions of each item according to the participant's personal experience
3. Give two examples of Behavior for each Item
C. Idiographic Expansion
1. Rank order items according to personal preferences
2. Explain reason(s) for ranking
D. Follow ranking to administer a general, all-purpose homework Interactive practice exercise, about the origin, rate, frequency, intensity, and consequences up to the first five or six items (L'Abate, 2011c).
D. Evaluate results objectively with the same battery of tests used to establish an initial baseline.
E. Administer another PIPE or add adjunct or alternative pre-para- or post therapeutic approaches (L'Abate, 2013d)

Fig. 8.4 Steps in the development of a PIPE or workbook. PIPE programmed interactive practice exercise

Sometimes, if the behavior represented in a particular item is strongly ingrained in the individual's affective, cognitive, and behavioral repertoire, participants may be asked to produce and reproduce it at certain times and places to achieve greater control over it, following the principle that "If we learn to approach and start a troublesome behavior, we can learn to stop it" (L'Abate 1984), contrary to many behavioral dogmas. Through this process, therefore, as shown in figures to follow, it is possible to transform thousands of passively inert test instruments into active and interactive methods of treatment, linking evaluation with treatment in ways that would be difficult and expensive to achieve in self-help, preventive, promotional, or psychotherapeutic interventions using F2F TB approaches.

Therefore, to reiterate an important point, workbooks (Hooper et al. 2014; L'Abate 1992, 1996, 2011c, 2013b) can be divided into being (1) *independent* from RCT when produced from another theory or model; (2) loosely *related* to RCT, as in externalizations and internalizations (Fig. 8.7); and (3) directly *derived* from specific models of RCT. Three original workbooks about depression, negotiation, and intimacy were published in L'Abate (1986). One workbook, Planned Parenting (L'Abate 2011c), includes all the models of RCT using concrete questions just as much as a concrete, simple interview (L'Abate 2009) has been reduced to workbook format. Models[1, 4, 5, 9, and 12] can be administered through structured enrichment programs for couples and families (L'Abate and Weinstein 1987). Intimacy (Model[15]) that can be evaluated with a Sharing of Hurts workbook (L'Abate 2010). Figure 8.8 shows how Model[11] can be used to link it with a classification of workbooks connecting a model of the theory to replicable interactive practice exercises.

Fig. 8.5 Self-help workbooks for individual, couple, and family lifelong learning

Individuals

Character Strengths
Emotional Expression
Development of Emotional Competence
Multiple Abilities
Normative Experiences: Form AB5C
Normative Experiences: Form IPIP
Normative Experiences: Form PSC
Priorities
Self-awareness
Self- Others Importance
Social Skills
Speak UP For Yourself
Who Am I? Aspects of Identity Formation

Couples

Premarital Preparation
Relational Quality1
Relational Quality
Relational Quality3
Relational Styles
Sexual Motivation

Families

Foster/Adoptive Care
Planned Parenting

Workbooks for Preventive and Health Promotional Lifelong Learning

Figure 8.5 includes workbooks that can be used when no specific clinical concern is present or detected, but there is interest and motivation to learn more about oneself in individuals, couples, or families.

These workbooks, therefore, could be used in self-help (Harwood and L'Abate 2010), prevention (L'Abate 1990), and promotional (L'Abate 2007d, 2013c) activities with functional or semi-functional participants, especially those who are at risk for possible breakdown, such as an adult children of alcoholic parents. These individuals, couples, and families may not be classified as yet according to a psychiatric label, but they may evidence prodromal characteristics that may foretell future disorders, especially in children.

Workbooks for Psychiatric Classification

Figure 8.6 includes workbooks that were derived from list of symptoms in psychiatric diagnoses found in the DSM-IV (Author 1994, Millon et al. 1999) and other sources, showing that through programmed DW, it is possible to link evaluation with specific treatment in ways that would be difficult if not impossible to achieve through F2F TB interventions.

Disorders of Internalization

Children and Youth

Anxiety
Anxiety, Depression, and Fears
Asperger Disorder
Depression
Post-Traumatic Stress
Separation Anxiety

Adults

Anxiety
Depressive Personality
Loneliness
Phobias
Post-Traumatic Stress Disorder
Procrastination
Signs of Depression

Disruptive Developmental Disorders

Anger
Conduct Disorder
Hyperactive/Attention Deficit
Juvenile Troublemaking
Oppositional Defiant

Disorders of Externalization in Adults

Addendum to Relational Training
Anger, Hostility, Aggression
Troublemaking

Workbooks for Conflicting Couples and Families

Children and Families

Bing Eating
Divorce Adjustment in Children
Domestic Violence
Lying
Shyness
Stealing
Temper Tantrums
Time Out
Verbal Abuse

Couples

A theory-derived workbook for intimate couples
Arguing or Fighting
Complaints
Depression
Difficulties
Intimacy
Sexuality
Violence

Families

Hurt Feelings
Intimacy
Negotiation
When Parents Argue: From the Child's Eyes
When Parents and Child Argue: From the Child's Eyes

Fig. 8.6 Workbooks for participants with psychiatric diagnoses. (Adapted from L'Abate 2011c)

Workbooks from Research with Single- or Multiple-Score Tests

Another way to link evaluation with treatment is found in developing workbooks directly from items found in factor analyses, single- and multiple-score tests, as shown in Fig. 8.7.

Single Score Tests

Children: Mixed Internalizing and Externalizing Disorders

School Conduct Problems
School Social Skills
Unusual or Troublesome Behavior

Adults

Butcher Treatment Planning

Axis II Cluster C Internalizing Personality Disorders

Beck Anxiety
Beck Depression
Hamilton Anxiety
Hamilton Depression
Help-seeking (Dependent)
Self-suffering (Masochist)
Serious (Depressed)
What Are My Concerns

Axis II Cluster B Selected Externalizing Personality Disorders

Anger Expression
Compelling (Compulsive)
Distinct (Schizoid)
Exciting (Histrionic)
Non-conformist (Negativistic)
Private (Avoidant)
Self-interested (Narcissistic)
Unpopular (Antisocial)
Unusual (Sadistic)

Mixed Internalizing and Externalizing Disorders

Personality Disorders, Form 1989
Personality Disorders, Form 1990
Personality Disorders, Form 1992

Multiple Score Tests

Personality Dimensions from the MMPI
Personality Dimensions from Neuroticism Extraversion Openness Inventory (NEO)
Personality Dimensions from Personality Assessment Inventory

Severe Disorders

Individuals

Mood Swings
Over-dependency
Severe Concerns
Sexual Abuse

Couples

Improving Relationships
Relationship Conflict
Couple Satisfaction

Families

Profile Form
Functioning

Fig. 8.7 Workbooks from research with single- and multiple-score tests. (Adapted from L'Abate 2011c)

		Self-Importance	
		High	*Low*
Importance of Others	*High*	*Functionality* Life-long learning exercises	*Cluster C Disorders* Depression Anxiety
	Low	*Cluster B Disorders* Acting-out Psychopathy Impulsivity	*Severe Axis I* Cluster A Disorders Mood Swings Schizophrenic

Fig. 8.8 Relationships among selfhood propensities (Model[11]) functionality, psychopathology (DSM-IV), and selected interactive practice exercises. DSM-IV Diagnostic and Statistical Manual of Mental Disorders, Fourth Edition (L'Abate, 2011c)

Model[1].
Emotional Problems in Youth (L'Abate, 2013b, pp. 198-212); Awareness: Enhancing Self-awareness (L'Abate, 2011c, pp. 689-696). Symptoms and Psychosomatic Inventory (L'Abate, 2013b, pp. 243-279)

Model [4]. Depression in Couples (L'Abate, 2011c, pp. 352-362);

Model [5]. Antisocial Behavior (L'Abate, 2011c, pp. 227- 250) for Acting out, Aggressive, and Criminal Cluster B Personality Disorders; Arguing and Fighting in Couples (L'Abate, 2011c, pp. 372-410); Procrastination (L'Abate, 2011c, 159-168); Lying (L'Abate, 2013b, pp. 219-223; Shyness in Children, pp. 233-236; Social Training, pp. 280-308; Stealing, pp. 309-313; Temper Tantrums, pp. 314-322; Time-out, pp. 323-328).

Model [8]. Who am I? Aspects of Identity Formation (L'Abate, 2011c, pp. 696-707).

Model [9]. Over-dependency (L'Abate, 2011c, pp. 259- 295) see also Model [11]; Sexual Abuse (L'Abate, 2011b, pp. 296-310); Binge Eating (L'Abate, 2013b, pp. 168-171; Domestic Violence/Child Abuse, pp. 192-197; Negativity, pp. 223-226; Sibling Rivalry, 237-242; Verbal Abuse, pp. 329-333).

Model [11]. Self-Other Importance (L'Abate, 2011c, pp. 579-585); Selfhood (L'Abate, 2011c, pp. 462-463); Speak Up for Yourself! (L'Abate, 2011c, pp. 707-716); Dissociative Experiences L'Abate, 2013a, pp. 172-182).

Model [12]. Priorities (L'Abate, 2011c, pp. 618-623);

Model [14]. Kaplan Drama Triangle: Parentification, Cluster C personality disorders, Drama Triangle, Parental Alienation Behavior, Bullism, and Stockholm Syndrome (Hooper, L'Abate, Sweeney, Gianesini, & Jamkoski, 2014).

Model [15]. Hurt Feelings (L'Abate, 2011c, pp. 499-526; pp. 475-499);

Model[16]. Negotiation (L'Abate, 2011c, pp. 446-475). Divorce Adjustment in Children (L'Abate, 2013a, pp. 183-191; Planning Problem Solving (L'Abate, 2013b, pp. 227-232)

Fig. 8.9 Matching RCT models with workbooks or interactive practice exercises. RCT relational competence theory (L'Abate 2011c, 2013a)

Figure 8.8 shows the relationship between Model[11] and an overall classification of workbooks according to functional and dysfunctional criteria.

Figure 8.9 includes an even more specific matching between RCT models and workbooks, a matching that cannot be achieved in F2F TB psychotherapy.

Research Results

Research about the effectiveness of workbooks was conducted from the very beginning, starting 30 or more years ago but reported more recently (L'Abate et al. 1992; L'Abate 2004b, pp. 75–92) with unexpected paradoxical and sometimes inconsistent results. For instance, in "few studies control groups obtained higher gain scores than experimental groups suggesting that this was an important area to investigate in the future" (L'Abate 2004b, pp. 91–92). To find a more definitive answer, Smyth and L'Abate (2001) performed a meta-analysis of 18 workbooks, 12 in mental health and 6 in physical health. The overall effect size for mental health outcomes was $d=0.44$, while the overall effect size for physical health outcomes was $d=0.25$.

Results from this analysis as well as from the studies summarized in L'Abate (2004b, pp. 75–92) suggested that workbooks may produce a medium effect size and a somewhat lower effect size for physical health, even though great variability was present for such outcomes. This effect size was quite similar to the one obtained from a meta-analysis of F2F TB psychological treatment in 90 studies conducted across a broad range of clinical settings (mean $d=0.41$; Shadish et al. 2000).

Here is where costs and cost-effectiveness come into being. If the same results are obtained by two different types of intervention, one would choose the less expensive intervention. This, however, is not an either/or but a both/and issue. Conceivably, F2F TB interventions may be needed with more severe cases, and even in these cases, adding PIPEs may decrease the length of treatment or reduce the possibility of relapse.

However, this was not the case with outpatients who received workbooks in addition to F2F TB psychotherapy (L'Abate et al. 2005). Those participants (individuals, couples, and families) who received workbooks showed a significantly greater number of sessions than those who did not received them. In an inpatient setting, however, Goldstein (L'Abate and Goldstein 2007), a problem-solving workbooks reduced significantly the length of hospitalization in decompensating women who complete that workbook versus a control group of women who did not receive it. This study needs replication just like all previous research conducted in this author's laboratory. The inconsistency and contradictions found in the area of research with PIPEs cry out for more adequate and controlled research that could not be conducted by just one investigator alone.

Replicable Theory-Derived Interactive Practice Exercises and Prescriptions

Applications in the Laboratory

Primary Prevention: Structured Enrichment Programs

This approach consists of written-down exercises to be administered by semiprofessional trainers under the supervision of a professional (L'Abate and Weinstein 1987; L'Abate and Young 1987). These exercises are administered verbatim from the text to couples and families (L'Abate 1990; L'Abate 1999d). There are two types of enrichment programs: one, theory-free and developed from existing evidence and literature and the second, theory related and model derived from RCT.

Theory-Free PIPEs

There are at least PIPEs not derived from any theory or model (see Appendix).

ERAAwC (*emotionality, rationality, activity, awareness, and context*): This model can be evaluated by administering an enrichment program isomorphic with this model (L'Abate and Weinstein 1987, pp. 376–383). L'Abate and Young (1987) present seven different case studies where this program was successfully administered.

Styles: The attachment, self-regulation, and competency (ARC) model can be evaluated by a series of questions isomorphic with the model (L'Abate and Weinstein 1987, pp. 317–375).

Priorities: This model can be evaluated through the administration of a program by the same title (L'Abate and Weisntein 1987, pp. 384–391).

Intimacy: An early version of an Intimacy Enrichment program was published verbatim (L'Abate and McHenry 1983, pp. 357–362). In another collection with hundreds of exercises and questions on a variety of topics (L'Abate and Weinstein 1987), one exercise addresses avoidance of intimacy (p. 162) and a complete program (No. 29) on helpfulness (pp. 300–309) contains lessons on (1) establishing levels of caring, hurts, and strengths; (2) seeing the good; (3) caring; (4) sharing of hurt feelings; (5) forgiveness; (6) protectiveness; (7) responsibility; and (8) enjoyment. Two case studies (L'Abate and Young 1987), illustrating specific applications of this program to issues of parentification (pp. 134–153) and to a psychosomatic family (pp. 163–179), describe how this program was applied with pre- and post-enrichment test batteries.

Crisis Intervention or Psychotherapy: Prescribed Therapeutic Tasks

In initial as well as subsequent interviews with clinical respondents, it is possible to ascertain directly the validity of the theory by evaluating the assumptions of distance and regulation, the ability to love and to negotiate, to see whether presence is mixed with power, how differentiated individuals are according to a continuum of likeness, what interpersonal style they are using, what personality propensities are prevalent, what priorities are present and influential, and whether there is any sharing of hurts and of fears of being hurt. In psychotherapy, after a through history and the administration of objective tests, it has been found useful to administer the following tasks in the author's office and, in many cases, prescribe them as homework assignments.

Interpersonal styles: Through F2F interviews and direct observation of couples and families, especially in clinical, critical, or criminal relationships, it is possible to discern relatively easily whether their styles are abusive–apathetic (AA), reactive–repetitive (RR), or conductive–creative (CC), as in the ARC model. The latter styles are not usually visible in clinical relationships, unless used to present a positive facade. However, usually this facade crumbles after a structured interview and the administration of a test battery. Once they are observed, these styles can be prescribed paradoxically, to see whether they can be changed (Weeks and L'Abate 1982). Many other tasks, like time-out, sibling rivalry, etc., were derived from clinical practice, where repetition of the same instructions was found to be more useful if administered in writing.

Drawing lines is a task administered in therapy as well as in homework assignment in the codependency workbook. This task is drawn from the selfhood model and is to be administered to so-called codependent individuals (addicted to the addict) or couples involved in symbiotic relationships (Jordan and L'Abate 1995).

Intimacy (Model[15]): This Model Is Evaluated in Therapy with Two Tasks

The *Sharing of Hurts* exercise (L'Abate 1986, p. 235, 1997b, pp. 320–321, 1999a, c, e, f, 2013c, pp. 227–230) requires partners to face each other on a sofa or two chairs, to close their eyes and hold each other's hands. They are asked to concentrate on their physical sensations first, such as those elicited and expressed by holding each other's hands, before concentrating on their hurts. Once the request to concentrate on their hurt is given, the professional is to wait for the outcome. One may repeat the request for a second time, but no more than twice altogether. Once they are in touch with the hurts that are dwelling inside their bodies, partners are asked to acknowledge and, if possible, share them ("I hurt, I am hurting"). This task has also a diagnostic function to evaluate whether partners can share their hurts or are defending against disclosing them (the leaves of the artichoke!).

On the basis of Pennebaker's (1997) work and research, most participants, whether individuals, couples, or families, could be asked to write from the very outset of therapy, after a through objective evaluation, to write about their hurts for 20 min a day for 4 consecutive days. In couples and families, respondents had to make an appointment with each other to share, compare, and discuss what they had written about their hurts. Variations on this assignment consist of listing "hurts given" and "hurt received," including also targets of given hurts and sources of received hurts. On the basis of these homework assignments with clinical couples, it could be seen readily that the process of intellectualization and other defenses—the leaves of the artichoke—was still present. Often, even though they may be cognizant of the inflicted hurts, partners were not ready as yet to share them in an affective fashion. Hence, when couples brought their lists of hurts to the therapist, this homework assignment was very informative from the outset of therapy. However, most couples were not ready as yet to share their mutually inflicted hurts in a cathartic fashion, at least not in front of the therapist and not at the beginning of therapy. This area of sharing hurts through writing is completely open to clinical and preventive applications (L'Abate 1986, 2011, 2013c).

Hugging, Holding, Huddling, and Cuddling (3HC): The second task consists of partners or families hugging, holding, huddling, and cuddling each other for a predetermined length of time, without any erotic moves (L'Abate 2013c, pp. 153–162). It requires nothing more that being together without any demands for perfection, production, performance, or problem solving. Traditional treatment approaches, whether behavioral or otherwise, are directed usually toward "doing something" or "performing," requiring problem-solving ability and activity either on the part of the therapist, the identified patient (IP), or a child's caretaker. Why not teach respondents how to enjoy "doing nothing together" as the Italians call "dolce far niente" (sweet doing nothing)? Instead of action or activities that are part of the American culture, why not use tasks that require no solution or activity, but that instead allows family members to learn being available to each other nonverbally without doing anything?

Such a therapeutic orientation, relational in nature, derives directly from the modality of "being" or "presence." Loving someone means being physically together in a way that allows direct, frequent, and consistent physical contact. This contact is necessary to feel emotionally available to and close with another intimate in a nonverbal fashion. The close physical presence of all family members without demands for performance, production, perfection, or problem solving, i.e., "unconditional love," defines "presence" as being the major glue that holds families together and makes them function well. The inadequacy of presence brings about mixed priorities, with emphasis on performance and production. Under these circumstances, it is possible to see an increase in symptomatic behavior in any one member of the family. Doing and having characterize some aspects of the American culture, while presence or being characterize some Mediterranean and Latin cultures (Spiegel 1971).

Conclusion

Either by themselves or in conjunction with medical, neurological, psychiatric, and psychological approaches, PIPEs or workbooks can perform self-help, preventive, promotional, psychotherapeutic, and rehabilitative functions that are either time consuming or difficult to perform in F2F TB treatments. Only future research will determine which reason for referral will be helped by which approach. Fortunately, the field of mental health in the last generation has been expanded by so many different approaches that will allow professionals to investigate which approach is more adequate, effective, and specific to deal with particular referral questions, concerns, and symptoms.

This proposal has reviewed preliminary evidence to support a developmental, contextual theory of intimate relationships. Its validity is necessary to establish a nexus between theory and practice, whether in the laboratory or in sickness prevention, health promotion, psychotherapy, or rehabilitation. The administration of workbooks, then, can be guided by theory and not by a random, hit-or-miss, arbitrary, and whimsical process. There is no way that this author by himself can validate the theory or the usefulness of workbooks that have been developed. This task will fall on better and younger shoulders than on this author's.

Chapter 9
Conclusion: Implications for Evaluation, Therapy, and Training

The foregoing, admittedly, radical arguments present implications for how the evaluation and improvement of human relationships will occur in the near future.

Evaluation

Many theoretical models will need to be revised to encompass all types of intimate relationships rather than view personality, couple, or family relationships as separate and independent constructs from each other. Instead of well-validated theory-free test instruments to evaluate couples and families without taking account of the individual personalities involved, or evaluating personalities in a relational vacuum, we need validated theory-derived and theory-related instruments to evaluate individual, couple, and family relationships according to a relational perspective that links and integrates rather than divides those relationships (Cusinato and L'Abate 2012; L'Abate 2013b; L'Abate et al. 2010). Here is whether constructs such as intimacy and identity may fulfill integrative functions unavailable in the separate fields of family and personality psychology (L'Abate 2013a).

Therapy and Training

The training of marriage and family therapists needs to be revised and updated to meet the challenges of these changes, including distance or remote writing and the Internet to deliver adequate mental health services to as many people as possible at the least possible cost (L'Abate and Sweeney 2011, in press; Barnett and Shale 2012; L'Abate 2013b, c). Here is where the growing, newly founded Coalition for Technology in Behavioral Science will fulfill an important function in meeting those challenges. Furthermore, couple and family therapists, in addition to necessary multigenerational and multicultural training (Bray et al. 1987; Hooper et al. 2014; L'Abate et al. 1994), could supplement or supplant face-to-face (F2F)

L. L'Abate, *Concreteness and Specificity in Clinical Psychology*,
DOI 10.1007/978-3-319-13284-6_9

talk-based (TB) contacts with easily reproducible, replicable programmed, distance or remote writing. In line with the two emerging constructs, there are workbooks available about intimacy as hurt feelings (L'Abate 2011b, pp. 501–528) and about aspects of identity formation (L'Abate 2011b, pp. 696–707). Furthermore, above and beyond therapy, clinicians will need to pay attention to issues of prevention with special groups, such as HIV/sexually transmitted disease (STD) couples and families (Pequegnat et al. 2001; Pequegnat and Bray 2012).

Appendices

Programmed Interactive Practice Exercises

Luciano L'Abate and B. Grace Ratliff

Intake/Follow-up Questionnaire

The first part of this questionnaire can be administered at Intake. The remainder can be administered after completion of a workbook or a series of interactive practice exercises. For a more detailed ecological intake look up L'Abate (1992, 2008).

Name__________________________________ **DOB**____**Date**_____**M F**

1. Education

a. Elementary School
b. High School
c. College (Name major____________________________)
d. Graduate school (Name title(s)____________________________)
e. Professional School (Name title(s)_____________________________)

2. Current status, check which applies to you:

a. Married
b. Divorced
c. Remarried
d. Widowed
e. Single (never married)
f. In committed relationship

3. Current job or position:

a. working: What kind of work do you do?
b. retired from what kind of work?
c. unemployed because (please explain)
d. handicapped (please explain)

L. L'Abate, *Concreteness and Specificity in Clinical Psychology*,
DOI 10.1007/978-3-319-13284-6

4. Family composition:

a. Partner
   i. Education
   ii. Occupation
b. Children (list age, sex, and current occupation if applicable)
c. State age, sex, and occupation of anyone else living in your household:
d. If you have children in school, how are they doing?
   i. very well
   ii. well
   iii. not well (please explain)

5. Medical history:

a. How healthy are you?
   i. very healthy
   ii. somewhat healthy
   iii. not so healthy
   iv. Comments or exceptions:
b. How healthy is your family as a whole
   i. very healthy
   ii. somewhat healthy
   iii. not so healthy
   Comments or exceptions:

6. Mental health:

a. How satisfied are you with your life?
   i. very satisfied
   ii. somewhat satisfied
   iii. not very satisfied (please explain)
b. Please give any information that will help us understand your current status and level of satisfaction.

1. Since the completion of a series of Practice Exercises of Workbook, you have worked steadily at the same job for:

a. how many years?
b. changed jobs times.
c. been unemployed for (length of time).
d. Other:

2. Current work

a. How satisfied are you with your current job?
   i. very satisfied
   ii. satisfied
   iii. not satisfied
b. How well did completing this workbook help you in coping with your current job?
   i. very well
   ii. OK
   iii. not very well
c. What might workbook have done to prepare you better for your current job?

8. Workbook (write title of completed workbook_............................
   a. On a scale from 1 to 5 (1 = completely satisfied; 5 = completely dissatisfied), how satisfied were you with the workbook you completed? Circle one: 1 2 3 4 5
   b. Have there been significant life changes (births, deaths, weddings, moves, job changes) in your immediate family since workbook ended? If yes, please explain.
   c. Have you or members of your family received further professional help or therapy since the termination of workbook here?
   d. If you and your family are having problems, what do you think we should do or should have done to prevent those problems?
   e. All things considered, which of the following best describes your life and the lives of your immediate family since completing this workbook?
      i. better
      ii. same
      iii. worse
   f. Which of the following best describes your initial problem after completion or a workbook
      much better
      no change
      worse
      much worse
9. While working on interactive pratice exercises,, did you notice changes in you and in members of your family? Please explain your answer.
   h. Since you finished a workbook or a series of interactive practice exercises, have there been improvements in ol problems that were not directly dealt with a workbook or the like? Please explain

After completing the questionnaire, please return it to whoever administered to you.. Thank you for your help. We will appreciate any suggestions that will help us to improve our services to families. Feel free to add other comments on the remainder of this page.

1. Current status:

married
divorced
remarried
widowed
in relationship

2. Current job or position:

3. Family composition:

a. Spouse: Education Occupation
b. Children (list age, sex, and current occupation if applicable)
c. State age, sex, and occupation of anyone else living in your household:
d. If you have children in school, how are they doing?
   very well
   well
   not well

4. Work history:
Since termination of family intervention, have you worked steadily at the same job for how many years?
changed jobs times.
been unemployed for (length of time).
Other:
5. Current work:
a. How satisfied are you with your current job?
very satisfied
satisfied
not satisfied

Practice Exercise

Structured Interview Derived from a Theory of Relational Competence

The purpose of this interview is to find out as much as we can about how you get along with your own selves and with each other. For individuals, the "Who?" could be changed to "Do you?"

Name______________________________________Age____Date_____

Model 1. Information Processing
***Emotionality*:**
How are feelings expressed (in individual, couple, or family)?
Who laughs?
Who cries?
Who does not cry or laugh?
What is crying or laughing about?

***Rationality*:**
Who acts and thinks like a computer?
Who thinks before acting?
Who thinks most or all the time?
What do you think about?
Who acts without thinking?

***Activity*:**
Who keeps busy and works all the time?
What do you do most of the time to keep yourself busy?
Is there a couch potato here?

***Awareness*:**
Who is self-conscious?
Who is not self-conscious?
What are you aware of?
What are you not aware of?
Why should anyone be aware?
Aware of what?
Are you aware of something but are afraid to share it with those you love and who love you?

***Contest*:**
Who worries about other people?
Who does worry about what the neighbors will think?

Model 2. Levels of Description and Explanation
Who wants to make a good impression on others?
Who does not care to make as good impression on others?
How do you behave outside of your home and how do you behave when you are at home?
Same____
Different____
Opposite____
How do you feel about your own self?
Good___
Bad___
Indifferent___
How did you learn to feel that way about yourself?

Model 3. Settings
How much of your time is spent at:
Home___
School/work___
Shopping___
Free time___
Going from one place to another___
How much time do you spend on survival rather than enjoyment activities?
Where do these activities take place?

Model 4. Ability to Love
Who is close to whom?
Who keeps distant from whom?
Why are you close/distant from whom?
Who goes from one extreme to the other?

Model 5. Ability to Control Self
Who waits a long time to answer or to act?
Who is fast in responding and acting?

What about are you slow or fast?
When?
With whom?
With what?

Model 6. Models 4 and 5 Combined
How do you see yourself in relationship to loved ones?
Do you love each other?
How do you show your love?
How do you react to each other?
Fast___
Slow___
In-between___

Model 7. The Triangle of Living*: Its Three Modalities*
a. *Having production*

1. *Money*

   a. What does money mean to you (your marriage or family)?
   b. What kinds of conflicts are there about money?
   c. Who is in charge of money?
   d. Who is in charge of buying?
   e. Who is in charge of taking care of things in the house?

2. *Goods*

   a. What do goods (possessions, material things) mean to you (your marriage or family)?
   b. What kinds of conflicts are there about goods (gifts, things, purchases)?
   c. Is there a hoarder in this house?

b. *Doing performance*

3. *Services*
   a. Who performs what chores (or services) in this marriage/family?
   b. Who makes decisions about chores (or services) and who carries them out?
   c. Who does what in the house?
   d. Who shops for food?
   e. Who cleans the house?
4. *Information*

   a. What kind of information is allowed in this marriage (family)?
      TV workbooks (what kind, for how long) and movies
      Newspapers and/or magazines
      Books (who reads what?)
      Relatives (get-togethers, frequency of meetings, feelings about visits, etc.)
      Friends and neighbors
      Others (visitors, drop-ins, entertainments, etc.)

c. Being present

1. *Intimacy*

a. What does intimacy mean to you, this marriage, or this family?
b. How is intimacy shown or demonstrated?
c. Is intimacy used as a commodity to bribe or blackmail family members?
d. How do you share joys?
e. How do you share hurts?
f. Who is available emotionally to whom?
g. Who prefers to do things rather than being close to those you love?
h. Who prefers to have money and things rather than being close to loved ones?
i. Who loves unconditionally without demands for perfection, performance, or production of goods and money?
j. Who has ever experienced or expressed unconditional love?
i. How?
ii. When?
iii. Why?

2. *Importance*

a. How important are you to yourself and to others in the marriage or family?
b. How is this importance shown or expressed inside the family?
c. How is this importance shown or expressed outside the family?
d. How do you fail to show your individual importance?
e. Which of the preceding questions is most important?
i. To whom?
ii. How?
iii. Why?
f. How does this arrangement work for you (your marriage or your family)?

d. *Balance of having-doing-being*

a. Which of these—having, doing, being—is most important to you?
b. Why? (i.e., what does it get you?)
c. Are you satisfied with the way you rank these resources?
d. If you are satisfied, why?
e. If you are not satisfied, why not?
f. How could you do better?

Homework
After answering these questions, discuss them with your partner or family, if possible at a preordained appointment.

Model 8. Self-Identity Differentiation

How much do you resemble loved ones: parents, caretakers, brothers and sisters, relatives, and other people?

How strong was or is this resemblance? Very very close, close enough, not close at all, different from someone, the opposite of someone, or completely without any resemblance to anyone?

Model 9. Stiles in Intimate Relationships

What is you preferred style in dealing with loved ones?
How courteous are you with each other?
How respectful are you of each other's feelings?
Do you think and plan before answering to each other?
Do you answer immediately without thinking about the consequences?
Do you ever become abusive and fowl-mouthed when dealing with and answering to loved ones?
How?
When?
Why?

Model 10. Interactions in Intimate Relationships

How much do you do above and beyond home chores, school, or work responsibilities? Do you leave time to yourself?
How do you have and use extra free time?
Do you belong and are you active in any charity or social organization?
Do you have any hobbies or other interests outside of home, family, school, or work? How much has your relationship changed over time? Much improved, improved, the same, worse, much worse?
How?
Why?

Model 11. Selfhood

How important are you to yourself?
How important are you to loved ones?
How important are loved ones to you?
Are you more important than your loved ones?
Are your loved ones more important than you?
Is anybody unimportant to anybody?
How?
When?
Why?

Model 12. Priorities

Besides each other who else is more important to you?
What other people are more important than your family?
Who are they? Are they more important than other people?
What place is more important than other place?
What activities are more important than other activities?
What things are more important than other things?

Model 13. Distance Regulation

Who pursues whom in your intimate relationship?
When?
How?
Who keeps away from whom?
When?
Why?
Who do you go to when you need or want something or help?
Who do you keep away from?
When?
Why?
Who sends you away when you need or want something?
Who wants something from you and sends you away because whatever you do or say is not good enough?

Model 14. The Deadly Drama Triangle

Does anyone here ever play the part of the victim?
Who becomes the persecutor?
Who becomes the rescuer?
Do you ever switch parts, the victim becomes the persecutor and the rescuer becomes the victim?
Are you aware of this deadly triangle in your life?
When?
How?
Why?

Model 15. Intimacy

Do you ever share past and present joys?
With whom?
When?
Do you ever laugh together?
When?
How?
Why?
Do you ever share past and present hurt feelings?
With whom?
Have you ever cried together?
Have you ever seen any loved ones cry together?
When?
How?
Why?
Why not?
Do you ever forgive yourself for past or present transgressions (errors or mistakes)?
How?

When?
Why?
Why not?
Do you ever forgive others for past or present transgressions?
How?
When?
Why?
Why not?

Model 16. Negotiation and Problem-Solving

a. Who makes decisions in this relationship?
b. How do you make decisions?
c. Who makes big decisions and who makes small decisions?
d. Who carries those decisions out?

Who does not want to make any decisions?
How do you solve disagreements?
How do you solve problems?
Do you ever sit down to talk things over?
What do you think about all the questions you were asked above?

Linking Evaluation with Treatment: An Experimental Example What Kind of Concerns?

ID______________________________________**Age** _____**Sex**___**Date**______

The purpose of this experimental checklist is to find what kind of concerns are effecting your life at the present time. Please read the statements below and rate them according to whether they apply to you most of the time, sometimes, or not at all.

	This statement applies to me: Most of the time	Some-times	Not at all
1. Helplessness (feeling completely unable to cope or to deal with a situation).................................	_____	_____	_____
2. Feelings of worthlessness	_____	_____	_____
3. Loss (feeling completely lost and alone)..............	_____	_____	_____
4. Feelings of inferiority..	_____	_____	_____
5. Abandonment(feeling abandoned and left-out)................	_____	_____	_____
6. Feeling guilty...	_____	_____	_____
7. Comfort (not having anyone to comfort and support you)...........	_____	_____	_____
8. Feeling like a failure..	_____	_____	_____
9. Closeness (not having anyone to be close to and to share your hurts with).............................	_____	_____	_____
10. Fear of criticism...	_____	_____	_____
11. Love and loss of love (unable to be loved by someone important to you)........................	_____	_____	_____
12. Perfectionism..	_____	_____	_____
13. Protection (feeling no one looks after you)...........	_____	_____	_____
14. Afraid to make mistakes-..	_____	_____	_____
15. Nurturance (feeling without sufficient love or care from anybody).......................	_____	_____	_____
16. Wanting acceptance and approval...........................	_____	_____	_____
17. Rejection (being rejected by someone you love)....	_____	_____	_____
18. Wanting to achieve well..	_____	_____	_____
19. Overdependence (relying too much on someone else)..............	_____	_____	_____
20. Self-criticalness (being very hard on yourself).........	_____	_____	_____

Instructions for Scoring:

Now add all of the *odd-numbered* statements (1,3, 5, etc.) together, giving 2 points for check marks made under "Most of the time" and 1 point for check marks made under "Sometimes." Do the same, that is, add up all of the *even-numbered* statements (2, 4, 6, etc.), giving 2 points for checks under "Most of the time" and 1 point for check marks made under "Sometimes."

Totals for odd-numbered statements_____________

Totals for even-numbered statements_____________

If your total for odd-numbered statements is a great deal (5 points or more) higher than the total for even-numbered statements, then your concerns may stem from depending too much on others.

If your total for even-numbered statements is a great deal (5 points or more) higher than the total for odd-numbered statements, then your concerns may stem from being too self-critical.

If your two totals are within a few points (less than 5) of each other, then your concerns may stem from both depending too much on others and being too self-critical.

Whatever the conclusion, regardless of your scores, rest assured that these concerns are normal to everybody and *they can be dealt successfully if they are shared with those who care about you and, hopefully, if you keep on working on improving yourself.*

In addition to setting up a baseline, this still experimental checklist can be converted into interactive practice exercises by asking participants to define each behavior item and give two examples for that behavior/item (nomothetic task). On completing these definitions and examples, participants can be asked to rank-order those items according to their importance to the individual (idiographic task). These rank-order can be considered as treatment plan where each item from the first to the fifth or sixth in importance could be addressed in single sessions using a general format found in L'Abate (2011c).

If the concerns are related to dependency, a series of interactive practice exercises for depression can be found in the same source (2011c). If concerns about self are very high, in comparison to dependency concerns, then various series of interactive practice exercises for acting-out, externalizing personality disorders are available in two sources (L'Abate 2011a, 2013b).

Experimental Ecological Questionnaire
The Ecology of the Relational Contexts Constructive Patterns: Checklist of Behaviors Necessary to Discriminate Levels of Functioning in Individuals, Couples, and Families

Instructions:
Frequency means how often a behavior occurs from minimal (1) to maximal (5).
Duration means how long a behavior lasts from short (1) to long (5).
Intensity means how strong a behavior is from weak (1) to very strong (5).
Satisfaction means how much pleasure a behavior produces from little (1) to great (5).

Circle the number that best represents how often, how long, how strong, and how satisfying a behavior listed below is from 1 to 5.

If an activity is not included in this list, there are two available spaces where such an activity can be added. Write the name of that added activity.

Individuals	Frequency	Duration	Intensity	Satisfaction
Nutrition: weight, height, diet, vitamins and supplements, herbs	1 2 3 4 5	1 2 3 4 5	1 2 3 4 5	1 2 3 4 5
Physical activities: exercise, sports, hunting, games	1 2 3 4 5	1 2 3 4 5	1 2 3 4 5	1 2 3 4 5
Pleasant and pleasurable activities: hobbies, collecting, gardening and similar activities	1 2 3 4 5	1 2 3 4 5	1 2 3 4 5	1 2 3 4 5
Reading: preferred books, magazines, newspapers	1 2 3 4 5	1 2 3 4 5	1 2 3 4 5	1 2 3 4 5

Individuals	Frequency	Duration	Intensity	Satisfaction
Television: how much time spent, programs watched, reliance on tapes, disks, etc.	1 2 3 4 5	1 2 3 4 5	1 2 3 4 5	1 2 3 4 5
Computer and Internet use: enrichment: education extra-home, school/work interests	1 2 3 4 5	1 2 3 4 5	1 2 3 4 5	1 2 3 4 5
Friendships: nature of friends and frequency of meetings	1 2 3 4 5	1 2 3 4 5	1 2 3 4 5	1 2 3 4 5
Correspondence: writing versus computer-driven e-mails, etc.	1 2 3 4 5	1 2 3 4 5	1 2 3 4 5	1 2 3 4 5
Use of car: strictly for work and shopping purposes, joy riding/ vacations	1 2 3 4 5	1 2 3 4 5	1 2 3 4 5	1 2 3 4 5
Abuse: alcohol, smoking, drugs, Internet	1 2 3 4 5	1 2 3 4 5	1 2 3 4 5	1 2 3 4 5
Volunteering: where, when, for how long?	1 2 3 4 5	1 2 3 4 5	1 2 3 4 5	1 2 3 4 5
Other	1 2 3 4 5	1 2 3 4 5	1 2 3 4 5	1 2 3 4 5
Other	1 2 3 4 5	1 2 3 4 5	1 2 3 4 5	1 2 3 4 5
Couples and families				
Attending movies, plays, concerts, symphonies, or operas	1 2 3 4 5	1 2 3 4 5	1 2 3 4 5	1 2 3 4 5
Camping and hiking	1 2 3 4 5	1 2 3 4 5	1 2 3 4 5	1 2 3 4 5
Cooking together	1 2 3 4 5	1 2 3 4 5	1 2 3 4 5	1 2 3 4 5
Eating together	1 2 3 4 5	1 2 3 4 5	1 2 3 4 5	1 2 3 4 5
Eating out	1 2 3 4 5	1 2 3 4 5	1 2 3 4 5	1 2 3 4 5
Playing cards or board games	1 2 3 4 5	1 2 3 4 5	1 2 3 4 5	1 2 3 4 5
Shopping together	1 2 3 4 5	1 2 3 4 5	1 2 3 4 5	1 2 3 4 5
Vacations	1 2 3 4 5	1 2 3 4 5	1 2 3 4 5	1 2 3 4 5
Watching at home together versus apart: movies, CD-rom, TV	1 2 3 4 5	1 2 3 4 5	1 2 3 4 5	1 2 3 4 5
Other	1 2 3 4 5	1 2 3 4 5	1 2 3 4 5	1 2 3 4 5
Other	1 2 3 4 5	1 2 3 4 5	1 2 3 4 5	1 2 3 4 5

Feel free to add any comments that may relate to the activities listed in this form by adding more information about these activities

Intake/Follow-up Questionnaire*

The first part of this questionnaire can be administered at Intake. The remainder can be administered after completion of a workbook or a series of interactive practice exercises. For a more detailed, experimental, ecological intake look up L'Abate (1992, 2008a).

Name________________________________**DOB**________**Date**______

1. **Education**
   a. Elementary School
   b. High School
   c. College (Name major____________________________)
   d. Graduate school (Name title(s)____________________________)
   e. Professional School (Name title(s)______________________________)
2. **Current status, check which applies to you:**
   a. Married
   b. Divorced
   c. Remarried
   d. Widowed
   e. Single (never married)
   f. In committed relationship
3. **Current job or position:**
   a. working: What kind of work do you do?
   b. retired from what kind of work?
   c. unemployed because (please explain)
   d. handicapped (please explain)
4. **Family composition:**
   a. Partner
      i. Education
      ii. Occupation
   b. Children (list age, sex, and current occupation if applicable)
   c. State age, sex, and occupation of anyone else living in your household:
   d. If you have children in school, how are they doing?
      i. very well
      ii. well
      iii. not well (please explain)
5. **Medical history:**
   a. How healthy are you?
      i. very healthy
      ii. somewhat healthy
      iii. not so healthy
      iv. Comments or exceptions:

b. How healthy is your family as a whole
  i. very healthy
  ii. somewhat healthy
  iii. not so healthy
Comments or exceptions:

6. Mental health:

a. How satisfied are you with your life?
  i. very satisfied
  ii. somewhat satisfied
  iii. not very satisfied (please explain)
b. Please give any information that will help us understand your current status and level of satisfaction.

1. Since the completion of a series of Practice Exercises of Workbook, you have worked steadily at the same job for:

a. how many years?
b. changed jobs times.
c. been unemployed for (length of time).
d. Other:

2. Current work

a. How satisfied are you with your current job?
  i. very satisfied
  ii. satisfied
  iii, not satisfied
b. How well did completing this workbook help you in coping with your current job?
  i. very well
  ii. OK
  iii. not very well
c. What might workbook have done to prepare you better for your current job?

8. Workbook (write title of completed workbook_............................

a. On a scale from 1 to 5 (1 = completely satisfied; 5 = completely dissatisfied), how satisfied were you with the workbook you completed?
Circle one: 1 2 3 4 5
b. Have there been significant life changes (births, deaths, weddings, moves, job changes) in your immediate family since workbook ended? If yes, please explain.
c. Have you or members of your family received further professional help or therapy since the termination of workbook here?
d. If you and your family are having problems, what do you think we should do or should have done to prevent those problems?
e. All things considered, which of the following best describes your life and the lives of your immediate family since completing this workbook?
  i. better
  ii. same
  iv. worse
f. Which of the following best describes your initial problem after completion or a workbook

much better
no change
worse
much worse

9. While working on interactive pratice exercises,, did you notice changes in you and in members of your family? Please explain your answer.

h. Since you finished a workbook or a series of interactive practice exercises, have there been improvements in ol problems that were not directly dealt with a workbook or the like? Please explain

After completing the questionnaire, please return it to whoever administered to you.. Thank you for your help. We will appreciate any suggestions that will help us to improve our services to families. Feel free to add other comments on the remainder of this page.

1. Current status:
married
divorced
remarried
widowed
in relationship

2. Current job or position:

3. Family composition:
a. Spouse: Education Occupation
b. Children (list age, sex, and current occupation if applicable)
c. State age, sex, and occupation of anyone else living in your household:
d. If you have children in school, how are they doing?
very well
well
not well

4. Work history:

Since termination of family intervention, have you worked steadily at the same job for
how many years?
changed jobs times.
been unemployed for (length of time).
Other:

5. Current work:

a. How satisfied are you with your current job?
very satisfied
satisfied
not satisfied

Feel free to add whatever else you can tell about yourself and your family that is relevant to helping you and your family.

To be administered after completion of a Workbook or a Series of Programmed Interactive Practice Exercises.

Copies of Informed Consent Forms can be found in previous publications (L'Abate 2011a, 2013b, c) or could be available online.
Administer this Form after every Practice Exercise (PE) is completed.

General Practice Exercise Feedback Form*

Name__________________________________**Date**________________

Workbook Title_________________________________**PE Name**____________

Now that you have completed this exercise, please respond to the following questions concerning the assignment itself.

1. How useful did you find this exercise for understanding the workbook topic?
a. very useful
b. quite useful
c. somewhat useful
d. slightly useful
e. not useful at all

2. How important is the concern, skill, or attitude addressed by this exercise?
a. very important
b. quite important
c. somewhat important
d. slightly important
e. not important at all

3. Put into your own words what you got out of doing this exercise

....
....
....
....
....

4. How could this exercise be improved or changed?

....
....
....
....
....
....
....
....

*To be administered after completion of each practice exercise.

Life Stages

ID____Age _____Sex___ Date______

This series of interactive practice exercises covers most of the family life stages. One can start from the beginning exercise or from whatever life stage is relevant to participants.

Exercise 1. Growth and Togetherness

a. How did it feel to grow inside your family of origin?
b. How did it feel to grow away from your family of origin?

Exercise 2. Ties that Bind

a. There are ties that bind every family together. What ties bind you together as a couple and/or as a family?
b. What ties bind your children with each other and with you as parents?
c. Houses have rooms that let us be together and rooms that let us be apart. What rooms in your house let your family be together?
d. How do you feel about being together?
e. What rooms in your house let you be apart?
f. What do you do in these rooms?
g. How do you feel about being apart?
h. If you were to change anything about the way your family spends its time together and its time apart, how would your change it?

Exercise 3. Feelings and Emotions

a. What feelings does this family like?
b. What feelings does this family not like?
c. What happens to your family when someone feels hurt?

Exercise 4. Learning from Each Other

a. On a sheet of paper, write down a list of several things you think you have learned from each member of your family.
b. Each family member should read his or her list aloud.
c. After all the lists have been read, write whether you heard any of these things before.
d. All families experience happy times and sad times. What has your family learned from your sad times together?

Exercise 5. Adulthood

a. How did you know when your parents knew that you were adults, with your own lives to lead?
b. How would you like your parents to let you know someday that they know you are adults?

c. Write about an event that might bring this family together.
d. Write about an event that might break this family apart.

Exercise 6 Parenthood and Grandparenthood

a. Write about the time when the children in this family will become parents and the parents will become grandparents.
b. Write about what becoming a grandparent means to this family.

Exercise 7. Your Grandparents

a. Write about your own grandparents.

    i. What are or were they like?
    ii. What (is/was) your relationship with them?
    iii. What (do/did) they mean to you?

b. What does becoming a grandparent mean to you?
c. What does becoming a parent mean to you?
d. List some positive and some negative aspects of being a grandparent.
e. Share your list with each other.

Exercise 8. Similarities and Differences

a. What similarities and differences do you see between grandparents and parents in general?
b. How would you like to relate with your children when they become parents?
c. How would you like your parents to relate to you when you are a parent?
d. How do you think parenthood and grandparenthood will affect this family?

Exercise 9. Types of Grandparents

There are many types of grandparents. For example, there is the grandparent who is a playmate, the grandparent who spoils the child with expensive toys, the grandparent who is a substitute parent and takes care of the children, the grandparent who visits and is visited occasionally, perhaps twice a year, and the grandparent who is a babysitter for the children.

a. What kind of grandparent would you like to be?
b. Why?
c. What kind of grandparent would you like your parents to be to your children?
d. Why?

Exercise 10. Let Us Pretend

a. Pretend your parents have told you they would like to buy your child an expensive toy, and it is not a special occasion. Your child is used to getting "big" toys only on special occasions such as birthdays and Christmas. Discuss this gift with your partner and after discuss this gift with your parents.
b. Pretend your parents have asked you to go fishing with them this weekend so they can spend some time with you. Your child asks you to take his or her scout group on an outing the same weekend. You have not given anyone an answer yet. Discuss this with your parents.
c. What did you learn from acting out these situations?

d. These pretend situations are typical of issues that may arise when you become grandparents and parents. Can you think of some other issues that might arise between you as parents and grandparents?

Homework
During the coming week discuss some other issues that might arise and how you could handle them positively, in a way that would bring the family together.

Practice Exercises About Leisure in the Family Life Cycle

ID____ Date______

Exercise 1. Leisure and the Family Life Cycle
a. How does your family spend your leisure time together?
b. Comment on how a family that does not have fun together will soon look elsewhere for its fun.

Exercise 2. Defining Leisure
a. What is a leisure activity?
b. What is the difference between leisure activity and work?
c. What would happen in a family when there is no leisure time?
d. What would happen in a family when there is nothing but leisure time?

Exercise 3. Fun in Life Stages
a. Describe your leisure self as a child: What did you do to have fun as a child?
b. Now describe your leisure self as an adolescent.
c. As a young adult.
d. As a partner in marriage.
e. As a parent in the family.
f. At middle age, your children grown and away from your home.
g. At retirement.

Exercise 4. Leisure in Groups
a. What are some leisure activities that only males do in this family?
b. What are some leisure activities that only females do in this family?

Exercise 5. Where the Fun Is
a. Name all the places where you spend leisure time together. For example, many families spend time together in the TV room.
b. What new places could you develop?

Exercise 6. Types of Leisure
Two primary types of leisure activities are person-to-person, such as two people taking a walk together, and person–object activities, such as watching a movie or TV. Person-to-person activities require people to communicate with each other. Person–object activities may involve communication but mainly involve people focusing their attention on a solitary activity or an object rather than a person.

a. What kinds of person-to-person leisure activities does this family engage that do not involve outside persons.
b. What kinds of person–object activities does this family engage in?

Exercise 7. Developing New Enjoyments

a. We want each of you to give two examples of person–object leisure activities and two examples of person-to-person leisure activities that you would like to see in this family.
b. These must be the activities that you are not currently doing in this family. As a family, choose one activity of each type that you can do this week.

Homework

During the coming week, do the activities that you have just decided on—one person–object activity and one person-to-person activity.

Retirement

ID____**Age** _____**Sex**___ **Date**______

The purpose of these interactive practice exercises is to prepare you for and adjusting to retirement. Writing about retirement beforehand can make this period of life more pleasant and satisfying for the retired person and for the rest of the family.

Exercise 1. Feelings About Work

a. Before dealing about what it means to retire, let us first write about the place work has in this family. Please complete the following sentences, writing as many things as you can:

   i. "I work because I…"
   ii. "When I am not working, I…"

b. Choosing to work out of financial necessity.
c. Working for enjoyment versus being a workaholic.
d. What is the difference between unemployment and leisure?
e. What is the difference between unemployment, leisure, and retirement?

Exercise 2. Attitudes Toward Retirement

a. Retirement means the separation of a person from the work for which he or she has been paid. People have very different ideas about what retirement means.

   i. One person may feel that after many years of doing his or her share for the growth and prosperity of society, he or she has earned the right to share in that prosperity without having to continue to work. Please comment on this statement.
   ii. Another person may feel that after a certain age the older worker is no longer capable of doing his or her job and should be legally required to step aside to let a more capable, younger person take over.

b. Which of these two views describe the attitude of the members of this family toward retirement?
c. Do you think about retirement as leaving something or as heading toward something?

Exercise 3. Preparing to Retire

In a way, the preparation for retirement startsfrom the day a person realizes that he or she will some day leave his or her job for good. A person's attitude while preparing for retirement can affect how happy that person will be in retirement.

a. How might a person's income and enjoyment of his or her job influence one's attitude toward retirement and one's enjoyment of retirement?
b. How does one's family affect the retiring person's attitude toward retirement, preparation for it, and adjustment to it?

Exercise 4. Feelings About Self in Retirement

a. How will retirement affect how members of this family feel about themselves as they near retirement?
b. Are goals set aside for yourself in your work that you have not reached or will not have reached by the time you retire?
c. How do you feel about not reaching these goals?
d. Name some things you will be able to do in retirement—things you enjoy but have been unable to do.

Exercise 5. Retirement as a Transition

Retirement can be both an end and a beginning.

a. What things will retirement end for members of this family?
b. In what ways will retirement be a beginning?
c. Overall, will retirement be more of an end or more of a beginning for members of this family?

Exercise 6. Family Relationships During Retirement

a. What will be the effects of retirement on marital and family relationships?
b. How you would like the family to be during your retirement?
c. Are you satisfied with how your family is reacting to your retirement? Please explain.
d. How does the rest of you here today feel about this retirement?
e. Would any of you change as a result of this retirement?

Practice Exercises for Seniors

ID____**Age** _____**Sex**___ **Date**______

Successful adaptation to old age required both accommodation to one's own internal needs and conformity to society's demands. These practice exercises were designed to include the elderly person's family to provide experiences that may help older families adjust to the postretirement stage of the life cycle. In this workbook successful aging means that a person typically must make a lot of adjustments upon entering late adulthood. Some people experience more changes than others as they get older and must therefore make more adjustments than others. No one way of adjusting to old age works for everyone.

Exercise 1. Successful Aging

a. ***Recognition of aging and definition of limitations***

i. How did you recognize you were getting old?
ii. How do you define "old age?"

b. ***Redefinition of physical and social life space***

i. What restrictions on your physical space are occurring to you?
ii. What restrictions on your social life space are occurring to you?

c. ***Substitution of alternative sources of satisfaction***

i. What substitutions or alternatives have you considered instead?
ii. What changes have you made to get what you like, need, or want in old age?

d. ***Reassessment of criteria for self-evaluation***

i. What changes have you made to redefine your own self?
ii. How are these changes working for you?

e. ***Reintegration of values and life goals***

i. How have you been able to put together your values?
ii. How have you been able to put together your own values?

Exercise 2. Reactions to Old Age

a. How did each of you react to one of you being old?
b. What did these reactions have to do with how old you are?
c. What can you do to help whoever is becoming old in your family?
d. Please complete the following sentences:

   i. Old people are…
   ii. When people get old, they should…
   iii. Young people are…
   iv. When people are young, they should…
   v. If I were older, I would…
   vi. As an older/younger person, I am…
   vii. The typical picture of an older person is…
   viii. The typical picture of a younger person is…

e. Read and share aloud your responses to those sentences.
f. What do your responses say about how you view old people?
g. How do those of you who are older differ from the younger members in the ways you reacted to old age?

Exercise 3. Adjusting to Old Age—Staying Active

One way that some people adjust to old age is to try to stay as active as they were during their middle years. They continue to be active in clubs and organizations and keep an interest in hobbies or find substitutes for them.

a. Have any of you, who are older, adjusted to old age in this way?
b. What are some of the pros and cons of dealing with old age in this way?
c. Disengagement: another way that people can adjust to their old age is by gradually cutting down on how active they are—by dropping club memberships, seeing friends less often, and spending more time with their families or with hobbies.
d. Does this describe anyone here?
e. What are some of the pros and cons of this adjustment to aging?
f. Continuity: another way that people adjust to old age combines the two ways that we have already introduced above. People who adjust in this way become less active physically and socially but keep to the same schedule that they always have, such as getting up and going to bed at the same time, maintaining their hobbies and interests, and staying interested in the kind of work they did.

    i. Has anyone here adjusted to old age in this way?
    ii. What are some of the pros and cons about this way of growing old?

Exercise 4. Satisfaction in Old Age
a. How well have the older people here adjusted to old age?
b. Are you satisfied with your life as an older person?
c. What would you like to change or improve?
d. What can the family do to help you?
e. Can those of you who are older remember what your ideas were of old people when you were children? What were they?
f. How do these childhood ideas about old people help or hinder your attempts to grow old successfully?

Exercise 5. Recognition of Aging and Limitations
a. How do we become aware that we are getting older?
b. What are some of the differences in how different generations see getting old?
c. What are some of the similarities?
d. What is it like for you to realize that you have lived most of your life?
e. What did you feel like when you first became aware that you were getting old?
f. In what ways do you feel different about getting older now?

Exercise 6. Dealing with Limits Imposed by Society
a. What are some of the ways our society makes people aware that they are growing old?
b. Retirement is one way that our society increasingly limits the part the older person plays in our society. What experiences have you had with limits placed on you by society?
c. How can you best cope with these?

Exercise 7. Dealing with Physical Limitations
a. Have you felt a loss or a reduction of the physical strength or stamina or the mental sharpness of your younger years?
b. If yes: What is it like to experience this?
c. If no, ask: If you have not had this experience, how might you feel when you do?
d. What can you do to delay or make up for loss of ability or skills?

Exercise 8. Dealing with Fragile Health

In addition to affecting our abilities, advancing age eventually affects our health.

a. Has poor health been a problem for you?
b. How has poor health limited your life space?

Exercise 9. Changing Life Space and Retirement

a. Have you pulled back from the amount of physical space you once lived in?
b. If yes: Was this an easy decision or one you made reluctantly?
c. If no: How satisfied are you with the present space arrangements?

Exercise 10. Adjusting to Less Physical Mobility

Decreased physical mobility is another fact of life for older people.

a. What does it mean to you not to be able to get around as easily or as quickly as you used to?
b. Do you depend on others to get around?
c. If yes: How does it feel to you, who were once very independent, to have to rely on others?
d. How do the rest of you feel about having an older person dependent on you?

Exercise 11. Adjusting to Lowered Social Influence

Sometimes the loss of influence and social activity in retirement makes an older person withdraw even further from society.

a. Have any of you experienced loneliness or isolation in retirement?
b. How can the family help?
c. How can friends help?

Exercise 12. Finding Alternative Means of Personal Satisfaction

a. Distinguish among

    i. Likes
    ii. Needs
    iii. Wants

b. What are the differences among

    i. Likes
    ii. Needs
    iii. Wants

c. What are the similarities?
d. Is what a person likes the same as what a person needs?
e. Is what a person needs the same or different from what a person wants?
f. Can you recognize the difference among the likes, needs, and wants of an older family members and those of the younger ones?

Exercise 13. Effects of Aging on Likes, Needs, and Wants

a. How does the transition to old age affects what a person likes, needs, or wants?
b. Do the changes in old age make this distinction easier or harder for those of you who are older?

c. As you have grown older, have your likes become your needs and your needs become your wants, or have your wants become your needs, or likes before your wants?

Exercise 14. Meeting the Need for Companionship

a. How do the older members of this family take care of the needs for companionship and friendship?
b. How has old age affected your need for companionship?
c. How has old age changed the way you go about finding companionship?

Exercise 15. Learning to Enjoy Leisure

Some people who have worked hard most of their lives, especially those who have been self-employed, have difficulty adjusting to the leisure that society permits older people. These people have difficulty accepting and enjoying leisure.

a. Has anyone here had similar problems adjusting to retirement and old age?
b. What specific things can you do to fill the gap left by retirement and make better use of your leisure time?

Homework

During the coming week, make three lists of (a) likes you prefer, (b) needs that are necessary for survival, and (3) wants necessary to enjoyment. Write down specific steps that you can take to meet them. If possible, share these lists with your family members or friends.

Identifying New Criteria for Self-Evaluation

ID____Date______

Exercise 1. Valuing Yourself

a. Write three responses to each of the following half sentences:
   i. I feel good about myself when I…
   ii. My worth and importance as a person depend on…
   iii. My importance to others is based on…
b. Is your sense of importance based on:
   i. Being emotionally available to yourself and intimate others
   ii. Whatever you do or perform
   iii. Whatever you have in money and possessions
c. Which of these three possibilities is more important to you?
d. Why?

Exercise 2. Importance of Physical Attractiveness

a. How have you adjusted to changes in your body and physical appearance?
b. What does beauty and attractiveness mean to members of your family?
c. Are these terms the same or are they different?

d. Have your ideas about beauty and attractiveness changed as you have gotten older?

Exercise 3. Self-Worth as a Child

a. What do you remember about the things that made you feel good about yourself, things that made you feel worthwhile as a child?
b. Were they the things about your personality, things that you did or did not do, or things that you owned?

Exercise 4. Self-Worth as an Adolescent

a. What do all of you remember about what made you feel good about yourself as a teenager?
b. What things made you respected, valued, or liked by others?

Exercise 5. Self-Worth as an Adolescent

a. What made you feel good about yourself as an adolescent, during your school and extra-school life?
b. What things made you liked and appreciated by others, or valued by society?
c. Were they the things about your

    i. Personality
    ii. Things you did
    iii. Skills you had
    iv. Things you owned?

Exercise 6. Self-Worth in Adulthood

a. What made you feel good about yourself as an adult, during your career and working life?
b. What things made you liked and appreciated by others, or valued by society?
c. Were they the things about your

    i. Personality
    ii. Things you did
    iii. Skills you had
    iv. Things you owned?

Exercise 7. Self-Worth in Old Age

a. What will help the older members of this family feel good about themselves?
b. Is it fair or realistic for older people to evaluate themselves or be evaluated by society on the same basis that a younger person is evaluated?
c. What do all of you value in your older family members?

Exercise 8. Reintegrating Values and Life Goals

a. Listing your life goals and values

    i. Write down five goals in your life.
    ii. Five things that you have worked for or tried in whatever way to make a part of your life—past or present.
    iii. Five values that you have now or have had in the past—principles that you believe in, that you try, or have tried to live your life by.

b. Share with intimate others what you have written?
c. How have your goals and values changed over the years?
d. What events or experiences led to the change in your goals and values?

Exercise 9. Unmet Goals

a. Do you have any "unfinished business" from your younger years or any goals that you had wanted to reach but did not by the time you retired or became ill?
b. How do you feel about not having reached these goals?
c. How realistic is it for you to continue to try to achieve them?

Exercise 10. Setting New Goals

a. What new goals can you, who are older, set for yourselves?
b. What strong points, or abilities do you have now that you could use to achieve these goals?

Exercise 11. Changing Values

a. What values have remained unchanged from your younger years?
b. What values have developed since you retired or became aware that you were getting old?
c. How have the passing of time and the changes in growing old affected your values?

Exercise 12. Realistic and Unrealistic Values

a. What values do you have that are difficult to abide by because of the limitations of old age?
a. What kinds of problems can come up in trying to be true to unrealistic values?

Exercise 13. Respecting and Learning from the Elderly

a. What are some things that people can learn from the elderly in general and the older members of this family in particular?
b. What can society do or not do to make life more pleasant and comfortable for the elderly?
c. How can the older members of this family best cope with their situation until these changes come about?
d. How can other family members help?

Widowhood

Name____Age _____Sex___ Date______

One of the most traumatic events a person is likely to experience is the loss of a spouse. The surviving spouse is suddenly faced with reorganizing an entire life alone. In addition to facing the loss of the spouse, the widowed person must now also cope with changed financial and social status. With all these new stresses, it is not surprising that there is a high rate of suicide following the death of a spouse, with the highest rate occurring during the first year of widowhood. Adjusting to widowhood is a particular concern for women, who are four times more likely than men to be widowed and more likely to be widowed at a younger age. The main psychosocial task for widowed persons after the grief period is to restructure their lives and reinvest themselves in the future. Although many widows could benefit from help in accomplishing this task, such help is typically inadequate, even nonexistent.

The purpose of this workbook is to help the widow successfully confront the tasks and problems associated with widowhood.

Exercise 1. Grief

Many feelings of grief are experienced after the death of a spouse. Many people believe that they should be "finished" with their grieving after a certain period of time, yet it often takes longer than we expect.

a. Get in touch with those feelings of loss and abandonment.
b. Share those feelings with those you love and who love you.

Exercise 2. Feelings About Death

a. Think about the moment when your partner died.
b. Were you with him/her or did you learn about it later?
c. How did you feel at that moment?
d. Do you go through that moment again very often in your mind?

 i. How often?
 ii. Do you try to put that moment out of your mind?
 iii. Why?

Exercise 3. Feelings—Here and Now

a. How do you feel now—right here—when you think about that moment?
b. How do you think you will feel in the near future?
c. How do you think you will feel in the distant future?

Exercise 4. Grieving

a. Do you think that your family has allowed you to grieve?
b. Do you ever push tears away so that family members would not be impatient with you?
c. What about your friends? Have they allowed you to grieve?
d. Do you feel as if they were impatient with your grief?

Exercise 5. Tea and Sympathy

a. Have you ever been annoyed with the expressions of sympathy that family and friends have given you?
b. What kinds of comments have annoyed you the most?

Exercise 6. Support and Grief

a. Who do you think has best understood your grief?
b. In what way has this person understood your grief better than others have understood it?

Exercise 7. Loneliness

After the death of a partner, loneliness can be especially painful. Trying to run away from those feelings is not only difficult but can also be more destructive than facing the painful feelings themselves. As so many things have to be taken care of after the death of a partner, it is often quite some time before loneliness sets in.

a. When were you first aware of loneliness?
b. What were the circumstances that led to your awareness of this feeling?
c. Can you describe how you felt?
d. At what particular times do you feel most lonely?
e. What did you do about it?

Exercise 8. Recognizing Loneliness
As so many things have to be taken care of after the death of a spouse, it is often quite some time before loneliness sets in.

a. When did you become aware of loneliness?
b. What were the circumstances that led to your awareness of this feeling?
c. Can you describe how you felt?

Exercise 9. When I Feel Lonely
a. At what particular times do you feel most lonely?
b. What do you do about it?

Exercise 10. Avoiding Loneliness
Some widows/widowers who are lonely attempt to deal with their loneliness by overeating, overdrinking, or oversmoking more than they normally do.

a. Have you been doing any of these things?
b. Have any of these things helped?
c. In what way?
d. How long does the satisfaction from (eating/drinking/smoking) last?

Exercise 11. Getting Busy
People use other means of getting away from their loneliness, such as shopping, working, telephoning a friend, or going out to lunch, dinner, or a movie with someone.

a. Have you done any of these things?
b. Have they helped?

Exercise 12. Overcoming
a. When you cannot do any of the things that are mentioned above, what do you do to overcome your loneliness?
b. How can you use the resources within you to deal with your loneliness?
c. How can you help yourself?

Homework
During the coming week, go over your answers to the questions asked in this workbook and see whether there is something more or different that you can add to your previous answers.

Back to Reality

ID____________________________________Age ____Sex___ Date_____

The purpose of this workbook is to deal with the inevitable practical matters that one must face after the death of a partner.

Exercise 1. Finances

a. How familiar are you with the finances available to you?
b. What was the outcome of your partner's last will and testament?
c. Are you ready and up to deal with finances?
d. Are you going to deal with them by yourself or will you ask for help?

Exercise 2. Financial Awareness

When your partner (spouse) died, were you aware of how much or how little money you were going to have? Did you feel financially secure or insecure?

Exercise 3. Benefits

a. Did you know about Social Security or Veteran's Administration benefits?
b. Did someone help you check on these, or did you do it alone? Are they something that still has to be looked into?

Exercise 4. Financial Advice

a. Did anyone try to give you advice on what to do with your money?
b. Were you grateful for this advice, or did you resent it?
c. Did anyone try to get you to invest all your money in a speculative venture?
d. How did you handle that?

Exercise 5. Spendthrift or Miser

a. Perhaps after your partner (spouse) died, you had never had so much money at one time.
b. Did you spend some of it recklessly because there was so much of it?
c. How did you feel about doing that?
d. How do you feel about it now?
e. Did you become concerned about money, becoming very frugal because you have to use this money for the rest of your life?
f. Are you still treating it that way?

Exercise 6. Lifestyle Changes

a. Have you had to make any changes in your life because of money? Are there things that you had that you can no longer have?
b. Are you angry about that? Are you perhaps angry with your husband for leaving you in that position?

Exercise 7. Decisions

a. Are there any positive decisions you have made about how you handle your money?
b. Responsibility for finances is scary, yet it can also give a feeling of independence and self-sufficiency.
c. How do you feel about your responsibility and your independence?

Exercise 8. Children

The death of their parent has affected your children. This effect on them has, in turn, had an effect on you. Your relationship with your children is different now that they have only one parent. We are going to discuss some of the problems that may arise in that new relationship.

Exercise 9. Children's Behavior

a. Have you noticed any changes in your children's behavior since their parent died?
b. What are they?

Exercise 10. Sudden or Slow Death and Children

a. If their parent had an extended illness and suffered a great deal, what effect do you think this had on them?
b. What effect do you think the suddenness of their father's death had on them?

Exercise 11. Sharing and Withholding

a. Do your children ever discuss their feelings about their parent's death with you?
b. How do you feel when they talk about their feelings?
c. What do you think is the reason they do not talk about it?

Exercise 12. Resisting Old Age

It is not an easy thing for anyone to adjust to old age. What are some ways in which people resist old age or deny that they are getting older and more prone to health problems?

Exercise 13. Retirement and Redefining Physical and Social Life Space

What are the demands and strains that growing old puts on a person's physical mobility, on marital and family relationships, on social activity, and on one's influence in general?

Exercise 14. Middle Age and Retirement

In many ways the period between ages 45 and 55 is the time when a person is most socially active and influential. What experiences did you have between 45 and 55 that made it difficult for you to retire?

Exercise 15. Sharing or Shielding

a. What about you—do you ever tell your children what your feelings are about their parent's death?
b. Are there times when you try to keep your feelings from them?
c. If yes: Is it to protect them or what?

Exercise 16. Staying the Same

a. Do you attempt to keep things in your children's lives the way they were before their parent died?
b. How?
c. If things are not the same, why are you trying to keep them that way?

Exercise 17. Making Up the Loss

a. Have you sometimes spoiled your children since their parent died?
b. In what way?

Exercise 18. Resentments

a. Are there times you resent your children's dependence on you?
b. Have there been times that you have changed roles with your adult children?
c. Have they taken parent or adult responsibilities away from you?
d. Do you resent this?
e. Although these changes may present problems in your relationship with your children, remember that the new relationship you create can be as rewarding or more rewarding than the old relationship.

Exercise 19. Remarriage, Dating, and Sex

Often, friends or relatives pester recent widows about remarriage. That can hurt or annoy you, yet remarriage, dating, and sex are topics that come into the minds of all widows or widowers at some point.

Exercise 20. Remarriage

a. Have you thought at all about remarriage?
b. How soon after your partner (spouse)'s death did you start thinking about it?
c. Were your thoughts negative or positive?

Exercise 21. Then and Now

a. Are your thoughts about remarriage different from when you first started thinking about it?
b. How are they different?

Exercise 22. Dating

a. Have you thought about dating?
b. What are your thoughts about it?
c. If he/she has dated, ask: How did things go on your first date?
d. If you are still dating, what do you think now in comparison with what you thought when you first started to date?

Exercise 23. Whom to Date

a. If you do date, do you date only (wo)men who are marriageable?
b. If you do not date, would you, if you did date, date only person who are marriageable?
c. What are your reasons?

Exercise 24. Sexual Desires

a. Do you have a desire for sex?
b. When did you first become aware of this desire?
c. What were your thoughts about your desire for sex?
d. What do you think the reasons are that you have not thought about sex again?

Exercise 25. Sexual Attitudes

Whether or not you have had sex again, are your thoughts about sex different now than they were when you first thought about it?

Exercise 26. Loving Again

a. Do you think that you can love a (wo)man again?
b. What are your reasons?

Building a New Life

ID____Date______

After you become a widow(er), you have to build a new life. You are no longer a wife (husband or partner) so you no longer play that role. You must make changes in your personal, family, and social life, and you may have to build a new life outside your home. For many, it means returning to the working world. For some, it is not returning to but entering the working world for the first time. In this workbook, we are going to discuss about some of the changes in building a new Iife.

Exercise 1. Changes

a. Can you think of some ways in which your life has changed since your partner's death?
b. Do you think these are good or bad changes?
c. Why?
d. If bad: What do you think you could do to make them good?

Exercise 2. Family and Change

a. What are some of the ways in which your life is different in relation to your immediate family?
b. Are these positive or negative changes?
c. If negative, ask: How could you make some positive changes?
d. What about relationships with other relatives and in-laws?

Exercise 3. Friends and Change

a. Have you noticed a big change in your relationships with couples who were friends of you and your husband?
b. If yes, ask: When did you first notice that change?
c. Why do you think these relationships have changed?
d. Does this change bother you?
e. Are you interested in continuing these relationships?
f. Why?

Exercise 4. New Friends

a. Have you formed any new relationships since you became a widow?
b. If no: What do you think the reasons are that you have not formed any new relationships?
c. If yes: How did these new relationships come about?

Exercise 5. Beginning Again

a. Have you made any changes in your life outside your home, such as going to work or to school?

b. If yes: What changes?
c. If no changes: What do you think the reasons are that you have not made any such changes?
d. Do you want to?
e. What are some ways to go about it?

Death and Dying

ID____Date______

Exercise 1. The Meaning of Death The goal of this exercise is to get all members of the family to express their feelings about death honestly. If this workbook is to be effective, every member must attend and participate fully in all the sessions. What does death mean to each of you?

Exercise 2. Definition

a. What does death mean to you?
b. What do you think about life after death?

Exercise 3. Worrying About Death

a. If you knew that you would die tonight, what would worry you the most?
b. If you could choose the time, place, and way of your dying, what would they be?
c. If you were told that you had 3 days to live, how would you spend those 3 days?

Exercise 4: A Time to Die

a. What is the right age for someone to die?
b. What is the worst possible age to die?

Exercise 5 Death as a Person

a. If you had to imagine death as a person, what would this person look like?
b. What did you think of each other's answers, and who do you think had the best description?

Exercise 6. Reconsidering Answers

Thinking back over tonight's questions, would you like to change any of your answers?

Exercise 7 Homework

Suggest that they continue discussing tonight's questions among themselves during the coming week.

Death and Its Consequences

ID____Date________

Exercise 1. Shock and Denial

The purpose of this exercise is to work on feelings of shock and denial. We are going to be a little more direct than we were in the last session.

Exercise 2. Finding Out

a. How did you feel when you first found out that your loved one is going to die?
b. Did you really believe it was true when you were told?
c. Why did not/did you believe it?
d. How do you feel about it now?

Exercise 3. Reactions to Death of Loved One

a. What did you do or say when you first learned of (name person)'s death?
b. Did you really believe it was true when you were told?
c. Why did not/did you believe it?

Exercise 4. Reacting to Death

a. What did you do or say when you heard the news?
b. Do you think that (name person) knows (she/he) is dying?
c. Do you think that (she/he should be/should have been) told?
d. What did you do or say when you heard the news?
e. How do you feel about it now?
f. Do you find yourself still thinking of (name person) as alive?

Exercise 5. Discussing Death

a. Do you or would you like to discuss with (name person) the fact that (she/he) is dying?
b. Do you discuss among yourselves the fact that (name person) is dying?
c. If the answer is no, ask: Why not?
d. Do you discuss (name person)'s death among yourselves?
e. If the answer is no, ask: Why not? If the answer is yes, ask: In what way?

Exercise 6. Dealing with Realities

a. What has been done with (name person)'s room, clothes, belongings?
b. Does this bother you? In what way?

Exercise 7. Externalizing Feelings

This exercise is an attempt to get the family members to externalize the feelings of anger, resentment, and hostility that usually accompany the dying and death of a family member.

Exercise 8. Feelings About Death

a. Do you feel angry that this had to happen to your family?
b. Who or what do you feel most angry at?
c. Do you believe that the doctor is doing all that he or she can do?

d. Are the hospital personnel doing all they can?
e. Do you feel the doctors did all that was possible?
f. Did the hospital personnel do all they could have?

Exercise 9. The Fairness of Death
Do you feel it is unfair that this had to happen to your (name relationship) and to your family?

Exercise 10. Helplessness and Frustration
a. Do you feel helpless and frustrated when you think about (name person)'s dying?
b. Have you wished that this could be happening to someone else? If answer is yes, ask: Who?

Exercise 11. Resentment
a. Do you resent what (name person)'s dying is doing to you and to your family?
b. Do you resent what (name person)'s death has done to you and to your family?

Exercise 12. Feeling Like Screaming
a. Have you felt like screaming since you found out that (name person) is dying?
b. Have you felt like screaming since (name person) died? If the answer is yes, ask: Have you actually screamed? Encourage discussion about expressing feelings openly.

Homework
Before another practice exercise each of you work on ways of getting your feelings outside yourself. Try punching a pillow or one of those inflatable clowns. Maybe you would like to drive out in the country and just scream your head off. Or just cry—alone or together. The main thing is not to bottle up your feelings—let them out!

Death and Other Consequences

ID____**Date**________

Leftover and Guilt Feelings
This exercise deals with any remaining vestiges of denial or bargaining (A questions) or with guilt feelings surrounding the death of a family member (B questions). The goal is also to help family members externalize their feelings of sadness and depression.

Exercise 1. Getting Feelings Out
a. Have any of you tried direct ways of getting your feelings out, such as screaming or kicking things?

Exercise 2. Bargaining and Preventing
a. Have you engaged in bargaining about (name person)'s death? I mean, have you found yourself saying: "Just give (him/her) one more year, and I'll…"?
b. Do you believe that you could have done anything to prevent (name person)'s death?
c. If appropriate, ask: Did you fail to notice how sick (he/she) was getting?

Exercise 3. Hoping for a Miracle

a. Do you find yourself hoping for some kind of miracle cure at the last moment?
aa. Do you think this is an unreasonable hope?
b. Do you feel there were times when you neglected (name person)? If yes, ask: How does this make you feel now?
bb. Do you regret the times you were unkind or thoughtless toward (name person)?

Exercise 4. Sadness and Loss

a. Do you sometimes feel overwhelmed by feelings of sadness and loss?
aa. Do you think these feelings will ease as time passes?
b. Did you ever resent (name person) during (his/her) illness? If answer is yes, ask: Why?
bb. Think of specific answers, such as expenses, nagging, complaining, family inconvenience, and personal inconvenience.

Exercise 5. Losses and Gains

a. Have you thought about what sort of things you will lose when (name person) dies?
b. Did you ever feel that (name person) was becoming a burden before (she/he) died?
c. Can you see your shortcomings toward (name person) as human failings?
d. Can you forgive yourself?

Exercise 6. Dreaming of Death

a. Have any of you dreamed about (name person)'s death?
b. If answer is yes: Would you like to share those dreams?

Exercise 7. The Finality of Death

a. Can you accept death?
b. If yes: why?
c. If no: why?

Exercise 8. Bargaining and Hoping

a. Are you still bargaining or hoping for a miracle?
aa. If someone says yes, ask: How do the rest of you feel about this?
b. Do you sometimes feel almost overwhelmed by feelings of sadness and loss?
bb. Do you think these feelings will ease as time passes?

Exercise 9. Feeling at Peace

a. Do you feel more peaceful about (name person)'s dying now than when we first began these sessions?
b. Do you feel more peaceful about (name person)'s death now than when we first began these exercises?
c. If yes, ask: Why do you think this is so?

Exercise 10. Forgetting About Death

a. Do you find yourself doing things and forgetting for a moment that (name person) is dying?

b. Do you find yourself doing things and forgetting for a moment that (name person) is dead?
c. How does this make you feel?

Exercise 11. Accepting Death
a. Do you think that (name person) has accepted the fact that (she/he) is going to die soon?
b. Do you think the other members of this family have accepted (name person)'s death? Have you accepted it?

Exercise 12. Looking to the Future
a. Have you begun to think about what it is going to be like for this family in the future without (name person)?

Homework
Make a list during the coming week of everything (name person) used to do for you or for the family. List everything you can think of—even little things. Make sure you keep your list for the next practice exercise.

Reconstructing the Family

ID____**Date**________

The purpose of this exercise is to begin the job of reconstructing the family so that it can function without the dying or dead member.

Exercise 1. What Has Been Done for You
a. Last week when you ended the previous exercise, you were asked to make a list of all the things (name person) used to do for you and for the family. Do you have your list?
b. Read and share your list with whoever cares about you and the dead family member.
c. Were there any surprises on any of the lists?

Exercise 2. Taking Over
a. Now, using your own list, beside each item write the name of the surviving member of the family who could take over each item.
b. What about any items that were not assigned? Who will do them?
c. Do you think you can do the things assigned to you by others?

Exercise 3. What You Can Do for Each Other
a. Now make a list of the things the other people in the family do for you.
b. Now, read your lists.
c. Did you realize how many things you do for each other?
d. Is this family working together rather well? What do you think?
e. Have any of you who are older adjusted to old age in this way?
f. What are some of the pros and cons?

Homework

During the coming week think and write down some possible sources of conflicts about sexuality between parents and adolescents. If at all possible, set a family conference time well 24 h ahead and discuss no longer than 1 h with someone taking down notes of what has happened.

Adjusting to Divorce

ID ______________________________ ***Date*** __________

Exercise 1: Adjustment to the Past: How Did You Adjust to the Stress of the Divorce?

a. During the divorce process
b. Immediately after the divorce process
c. Some time (weeks/months) after the divorce

Exercise 2. Separation from Our Pasts (Optional)

a. Close your eyes and imagine you have a piece of cord and a pair of scissors in your hands.
b. Think of all the painful experiences that keep hanging in your mind from the past as represented by the imaginary cord.
c. Now pretend to cut the piece of cord in two and throw away the piece that represents painful experiences and keep the part of the cord in your hand that represents joyful experiences.
d. Keep that piece of cord in your mind to remember joyful experience.

Exercise 3. Meeting with Your Former Mate (Partner)

a. Describe your last meeting with your former mate.
b. Write about the emotions that dominated that meeting.
c. How would you have liked to change that meeting?

Exercise 4. Self-Image

a. Describe three of your traits that you like.
b. Now please describe three traits that you dislike.
c. Write how you might change the traits you do not like.
d. Are these changes realistic?

Exercise 5. Independence

a. Describe three things you have done since your divorce that you did not do while you were married—three things that show new independence for you.
b. What things might you do for more independence for yourself?
c. Please describe what these things might be and how you might accomplish them.

Exercise 6. Mourning the Loss: Death of a Relationship

a. Write how your divorce represents a death to you.
b. How might your divorce be a new beginning for you?

Exercise 7. Testing Reality

a. Describe the parts of your life that are realities.
b. Describe the parts of your life that are fantasies.
c. Describe how your fantasies might become realities.

Exercise 8. Being Aware of Your Emotions

a. Describe how it feels to have each of the following emotions. Give an example of each as it pertains to your life.

    i. Depression
    ii. Hostility
    iii. Self-pity
    iv. Guilt
    v. Remorse
    vi. Anxiety
    vii. Fear
    viii. Anger

b. Which of these emotions have you experienced since your divorce?

Exercise 9. The Children (If You Have Them)

a. Write about your children's mourning.
b. How did they show or not show their feelings?
c. Write how each child mourned the loss in different ways.

Exercise 10. Guilt Over the Children

Children are a common focus of fear and guilt when parents get a divorce.

a. Both of you describe the fears or guilt that you have experienced concerning your children.
b. How might each of you change those fears and guilt into commonsense precepts concerning your children?

Exercise 11. Children, Too, Must Mourn

In a divorce, children go through the same process of mourning as their parents do.

a. Describe the feelings and behaviors of your children after your divorce.
b. Children also have fantasies. How might each of you establish a climate in which your children can express all the feelings that the shock of separation has triggered?

Exercise 12. Connecting with Your Children

You and your children are interdependent individuals.

a. Both of you describe your children as individuals who are unique and separate from you.
b. Now both of you describe new ways of being with your children.

New Realities

ID ____ ***Date*** ____________

Exercise 1. New Beginnings

a. Describe the experiences you have had since your divorce that have made you feel, think, and act like a single person again.
b. If there are none, what might you do to make your single status more real to you?

Exercise 2. Rethinking Values and Priorities

a. Describe the values and priorities that have changed since your divorce.
b. Which values and priorities would you like to change, and how would these changes affect your life?

Exercise 3. Inner Resources

a. Describe any accomplishments that you have made since your divorce, especially those you thought were impossible.
b. Describe a recent crisis in your life, one that has occurred since your divorce. Please give details of the outcome and how you might handle the situation now.
c. Describe any inner resources that you have discovered in yourself since your divorce.

Exercise 4. The World of Work

Career planning must be reviewed by many divorced men and women.

a. Describe any interests or needs that are not being met by your current job or that may not be met in the future.
b. When you seek employment, what realities must you deal with?
c. Describe how you might deal with these realities.

Exercise 5. Assertiveness

The ability to be assertive—to express yourself directly, honestly, spontaneously, and effectively—is vital to every situation you face as a divorced person.

a. Describe a recent situation in which you should have been more assertive.
b. Please read the following assertive statements. As you read them, be aware of the feelings you are experiencing.

Assertive Statements

Statement 1

I realize you are very busy now, but I ordered my steak rare and this one is well done, so you will have to take this one back.

Statement 2

I know you are enjoying that television workbook, but I asked you to do the dishes before you turned on the television. I will have to ask you to turn off the television until the dishes are done.

Statement 3

I know you stopped by to visit me, but I am on my way to an appointment, so we will have to get together later this afternoon?

Statement 4

I realize you asked the other person if you could be of assistance, but I was here before she was, so I will have to ask you to help me first.

a. Now please describe how it feels to be assertive.
b. How might you become more assertive?

Exercise 6. Living Alone Versus Feeling Lonely
Loneliness has little to do with living alone.

a. Describe how it feels to be lonely.
b. Describe the times when you feel the loneliest.

Exercise 7. Relating Socially
Divorce signals a period of experimentation with new ways of relating to other people.

a. Describe your relationships with your relatives and ex-relatives since your divorce.
b. How might these relationships be improved and what benefits might be gained from continuing these relationships?
c. What benefits have you received from these new relationships?

Exercise 8. Relating Sexually
Sexual relationships are important parts of our lives.

a. Describe the characteristics you might look for in a new sexual relationship.
b. How would a relationship now differ from your former marriage?
c. Are the characteristics you described realistic ones for you?

Exercise 9. New Degrees of Commitments
There are different degrees of commitment.

a. Please describe what being committed means to you.
b. What commitments did you make in the past, before your divorce?
c. Why did these commitments work or not work for you?
d. How might each of you make commitments that will be more satisfying in the future?

Exercise 10. Committing Yourself
Commitments may lie in the areas of emotional support, parenthood, status, and economic security.

a. Describe any new commitments you have made since your divorce.
b. What new commitments do you see yourself making in the near future?

Exercise 11. Remarriage
Three out of four divorced persons remarry.

a. Please close your eyes and concentrate on being married again.
b. Keeping your eyes closed, let your thoughts drift and imagine the happiest moment the two of you would have together.

i. Where would you be?
ii. What would you be doing?
iii. Try to be aware of what you are feeling as you do this exercise. When you have finished fantasizing you may open your eyes.

c. Now describe your fantasy in as much detail and as clearly as possible, being aware of the feelings you experienced.
d. Explain why your fantasy could or could not become a reality.

Exercise 12. Sharing Our Fear

a. Write three things that you have been afraid to talk about.
b. When we are too frightened to talk about our fears, we never do find out if our fears will really happen because we never give ourselves a chance to find out.
c. What do you think might happen if you were to talk to a loved one about one of things you listed in part a?

What do you think might happen if you were to talk to another loved one about the same thing or another thing you listed in part a?

Exercise 13. Assuming Responsibility

Sometimes when people have problems, it is hard to tell what caused these problems. As a matter of fact, people who have nothing at all to do with the problem may feel that the problem is their fault; this frequently happens when married people have trouble and decide to get a divorce. Complete each sentence.

a. Children complete this sentence "I think Mommy and Daddy got a divorce because…."
b. Children complete this sentence "I think Mommy and Daddy have problems because…."
c. Children complete this sentence: "I think Mommy and Daddy aren't together anymore because…."
d. Now both parents (separately) finish the following sentence with a statement that only talks about your own behavior. Finish this sentence: "(Name) and I got divorced because…." Come up with three different endings.
e. Now both parents need to collaborate in order to complete a different sentence. Come up with three endings, but this time you must agree on the endings. Please make your statements as clear and concise as possible. You have 5 min to complete this task. "We got a divorce because we…." The children should be quietly observing the collaborative process. Now both of you, in unison, tell each of your children what your responses were. Tell each child in a way that will convince him or her as you say it. Ok, look at the first sentence and get it fixed in your minds. When you are ready, look up.
f. Now tell each child in unison your first sentence. Remember to begin with (his/her) name and to look directly at (him/her). Make sure your children are looking directly at you both while you speaking. Repeat for Sentences 2 and 3. Repeat entire exercise for each child.

Exercise 14. Hearing and Sharing

a. Children complete the following sentences. "Daddy and Mommy got divorced because (use 'we' statements from joint parent exercise) not because (child statements)." Repeat for three statements.

Homework

This week you need to say to each of your children every day the following sentence: "*Even though things are different now, I can take care of myself and I can take care of you.*" For the parent with whom the children live, bedtime is a good time. The other parent may have to rely on the telephone.

Adoption

***ID*______________________________________*Date*________**

Exercise 1. Definition

a. Define the word "adoption."
b. Could you agree that adoption means that a family takes into their home a child who was not born to them and makes that child their own.

Exercise 2. Decision to Adopt

a. What made your family decide to adopt a child?
b. Did your partner and you agree together?
c. How?

Exercise 3. Process of Adoption

a. How did you go about adopting a child?
b. You were able to adopt (child's name) through a public agency.
c. What did the agency require you to do in order to adopt (child's name)?
d. Talk to your child about the interviews with the agency.
e. Ask your children if they fully understand the things that the agency required?
f. Does anyone have any questions about how the agency helped to choose this family for (child's name)?

Exercise 4. First Sight

a. What do you remember most about the first time you saw (child's name)?
b. Where and when did you first saw your child?
c. You could show your child any photos you have of that occasion.
d. How did you feel when you first saw (child's name)?
e. Ask your adopted child: What is the first thing you remember about seeing your parents?
f. If the child was old enough at the time of adoption, ask: How did you feel when you first saw your parents, and sisters and brothers?

Exercise 5. Adoption and Love

a. Does everyone here understand what adoption means to different members of the family?
b. Who chose to adopt (child's name) into this family?

c. Can see that adoption means more than just wanting to love and raise a child as your own. A family must work hard, with the help of an agency, to adopt a child. Do you agree?

Exercise 6. Finding-Out

a. (Child's name), how old were you when you first found out that you were adopted?
b. How did you find out that you were adopted? Who told you?
c. What do you remember being told about your adoption by your parents?

Exercise 7. Telling It

a. How and when did you decide to tell (child's name) about (his/her) adoption?
b. If you used the word adoption in talking with (child's name) before (he/she) understood what it meant, what do you remember about talking with (child's name) the first time (he/she) really knew what adoption meant?
c. If you told the child when he or she was older (5 years), what do you remember about the first time you talked with (child's name) about the adoption?
d. How did you tell him/her? If the child was told by a schoolmate, friend, or relative, ask the child: You say that (person's name) told you that you had been adopted.
e. How old were you at the time?
f. How did (person's name) tell you this? What did (he/she) say?

Exercise 8. Feelings

a. Ask the child: How did you feel when you were told that you were adopted?
b. Did you share these feelings with anybody else?

Exercise 9. Hurt

a. If your child was accidentally told by a friend and indicates that it was painful, if your child did not like the way you told him or her, or if your child had any other negative feelings about the experience, tell your child: I understand that you were (hurt/felt rejected/angry) when (name) told you that you were adopted.
b. Why don't you pretend that you are us and you are telling your child that he or she is adopted?
c. Go ahead—act as if you were us; one of us can pretend to be you. How would you tell your child that she/he is adopted?
d. Have the child act it out with one of you. How did it feel to tell and to be told this way?

Exercise 10. Telling It Again

a. How did you feel when you told (child's name) that (he/she) had been adopted?
b. We can understand that it was difficult to tell (child's name) about the adoption, and we can imagine how nervous you probably were. Since you have been learning about how it feels to tell your child that he or she is adopted, why don't you pretend you are telling (child's name) for the first time? Go ahead—act it out.
c. How did it feel to tell (child name) this way? We hope that you can better understand how (child's name) felt when he/she found out that (he/she) was adopted and that (child's name) understands better how it feels to tell someone about adoption.

Newly Weds

***ID*____________________________________*Date*_______**

Exercise 1. Adjusting to Marriage

a. What have been the biggest adjustments or changes each of you has had to make to live with your spouse?
b. What adjustments have been the most fulfilling?
c. What adjustments have been the most difficult?

Exercise 2. Stress in Marriage

A certain amount of stress is part of any marriage.

a. What kinds of stress has your marriage brought on?
b. How have you dealt with these stresses?
c. What effect has dealing with these stresses had on your relationship?

Exercise 3. New Roles

Now that you are married, each of you has new social roles—those of husband and wife.

a. What do these roles mean to each of you?
b. How can each of you make it easier for the other to adjust to this new role?

Exercise 4. Separateness–Togetherness

a. What does each of the following statements mean to you?

   i. Each spouse must achieve emotional separation from his or her family.
   ii. Together you must gain a sense of identity as a family unit.

b. Write your answer here.

Exercise 5. After the Honeymoon

For most newlyweds, the first transition is from the euphoria of the honeymoon and the first months of marriage to the more down-to-earth matters of daily life.

a. Have you experienced such a transition?
b. If you have, how did you first notice it, and how have you dealt with it?
c. If you have not experienced this, is this transition something you expect to experience?
d. How does each of you expect to deal with it?

Homework

During the coming week, be aware of the adjustments you have had to make to married life and discuss them with each other. Write them down and bring them to the next meeting.

Expectations

ID__________________________________**Date**__________

Exercise 1. Did You Do Your Homework?

a. What adjustments have you become aware of during the past week?
b. Allow full discussion of implications of new adjustments.

Exercise 2. Definition

a. What is an expectation?
b. Would you agree that an expectation is an assumption that specific behavior will occur?

Exercise 3. Great Expectations

a. Close your eyes and think back to a few months ago—before you were married. Recall what you thought it would be like to be married to each other.
b. How close were those images to what married life is really like?

Exercise 4. Unrealistic Versus Realistic Expectations

a. How are expectations different from hopes and wishes?
b. Would you agree that a hope is less likely than an expectation to be fulfilled and that a wish is a completely unrealistic expectation?

Exercise 5. "I Want a Girl Just Like the Girl…"

a. In what ways do we confuse what we want or what we hope for with what we can legitimately expect?

Exercise 6. Owning Hopes and Wishes

a. Think about what expectations you have of each other that may actually be hopes and wishes.
b. Make a list of at least three expectations that are really hopes and wishes.
c. How do you feel about what your partner has listed?

Exercise 7. Relationship Building

a. What are some ways in which not talking about unfulfilled expectations can hurt the relationship you have developed?
b. How does communicating unfulfilled expectations help your relationship?

Homework

During the next week, be aware of instances in which you feel you have not lived up to what you expected. Also, be aware of instances in which you do live up to what you expected. When either instance occurs, talk about it with each other. Try to figure out whether the expectation was legitimate, or was a hope or wish disguised as an expectation.

Discovering Each Other

***ID*____*Date*__________**

Exercise 1. Discuss Homework (Expectations)

Exercise 2. Images

a. Write down the answers to these questions:

   i. If your partner were an automobile, what make or model would he or she be? Why?
   ii. If your partner were a jewel, what kind of jewel could you like him or her to be?
   iii. If your partner were a flower, what kind of flower would you like it to be?

b. Add another item if you like.

Exercise 3. Finding Out About Oneself

a. Now, read your lists to each other.
b. Are you surprised at any of the strengths your partner listed for you?
c. How do you feel about each other's lists?

Exercise 4. Weaknesses

a. Just as in the last exercise, make two lists—one of your personal weaknesses and one of your partner's personal weaknesses.
b. Now we would like you to read your lists to each other.
c. How do you feel about each other's lists?
d. How accurate do you think your partner's perception of you is?

Exercise 5. Spiraling

a. What happens when we act according to how we think our partner wants us to act rather than according to how we want to act?
b. Can we agree that this creates a situation like a spiral—each partner acting more and more in accord with what he or she thinks the other wants?
c. Can you think of any spirals in your relationship?
d. How do these spirals affect your relationship?
e. What are some possible ways of stopping the spirals?
f. How might you stop a spiral by using what you learned in the exercises about your self-perception and how your partner perceives you?

Homework

During the coming week, pay attention to situations in which you may or may not act according to how you think your partner wants you to act. Discuss these situations with each other in terms of your self-perceptions and your partner's perceptions.

Dealing with Parents and In-laws

***ID*____*Date*_______**

Exercise 1. Checking on the Homework

a. Did you do your homework?
b. What did you learn from it?

Tonight's lesson focuses on your relationships with your parents and in-laws.

Exercise 2. Shifting Loyalties

Now that you are married, your loyalties have shifted from your parents and families to each other.

a. Has this changed the relationships you have with your own parents?
b. If no, how have you been able to keep the same relationship with your parents? If yes, what are some of the changes?
c. How does each of you feel about these changes?
d. Do you know how your parents feel about these changes?

Exercise 3. Gaining In-laws

a. A saying that crops up at many weddings is: "I haven't lost a son (daughter), I've gained a daughter (son)." What does this saying mean to each of you?
b. Is this saying applicable to each of you and your parents and in laws?

Exercise 4. Choosing Sides

Newly married couples often find it difficult to decide with whose parents to spend major holidays.

a. How are you dealing with this issue?
b. How do you feel about having to decide between two sets of parents?
c. How do your parents feel about these decisions?

Exercise 5. Letting Go

There are many subtle ways parents can show their regrets at letting go of their children, for example, phoning too often or dropping by unexpectedly.

a. Have you noticed any of these subtle behaviors in your parents?
b. Has your partner noticed these subtle behavior changes in his or her parents?

Exercise 6. Running Interference

Parents and in-laws have many ways of interfering in their children's new marriage.

a. Have you experienced any interfering by your parents?
b. How do you feel about your parents' interfering in your marriage?

Exercise 7. Dealing with In-laws

The last three exercises have dealt with some issues that may arise between you and your parents and in-laws.

a. What are some productive ways of dealing with in-laws?
b. What are some effects of dealing with in-laws positively?

Homework
During the coming week, think and write down about the effects your parents' marriages have already had on your marriage. Make a list of things your parents do that you notice you yourself might be doing now. Bring your notes to the next meeting.

Trust

ID_________________________________***Date***________

Exercise 1. Checking on the Homework (Parents and In-laws)

a. Did you do your homework?
b. What did you learn from it?

Tonight's lesson deals with trust and developing trust in your relationship.

Exercise 2. Defining and Developing Trust
a. What does trust mean to you?
b. What are some ways in which you trust each other? For example, you trust each other to be home for dinner, do the shopping.
c. Would you agree that trust means counting on another person?
d. How do you think a person develops trust?
e. How do you two develop trust?
f. How might trust be destroyed between you two?

Exercise 3. Trust Means Caring
Trust is involved in most of our daily human relationships. For example, an employer trusts employees to work competently; they in turn trust the employer to pay their salaries.

a. Is this kind of trust different from trust in a marriage?
b. Try to define kind of trust you and your partner have.
c. Does the kind of trust resemble a concept close to "caring?" If not, could you agree that trust between a husband and a wife involves caring?
d. How does caring relate to trust between you two now that you are husband and wife?

Exercise 4. Being Open with Each Other
Trust rests on both partners' willingness to be open and honest.

a. Each of you tell the other two subject areas that you would like to be more open to discussion.
b. How can you promote more discussion on these topics?
c. What are your feelings about the topics your partner named, that is, what surprised you, annoyed you, angered you, or pleased you?

Homework
Discuss the issues you named in the last exercise. You do not have to come to any resolution about them, but just begin to practice talking about some of the topics you are afraid to discuss with your partner. Keep written running notes to bring to the next meeting.

Personal and Marital Goals

***ID*______________________________________*Date*________**

Exercise 1. Checking on the Homework (Trust)

a. Did you do your homework?
b. What did you learn from it?

Exercise 2. Professional Goals

a. What are your professional goals?
b. Are you likely to achieve them fully, or will you continue working toward them for a long time?
c. What role does your marriage play in achieving these goals?

Exercise 3. Personal Goals

a. What are your personal goals, goals that are not necessarily tied to professional goals?
b. Do you think you can achieve them fully, or might you always be working toward them?

Exercise 4. Marital Goals

a. What are your goals for your marriage relationship?
b. Will these goals ever be achieved?

Exercise 5. Contrasting Goals

a. What are some of the similarities and differences in your professional, personal, and marital goals? That is, how are they generally alike, and how are they generally different?
b. Would you agree that professional goals are more likely to be fully achieved than personal goals or marital goals?
c. What does it mean that personal and marital goals have to be worked at throughout the relationship?

Exercise 6. Triangles

a. What is an equilateral triangle?
b. What happens when one side of an equilateral triangle becomes longer than the others?
c. Could you say that a marriage is an equilateral triangle whose three sides are I, you, and we?
d. What happens when the sides become unequal? Do you think there are any unbalanced sides in the triangle in your marriage?
e. What are some ways of keeping your triangle balanced?

Homework

Although you have completed this workbook, hopefully you will continue to work on the issues covered in these practice exercises. In the next week, try to identify two other triangles in your marriage that you must keep in balance and share with each other.

Deciding Whether to Have a Baby

ID____________________________________**Date**________

Exercise 1. Who Am I? Who Are We?

a. Answer this question? Who am I?
b. Take a few deep breaths and think about yourself as you are now. Let your thoughts float freely. Think of yourself in as many ways as you can. When you are ready, open your eyes and introduce yourself to your partner. Each spouse should state at least five self-definitions.
c. Were you surprised at anything your partner said?

Exercise 2. Personal Goals

a. Think about yourself in the future: Who do you want to be?
b. What goals do you have for yourself as an individual, say 5 years from now?
c. 10 years from now?
d. For the rest of your life?

Exercise 3. Who Are We?

a. Think about who you two are as a couple.
b. Take a piece of paper and a pencil and draw a coat of arms for you as a couple. Include anything you consider important to who you are as a couple. You may draw some pictures or write several of your marriage's mottos on the crest.
c. Now describe your crests and explain to each other why you included each part of your design.
d. How are your designs similar? How are they different?

Exercise 4. Marriage Goals

a. Think about your future goals as a couple. Think of several goals for you two as a couple and write them down on the other side of the papers on which you drew your coats of arms. Your goals may relate to many different areas of your marriage—financial, recreational, sexual, or emotional.
b. Read your own list. What similarities do you see in your two lists? What differences are there?

Exercise 5. Priorities as a Couple

a. You have heard and thought about the goals you and your spouse have for your life together. Rank these goals according to their importance to you as a couple.
b. Share your lists and develop a list for your two as a couple.
c. Draw a circle and write the goal most important to you as a couple on the circle; draw another circle enclosing the first one and write the goal that is next in importance. Draw a circle for each of the goals on your list. Explain each of your choices. Take turns explaining your choices.
d. How did it feel to negotiate your priorities for the future?

Exercise 6. Babies and Change

a. Now imagine the thought of you, as a mother and as a father. Will the baby change your priorities as individuals and as a couple?

b. What will happen if you put your baby ahead of yourselves as individuals and as a couple?
c. What will happen to your priorities after the child is grown and gone?

Exercise 7. Reliving the Past Through Children

a. Tell about one or two goals you have not been able to reach.
b. Now, pretend you are talking to your child.

   i. Tell your child about your disappointments, then describe the pitfalls you have experienced, and tell the child how he or she could avoid difficulties by learning from your mistakes.
   ii. Tell your child how happy you will be if he or she succeeds where you failed and how disappointed you will be if he or she also fails.

c. How did it feel to have a child in order to redo the areas in which you made mistakes?

Exercise 8. Children as Extensions of Us

a. Think of one or two achievements you prize most and tell each other about them.
b. Now, pretend that you are talking to your child. Tell him or her how good it felt to succeed, how you went about it, and how happy it will make you to know that he or she will follow in your footsteps.
c. How did it feel to have a child in order to build up your self-importance?
d. Do you need a child to feel better about yourself?

Exercise 9. Gains and Losses

a. Think of some reasons of your own for having a child.

   i. What might you gain if you have a child?
   ii. What might you lose if you have a child?

b. Make a list, one column for your gains and one column for your losses.
c. Now, share your lists with each other.

   i. What similarities do you see in your lists?
   ii. What differences do you see?

d. Which is your most important gain and which is your most important loss?
e. Right now, which outweighs the other—gains or losses? Why?

Exercise 10. Past and Future

a. Close your eyes and try to see yourself as a child again. You are with your parents. Let yourself go back to different times in your childhood. Feel your resentments and hurts, feel your happiness and pleasures as you did when you were a child.
b. When you are ready, open your eyes. Share your memories with each other. In your relationship with your parents, what made you happy? What hurt you or made you angry?

Exercise 11. Parenthood

a. Close your eyes again. This time, imagine yourself as a parent with your own child, in a situation just like the one in which you saw yourself and your own parents just a few minutes ago.
b. How do you feel as the mother or father? What do you do?
c. When you are ready, open your eyes and share your experiences with your partner.
d. What could you do to help yourself be you as a parent rather than a carbon copy or a mirror image of your own parents?

Qualities of Parenting

ID______________________________Date_______________

Exercise 1. Clarify Your Expectations of Yourselves as Parents

a. On sheets of paper, write classified ads. One will say "Mother Wanted"; the other will say "Father Wanted." In your ad, list all the qualities you think a mother or father needs to do a good job of parenting.
b. Now, read your ads.
c. The following question is for the husband. Do you have any qualities you want to add or delete from your wife's ad? Why?
d. The following question is for the wife. Do you have any qualities you want to add or delete from your husband's ad? Why?
e. Were you surprised by anything in your partner's ad?
f. What similarities and differences do you see in your ads?

Exercise 2. Do I Have the Qualities for Parenting?

a. Now write another ad. This time, the wife's ad will say "Woman Available to Mother" and the husband's ad will say "Man Available to Father."
b. List all your qualifications and limitations in your ads.
c. Read your ads now.
d. Do you think you have what it takes to fill the mother-wanted and father-wanted ads you wrote? Explain why or why not.
e. What areas of parenting do you think you will have to work on especially?
f. How do you think your spouse can help you to be a good parent?
g. How do you feel about your spouse's qualifications?

   i. What are his or her weak points?
   ii. What are his or her strong points?

h. How can you support each other?

Exercise 3. Is Perfection the Goal?

a. If somebody said, "I never make mistakes," what message would you get from that statement?
b. Think of a mistake you made recently. Point your finger at yourself and tell about your mistake, scolding yourself. When you have finished blaming yourself, say, "I made a mistake and I forgive myself."

c. How did it feel to blame yourself?
d. How did it feel to forgive yourself?
e. How willing are you to be a less than ideal parent?

Exercise 4. Limits and Fulfillments

a. Please get up, stand back to back, and lock arms. One of you will pick a direction and try to go that way. The other will try to go in the opposite direction. You will have a choice—by touching only, you may try to convince your partner to go in your direction, or you may change your mind and go in your partner's direction.
b. How strongly did you feel about going in your own direction? Did you change easily or did you resist?
c. What did you like or dislike about the way your partner tried to convince you?
d. How flexible do you think you could be in setting limits and in allowing your child independence and freedom?
e. How would you go about teaching your child values?
f. How would you feel if your child decided to go in his or her own direction and not accept your values?

Exercise 5. Negotiating Differences

a. If you decide to become parents, you will have many responsibilities related to child care. Think of as many child-care tasks as possible.
b. How would you like to see these responsibilities divided?
c. How much do you agree on the way you would like to divide these responsibilities?
d. In dividing these responsibilities, what differences are there between you? Which of your assignments of responsibilities do you consider nonnegotiable?
e. Are you willing to negotiate all the other assignments?

Exercise 6. Critical Times

a. Think of a time when you had to deal with a crisis. Tell:

   i. What the crisis was
   ii. How you behaved
   iii. How you handled the problem
   iv. How you coped with it emotionally

b. Now imagine that you have a child who is mentally retarded or physically handicapped. How do you think you would be able to deal with this situation, emotionally, financially, and practically?

Exercise 7. Jealousy

a. When was the last time you were jealous of your spouse's being with another person or being very absorbed in a project or activity?
b. How did you show that you were jealous?
c. How does your partner react when you are jealous?
d. How frequently do you get jealous?
e. Some partners become jealous of the partner's relationship with their child. How willing and able do you think you would be to share your partner with a child?

Exercise 8. Looking at Your Marriage

a. You are currently a couple without a child. If you decide to have a child and you want to be a couple after your child leaves home, you will have to work at keeping your relationship strong while your child is at home. What are the strengths of your marriage?
b. What are the weaknesses of your marriage?
c. How could you use the strengths in your marriage to keep your relationship satisfying if you have a child?
d. If you do not have a child? How do you think having a child might affect your working on the weaknesses in your marriage?
e. How well do you think your marriage would survive parenthood?

Exercise 9. Sharing Space and Time

a. In the next two exercises, you will have a chance to experience your relationship as it is now and imagine what it might be like if you had a child. We like you to sit on the floor. Spread out and take as much room as you want. Close your eyes and relax. Enjoy the feeling of being in your own space, taking up as much of the floor as you want, knowing that the space is yours. When you are ready, open your eyes and look at your partner. If you want to share your space and your feelings or if you want to enjoy the moment by yourself, let your partner know by a look, a gesture, or a body movement.
b. Depending on whether they both stayed apart or shared the space, answer the following questions. How did it feel to be in your own space? How did it feel to enjoy the moment by yourself? How did it feel to enjoy the moment with your partner?

Exercise 10. Is Three a Crowd?

a. If you do decide to have a child, you will have to share your space and time with one more person. How will it feel to lose some of your space and some of your time alone together?
b. What are some good points and some bad points about sharing your space and time with a child?
c. For you, do the good points outweigh the bad, or do the bad points outweigh the good ones?

Homework

In the coming week, if you can, role-play parenting situations pretending to be a parent and to give you an idea of what it might be like if you were a parent.

Financial Costs

ID____***Date***________

Exercise 1. Can Two Live Cheaper Then One?

a. You have heard that "two can live as cheaply as one." Do you think that three can live as cheaply as two?
b. Some have estimated the cost of raising a child to age 18 (not including college) at over $ 200,000.00. Put yourselves in the following situation: You have made

out a monthly budget, but this month your child seems to be growing out of every shoe and every piece of clothing. The roof has a leak and needs to be fixed. Discuss how to deal with your financial pressures.

c. Do you think you are willing to commit yourselves to the large financial outlay necessary for a child?

Exercise 2. Something's Got to Give

a. Both of you work, you are involved in the activities of several organizations, and you have been invited to three parties this month. Your son has been having difficulty making friends at school because his classmates do not live in your neighborhood. In order for him to socialize with his classmates, you would have to drive him to their homes—30 min each way. Your child's teacher has suggested that you do more informal sports activities with him, but this means you will have to give up some of your own activities. Discuss your child's needs and your own needs. Discuss what activities you would and would not be willing to give up and what alternatives there are.
b. How did it feel to negotiate your commitments and needs with your partner?

Exercise 3. Children Should Be Seen, Not Heard

a. You have just come home after a very hard day. The baby sitter greets you at the door and tells you that your 5-year-old daughter has been in a bad mood all afternoon. The living room is strewn with toys. Your child is bawling loudly; when she sees you, she picks up a toy and hurls it at you. What do you do?
b. How did it feel to have to deal with your child when you were so tired?

Exercise 4. A Chip Off the Old Block

You have next Monday off, and you two decide it will be fun to go off on a weekend with your teenaged daughter, with whom you have not spent too much time recently. When you tell her about your plans, she tells you it is out of the question because there is a party Saturday night. Discuss your feelings about her response and decide how you will react—what you will do and what you will say?

Exercise 5. A Bundle of joy

a. Your 12-year-old son comes home from school with some games you know are not his. You ask where they came from, and he tells you that he took them from a classmate who has been ripping off his lunches for the past 2 weeks. Your child is very definite that his behavior is justified and tells you that what he did was right. What do you do?
b. How did it feel to be in conflict with your child over values?
c. How willing do you think you would be to let your child take responsibility for his actions and accept the consequences of his behavior?

Exercise 6. Evaluating the Issues

a. Which of the situations presented above was the most difficult for you to deal with?
b. Can you think of any other situations you would have difficulty with?
c. Can you think of some support you could give your spouse with his or her difficulties?

d. Based on your reactions to these role-plays, do you think you would be willing to deal with a child for 18 years on a day-to-day basis? Why? Why not?

Homework
Between now and our next exercise, spend an extended period taking care of a child. You may babysit for two evenings or spend part of a day with a child. Think and talk about the experience together.

Decisions and Consequences

ID____***Date***______

Exercise 1. Consider Past Homework

a. Before beginning this exercise, consider the homework, if you did perform it. How old was the child you took care of?
b. How many hours did you spend with the child?
c. What did you like about the experience? What did each of you dislike about the experience?
d. What did you learn about your desire to become a parent? In this exercise, focus on the consequences of deciding to have a child and of deciding not to have a child.

Exercise 2. Consequences of Not Having a Child
a. Think about the consequences if you decide not to have a child. Please write:

   i. "If I decide not to have a child, then…."
   ii. Under this, list as many consequences—good and bad—as you can think of.

b. Now read your lists.
c. Which are the three most important consequences on your list?
d. Now look over your whole list.

   i. How many consequences are pleasant for you?
   ii. How many are unpleasant?

Exercise 3. Consequences of Having a Child
a. Now turn your paper over and write, "If I decide to have a child, then…." Again, list as many consequences both good and bad, as you can think of.
b. Again, look down your list and pick out the three most important consequences. Tell each other what they are. Which of the consequences on your list are pleasant for you?
c. Which are unpleasant?

Exercise 4. Reevaluation 1
a. Now look back to the list of consequences of not having a child. Change the first part of the sentence to "If I have a child."
b. Now see if you can retain the consequence by adding conditions that will make the sentence true for you. Here is an example: Suppose you first wrote, "If I don't have a child, I (or my spouse) can keep working." To rewrite the sentence, you might say, "If I decide to have a child, I (or my spouse) can keep working as long

as I resolve my questions about the appropriateness of day-care centers as good substitutes for a parent. ”

c. Are there any sentences you cannot rewrite?
d. What did you learn from rewriting your list?
e. What did you learn from listening to your partner’s rewritten list?

Exercise 5. Reevaluation 2

a. Now try to rewrite the second “If I decide to have a child” list. Begin with “If I don’t have a child” and add conditions that will make the sentence true for you. For example, suppose you wrote first, “If I decide to have a child, I will feel very close to my partner.” You might rewrite the sentence as follows: “If I decide not to have a child, I will feel very close to my partner because we will be able to buy a vacation house and spend most weekends together, away from it all.”
b. Rewrite as many sentences as you can.
c. Please read your new sentences.
d. Are there any sentences you cannot rewrite?
e. What did you learn from rewriting your list?
f. What did you learn from listening to your partner’s rewritten list?

Exercise 6. Wrap-up

a. What has this workbook taught you about yourself and your willingness and ability to be a good parent?
b. What have you learned about your spouse’s ability and willingness to be a parent?
c. Are there any issues you need to consider further before you make your decision?
d. How do you plan to go about clarifying your views on these issues?

Expecting a Baby

ID____**Date**__________

Exercise 1. Changes During Pregnancy

a. Close your eyes and think of all the ways your life has changed since this pregnancy began. Think of all the things, good and bad, about the way you live or feel that are different now that a baby is on the way. Allow 5 min.
b. After opening your eyes. Describe what you came up with. After you speak, talk to your partner and ask: Were you aware of all these changes in (name)?

Exercise 2. What Do We Want?

a. Ask your partner, “What do you want?” After the partner answers, switch roles.
b. How did it feel to say what you want?

Exercise 3. Information About Pregnancy

a. Answer the following questions separately. Was this baby planned? Was the pregnancy wanted?
b. How did you feel when you first learned the news?
c. How have your feelings about this pregnancy changed since the beginning?

d. After your spouse answers each question, answer the question: "Were you aware (he/she) felt this way?"

Exercise 4. The Meaning of Motherhood

In a few months, you will become parents, something very new to you. Right now think about what it means to be a mother.

a. What does the word *mother* mean to you?
b. Now think about your own mothers. In what ways do you think being a mother in this family will be like your own mother?
c. What things will (wife's name) do that will be the same as things your mothers did?
d. What things will (wife's name) do differently?
e. If your mother was absent during your childhood, use a female guardian, or mother figure for comparison.

Exercise 5. The Meaning of Fatherhood

a. What does the word *father* mean to you?
b. Now think about your own fathers. Remember them as well as you can. What things will the father in this family do that are like things your fathers did when you were growing up?
c. What things will be different?

Exercise 6. Similarities and Differences

a. Can you see some things about the two roles, mother and father, that are alike?
b. What things are different?
c. How do you feel about yourself as the mother or the father you described?
d. How do you feel about (partner's name) as a mother or father?

Homework

Before completing the next exercises, look at some parents on television. Just pick any set of parents to study. Notice the situation, the kind of people they are, and what happens to them. Keep two sets of parents in mind you can talk. They can be on commercials, soap operas, news reports, or anywhere on television.

Feelings About Pregnancy

ID____ ***Date***________

Exercise 1. Homework

a. Did you watch your two sets of television parents?
b. Describe your sets of parents first?
c. Were these the kind of parents you would like to be? Do you think the parents on television were close to real life?
d. Why did you choose these particular parents?

Exercise 2. Expressing Feelings

a. Yelling helps get old feelings out along with held-in feelings, so stand up and start slapping your chest gorilla-style!

b. Now as you slap, yell "Ahhhh-h-h" as loud as you can for about 30 s. Let go completely on this one. Could your neighbors hear you? If not, do it again.
c. How did it feel—just letting everything go? How does your body feel right now?

Exercise 3. "Good" and "Bad" Feelings

a. Complete the sentences below with the first thought—good or bad—that comes into your mind. Do each one several times. Just complete these sentences as you naturally would:
   When I learned about the baby coming, I felt…
   Sometimes I wish this baby would…
   Pregnant women look…
   I get scared when I think about…
   My life has never been so…
   When the baby comes, I am going to miss…
   I worry too much about…
b. Answer each question, and then go through the entire set again.
c. Were you surprised at some of the answers?
d. If you were, explain why.

Exercise 4. Settling Arguments

a. Flip a coin to decide which side you argue first—pro or con. For the pro side, tell all the good, fantastic things about having this baby; for the con side, come up with the things that are not so good.
b. After a minute switch sides–if you are pro, you become con and vice versa. Each of you needs to argue each side three times.
c. How did you feel about taking sides like that? Which was easier for you?
d. What did you learn from this debate?

Exercise 5. Anticipating Your Baby's Birth

a. Close your eyes and relax for a while. Become as relaxed as you possibly can. Feel your whole body becoming quiet. Now picture a movie screen in your mind. The lights are coming up and a show is beginning. It is the story of the arrival of your baby. It is the story of how you want the baby to be. Just let this story of your child's birth unfold in your mind as you would most like to see it happen.
b. Where will you be when labor begins? Is it day or night? What is the hospital like? What happens next? Move in close to the picture. Have you missed anything? What happens when you come home with the baby?
c. Which of you would like to share your story first?
d. Include how they felt in their fantasies. How did you feel about visualizing this big event?
e. How much of this do you think will really come true?

Homework

Before the next exercise, listen to some music and pick a "family song." Choose a song you think best represents the way you operate or feel as a family. Bring a recording, lyrics, or be prepared to sing the song next time. Each partner is to do this independently.

Closeness

ID____**Date**________

Exercise 1. Your Family's Song

a. Have you done your homework? Share your family songs (Each partner needs to present his or her song).
b. Why did you choose that particular song?
c. What do you think of each other's songs?
d. How do you feel when you listen to each of them?

Exercise 2. Successful Arguments

a. Now you are going to have an argument with each other. Think of something that really makes you angry. This fight will be a little different from the ones you usually have.
b. Think of a fierce animal. Then, in this argument, pretend that you are that animal. Your only words will be animal sounds, but you can use gestures and actions that you think your animal would use (Limit this argument to 3–5 min).
c. How did it feel to be a fighting animal?
d. Did this argument remind you in any way of others you have had? If it did, explain the similarities.

Exercise 3. Nonverbal Expression

a. Sit very close together on chairs or on the floor. In the next 10 min, talk with each other without using words. Think of something important and beautiful you want the other person to know. You may use your eyes, your hands, your elbows; just do not speak. Think very hard about understanding what your partner is saying to you through a touch or a look. Do this for 10 min
b. How did it feel to talk without words? Did you feel understood?

Exercise 4. Difficult Situations

a. To better understand yourself and your partner, think at how you would handle a difficult situation such as these:

   i. *You are usually in charge of the budget. This month, there is not enough money to pay the bills. You feel guilty about having bought some frivolous things for yourself after your spouse praised you for being such a good money manager. Now you realize that you need more supplies for the baby. What do you do?*
   ii. *It is 2 weeks before the baby is due. You are out shopping together and labor begins. What do you do?*
   iii. *The baby has arrived and has been home about a week. You start feeling depressed, so low that you find it hard to go on. Taking care of this baby until he or she grows up seems impossible. What do you do?*

b. After reading each situation, think a few minutes and answer individually.

Exercise 5. Drawing Your Family

a. Use several sheets of paper and a drawing pencil: Draw yourself. Take about 5 min to do the best self portrait you can.
b. Now draw the two of you as a couple. Again, take 5 min to draw.
c. Draw yourselves and your baby as you think the baby will be a few months from now. Allow slightly more time for this drawing.
d. Now look at your pictures. Place the pairs of pictures side by side and compare them. What is different about how you see yourselves? What things did you draw similarly?
e. How do you feel about these drawings?
f. Which is your favorite? And why?

Feelings

***ID*____ *Date*_________**

Exercise 1. Using Your Bodies

a. Stand in the middle of the room, back to back. Now learn to talk with each other, using only your backs.
b. Try expressing different emotions: anger, love, sorrow, joy. Try to communicate the emotions named.
c. What else can you express this way?
d. Can you have a conversation?
e. How did you like talking this way?
f. Did you learn anything?

Exercise 2. Positions in the Family

a. Think about your position in this family. Right now, you are still a couple. What does that mean?
b. In a few months, you will become a family of three. What does being a family mean? How is it different from being a couple?
c. What are some things you will be able to do that you cannot do now?
d. What are some things you will probably stop doing after the baby comes?

Exercise 3. Expressing Weakness

a. Pretend you are a walking rag doll. Your spouse/partner must support and help you so you do not topple over.
b. Remember, you have no strength. Make your partner really work to hold you up.
c. Switch roles. How did it feel to be weak and helpless?
d. How did it feel to give support?
e. Which did you like better? Why?

Exercise 4. Expressing Strength

a. Who do you think is stronger in this family?
b. In what ways?
c. What are some other kinds of strength?
d. Tiny babies are helpless in many ways, but they do have strengths. What does a baby do that is strong?

e. How will you feel being responsible for a small, helpless person?
f. Can you make a statue with your body, showing how it feels to be strong? Try a statue that is strong and brave.
g. Now make one that shows how you feel when you admit that you are wrong.
h. How did you like becoming "statues of strength"?

Exercise 5. Dividing Labors

a. Does each of you have certain chores or tasks you do regularly? For instance, who washes dishes? Rakes leaves? Takes out the garbage? Keeps the budget? Makes the bed?
b. How did you decide who would be in charge of a task?
c. How do you handle the chores that neither of you wants to do? After the baby comes, will this arrangement of labor change?
d. What are some chores that the new baby will create?
e. Which ones do you worry about?
f. Do you know as much about child care as you would like to?

Exercise 6. Your Baby's Name

a. Have you decided on names yet?
b. Where did the names come from?
c. If no name has been chosen, what names are you considering?
d. Choose which response fits your response best:

   i. Not a family name: What does that name mean to you?
   ii. Whose idea was it?
   iii. What does it mean to have someone else carry on your name?
   iv. After a relative: What is it about this (aunt, uncle, grandmother) that made you decide to name your child after him/her?

e. How does he/she feel about it?
f. If they have chosen a name for only one sex, ask them what they will name a baby of the opposite sex.
g. What do you think a name is, anyway?
h. Do you think people act in certain ways because they have certain names?
i. How do you like your own names?

Exercise 7. Your Baby's Appearance

a. Close your eyes and try to imagine your child, first as a baby, then as an older child.
b. Considering the way you look—your coloring, height, and weight—what do you think your child will look like? Think about this for a few minutes. Try to see your child clearly in your mind.
c. Now describe what you see as clearly as possible.

Cohabitation

ID____**Date**____________________

Exercise 1. Living Together Versus Being Married

a. What does it mean to live together as an unmarried couple?
b. How living together compares with being married—how they are similar and how they are different?

Exercise 2. Choosing Not to Choose Marriage

a. Why did you choose to live together rather than get married? Discuss this:

    i. Psychologically
    ii. Emotionally
    iii. Practically
    iv. Familiarly

b. Would you live together for 5 years?
c. Would you live together for 10 years?
d. What are the long term implications of living together without marriage?

Exercise 3. Dependency and Loss; Freedom and Independence

a. Does marriage signify a loss of freedom or independence?
b. If the answer is yes: In what ways have you sacrificed freedom and independence by choosing to live together?
c. If the answer is no: In what ways have you become more free or independent by choosing to live together?

Exercise 4. Similarities and Differences

a. Can you think of some other ways in which living together is similar to being married?
b. What are some ways in which living together is different from being married?
c. How does living together compare with dating?

Exercise 5. Dating and Choosing

d. Has either of you ever dated someone else?
e. If the answer is no: Do you ever feel confined by not being able to date other attractive men or women?
f. If answer is yes: How is your relationship with other partners different from your relationship with each other?

Exercise 6. Dating and Screening

a. Do you find a greater sense of security in living together as opposed to dating?
b. If you can, give specific examples of when you felt this security.

Exercise 7. Cohabiting and Dating

a. In what other ways is living together different from dating?
b. In what ways is living together similar to dating?
c. If you can, give specific examples of similarities between the two.

Homework
Think about how living together has changed your lives. List at least five ways in which your life has changed since you started living together.

Broadcasting It

ID____ **Date**________________

Exercise 1. Letting Parents Know
a. Do your parents know that you are living together?
b. How does your family feel about your living together?
c. Are you satisfied with the way your family has reacted to your living together? If the answer is no: Can you think of any way you might help your family to understand and accept the fact that you two are living together?

Exercise 2. External Pressures
a. Has there been any pressure from your friends either to break up or get married? If the answer is yes, how have you dealt with these pressures?
b. Do you still associate with the same circle of friends since you started living together, or have you felt the need to find new friends?

Exercise 3. Legal Implications
a. Are you aware of the legal implications of living together as an unmarried couple?
b. Make sure you both know about these implications.

Exercise 4. Letting Employers Know
a. Do your employers know that you are living together? If the answer is yes, ask: Have you felt any pressure from them either to get married or to break up?
b. How have you dealt with these pressures? If the answer is no: How do you feel about having to keep this information from them?

Exercise 5. Finding a Place to Live
a. Have you had any problems finding a place to live?
b. How were those problems resolved?

Exercise 6. Cohabitation and Bureaucracy
a. Have any other authorities caused you problems about living together?
b. How were those problems resolved?

Two Selves

ID____ **Date**________________

Exercise 1. Looking at Yourself
a. What do you see as your strong points as a person?
b. What do you see as your weak points or the things about yourself that you would like to change?

Exercise 2. Similarities and Differences

a. List how you are similar in your personalities.
b. List how different you are in your personalities.

Exercise 3. Likes and Dislikes

a. Write, how have your likes and dislikes changed since you met your partner?
b. In general, do you see yourself as having become more similar or more dissimilar since you met each other?

Exercise 4. Privacy and Separateness

a. Has either of you felt the need for more privacy, or more separateness? If the answer is yes: Can you think of any ways in which you can deal with your needs for privacy?
b. How can you reconcile the desire for privacy from the desire for separateness?

Homework

Think of five areas in which you two complement each other, or fit together well, and five areas in which you do not fit together well.

Sharing Responsibility

ID____________________________________**Date**________

Exercise 1. Decision Making

a. Who makes the decisions in your household? Make sure you arrive at an agreement on this answer.
b. Are there any ways in which decision making could be shared more fairly?

Exercise 2. Household Duties

a. How are your household duties distributed? Answer specifically.
b. Who shops for food?
c. Who cooks?
d. Who takes out the garbage?
e. Who keeps the house clean?
f. Are there any ways the household duties could be distributed more fairly?

Exercise 3. Financial Responsibilities

a. How do you share financial responsibilities?
b. Are there any ways in which you could distribute finances more fairly?

Exercise 4. Fantasy Trip

a. Try something a little different. Close your eyes. Imagine you are 70 years old. You are thinking back over the course of your life. Describe for us what you have done with your life.
b. Describe for us some of the happiest times of your life.
c. Describe for us some of the saddest times of your life.
d. If you could, how would you change your life?
e. Open your eyes. What was your reaction, (name) to what (name of partner) had to say?

Fears, Hopes, and Expectations

ID____**Date**______

Exercise 1. Fears About Cohabiting

a. What are some of the fears you had, or still have, about living together?
b. What are some of your hopes about cohabiting?

Exercise 2. Expectations About Cohabiting

a. What were some of your expectations about living together before you moved in with each other?
b. In what ways have your expectations been fulfilled?
c. In what ways have your expectations not been fulfilled?

Exercise 3. Looking Into the Future

d. How do you see your relationship progressing in the future? Make sure you are specific.
a. What do you expect from this relationship in 5 years?
b. What do you expect from this relationship in 10 years?

Exercise 4. Pressures to Marry

a. Have you pressured the other to get married? If the answer is yes, how have you dealt with these pressures?
b. If you have satisfactory way of dealing with them, can you think of any constructive way of handling these pressures?

Exercise 5. Pressures to Break Up

a. Has either of you pressured the other to break up? If the answer is yes, how have you dealt with these pressures?
b. If you have no satisfactory way of dealing with this, can you think of any satisfactory way of handling these pressures?

Exercise 6. Having Children

a. Have you thought about having children with each other someday?
b. Have you thought about buying a house for both of you?
c. How will this affect your relationship?

Homework

If possible, try to develop a contract specifying as clearly as possible your commitment to each other and your relationship with each other. Do not make any commitments that you do not wish to make. Just state as clearly as possible your commitment to each other as you see it at this time. Do start writing anything down during this week, but do think about your commitment to each other.

The Contract

ID____**Date**______________

a. Do you want to draw a contract? If you do not, do not go any further in this exercise. If you do want to draw a contract, do go on. For instance:
b. Is either of you willing to commit yourself to a specified length of time for this relationship? If so, how long?

c. Are you willing to commit yourselves to marriage to each other at some time in the future? If so, when? If there is no definite commitment: Are you willing to consider marriage at some point in the future?
d. Are you willing to give up other sexual partners?
e. Is either of you willing to devote part of your time—daily, weekly, monthly, or yearly—purely for the enjoyment and satisfaction of the other partner? If so, how much time and how often will you give it?
f. Is either of you willing to assume responsibility for any part of the household duties? If so, which duties?
g. Is either of you willing to assume responsibility for any part of the financial burdens? If so, which part?
h. Is there anything that we have left out that either of you would like to add to this contract?

Homework
During next week, look over what you have written in the contract and correct or change whatever you do not agree with. Make an appointment 24 h in advance to discuss possible changes or corrections to eventually finalize your contract. After you have reached a contract agreeable to both, do sign it and makes copies for your records.

Conflict Resolution

ID___________________________________**Date**_______________________

Exercise 1. Reality and Fiction
a. What is a myth? To understand the realities of a marital relationship, it is helpful to first recognize the unrealities.
b. Think back to the time just before you were married and recall what you thought marriage would be like.

Exercise 2. Apparent Discrepancies
a. Describe what "being in love" was like during your courtship.
b. Give examples that point out the differences in your behavior and feelings when you were dating and now.
c. Do you expect to remain in a constant state of romantic love while married to your partner? If the answer is yes, how will you achieve this? If the answer is no, what will replace this romantic love?

Exercise 3. Real or Imagined Differences
a. A second myth about marriage is that men and women differ inherently in attitudes and behavior and that these inherent differences cause most marital troubles. *Take several minutes to write down two lists of adjectives: one list describing male characteristics and the second female. The heading can be Males are—: Females are—. Next, share your lists by reading them aloud.*
b. Which of these characteristics fit the two of you? Is either of you aware of stereotyping in your list?

c. The recent trend is to view differences between the two of you as minimal and to recognize that in fact you have any number of choices in defining your particular sex-role relationship. *Turn to your partner and ask*: Can you think of times when you may be doing jobs traditionally considered a man's? *Turn to husband*: A woman's?

Exercise 4. Fighting for a Good Marriage

a. Another common myth about marriage is that "if we argue, disagree or fight, we must have a poor marriage." How do both of you respond to disagreements between you? Ask questions, if necessary, and deal with the ways you have been able or unable to negotiate their differences.
b. What are the ways in which your partner shows respect for your viewpoint or your wishes in a given situation? Give an example.

Homework

All spouses have disagreements. During this workbook, work toward marital bargaining exercises so that each of you gets the maximum benefit from this experience, that is, both of you win. Living together means that no one person can have everything he or she wants, so there is always some giving and taking. Be aware, during the coming week, of the times you meet each other halfway. This may involve a television program, vacation plans, sex, or an evening out.

Focus on the Relationship

ID______________________________________**Date**__________

Exercise 1. Who Am I?

a. Ask the other, "Who are you?" Decide which of you is starting. For whichever one of is starting, repeat the question ten times; each time your partner will give you a different but true answer. Write down your answers and make sure your partner does not repeat an answer. Stop when you have reached eight. You may answer with descriptive words or phrases.
b. Now ask each other the question, "What can you give me?"
c. What are your feelings about the exercises you just did with each other?
d. Perhaps you are beginning to see some ways in which your behavior has an impact on your partner.

Exercise 2. Relationship Rules

a. The two of you add up to more than the sum of your parts, your marriage consists of each of you and the way you behave in relation to each other. In a marriage, once the relationship has been established, both partners work to maintain the balance of their relationship. You do this by establishing (early in marriage) the rules of your relationship and by following them. Some of these rules are open; others may be hidden. Can you think of some of the rules of your relationship?
b. In some marriages, when the man comes in from working all day, the rule is that no one talks until he has a half-hour to rest and read the paper. He, in turn, may have agreed that his wife may sleep late on weekends while he fixes breakfast. She may fix his favorite meals, keep his clothes straight; he may compliment her

for these acts, buy small gifts. In other families the rule is that when one partner is irritable, the other must not comment on his or her mood. Sometimes, the rules have to do with who makes certain decisions.

c. Are you aware of your rules about decision making?

Homework

You may still be wondering about the rules you operate under. Take some time during the coming week to write down all the rules you can think of that apply to your relationship. Do this separately, then share and discuss your lists with each other. See whether you can come up with a super-list that includes items from both lists.

Communication in Marriage

ID______________________________________**Date**_____

Exercise 1. Definition

a. What does the word communication mean to you?
b. What are the ways in which you have communicated with each other in the past?
c. What about nonverbal communication?
d. What about actions?
e. Facial expressions? Gestures? Are you aware of the nonverbal communication your partner typically uses or that you use?
f. There is no "not" communicating.

Exercise 2: Communicating Feelings

a. Face each other for this exercise. *To one partner*: Remain silent and concentrate on a feeling that you would like to convey to your partner. Now communicate this feeling to your partner without saying a word. You may touch your partner, but do not speak.
b. *Ask second partner*: What was the feeling message that you received? Ask first *partner*: Was that the feeling you sent?
c. Husband ask your wife a question. Make this a question that you would like an answer to now.
d. Wife, you are to remain silent and distracted. Husband, you are to insist that she answers you, and you may ask the question in a number of ways. What is she communicating to you by her silence?
e. What did you feel as you were doing the exercise?
f. Explain nonverbal canceling.
g. Say a sentence or two to the other and cancel the word message with a nonverbal disqualification.
h. What was the message that each of you received?
i. What were your feelings about the verbal message? The nonverbal?

Exercise 3. Incongruent Stances

a. The four types of manipulative roles are:

   1. Placating: pacifying, smoothing over differences, being nice, covering up.

2. Blaming: judging, bullying, comparing, complaining. For example, "It's always your fault"; "Why don't you…?" "If you would…."
3. Avoiding: being quiet, pretending not to understand or changing the subject.
4. Preaching: lecturing, using outside authority, proving you are right by explaining or using logic. For example, "You should…." "You must".

b. Play the role of a blamer and the other is to take the role of a placater. Allow 3 or 4 min to play a scene of your choosing. The scene may be a general issue between them or something as specific as an upcoming vacation to the beach.
c. Next, one of you must avoid and the other must preach.

i. Which role was the easiest to play?
ii. Which role was the most difficult?
iii. What did you learn about yourself? About your spouse?

Exercise 4. Speaking for One Self: "I" Statements
a. Talk together for a couple of minutes about an issue that concerns you, but only use sentences that begin with the word "It." Do not ask questions; begin every sentence with "It." Discuss briefly the experience of using only "It" statements.
b. Now use only sentences that begin with "You."
c. Again, discuss briefly. Now do the same thing, using only "We" statements.
d. Now talk with each other, using only statements beginning with the pronoun "I." No questions are permitted, only "I" statements. Again, discuss your experiences with "it," "you," and "we" statements. Saying "I" means that I take responsibility for my end of the relationship. When I speak for myself rather than others, I express my own sensations, thoughts, feelings, and intentions. It also means that I avoid telling others what they sense, think, feel, or intend. When I use the word "I", I disclose much of myself. I take a chance and let the other person know something about myself. This is what a relationship is about.

Homework
During the coming week, try to make three "I" statements a day to your partner.

Communicating Hurt Feelings

ID______________________________________**Date**________

Exercise 1. The Message Sent Is Not Necessarily the Message Received
a. We are going to give you some examples of statements to make to each other. Only the husband should read these statements. Ask your partner as naturally as you can "Didn't we have chicken on Tuesday?" For the partner who did not read the question, what is the message you received? Message may carry different meanings: (a) You (*husband*) are irritated and are warning her; (b) you do not mind but are curious to see if your memory is accurate because you are taking a memory course.
b. The wife should read the next statement: "It is cold in here." After you send this message to your husband, he will respond by telling you the message he received. Following his response, allow several minutes to think of the various messages she might be sending in addition to the words.

c. The husband should read the last statement: "No thank you," to a second cup of coffee.

Exercise 2. Accuracy in Communication

a. As you move toward negotiating with your partner, it is important that you work for accuracy of communication. This does not mean agreement but that the message sent is the one received.
b. Total, complete understanding is a utopian goal. It is hard to achieve, but when it happens it is called "shared meaning." It feels good and works like this: I know that my partner understands what I mean, and my partner knows that I realize he or she understands me. Two skills are central to shared meaning: asking your partner to reflect the message you have sent and acknowledging the message. Asking a partner to reflect the message can be done by asking, "What do you hear me saying?"
c. Acknowledging is a way of giving feedback. Saying "I understand" is not giving feedback. Letting your partner know what message has been received is acknowledgment, and is prefaced by saying: "What I hear you saying is…." We would like the two of you to take a few minutes to discuss a real issue between you. It does not have to be a "heavy" one, just something you agree to discuss here, using the shared meaning process. Allow a few minutes to decide what you will discuss. An additional 3 min will be enough time for them to demonstrate your understanding of the shared meaning technique.

Exercise 3. Talking Straight

a. If you want a truly intimate and trusting relationship with your partner, you must resolve to level with your partner and to bring up all significant problems, concerns, and worries. To leave a significant problem or concern not discussed is similar to leaving an infection untreated. It will not go away; on the contrary, it will get worse. Another way of stating this communication rule is: Do not walk on eggs! Sharing feelings, even negative ones, implies respect for and trust in the partner. If there have been times when you have "walked on eggs," that is, not expressed your negative feelings openly, you may have ended up feeling hurt and angry. We want each of you to express how you feel hurt. Face your partner and take turns saying sentences that begin with the words "I feel hurt by…" Take a few minutes to tell your partner how you wish he or she would let you know he or she is angry.
b. How can you encourage your partner to be more expressive of hurt or angry feelings?
c. How did you both feel about sharing this way. Remember that your differences do not have to divide you and that talking about them can be constructive. There are some additional rules for an open discussion of your differences: Stick with one issue at a time; do not bring up past history to use against the other person; and remember to find some appropriate humor!

Homework

When you have something important to say to your partner during the next week, use the process of shared meaning.

Trust

ID________________________________**Date**____________

Exercise 1. Openness and Honesty

a. Openness and honesty permit trust to develop. Are there topics that you do not feel you can be honest with your partner about?
b. What prevents you from being totally open about this?
c. We would like each of you to tell the other three subjects that you would like to be more open to discussion between you.

Exercise 2. Congruence

a. Verbal openness is only one kind of honesty. Sometimes we say one thing but by our behavior we communicate another. For example, you may say you love your partner, but you may be constantly irritable and inconsiderate of your partner's feelings, complaining, or keep the other waiting.
b. Can you think of examples of incongruities between your own words and actions that diminish the trust between you and your partner?
c. As you can see, honesty is more complex than being verbally honest.

Exercise 3. Imperfection

a. Sometimes partners think that they must be perfect in the eyes of the other or they will be less lovable.
b. Do you allow yourself to be imperfect (i.e., human)?
c. When did you last make a mistake and admit it openly?
d. Trust can best be seen as a two-way street. If you can face and share your feelings and faults, your hostilities and fears, secrets and shames, you will help your partner to face those things. Building this kind of trusting relationship requires the constant exercise of truthfulness and courage. Perhaps you have begun to work this out. If so, the rewards will be great.

Exercise 4. Styles of Relating

a. Just as couples differ in the amount of trust they have achieved, they also differ in other basic ways. One of these has to do with modes or styles of relating to each other.
b. Sometimes partners struggle for status. It is as if they were saying to each other, "I am as good as you are." If spouses consistently compete in this way, we say that they have a symmetrical marital relationship.
c. What are the areas that the two of you compete in?
d. How do you feel when this happens?
e. Another way of relating to each other is for one of you to be in charge and for the other to obey. If it were always that way for the two of you, we would say that you have a complementary marital relationship. This kind of relationship is rare, and it would surely end in dependency, anger, and dissatisfaction.
f. Each partner needs to answer the following question. What are the areas of your marriage that you are responsible for?

Exercise 5. A Parallel Relationship

a. A give-and-take marital system, which is a combination of the symmetrical and the complementary styles, is called a parallel relationship. This means that each of you has areas that you take the initiative in and that you are in charge of, and that occasionally you have a "status struggle" in which you are working out or even battling out your relationship. How does this sound to you?
b. The parallel relationship is satisfactory because each of you feels equal, knowing that neither of you will win all the issues at the expense of the other. Because you are here and working to improve your relationship, it is safe to assume that you want to collaborate, that is, to work together and cooperate rather than compete.

Homework

During the coming week, be aware of the areas of competence that each of you has and uses. Sit down together and tell each other the situations that you believe each of you handles well. These may concern children, home, social planning, driving, shopping, and work. If some areas are not clearly assigned, one of you take responsibility for it during the coming week. You may want to bargain as you divide responsibilities.

Quid Pro Quo

ID______________________________**Date**____________

Exercise 1. Rules of Communication

a. Speaking for self ("I" statements)
b. Avoiding manipulative styles (blaming, placating, avoiding, and preaching)
c. Checking out and acknowledging (shared meaning)
d. Matching verbal and nonverbal messages
e. Not using past history against the partner
f. Sharing feelings, even negative ones

Exercise 2. The Ideal Partner

a. State as factually as possible the characteristics that you would like to see in the other, characteristics that would make your marriage more workable. Who would like to begin? The partner who is to listen first, is to remain silent.
b. After the speaker has finished, the listening partner needs to summarize what she/he heard his/her partner saying. Do not use attacking or defensive words. However, the listening partner may add comments about himself or herself.
c. Repeat exercise and reverse positions.

Exercise 3. Destructive Patterns

a. Tell each other the ways you, yourself, contribute destructively or are failing in your relationship.
b. How could you change to improve your marriage? Again, the listening partner is to remain silent. After one partner has finished speaking, the other partner needs to summarize only.
c. Repeat the two-part exercise with the other partner. Do not respond at this point to what the other says.

d. Now you are ready to present your wishes, desires, and needs to each other. We want the partner who goes first to describe your principal wishes or desires for you in this marriage. Make these as specific as possible so that you will know, and your partner will know, how to fulfill the wish. As you name your wishes, your partner will write them down.
e. Six to eight items will be enough because these will be important wishes. Repeat, having other partner speak.

Exercise 4. Fulfillment

a. Study your partner's list of wishes carefully for 5 min.
b. Then each of you will identify one desire or need of the other that you feel can be fulfilled. Allow 5 min.
c. Tell your partner the item that you have selected and how you think it can be worked out between you.
d. Discuss it freely until you are satisfied. At that point you can move to your partner's selected item.
e. You have just negotiated successfully for something each of you want! How do you feel about the discussion you just had?
f. Although this is the end of this section, it is the beginning of learning to give and take for change in your marriage. It will require a lot of practice, but you will usually be negotiating only one issue at a time, not two, as we have

Homework

During the coming week, try to negotiate an important issue. Make an appointment at least 24 h ahead. Allow an hour and a quiet place to do this and be aware of the skills each of you use. Keep writing what is happening. It is important that whatever happens between you becomes a written record.

Let Us Pretend

ID__________________________________Date__________

Exercise 1. First Wedding Anniversary

a. Tonight is your first wedding anniversary. Now, to start the exercise, you both need to answer questions separately without the other hearing the answers.

For the female: I want you to pretend that it is your first wedding anniversary and you have spent most of the day cooking a special dinner for (husband's name). Try to feel as if this is actually happening. What are his favorite foods?

i. Which ones do you prepare best?
ii. That is good. Now how will you fix the table?
iii. What will you wear?
iv. Ok, dinner is just about ready and your husband is coming in from work. Now let us go back in so you can talk with your husband.

For the male: Tonight is a very special evening and your first wedding anniversary and you made surprise plans to take your wife out.

i. What restaurant will you take her to?

ii. You have made the reservation, ordered the meal, and paid for it. What did you order for yourself and your wife?
iii. Try to feel as if this is actually happening. What will you wear?
iv. Now you are coming home from work to tell your wife your plans for the evening. Let us go.

b. Act out this scene if you can.

   a. How did you feel about that?
   b. In what way did you handle the conflict?
   c. Are both of you satisfied with the outcome?

Exercise 2. Avoidance and Denial
One of the methods people use in conflict is avoidance.

1. Did you use it tonight?
2. Do you use it at other times?
3. Sometimes people will deny that a conflict exists. Others may say that the conflict is just not important. Are these bad ways or good ways of handling conflict?
4. Some people physically avoid conflicts by leaving the room. How is this bad?
5. One other way to avoid conflict is to make irrelevant, distracting remarks. Can you think of any examples?
6. Do you ever use any of these methods?

Exercise 3. Engagement
The opposite of avoidance is engagement, or going beyond arguing.

a. How is engagement better than avoidance?
b. There are two kinds of engagement—destructive and constructive. Can you give some examples of destructive arguments?
c. One very bad way to argue is to spread the conflict to other topics. Can you give some examples of this?
d. Why is it bad?
e. The best kind of arguing is constructive engagement. What are some ways to argue constructively?
f. Sticking to the point and listening are important. Try to come to an agreement and get closer to your partner rather than rejecting your partner. We are going to work on these things during our sessions together.

Homework
During this coming week, we want each of you to keep a separate list of your arguments. If they are too personal to talk about here, just write something down to remind yourself what they were about. Next, write down the methods you use while arguing, for example, avoidance, sticking to the point, or degrading. Please be as honest as possible.

Constructive Steps

ID______________________________________**Date**________

Exercise 1. Old Ways

a. How did the homework assignment work out? Do you have the sheets? You should get better at pointing out their methods of arguing as you progress through the program. Now take a minute to look at each other's summaries.
b. What methods did you use when arguing? Did you come to solutions that both of you were satisfied with? Make sure each person answers separately and refers to specific arguments.
c. How could you have solved these conflicts more effectively?
d. In what other ways could each of you have acted toward a mutual solution?

Exercise 2. Applying New Ways

a. Wife: Pretend you are about 7 months pregnant with your first child. Answer these questions separately without your partner hearing the answers. At 9:00 p.m. there is a television panel show in which authorities in psychology and psychiatry will discuss the naming of babies. They are going to discuss how names can affect the child. You and your husband have not decided on names, so this is a very important program. Both of you want to watch it. Are there any questions?
b. Husband: There is a special program on television at 9:00 p.m. that you are looking forward to watching. What type of program would it be? If you suggested a weekly series, name a much more special program. You have been waiting all week for this program. Are there any questions?
c. Pretend that you are both sitting in front of an imaginary or a real television set. Imagine it is a few minutes before 9:00 p.m. Again, act out the scene with as few interruptions as possible.

    a. How did you feel about that?
    b. In what ways did you handle the conflict?
    c. Are both of you satisfied with the outcome? Do not downgrade the way the other person handled the conflict. If one of you does, point out that he or she is not acting constructively.

Exercise 3. Follow a Specific Sequence

a. Now you are going to work on specific steps in arguing constructively. What are some of the steps one should take when arguing? Allow several minutes for discussion. You should at least include stating the problem, determining the solution, and choosing a solution. These are all very important, but how can you be sure the solution will be carried out?

    i. How does each of you feel after arguing?
    ii. How can you make your partner feel better after arguing?

b. It is often a good idea to return to the conflict in a general way and work out suggestions for similar future situations.

i. Are there any questions about what you have discussed?
ii. Now let us write down the steps you have come up with for ways of constructively arguing. Make a joint list.
iii. The list should include roughly the following:

I. An introduction and naming of the problem
II. Possible solutions and the implication of their solution
III. Practical plans for resolution
IV. Emotional reconciliation (cooling off)
V. An reaffirmation of the relationship
VI. Return to the conflict in a general way of making suggestions about future situations

Homework
Write down your conflicts and the methods you use in solving them. This time you can look at what the other writes and discuss how each of you has acted. Try to follow the constructive steps you have written down. The order does not matter—just use them.

Practice Makes Perfect

ID______________________________________***Date***_______

Exercise 1. Constructive Confrontations
a. Did you bring the homework assignment and the steps you wrote down last time?
b. Did you discuss with each other during the week the ways in which you handled your conflicts?
c. Did you ever start to argue again when discussing the conflict?
d. If the answer is yes, maybe the conflict was not really resolved constructively. What do you think?
e. If the answer is no, that is good, you must have really resolved the conflicts constructively. In which arguments did you not use the constructive steps?
f. Why not?
g. This issue will be dealt with further in down. How could you have handled this better?
h. In which arguments did you use the constructive steps?
i. How did you use them?
j. Were both of you satisfied with the outcomes? What do you think of these constructive steps?
k. Have they helped you?
l. Why or why not?

Exercise 2. Resolving Conflicts
Now we would like you to practice solving another conflict situation. Try to be constructive. Let us separate again for a few minutes.

a. To the wife: your husband has been acting like a stranger for several days—not like the man you married. He has been distant and cold, and this is worrying you. Tonight you are determined to overcome this barrier between you and reestablish closeness. Do you understand?
b. Ok, let us go back in.
c. To the husband: have you ever experienced the feeling of not wanting someone next to you, or of wanting nothing to do with that person?
d. Isn't it a feeling of wanting to be left alone?
e. Everyone feels this way at one time or another. Tonight this is how you feel about your wife. Has she ever done anything to make you feel this way? If the answer is no, then imagine something that would make you feel this way.
f. Are there any questions?
g. Ok, get back together. Why don't you go stand by the window?

How did you feel about this conflict? Remember that the situation was contrived and that the rejecting partner was instructed to act distant. Work with these feelings, using the constructive steps.

a. How did you handle the conflict?
b. Are both of you satisfied with the outcome? If either of you answers no, work through the conflict again, using the steps. It is not necessary to act the parts again.

Exercise 3. Conflicts and Feelings

a. Discuss feelings and conflicts. When you are angry, is it hard to follow the steps for constructive arguing?
b. Why or why not?
c. What are some other reasons?
d. What can both of you do to make sure your conflicts are constructive? Maybe practice would help.
e. An informal contract or agreement between you may also be helpful. In it each of you could promise the other to be responsible for your own behavior and to try your best to stick to constructive rather than destructive arguing. Would you like to try this? If you are interested, use the Conflict Resolution Contract as a guideline. Fill in the agreement and sign it. Do you have any other suggestions for dealing with emotions while arguing?

Homework

a. First, work on keeping the contract you have made.
b. Again, keep a separate record of all your conflicts and the ways in which you handled them. Feel free to discuss these records with your partner.
c. Last, think about the conflicts you have had in which one or both of you were not satisfied with the outcomes.
d. Bring up two of these conflicts again and try to solve them by using the steps you have learned. Use the forms to record your arguments at the end of this workbook.

Constructive Arguing

***ID*____*Date*_________**

Exercise 1. Contracts and Commitments

a. How did your contract work during this past week?
b. Did it help you stick to constructive arguing even though you might have been mad or upset? If the answer is yes, that's good. You must be taking it seriously. Why don't you continue the contract after the program ends? If the answer is no, a contract is a commitment to someone. It is not made to be broken. Is there some way you could renegotiate it to make it more effective?

Exercise 2. Improving Solutions

a. Make sure either of you have the list of constructive steps written for this exercise. Did you write down your conflicts during the week?
b. Did you discuss with each other the ways in which you handled the conflicts? How did your discussions go? In which conflicts did you argue constructively?
c. In which did you argue destructively? Why were you this way? If you argued destructively in some conflicts, why were you this way?
d. How could you have handled this situation better? If you had no destructive arguments, are both of you completely satisfied with the outcome?
e. Did you bring up two past conflicts in which you were not satisfied with the outcome?
f. Were you able to resolve them constructively?

Exercise 3. Trying Again

Practice solving a conflict situation very similar to last week's situation. Let us separate again. This is the same conflict as in a previous exercise, but the roles are switched.

a. *To the wife*: have you ever experienced the feeling of not wanting someone next to you, of wanting nothing to do with that person?
b. Isn't it a feeling of wanting to be left alone?
c. Everyone feels this way at one time or another. Tonight this is how you feel about your husband. Has he ever done anything to make you feel this way? If the answer is no, then imagine something that would make you feel this way.
d. Are there any questions?
e. Ok, let us go back in. Why don't you go stand by the window?
f. To the husband: your wife has been acting like a stranger to you for several days—not like the woman you married. She has been distant and cold, and this is worrying you. Tonight you are determined to overcome this barrier between you and reestablish closeness. Do you understand?
g. Ok, get back together. Act the scene out. If there are any serious problems, remember the steps for constructive arguing. How do you feel about the conflict this time?
h. Does it help to know how the other person feels?
i. How did you handle the conflict?
j. If you did not, try to settle it now. Are both of you satisfied with the outcome?

Exercise 4. Considering Options

a. Think of as many other ways as you can for making arguing less destructive. Can you think of some?
b. Why don't you list the ways we have talked about? Write down as many as you can think of together on a sheet of paper.
c. What else could each of you do to make the other person feel better when you are arguing?
d. Write down your answers. If something is bothering you, what are some of the most constructive ways of bringing up the topic with your partner? Write down your ideas. What if something is bothering your partner, how would you like him or her to tell you about it? Write down your answers and keep the list to refer to later. It may look something like this:

    i. Do not just criticize; bring out good points.
    ii. Start in a friendly manner.
    iii. Try to see the other person's point of view.

Make sure you have the steps for constructive arguing and the list of the other ways of making arguments less destructive. It may be necessary to renegotiate on your lists. Did you come up with any new ways of doing things in any areas progress has been made?

e. *You may have to review whatever step the couple is missing.*

Exercise 5. Pinpointing Conflict Areas

a. Tell each other a specific area in which you seem to have the most difficulty. Give an example of a conflict in that area. Write the conflict on a sheet of paper. Draw three vertical lines beneath the conflict.
b. Each of you answer the following question separately.

    i. How do you want things to work in this area?
    ii. One of you write a brief answer on the left side of the paper and the other write a response on the right side of the sheet. Now look at the page.

c. Here you have a conflict in what each of you wants in this area. Obviously, both of you cannot have your own way. So we are going to have to try to come up with a compromise.

    i. Any ideas about how this conflict could be handled so that both of you would be happy? If this causes too much fighting, switch to another conflict in this area where you have already gotten over your anger.
    ii. When you do decide on a compromise, write it down in the middle of the page, between your wishes as originally stated.

Homework

Now let us see if this is going to be a workable compromise. For the next week, please handle this conflict this way we just did. Many couples have difficulty explaining their conflicts. Do not give up if this is the case. Keep working with them in defining their conflicts.

Continued Pinpointing

ID__________________________________**Date**____________

Exercise 1. Practice, Practice, Practice

Repeat the procedure in the preceding exercise with a conflict in the area of next greatest unhappiness. Think how you succeeded in arriving at a compromise because you looked at things from both points of view. Also, you had already gotten your strong feelings about this conflict out of the way. Remember, you cannot solve problems when you feel too strongly about something, such as when you are too mad or too excited. When that is over, try to work toward a compromise.

Exercise 2. Responsibility

a. This workbook has also dealt with responsibility. Do you understand how?
b. You are responsible for doing things to make your marriage better. We cannot give you a happy marriage and spouse alone cannot make your marriage happy. You must both, as individuals and as a couple, be responsible for making changes and improvements in yourselves so that your marriage can continue to grow.
c. When conflicts come up in the future, try using this procedure to resolve them after you have worked through your feelings. Remember that compromises are a way for you to show each other that both of you are important.

Exercise 3. Specifying Feedback

a. Think about your sexual happiness and name specific issues that you think could be improved, making you happier sexually. Spend approximately 10 min to think about these issues.
b. Answer the following question separately.
    i. Which issues are you concerned about most?
    ii. How did each of you feel about what your spouse said?
c. Can you now think of ways you could make yourself and your partner happier sexually?
d. How about trying these things during the next week?

Exercise 4. Learning to Compromise

a. Do you still have conflicts about sex, things that one of you wants but the other does not? If conflicts still exist, use the compromise procedure outlined in a previous exercise. If you both are still experiencing sexual problems, you might want to work on workbook about sexual fulfillment for couples after completing this workbook.

Homework

During the coming week, continue to:

a. Acknowledge the nice things you do for each other
b. State disagreements positively
c. Do for each other the good things that you have agreed to do
d. Live up to your contracts

e. Use the compromise procedure
f. Abide by the results

Summing Up

ID__________________________________Date_____________

Exercise 1. Did you do your homework?

Exercise 2. Keeping Commitments
Now check on how you are coming along with the things you have agreed to do.

a. Are you acknowledging the nice things you do for each other?
b. Are you continuing to state disagreements more positively?
c. Are you continuing to do the additional nice things for your spouse that you agreed to do?
d. Are you living up to your contracts?
e. Have you abided by the compromises you reached in our sessions together?
f. Are you using the compromise procedure to settle disagreements at home?

Exercise 3. Reciprocity
Have you figured out the basic goal of this workbook? Want a hint? The key word is *reciprocity*. Have you ever heard of the Golden Rule? What is it? (Do unto others as you would have them do unto you) to reciprocity. The basic goal of this workbook has been to learn to make fair and even arrangements with each other. You do something positive for your spouse, and your spouse does something positive for you. Things work out only when we are fair with ourselves and with each other. Please comment at will.

Exercise 4. Collecting Feedback
a. What do you think we have accomplished working together? How do you feel about that?
b. Now on you will have to deal with your marriage and problems alone. Let us see how this is going to work out. Talk about ways to improve your marriage. If they begin to talk about past problems or hurt feelings, say: *We are not here to talk about the ways you have been defeating yourselves.*
c. Talk about ways to make things better. When the first conflict arises to conflicts or areas where you think improvements are needed, try using the techniques we have been working in this workbook to make things better.

Conflict Resolution Contract

Contract Between

ID____________________________and______________________________Date______

The problem:

The solution:

We, the undersigned, agree to abide by the terms of this contract for a period of

Signatures

Conflict Resolution Form

Argument or conflict

Specific methods used in handling the conflict

Satisfied with the outcome
Dissatisfied with the outcome

===

Writing a Couple or Family Contract

ID_____________________________Date____________________

Exercise 1. Practicing Compromises

a. Give an example of a conflict you are having in your family.
b. How would you like to see things work in regard to this conflict?
c. You can not solve problems or reach compromises when you feel too strongly about something. If you are angry, depressed, or even too excited, work these feelings out first, then go back to using this procedure to reach a compromise.

Exercise 2. Homework

For homework, do two things. First, write down ten nice things you have done for each other and how you showed your appreciation. If you praised the other person, please write down the words you used. Second, write down all the conflicts that you have in this coming week. Try to reach a compromise; write that down too. If you cannot compromise, do not fight about it; just write down the conflict.

Exercise 3. Reciprocity Necessary

Look at all the nice things that you all have done for each other and for voicing appreciation for those things. If you do have any unresolved conflicts, include them in the contract that is to be written during this session.

Exercise 4. Reciprocity

a. What does reciprocity mean in this context? Write down what you understand with this word.
b. Does reciprocity mean that if you want to place demands on others, you must be willing to have demands placed on you?
c. Try to work out some of the specific problems you are having with each other.

Exercise 5. Acceptable Limits

a. You need to answer the following question. What are some things that are important to you that your (son/daughter) is not now doing that you would like (him/her) to do? Write down the things you list. Be as concrete and as specific as possible. For example, a statement about improving specific grades in specific classes is more objective and specific than "doing better in school."

Exercise 6. Clarifying Conflict Areas

The following question is for the teenage child. What is important to you that you and your parents have conflicts about? Remember to be specific and write down your answers.

Exercise 7. Writing the Contract

Now, here we have lists of what you, the parents, want on the one hand and what you, the teenager, want on the other. Of course, all of you cannot have exactly everything you want, so let us work out some compromises and try to make two lists that are equally good and will require approximately equal amounts of giving on both sides. Try to combine items.

Exercise 8. Uncompromising Positions

a. If one side absolutely refuses to compromise on something very important to the other side, realize that one side may feel too strongly about this issue to come to an agreement. Try in the coming week to work out your feelings in the new way we have used in these exercises. Maybe we can add this desire to the contract in the next lesson.

Exercise 9. Maintaining the Contract

During the coming week, commit yourself to a couple or family conference at least 24 h ahead of the starting time. See whether the contract should be revised or kept as is.

Exercise 10. Renegotiating the Contract

How has this week gone? Did all of you keep your part of the contract? Address any of the problems in the contract and renegotiate the contract as necessary, following the guidelines in the preceding exercise. Remember, the power of the contract is that it is ironclad only for the past and present. You can change it for the future, but everyone must agree and sign. Ok?

Exercise 11. Goals

a. What do you think the ultimate goal of this contract is?

b. Would you agree that the goal is to get a feeling for give and take, for reciprocity, to learn to recognize and solve conflicts yourselves?

Exercise 12. Checking Up

a. Some families like to use the contract in some form indefinitely; others like to phase it out when everyone agrees they can and would like to do without it. It is up to you as to how long you wish to use it. Are there any questions? After each of the following questions, help them with any problems that have arisen in the area described. Besides the contract, have you remembered to let each other know that you appreciate the things that are done for you?
b. Have you continued to state your disagreements in a positive way?
c. Have you expressed your anger or displeasure without insulting the other person's character?
d. Do you feel you now have a better understanding of each other's position?

Confronting Change

ID____________________________Date__________________

We need to find out whether or not you want help.

Exercise 1. Meaning of Change

a. What does change mean to you?
b. Is the devil you have better than the devil you don't have?
c. Why do you want to change?
d. Things can stay as they are, or they can get worse. We want to help make them better. Which do you want?

Exercise 2. How Change?

a. How do you think change will take place in your family?
b. Who is going to be responsible for change in this family?
c. If any of you expect change to take place outside yourself, how is this stance going to help your family?
d. If any of you does not really want to change and wants to live with defeat, let's find out who that one is.

Exercise 3. Power to Defeat

a. Apparently you have taken on, or the family has given you, the power to the power to defeat and to keep things as they are or to win and change things for the better for you and your family. If you want to keep things as they are and you don't want things to change for the better, there must be a payoff for you. What is it? Do you get a kick out of or enjoy defeating defeat yourself. If you defeat others, how can you not defeat yourself?

Exercise 4. Investing in Sameness

a. Each of us can choose to stay the same and thus defeat others and ourselves, or we can choose to change ourselves. Which of these choices do you want?
b. Does anyone in your family have an investment in keeping things as they are?

c. By keeping things as they are now, no one has to change. Is that what you want?
d. If you really want to change, how does each of you want to change?

Exercise 5. For Whose Sake?

a. Why should any of you want to change anyway?
b. For whose sake should any of you change?
c. If anyone wants to change for somebody else's sake, it doubtful very seriously that change can occur.
d. If you change for someone else's sake, it means you already know what he or she wants from you—you have read that person's mind. It means pleasing that person rather than yourself. Under these conditions, it is impossible to change. Please comment on this statement.

Exercise 6. Change for One's Own Sake

a. If change is to take place, it must be to satisfy ourselves. How can we satisfy ourselves and others in the family?
b. Discuss any issues arising from this and earlier questions.

Homework

During the coming week, think about whether or not you want to change for the better. In writing, list reasons you should or should not change. Have a family conference to discuss the whole issue of change (for the better).

How to Live

ID________________________________**Date**____________

Exercise 1. Change or Staty the Same?

a. Do you want change for the better, or do you want things to stay the same or even get worse?
b. If no one makes a definite commitment, think about if you are you really committed to change for the better?

Exercise 2. Commitment to Change

a. If you seems committed to change for the better, write why you want to change.
b. If this question is difficult to answer try one of the following. What's in it for you if this family changes? Why is it important for this family to change?

Exercise 3. First Responsibility

a. Who is going to be responsible for change in this family?
b. If not everyone takes responsibility for change,, you may need to reconfront this issue with the family members who are not facing it directly.

Exercise 4. Second Responsibility

a. Who is responsible for the happiness of this family?
b. You can choose to live your lives happily or unhappily. Which choice do you want?
c. Some people are committed to living very unhappy lives. If you want this choice, you should have it. However, don't expect help to get it.

Exercise 5. Happiness

a. Since most of you have decided that you would like to live happy lives, explain what would make you happy.
b. Meake sure you answer in terms of what you would do to make yourself happy. Do not answer in terms of what others should do to make you happy.
c. The purpose of this exercise is to pin down individual responsibility, not relying on someone else for happiness. Please comment on this statement at will.

Exercise 6. More Happiness

What each of you can do to make yourself happy. Write down exactly what you are going to do that will please you. Remember, write down what you will do that will make you—not necessarily anyone else—feel good, proud, and excited about yourself.

Exercise 7. No-Loss Win

Now that you have written down what you will do to make you proud of yourself, go back over your list and think whether what you are going to do will represent a loss to someone else (your partner or any member of your family). If your winning means a loss to someone else, rewrite your win so that no loss occurs. If you cannot think of how to avoid a loss, cross that item off your list. Be sure not to give up an item on your list just for the sake of avoiding confrontation. Make yourself available to help each family member consider how to rephrase each behavior so that it will not imply a loss to anyone in the family. Help each member help other members consider behavior changes that will produce a win-win outcome for everybody in the family.

Homework

During this week consider in greater detail the changes that you are willing to make and that will make you feel happy and proud of yourself. Keep your list for the next exercise.

Goals for Change

ID____

Date__________

Exercise 1. Individual Goals

a. What do you want to get out of working on these practice exercises?
b. What goals do you want to accomplish by coming here?
c. Give only the goals you want for yourself.
d. Write your goals in the following sequence: primary goal, secondary goal, tertiary goal, and other goals.

Exercise 2. Couple or Marital Goals

What do you want out of your relationship? Again, list primary goal, secondary goal, and tertiary goal. Make sure to differentiate between goals as mates and goals as parents.

Exercise 3. Family Goals
List the goals of this family. What do you want this family to accomplish? Make sure that all these goals are written down: primary goal, secondary goal, and tertiary goal.

Exercise 4. Immediate Versus Long-Range Goals
Now that you have gone over all the goals each of you wants personally and as a family, separate goals you can reach in the near future and the goals you want to reach in the long range.

Exercise 5. Realistic versus Unrealistic Goals
Separate realistic from unrealistic goals.

Exercise 6. Abstract versus Concrete Goals
Separate abstract from concrete goals

Exercise 7. General versus Specific Goals
Separate Abstract from Specific goals.

Homework
During the coming week look up sources where various workbooks are described and chose the one that best fits into your needs, wants, or likes.

Assertiveness

ID____________________________________**Date**_________

Exercise 1. Give and Take
a. Do you know what the phrase "give and take" means?
b. How does it apply to your relationship?
c. Please write how you feel about the following statement: Would you both agree, then, that by "give and take" is meant that sometimes we must submit and allow our partner to have his or her way and that at other times we must stand firm and assert ourselves in order to make our own point of view heard.

Exercise 2. Assertiveness and Reciprocity: Definitions of Terms
Please define the following four terms and give an example for each:

a. *Assertiveness.*
b. Can you recall the last time you asserted yourself?
c. Could you describe the situation?
d. How did it feel to you?

1. *Submissiveness*
   a. Can you recall the last time you submitted yourself?
   b. Could you describe the situation for us?
   c. How did it feel to you?

2. *Dominance.*
   d. Can you recall the last time you dominated yourself?
   e. Could you describe the situation for us?
   f. How did it feel to you?

3. *Reciprocity*
   g. Can you recall the last time you reciprocated something?
   h. Could you describe the situation for us?
   i. How did it feel to you?

4. *How would you deal with the possibility that rather than a either/or possibility, there may be different shades of assertiveness, submissiveness, dominance, and reciprocity?*
5. *How* do you recognize each other's rights, privileges, needs, wants and desires, and, therefore, one partner does not always get his or her own way. Please comment:

Exercise 3. Reciprocity and Communication

a. Do you believe that reciprocity exists in your relationship?
b. Do you make yourself heard by your partner?
c. Are you doing a good job at communicating your point of view clearly
d. Compare your answers with your partner and discuss them in their pros and cons. Write down what happened during this comparison

Exercise 4. Balanced Assertiveness

a. Would you like your relationship to become more balanced in give and take and in reciprocity?
b. In the next sessions, we will be working on this by role-playing, or practicing, assertiveness and compromise in what we hope will be the beginning of a better balance in your relationship.

Homework

Follow up what you did in the previous exercise during the coming week. To become aware of the times when you asserted yourselves and the times when you were submissive to your partner. Write down when this happens. As awareness is an important initial step toward changing behavior.

Responsibility

ID____**Date**__________

Exercise 1. Assertiveness-Submissiveness

1. Recall and record times when you behaved assertively or submissively
   a.
   b.
   c.

2. How did you feel during this situation? For instance, did you feel anxious, angry, sad, or relaxed? Please explain

Exercise 2. Communication

1. Have you been able to communicate clearly your point of view to your partner?
2. When you want to communicate your point of view to someone else, whose responsibility is it to get the message across?

3. If you do not realize that it is your own responsibility to communicate clearly your needs, likes, and wants, whose responsibility is it?

Exercise 3. Assertiveness Skills:
Although it is our own personal responsibility to assert ourselves, sometimes we lack the proper skills to do so, or sometimes we just feel anxious about asserting ourselves to others. What is needed in these situations is practice, and that is what you are going to be doing—practice asserting yourselves. This also holds true for those who never compromise or listen to others. Again, practicing these skill is important.

Exercise 4. Pretending
Special materials: a large mirror
In the exercises that follows, present various situations to both of you. Try to get into these situations and role-play them through. Remember to follow the instructions carefully.

a. In this exercise, assert yourself to yourself. That is, we will describe a situation, and then you will respond to it. We want you to look into the mirror and talk at yourself. Close your eyes, relax, and listen carefully. You have just returned from the doctor's office, and he has told you that you have a very serious weight problem. You must lose 25 pounds or face serious health complications. You walk into the bedroom, look into the mirror, and strongly tell yourself that you will lose the 25 pounds. Whichever wants of you wants to go first, can go.
b. Rate each other however you like.
c. Both partners need to describe how they felt during the role-playing exercise and rate the other on the following:

    a. Eye contact and facial expression.
    b. Speech fluency and voice loudness.
    c. Duration of assertive statement, and the distance from the image in the mirror.
    d. The items on which you rated each other are just some of the important aspects of asserting ourselves. Praise them for their attempts at the role-playing exercise.

Homework
If you felt uncomfortable during these exercises, during the next week, when you are alone, practice asserting yourself at yourself (at least once a day) in the mirror. Make up your own situations if you wish and practice, keeping in mind the aspects of assertiveness that we just went over. If you felt comfortable with these exercises, observe *your* partner once or twice as he/she practices and give feedback (i.e., constructive criticism) on the areas that need work. Praise your partner when you feel he/she has done a good job of asserting himself/herself.

Continued Practice

ID___________________________________**Date**_____________

Exercise 1. Practice, practice, practice
If you felt uncomfortable in the last exercises:

a. Did you practice asserting yourself in the mirror?
b. How did it go?
c. If you felt comfortable in the last exercises:

    1. Did you observe your partner
    2. What do you think of how he/she did?

Discuss the strengths and weakness behavior of the assertive rehearsals that is practiced by the your partner.

Exercise 2. Role-Playing
a. Keep in mind the important aspects of assertiveness:

    i. Fluency,
    ii. Loudness of voice,
    iii. Eye contact,
    iv. Duration of response,
    v. Distance from the person being talked to, and
    vi. Facial and body expressions.

b. Now please relax and listen carefully, read the following situation: It is Sunday morning and you go outside to get the newspaper. You see that the paper has been thrown clear onto the other side of the lawn rather than on the porch as you have requested. Seeing the newspaper boy down the street, you catch up with him and firmly tell him what he did and how it should have been done. After the more submissive partner is done with the role-play, the other partner needs to judge the response according to the assertive dimensions listed earlier. Was your partner's response satisfactory? Attempt to get constructive criticism and praise. If necessary, have the role-player repeat the response in order to improve upon it.

Exercise 3. Requesting New Behaviors
a. Aside from the aspects of assertiveness with which we have been dealing with can you think of any other aspects of assertiveness that we should work with? One important aspect that comes to mind is requesting new behavior of the person to whom you are asserting yourself, such as telling that person what to do, where to go, to be quiet. If you have been using this technique in your role-playing, fine. If not, use the following example for guidelines: For example, in the last situation you might have asked the newspaper boy to go back and place the paper where it belongs. Repeat the last role-play, incorporating this response. See if you can use this technique in any of the role-playing situations we will do in the future.

Exercise 4. Repeat, Repeat, Repeat
Repeat the role-playing procedure used in the last exercise, using the following two situations:

a. You are driving home on the expressway at 55 miles per hour. All of a sudden a policeman pulls up and motions for you to pull over. He claims that you were doing 65 mph in a 55-mph zone and wants to give you a ticket. You strongly protest that he is mistaken.
b. You have worked the last three Saturday nights. It is finally your turn to be off. Further, you have planned a special evening with your spouse. Your boss comes up to you and says sternly that he needs you to work and orders you to work on your Saturday night off. You present your case authoritatively and refuse to work.

Homework
Each night, spend at least 30 min practicing assertiveness in (number) situations. The dominant partner can suggest situations for the partner to role-play. Discuss the good and the weak points in the behavior rehearsal.

Assertiveness in the Relationship

ID____________________________________Date_________

Exercise 1. Checking on Homework
a. How did the homework go?
b. Do you feel more self-confident as you continue to practice?
c. Have you noticed any improvements in your partner's ability to assert himself/herself?
d. Discuss specific improvements and the aspects that still need work.

Exercise 2. Continuing Role Playing
Up to now, you have been role-playing assertiveness in situations that are irrelevant to your relationship. This time, you are going to advance to situations that are relevant to your relationship. Again, we are going to pose some situations, and you will again role-play them assertively. However, this time we want you, the unassertive partner, to direct your response to (partner's name). The assertive partner's job will be to listen carefully to what is being said to you. However, do not respond to your partner's words—we will work on that shortly. The goal is to get the unassertive partner to practice asserting himself or herself directly to the partner.

Exercise 3. More Role Playing
a. The unassertive partner needs to relax, listen carefully, and try to get into the following situation. You've just come home from work about an hour later than usual. You had to stay late to finish a difficult job. As soon as you walk in the door, your partner comes running up to you, very upset, and says, "Don't tell me you've been working all this time. I know you've been out drinking again." You respond with your side, which is the truth.

b. How do you, the assertive partner, feel about that response? Which aspects of the response were good, or worthy of praise, and which aspects need further improvement.
c. Re-read the scene; let's see how you, the assertive partner, would respond. Your partner needs to watch and listen carefully.
d. Immediately following the response, ask how he (she) felt about the your partner felt about your role-play; then have the unassertive partner try the situation once again, taking cues from the dominant partner's modeled presentation.

Exercise 4. Yet More Role Playing
Repeat the process in the last exercise, using the following situations. The steps are:

1. Unassertive partner role-plays.
2. Listener (and enrichers) gives feedback.
3. Dominant partner models.
4. Unassertive partner gives feedback and role-plays the situation again.

   a. You are watching an exciting football game (soap opera) on the television, and your partner walks in and changes the channel—as she (he) does every time you are watching a good game (soap opera). You protest assertively.
   b. You have invited your mother over for dinner but when you get home, your partner says, "You must un-invite your mother because my mother is coming over (for the third time this week), and you know we can't have them both at the same time since they don't get along." State your point of view firmly.

Homework
Continue working on these types of exercises every night during the next week. Make up your own situations and role-play them. Remember, though, that you do not respond to each other's assertions. You are only role-playing!

Assertive Interactions

ID__________________________________**Date**__________

Up until now, you have practiced assertiveness, but you have not responded to each other's assertive statements. This time, we are going to work on a role-playing situation in which you will respond to each other.

Exercise 1. Receiving Messages
a. The following question is for the dominant partner. What do you think should happen when your partner clearly and appropriately communicates his or her point of view to you?
b. Wouldn't it be appropriate to pay close attention, praise your partner for expressing his/her point of view clearly and either agree (if the position is acceptable to you) or disagree, clearly stating your own position? The consequences are clearly communicated, assertive statements should be listening and considering plus praise plus agreement, or it should be listening and considering plus praise plus disagreement plus expressing the basis for disagreement. Praise does not necessarily mean just saying "good." Praise can be an expression of gratitude,

such as "Thank you for letting me know your point of view" or "I am glad you care enough about our relationship to tell me that."

Exercise 2. Practicing Some More

a. Keep these ideas in mind when you are doing some role-playing. This time, we are going to present a situation, and we want you, the unassertive partner, to respond assertively and clearly to your partner; then you, the dominant partner, will respond. Any questions?
b. You and your partner are standing before the closed front door of your house, and it is late at night. You are having trouble finding your keys and your spouse says to you angrily, "Why did you have to lose your keys now?"
c. After the role-play, both of you answer the following question. How do you feel about the way your partner responded to you? Discuss the good and bad points of each other's response, specifically the important aspects of assertive behavior.

Exercise 3. Assertiveness Versus Anger

a. A crucial point is that assertiveness must not be mixed up with anger—they are not one and the same. What is the difference between assertiveness and anger?
b. How can we act assertively without conveying anger?
c. If we were to rephrase negative, critical statements, using "positive" language, wouldn't we convey our messages without expressing or evolving hostility? Think of a few examples of how this might be done.

Exercise 4. Practicing Assertiveness

a. Repeat the procedure in the previous Exercise for the following situation.
   - □ You have disciplined your son by taking away his bicycle for a week. You go out for a while and come home to find that your spouse has ignored your decision and has allowed the child to go outside with his bike. You protest your spouse's treatment of your decision.
   - □ After a very exhausting day at work, you are not in the mood for sex. However, your spouse is, and he (she) makes sexual advances to you. Despite your tiredness, you decide to respond to your spouse's need and have sex. You begin to get aroused when the phone rings. Your spouse answers the phone and comes back, no longer interested in sex and oblivious to your needs. You respond that you feel unfairly treated.

Homework

During the next week, practice the behaviors you worked on today. That is, whenever a decision or conflict arises, state your case clearly using positive language, and pay close attention to what your partner says to you.

Lifemanship

ID____ ***Date***________

How did it go last week? Were there any instances in which you acted assertively toward each other? Discuss specific instances in which the unassertive partner acted assertively as well as how the dominant partner responded.

Exercise 1. Reviewing Goals

a. Up until now, you have been working on practicing assertive behavior, the unassertive partner, and the way in which you, the dominant partner, respond to that assertiveness. Do you remember what the goals of this workbook are? The goals of the workbook are to foster a balanced give-and-take relationship, including reciprocity and balance, on the dimension of assertiveness.

Exercise 2. Appropriate Assertiveness

□ Because both of you now should dhave a better understanding of assertive behavior, there are a few other important ideas we would like to review. When is it appropriate for us to assert our point of view? What are some examples of situations in which assertiveness would be appropriate?

□ When is it a good idea to not to assert ourselves? The rule here is that we do not assert ourselves when we are certain of the negative outcome from our assertiveness. Shouldn't we refrain from asserting ourselves when we know we are wrong or when our assertiveness might lead to some sort of trouble or negative consequence? Relate specific circumstance (past or hypothetical) in which assertiveness is not a good idea.

Exercise 3. Tact and Diplomacy

□ Also, it is important that we practice what some people have called lifemanship—fancy word for tact and diplomacy. What do these two words mean to you? If they do not understand the words, say: Don't they mean that when we are tactful and diplomatic we are sensitive to other people's feelings and therefore know what to do and say to maintain good relations with others?

Exercise 4. Compromising

□ What does the word compromise mean? How and when do we compromise?

□ We compromise when there is a disagreement or conflict, and the best way to compromise is to state positions clearly and then jointly work toward a position that is satisfactory to both persons. Well, would you agree that you should compromise in situations where there is conflict so that both of you can be satisfied?

Homework

If you learned to be assertive, you may ask to be administered another workbook in whatever area you may need to work on, either alone or with your partner.

Problem Solving in Courtship and Marriage

ID____ ***Date***______________

Exercise 1. Recognizing a Problem

a. When you want something and don't know how to get it or can't agree on how to get it, what do you do?
b. Give some examples.
c. When you are stumped about something, don't you have a problem?
d. What is the first step in solving a problem?

e. Isn't it recognizing and naming the situation as a problem?
f. Now, give some examples of recognizing and naming problems.

Exercise 2. Becoming Involved in Problem Solving

a. When you know you have a problem, what do you do?
b. Do you feel strong enough about it to make an effort to resolve it? Do you usually let the other person have his or her way and try to let the issue pass?
c. Give some examples.
d. Wouldn't you agree that what you do to solve a problem is get involved in solving it?
e. The second step in problem solving is involvement. Can you give some examples of involvement in problem solving?

Exercise 3. Generating Alternatives

a. When you have become involved in a problem, what do you do next?
b. Do you argue constructively or destructively?
c. Shouldn't you try to examine the pros and cons calmly and think of as many ways as you can to solve your problem?
d. How is being more flexible and empathetic (feeling what others feel) useful in generating alternatives that would be satisfactory to both of you?

Exercise 4. Assessing Alternatives and Picking Out the Best

a. When you have listened to the other person's solutions, what should you do next?
b. Shouldn't you pick out the best one?
c. Give an example of this.
d. Don't you need to consider whether a solution is realistic and practical?
e. Will other people let you? Do you have the resources?
f. List all the things you think you should consider in choosing a solution.
g. So the fourth step is what?
h. It is assessing the alternatives and picking out the best solution.

Exercise 5. Taking Action to Solve a Problem and Evaluating the Action

a. Once you decide on a solution, what do you do?
b. You take action. Give some examples.
c. Don't you also need to see whether your solution works?
d. So the fifth and sixth steps in problem solving are what?
e. You try the solution to see whether it works. When your solution works, you feel good and know that you can use it again in a similar situation. Can you give an example of using the six steps?

Homework

During this coming week, apply the steps in problem solving to any problem and see whether you are better organized than you have been in the past.

Developing Communication as a Resource for Problem Solving

ID____________________________________Date_________

Exercise 1. Reviewing Homework

a. How did your homework come out?
b. Did you successfully solve a problem in a way that both of you feel comfortable with?

Exercise 2. Opening Up to Each Other

a. What do you say to each other when you need help?
b. Are you able to send a clear message when you are anxious, angry, sad, happy, calm, or enthusiastic?
c. Give an example of how you appear when you are emotionally worked up.
d. What if you could remember to count to 10 before saying what you want?

Exercise 3. Rational Thinking and Emotion in Communication

a. What are the two basic personality features that all of us have?
b. Aren't they emotional and rational thinking?
c. How is thinking important in sending a clear message?
d. But don't we need emotion to give our messages determination, conviction, zest, and fluency?
e. Shouldn't emotion and thinking be balanced?
f. How should you behave at a wedding, a birthday, a holiday celebration, a funeral?
g. What behaviors would be inappropriate on those occasions?

Exercise 4. Verbal and Nonverbal Communication

a. Whether you are talking or listening, don't you use gestures and signals that communicate what you feel?
b. Are you sure you understand all of each other's hidden cues?
c. Can you name some?
d. Can't your cues contradict what you say if you are not sincere?
e. Shouldn't you learn each other's cues?
f. Why?

Exercise 5. Sensitive

a. How can you become more sensitive to each other and to what the other _ expects of you?
b. Can't you ask each other questions and compare each other's signals?
c. Also, can you study the way other people react at such events as weddings, birthdays, holiday celebrations, or funerals and discuss those reactions later?
d. Can you make it a habit to be more aware, to check and recheck each other's cues? e. Can you try to attend more social events together to develop greater sensitivity?
e. How social are you?
f. How social should you be?

Exercise 6. Monitoring Yourself

a. How can you develop empathy?
b. Don't you think that if you understand the way you feel, you will have more empathy for others?
c. Can you just ask each other how each of you feels and whether your behavior is appropriate?
d. We'd like you to spend 5 min imagining emotionally stressful events; then discuss those events.
e. Can you let yourself go—cry, laugh, rage, express some strong emotion?

Homework

In the coming week, plan to attend some event together with someone and compare each other's words, feelings, and nonverbal cues. See if you can give each other clear emotional cues.

Developing Conflict as a Resource for Problem Solving

ID____________________________________**Date**_________

Exercise 1. Reviewing Homework

a. How well did you learn to send clear emotional messages to each other in your homework? In this session we hope you are going to see how to develop even the conflict between you and between your goals as a resource for problem solving.

Exercise 2. Understanding Your Own Conflict

a. What do you do when you are in a dilemma?
b. Do you backtrack and take a second look?
c. Do you flip a coin, either figuratively or literally?
d. Shouldn't how you feel about the dilemma be your guide in how to handle it?
e. How good do you think you are in a dilemma?
f. Can you imagine several dilemmas and practice handling them?

Exercise 3. Mutual Conflict Techniques

a. How do you resolve or not resolve a conflict between you?
b. Do you listen to each other, or are you more interested in having your own way (as well as the last word)?
c. What signs of handling conflict poorly do you see in each other?
d. Can you see how unpleasant these habits are to your partner?
e. Could you try to be more patient, perhaps counting to 10 or 20 before having your final say?
f. What do you think about the saying "two heads are better than one" in your case?

Exercise 4. Positive Conflict

a. In what ways are your conflicts positive?
b. How can you be more positive?
c. Couldn't you make a habit of pausing and hearing out the other's side before expressing your feelings on the issue?
d. Would this be hard to do?

e. Wouldn't it show greater strength to swallow your pride and be patient?
f. How much does being calm contribute to a rational judgment that you won't regret later?
g. How could you disagree "agreeably"?
h. Isn't being close more important than just winning an argument?

Exercise 5. Sharing a Goal of Making Conflict a Resource

a. How can you improve your conflict techniques together?
b. After each conflict, can you try to analyze each other's negative habits?
c. Could you discuss them and make a pact to drop negative habits?
d. Shouldn't you reward each other for positive conflict habits so that you will learn to use the positive approach more than the negative?
e. How might you reward each other for making conflict positive rather than negative?
f. Might the best approach be to agree on and reassure each other in using the positive approach?

Exercise 6. Developing Better Conflict Techniques

a. Now that you understand about negative and positive habits in conflict, how can you make your conflicts more positive?
b. Couldn't you be more patient and open?
c. Couldn't you be mature enough to admit it when you are wrong?
d. Couldn't you perhaps train yourselves to stick to the issues, not personalities?
e. Can you forget about having the last word?
f. What else can you do?
g. Wouldn't disagreeing "agreeably" bring you closer together and improve your ability to solve problems?

Homework

During the coming week, try writing down what you do in a conflict. Discuss each other's negative and positive habits in conflict, and try to reward the positive ones.

This experimental workbook is included to illustrate how passive evaluation can be converted into a systematically interactive series of practice exercises. The behaviors included in Exercise 1 could be administered as evaluation by eliminating definitions and examples and asking participants to rate them on a three or five point scale from Always, Sometimes, or Never giving 2 points for behaviors rated Always, five one point for behavior rated Sometimes, and 0 points given for never, separating Odd and Even scores into two scores for

Depression in Youth

The purpose of this workbook is to help you deal with sad and unhappy feelings, thoughts, and behaviors that are painful to you and make it hard for you to do well in school, outside the school, and, perhaps, at home. This beginning practice exercise tries to help you learn more about these behaviors that are sad and unhappy to you.

Exercise 1. Definitions

Name__________________________________Gender____Date_____

The purpose of this practice exercise is to understand more fully what depression means to you.

---

1. Give the meaning of each behavior listed below as you understand it. Give two examples to make sure you understand each meaning. It might take you more than a day to write down all these meanings and their examples. Take your time. After you have completed this list, go to Exercise No. 2.

===

Behaviors **Meanings and Examples**

---

a. Feeling like I am a bad person

....

....

Example 1

....

....

Example 2

....

....

---

b. Feeling dumb and stupid

....

....

Example 1

....

....

Example 2

....

....

---

c. Thinking I am ugly

....

....

Example 1

....

....

Example 2

....

....

---

d. Thinking most other children or teen-agers hate me

....

....

Example 1

....
....

Example 2

....
....

----

e. Wishing I could run away

....
....

Example 1

....
....

Example 2

....
....

----

f. Having trouble getting along with other children or teen-agers

....
....

Example 1

....
....

Example 2

....
....

----

g. Feeling like killing myself

....
....

Example 1

....
....

Example 2

....
....

----

h. Hating myself

....
....

Example 1

....
....

Example 2

....
....

----

i. Feeling like things don't matter anymore

....
....

Example 1

....
....

Example 2

....
....

----

j. Causing problems for everybody

....

....
Example 1
....
....
Example 2
....
....
----

k. Feeling tired all the time
....
....
Example 1
....
....
Example 2
....
....
----

l. Feeling listless often
....
....
Example 1
....
....
Example 2
....
....
----

m. Easily upset
....
....
Example 1
....
....
Example 2
....
....
----

n. Getting down on myself easily
....
....
Example 1
....
....
Example 2
....
....
----

o. Feeling nervous and edgy
....
....
Example 1
....
....
Example 2
....
....
----

p. Having few friends

Example 1

Example 2

---

q. Feeling unusually fearful

Example 1

Example 2

---

r. Seeming too serious minded

Example 1

Example 2

---

s. Unable to enjoy life

Example 1

Example 2

---

t. Feeling sad very often

Example 1

Example 2

---

u. Feeling sullen often

Example 1

Example 2

....

----

v. Not knowing how to have a good time

....

....

Example 1

....

....

Example 2

....

....

w. Lacking in self-confidence

....

....

Example 1

....

....

Example 2

....

....

----

x. Depending too much on others

....

....

Example 1

....

....

Example 2

....

....

----

y. Lacking in sense of humor

....

....

Example 1

....

....

Example 2

....

....

----

z. Feeling sick often

....

....

Example 1

....

....

Example 2

....

....

----

xy. Not liking to go to school

....

....

Example 1

....

....

Example 2

....

....

---

xz. Feeling lonely

....

....

Example 1

....

....

Example 2

....

....

---

yz. Spending a lot of time sleeping or lying around

....

....

Example 1

....

....

Example 2

....

....

---

xyz. Thinking of myself as a failure

....

....

Example 1

....

....

Example 2

....

....

==

Exercise 2. Rank-ordering Behaviors

Go back to your definitions and examples and rank-order the behaviors defined above according to how hurtful and painful they are to you. Rank-order as No. 1 the most hurtful and painful behavior, rank as No. 2 the nest hurtful behavior until you reach a behavior or behaviors that are not hurtful or painful to you (N/A).

Behaviors	**Rank-Order**
a. Feeling like I am a bad person	_______
b. Feeling dumb and stupid .	_______
c. Thinking I am ugly .	_______
d. Thinking most other children or teen-agers hate me	_______
e. Wishing I could run away	_______
f. Having trouble getting along with other children or teen-agers	_______
g. Feeling like killing myself	_______
h. Hating myself	_______
i. Feeling like things don't matter anymore	_______
j. Causing problems for everybody	_______
k. Feeling tired all the time	_______
l. Feeling listless often	_______
m. I am easily upset	_______
n. Getting down on myself easily	_______
o. Feeling nervous and edgy	_______
p. Having few friends	_______
q. Feeling unusually fearful	_______
r. Seeming too serious minded	_______
s. Unable to enjoy life	_______
t. Feeling sad very often .	_______
u. Feeling sullen often .	_______
v. Not knowing how to have a good time	_______
w. Lacking in self-confidence	_______
x. Depending too much on others	_______
y. Lacking in sense of humor	_______
z. Feeling sick often	_______
xy. Not liking to go to school	_______
xz. Feeling lonely	_______
yz. Spending a lot of time sleeping or lying around	_______
xyz. Thinking of myself as a failure	_______

3. Why did you rank-ordered these behaviors they way you did? Please explain:

....

....

....

....

Homework: During the coming week, think about these behaviors and how you rank-ordered them. Perhaps, the more you approach these behaviors instead of avoiding them, the easier it will be for you to forget about them and for them to have an effect on your behavior. Before going on with the next practice exercise, you need to answer these two questions in writing:

(1). What will happen to you if you go on with the same sad and unhappy behaviors?

....

....

....

....

(2) What would happen to you if you were to change these behaviors from sad to contented and from unhappy to pleasant?

....

....

....

....

Standard Practice Exercise for Depression in Youth

Exercise No.___Title (name behavior)__________________

Name____________________________Gender______Date_____

The purpose of this practice exercise is to understand more about the behavior listed in the title above. Put in the Title behaviors that were rank-ordered from 1 to 6, completing one exercise at one time

1. How does this behavior apply to you? Please explain in detail:

....
....
....
....
....
....

2. How often do you behave this way?
a. Practically every day____
b. Once a week_____
c. Couple of times a month___
d. Once a month_____
e. Once every six months_____
f. Once a year_____
g. Once every few years______
Please explain further:

....
....
....
....
....
....

3. How did this behavior come about? Do you remember when it started? Check which answer fits best:
a. When I was a child (younger than 5 years of age)____
b. When I was in elementary school____
c. When I was in middle school____
d. When I was in high school_____.
e. Any other time______
Please explain further:

....
....
....
....
....
....

4. Is this behavior acceptable (OK) or unacceptable (non OK) to you? Why is this behavior acceptable (OK) to you? Why is it unacceptable (Not OK) to you?
Please explain:

....
....
....
....
....
....

5. Give 3 specific examples of how this behavior was hurtful and painful to you in the past:

Example 1:

Example 2:

Example 3:

6. Give 3 specific examples of how this behavior is hurtful and painful to you now:

Example 1:

Example 2:

Example 3:

7. Give 3 specific examples of how this behavior will hurtful and painful to you in the future:

Example 1:

Example 2:

Example 3:

Homework

Next week pretend (make up on paper in writing) to bring about or repeat this hurtful and painful behavior at pre-set times (for instance, at 8 am, 12 noon, 4 or 7 pm), at least three times (Mondays, Wednesdays, and Fridays or Tuesdays, Thursdays, and Saturdays. It may sound strange to you to be asked to repeat this behavior, especially when it is so hurtful and painful to you. However, keep in mind that *if you can start it, you can control it*. If you can learn to control it, you may be able to let go of it. Otherwise, this behavior may come back when you will be the one who is hurt.

For each time you pretend (make up) this behavior, write down what you thought would happen in detail. Make sure to answer in writing the following four questions:

a. what behavior did you start?
b. how did you start it?
c. how did it end?
d. what did this behavior get you?

Time 1 (write time you started__________):
a...
b...
c...
d...
Time 2 (write time you started__________):
a...
b...
c...
d...
Time 3 (write time you started__________):
a...
b...
c...
d...

Please, check which of the following shows how you feel about this practice exercise:

a. Completely useless-_____
b. Somewhat useless–_____
c. So-so ————-_____
d. Somewhat useful–-_____
e. Extremely useful–-_____

Explain in greater detail how you feel about this practice exercise and what you got out of it:
....
....
....
....
....
....

Concluding Follow-up Practice Exercise for Depression in Youth

Name________________________________ID______________Date__

The purpose of this practice exercise is to review whether this practice exercise was helpful to you or not.

1. Please answer which answer fits how you feel about this practice exercise:
   a. I did not like working on this practice exercise at all. I wish I never saw it ____
   b. I did not like this practice exercise at all, but I am glad I got to work on it_____
   c. I am delighted I got a chance to work on this practice exercise_______
   d. I am not only delighted about working on this practice exercise but I wish all children who suffer from the same painful experience had a chance to work on it_____
2. How helpful was it to work on this practice exercise? Please check the answer that applies to you.
   a. Not helpful at all____
   b. Somewhat helpful____
   c. Helpful_____
   d. Very helpful_____
3. Which practice exercise did you *like best or was it most helpful to you*? Please rank-order practice exercises from the one you liked best or was most helpful to you (Rank No. 1) to the one you liked next best (rank No. 2) and to on, to the one you did not like at all or that did not apply to you (N/A):

Behaviors **Rank-Order**

---

a. Feeling like I am a bad person ------------------------------------_______
b. Feeling dumb and stupid .--_______
c. Thinking I am ugly .---_______
d. Thinking most other children or teen-agers hate me------------_______
e. Wishing I could run away ---------------------------------------_______
f. Having trouble getting along with other children or teen-agers _______
g. Feeling like killing myself ---------------------------------------_______
h. Hating myself --_______
i. Feeling like things don't matter anymore -------------------------_______
j. Causing problems for everybody ----------------------------------_______
k. Feeling tired all the time--_______
l. Feeling listless often --- _______
m. I am easily upset --- _______
n. Getting down on myself easily -----------------------------------_______
o. Feeling nervous and edgy ---_______
p. Having few friends --- _______
q. Feeling unusually fearful ---_______
r. Seeming too serious minded ------------------------------------_______
s. Unable to enjoy life --_______
t. Feeling sad very often .--_______
u. Feeling sullen often .---_______
v. Not knowing how to have a good time -------------------------_______
w. Lacking in self-confidence ---------------------------------------_______
x. Depending too much on others ---------------------------------_______
y. Lacking in sense of humor -------------------------------------- _______
z. Feeling sick often --_______
xy. Not liking to go to school -------------------------------------_______
xz. Feeling lonely ---_______
yz. Spending a lot of time sleeping or lying around ---------------_______
xyz. Thinking of myself as a failure---------------------------------_______

==

4. Why did you rank-ordered practice exercises the way you did? Please explain your reason(s) for your rank-order of practice exercises:

....
....
....
....
....
....

5. Feel free to write any comments that might improve this practice exercise.

....
....
....
....
....
....

==

Equality

*ID*______________________________________*Date*_________

Exercise 1. Old Roles: Advantages and Disadvantages of Old Roles

Exercise 1. Responsibility Without Authority

What is the difference between Responsibility, that is: carrying out chores, versus Authority, that is, making decisions on who and what should take responsibility?

a. Authority without Responsibility: One can make decisions on who and what should be done without any responsibility.

Exercise 2. Responsibilities and Chores

a. Who has the responsibility in which particular areas in this family?
b. Make lists, one for each of you, including

    i. income
    ii. household chores
    iii. paying bills
    iv. yard work
    v. *Shopping*

Exercise 3. Role Reversal

a. Role-play a situation in which both of you are taking care of responsibilities, but you play each other's part. Here is an example: The husband coming home after a day of work to the wife who's had a day of kids and housework—the husband plays the wife and vice versa. After role-play each of you needs to answer the following questions:
b. How did it feel to be in your spouse's shoes?
c. How did it feel to see how you appear to others?

Exercise 4. Perks and Privileges

a. Who has particular privileges in this family?
b. Make lists, one for each of you, including

    i. who has the final say
    ii. who gets to spend an evening out each week
    iii. who makes decisions without responsibilities

Exercise 5. Privileges and Responsibilities

a. Role-play a situation in which one of you is meeting a responsibility and the other is enjoying a privilege. Each of you plays the part of your spouse. Example: The wife cooks dinner while the husband watches television or reads the newspaper.
b. After the role-play, answer the following question: How did it feel to be in your partner's place?

Homework
In the coming week, make a list of at least 10 advantages and 10 disadvantages that each of you has in your roles. Make sure you are specific. Write the advantages for the one of you on one side of a piece of paper and the disadvantages on the other. Do the same for the other. You will probably find that the husband's advantages are social, but his disadvantages are psychological. The wife's disadvantages may be both psychological and social. Keep in mind the husband may have psychological disadvantages, such as tension from his job, inability to express sadness.

Femininity Masculinity

ID____________________________________Date__________

Exercise 1. Femininity

a. Each spouse answers the following question:
   - □ What does femininity mean to you?
   - □ Now what does your spouse think?
   - □ Do you agree with what your spouse just said?
   - □ What does femininity mean to you?
   - □ List your answers.

Exercise 2. Masculinity

a. Ask the spouse who did not answer first in the preceding exercise:
   i. What does masculinity mean to you? Let him or her answer, and then ask the partner:
   ii. Do you agree with what your spouse just said?
   iii. What does masculinity mean to you?

b. List your answers.

Exercise 3 Overlaps

a. Do you see any overlap between these two lists?
b. If there is overlap, what do you think the overlap means?
c. Can we say that the overlap is characteristic of human beings?

Exercise 4. Differences

a. Where do the differences in the lists come from?
b. Are they due to stereotyping or are they true distinctions?
c. Go over each item in the lists and cross out the items you agree are due to stereotyping.

Exercise 5. Are They Real?

a. What can we conclude about true distinctions between men and women?
b. Can we conclude that, aside from physical differences, the differences between men and women are individual, not gender, differences?

Exercise 6. Uniqueness

a. All of us value our distinct qualities, which makes us unique. What satisfactions do you value and want to preserve in this relationship?
b. Keep a list as they respond. You have agreed, then, that you want to keep the following distinctions in your relationship: (*read the list*).

Responsibilities

***ID*____*Date*______**

Exercise 1. The Meaning of Responsibility

□ During the first exercise each of you made a list of your responsibilities. We often overlook the fact that our primary responsibility is for and to ourselves. What does "responsibility for yourself" mean?
□ A responsibility that should not be delegated to someone else.
□ Can responsibility for yourself mean taking responsibility for your behavior?

Exercise 2. Do Something for Yourself

□ All of us have a responsibility to ourselves to allow ourselves to grow and to enjoy life. Please think of something that you would like to do for yourself.
□ Be specific. Write down what each you say. Be sure that it is something that you can do at least once in the following week.
□ Now sign these contracts agreeing to whatever you said during the following week. Each spouse needs a copy of his or her contract.

Exercise 3. Knowing Yourself

□ We also have the responsibility to know ourselves. That means knowing and accepting as human our limitations as well as recognizing our strengths.
□ A strength that each of you has is the courage to ask for help in your marriage and caring enough about each other to want help.
□ Name five other strengths that you see in yourself.
□ You may want to alternate between the spouses, but make sure you each name five.
□ Another strength you may have is the willingness to learn from your errors.

Exercise 4. Setting Limits

□ If we know ourselves, we can know the issues on which we are willing to compromise and those on which we won't budge. We can then set limits and communicate those limits clearly to others.
□ This is a responsibility each of us has to your marriage. How do you communicate your limits to each other?
□ It may be helpful to discuss a recent and specific instance. Describe exactly what you both said and felt. Would it have helped if you had been clear in your own mind about what you wanted?
□ Try communicating more positively. Can you rephrase more positively what you said in that instance?

Homework

During the week, please be sure to keep your contracts with yourselves and try to rephrase your negative statements more positively.

Sharing Feelings

ID____________________________________***Date***_________

Exercise 1. Defining Yourself

- □ One way we can define ourselves—and an important aspect of marriage—is to share feelings with a spouse.
- □ How do you share your feelings?

Exercise 2. Feelings and Rejection

a. Are there some feelings you can't share because you are ashamed or fear that you'll be rejected?
b. Remember that any feelings you have is a feeling that many other people have. When we love and respect a person, we also respect that person's feelings. Do you agree with that?

Exercise 3. Steps in Sharing

There are several steps that may help you in sharing your feelings.

a. First, be sure you pick a time and place in which you will not be interrupted. Get your spouse's attention; be sure you are being heard.
b. Next, state your feelings clearly. If you have a negative feeling to express, such as anger, try to state it constructively. Stick to the issue, give the rational basis for your feeling, and, if you are asking your partner to do something about the issue, express a reasonable thing that your partner can do.
c. Finally, allow your spouse to give you feedback. Remember that both of you should try to state your feelings positively. Refer back to the steps if needed.
d. Now, one spouse, think of a feeling that you have recently wanted to share with your spouse but have not been able to.

Remembering the steps, role-play sharing that feeling now. Remember eye contact, tone of voice, and gestures. If you remembered all these things, you are half way home.

Exercise 4. Practice in Sharing Feelings

- □ Now it's the other spouses turn. Think of a feeling you want to share and would like to practice.
- □ If you have time, have each spouse role-play a second feeling. If the first feeling shared was a positive one; suggest that the second be a negative.

Homework

During the week practice sharing your feelings with each other using the steps given above. Remember, when you share your feelings and making sure that you are heard, you are saying that you are important, that you count.

Achieving Equality

***ID*___________________________________*Date*_________**

Exercise 1. Checking on Homework

a. The goal of this exercise is to review the sessions, showing that each one has provided a basis for equality between the spouses.
b. How did the week go?
c. Did you practice sharing your feelings with each other in a positive way?

Exercise 2. Ways to Achieve Equality

a. The purpose of this exercise is to help you achieve equality. What does that mean to you?
b. Does equality mean being the same, or can two different people be equal? In a previous exercise we talked about masculine and feminine roles, and you agreed on the distinctions you want to preserve. This was a conscious choice that you based on neutral grounds rather than on stereotypes. Would you agree that equality is neutral?

Exercise 3. Equality and Growth

a. Do you think that by taking responsibility for your own behavior and for your growth, you can approach your marriage as an individual on equal footing with your partner and help your marriage grow?
b. Please comments at will to answer the question above.

Exercise 4. Feelings and Equality

- □ Last week you learned how to share feelings with each other. How does being able to share feelings help you achieve equality?
- □ By sharing feelings we assert our importance so that neither of us is dehumanized.
- □ Please comment about the statement above.

Exercise 5. Equality and Sexuality

a. Another area in which equality is important is your lovemaking. One spouse needs to answer the following question.
   i. Do you feel equal to your partner when it comes to sex? Are you free to be an individual or free to choose the role you want to play?
   ii. The other spouse needs to answer the following question. How do you feel about what your partner said?
b. To have equality in your marriage means to be equal in every area, to be able to voice your feelings, and to have a choice. Can you agree on roles that would satisfy both of you?

Exercise 6. Adding Topics

Are there any other general concepts or areas you'd like to discuss tonight? If you discuss other areas, recognize each other's individuality and base any decisions on neutral grounds rather than stereotypes.

New Roles

***ID*_______________________________________*Date*__________**

Exercise 1. Doing for Yourself

- ☐ Because equality requires two equal individuals who are responsible themselves, we want you to think just in terms of yourself.
- ☐ What are 10 things that each of you would like to do for yourself? Each spouse should make a list. Be sure that each item is specific.
- ☐ Rather than an abstraction such as "take care of my body," try something more specific, such as "I will give myself a manicure once a week."
- ☐ List items that can be done at least once a week.

Exercise 2. Deciding Among Chores

- ☐ Stop after you both have 10 items. Now that you can approach the problem as equals and on neutral grounds, consider your responsibilities in your marriage.
- ☐ Divide the items up and decide who will do what. Write these down, too.
- ☐ Make sure they are specific and cover things such as spending time with the kids, household responsibilities, working in the yard and, paying the bills.
- ☐ After the lists have been made, make copies for both of you of what you both will do for yourselves and what you both will do for their marriage.

Exercise 3. Contracting

Do agree to these items by signing a contract with each other? You both need to sign and keep copies. Remember that you can renegotiate problem areas.

For additional Exercises related to Equality consults similar PIPEs in this volume and in previous publications.

Non-traditional Families

ID_______________________________________Date__________

Exercise 1. Identity and the Meaning of Parents

a. Do you know anything about your biological parents? If the answer is yes, continue this exercise; if the answer is no, end this exercise after this exercise. What does it mean to be a parent? What do parents do that make them different from other people?
b. Parents, then, are more than just the people who give birth to you. Your parents are the people who teach you and love you and feed you and provide a home for you.
c. How do you feel about these questions?

Exercise 2. Parents and Identity

a. (Child's name) has two sets of parents: biological parents and adopted parents.
b. Part of what makes each of us a person and helps answer the question "Who am 1?" is knowing something about the past—where we were born and what our parents were like.
c. Ask the adopted child: What do you know about your biological parents?

d. As the parents is there anything that you can add to this information about (child's name)'s biological parents?
e. Can you describe the physical descriptions of the biological parents?

Exercise 3. Who Am I?

a. What can all this information tell us about (child's name) as a person?
b. How does this help answer the question "Who am I?"
c. Try to think of comments that may give the child a physical identity, such as "(Child's name) will probably be tall because his father was tall," or comments that support a social identity, such as "(child's name) is very creative. His biological mother was artistic, also."
d. You could also encourage a statement from your adopted child by saying, "(Child's name), what can you tell me about yourself if I ask you, "Who are you?""

Exercise 4. Self and Environment

Especially if the parents know little about the biological parents, emphasize the importance of the following discussion about environmental influences on one's personality. Now you can probably see that if we know something about our biological parents, we have a better idea about why we look the way we do and why we might have certain talents. However, there is another part of our lives that is even more important in helping us understand ourselves.

a. What do you think this is?
b. The parents who raise you and love you are very important in helping you become a person. Ask any or all of your children: What sort of things, (child's name), do you know about your mother and father?

Exercise 5. Self and Identity

a. The following question is for the children. What does your knowledge of your parents tell you about yourselves, and how does it help you answer the question "Who am I?"
b. The following question is for the parents. Do you agree? Is there anything you would like to add?

Homework

During the coming week think and share with each other what it means to be oneself. Keep notes of what has been discussed and shared by everybody in the family.

Family Relations

ID____ ***Date***__________

Exercise 1. Draw a Family Picture

a. You needs to draw a picture of your family as you see it. Do this in no more than 5 min. Show everyone your picture and tell them about it. Make sure while sharing your picture you explain the placement of each person in the drawing.
b. How do you feel about your family pictures? Do you like them?
c. If you do not like a picture, explain why.

Exercise 2. Sibling Rivalry

a. Do you children do any bickering or fighting?
b. If the answer is yes, everyone in the family needs to answer the question: Why do you think the children fight with each other?

Exercise 3. Stop- Bickering

a. Parents, what do you do when your children fight or bicker?
b. If applicable: The next time your children start fighting you might want to have a time-out period to allow things to cool down. Does everyone know what a time-out period is?
c. During a time-out period each child is sent to a separate place to be alone for a specified time.
d. What do you think of the idea?

Exercise 4. Order your children to bicker

As long as the children bicker they are in control. Assume control by instructing them to bicker at a specific time (when both parents are home) and for a specific period of time (e. g., 15 min by the clock).

Exercise 5. Favorites

a. Children, do you think that your parents compare you with each other?
b. If they say yes, how does it make you feel to be compared with your sibling?
c. If the children answer no, parents, do you find yourselves comparing your children? If they say yes, everyone answer the question, why is it unfair to compare one person with another?

Exercise 6. Competition

a. Children, do you feel that you have to compete with your sibling for your parents' attention?
b. Everyone answer the following question. Do you think (child's name) gets special attention because (he/she) is adopted?
c. If yes, how does this make you feel, and what do you think you could do to change it?

Homework

During the coming week, if you children start to fight, stop and think of the real reason you're fighting. If you can't come to an agreement with each other, then you, (parents' names), should use a time-out period to cool things down then follow the instructions of Exercise 4 by giving them 15 min to fight.

Adoption and Extra familial Relationships

***ID*____*Date*________**

Exercise 1. Introduction to exercises

a. Did everyone here have a chance to do the homework assignment?
b. How did the time-out work? What happened?
c. What does your adoption mean to your relatives, friends, and neighbors, and how it makes you feel?

Exercise 2. The Reactions of Others

a. Do you have any friends in school or neighbors or friends at work who know about (child's name)'s adoption?
b. How do people react when they find out that (child's name) is adopted?

Exercise 3. Feelings

c. How does it make you feel to have people act this way when they find out you're adopted?
d. Does it bother you that people know that (child's name) is adopted? Is it a problem?

Exercise 4. A Private or a Public Matter

a. If you say that it is a problem, ask your child: Who is going to define your relationships with your family? Who is going to tell you whether or not it is important that you're adopted?
b. Do all of you tend to listen to other people's gossip, or do you consider it none of their business?
c. Is adoption a public matter, or is it something private to this family?

Exercise 5. Relationships

The fact that (child's name) is adopted should not interfere with (his/her) relationships with other people. (Child's name) you should be able to get to know people on the basis of who you are and what you are as an individual. The fact that you're adopted should not be the most important thing. What do you think? Do you agree or what?

Homework

We'd like you to do some homework again this week. We want you to think of positive things about each other that have nothing to do with adoption. Think of good things about each other as individuals.

Excessive Attitudes in Families

ID___________________________________**Date**____________

Exercise 1. Definition and Extremes

a. One of the things that gets in the way of our happiness is trying to be perfect. What does it mean to be perfect?
b. Ok, so being perfect is impossible. What happens to someone who tries to be perfect?
c. If we try to be perfect, you will fail. Does that mean we should n't try to do our best?
d. Then do we agree that we should do our best but we need not expect to be perfect?

Exercise 2. Trying to Be Perfect

a. A person who tries to be perfect is always on tiptoe, reaching for the impossible. Stand on your tiptoes and put your arms up in the air as if you were reaching for the sky.
b. What happens to you when you stand on your tiptoes like that?
c. It's hard to stand on tiptoes very long without losing your balance.

Exercise 3. Failing to Be Perfect

a. Sometimes members of your family may expect you to be perfect. They send you messages to let you know they don't like what you are doing. Take turns acting outme of the ways that family members show they dislike what you've done—act without talking. You may make sounds and use your face and body. Who will go first?
b. Who can make up a very short story to tell what might have happened to evoke the look or the sounds (name) has acted out? No one is allowed to talk except the storyteller. The story may be real or fantasy. Be sure each family member has a turn.

Exercise 4. Disappointing One Another

a. Now, think about how you feel when you know you've disappointed someone. Go around the circle and ask each of you needs to complete this sentence: "I often disappoint (family member's name) when I fail to…."
b. After each person completes answer the following question: "How does it make you feel when you know you've disappointed someone you love and who loves you?

Exercise 4. Asking for Help

a. There are some things that all of us want to do better, but sometimes we need help. If you can't ask your family for help, who can you ask? Think for a minute about something you'd like to do better and who in this family could help you.
b. Now, we'd like all of you to say what you'd like to do better. Then tell the other family members how they could help.

Homework

During this week, choose one room in the house to keep in perfect order. If you have your own bedroom, you could keep it perfectly this week. Discuss it as a family so that everyone has a room or a section of a room to keep perfectly. Next week we will talk about what it was to like keep a room in perfect order.

Overcoercion

ID____________________________________**Date**__________

Exercise 1. Discussing Homework (Perfectionism)

a. Discuss the homework you did for this week. How did it feel to try to keep things perfectly?
b. What did you learn from your homework?

Exercise 2. Definition and Extremes

a. Let's talk about giving and receiving orders. What does it mean to be a dictator?
b. To be a dictator, then, is to order someone around, to direct and redirect someone's activities. Who in this family always likes being told what to do and how to do it?
c. Would you agree that the person who is ordered around begins to feel unable to think for himself or herself? The things that person wants to do are always being interrupted.
d. What is the opposite of being ordered around?
e. If we were never told to do anything we wouldn't feel a part of the family. We need to be told some things so that we can learn.

Exercise 3. Too Many Demands

a. In this exercise, see how it feels to have too many demands. One of you should to go to the center of a circle and stand, comfortably balanced. Then your family will gently but firmly pull at different parts of your body when they are told to do it. Who will be first? If no one volunteers, ask a parent. Now, stand comfortably. The rest of you, take her or him by the leg, the arm, the shoulders. Now, firmly but gently, pull. Let each member have a turn inside the circle. How does it feel to be pulled in so many directions?

Exercise 4. Giving Orders

a. We use certain looks or body motions when we order someone around. Show all of us some of the ones you've noticed in this family.
b. Without talking take turns ordering someone around. Feel free to get up and use your hands, arms, legs, face, to get your message across.

Exercise 5. Not Needing Orders

a. All of us do some things for ourselves and for others without being told to do them. Think of three things you do without being told. Who will start?
b. Are there some things that you would like to try doing without direction? Think about it a minute, and then one of the parent can start. What is something you'd like to do without directions?

Homework

a. How many of you know the game Slave for a Day?
b. If someone has played it, let that person tell the family about it. This is going to be your homework. Set up a schedule so that each of you has a day to be slave. The one who is slave for that day must do everything the family asks from 5:00 p.m. until bedtime.

Oversubmission

ID____________________________________***Date***________

Exercise 1. Homework Discussion (Overcoercion)

a. Let's talk about your homework. How did each of you feel about being a slave?
b. How did each of you feel ordering the slave around?
c. What did you learn from the homework?

Exercise 2. Definition and Extremes

a. What does it mean to be a servant?
b. A servant waits on people, doing things for them that they could do for themselves. What happens to a person for whom things are done that the person could do for himself or herself?
c. Would you agree that that person becomes selfish and demanding and isn't given a chance to learn to do for himself or herself?
d. What happens to a person who never has anything done for him or her?
e. Doing some things for people shows we love them.

Exercise 3. Slavery Versus Sharing

a. Use this part of the exercise only if the family has not done the Slave for a Day as homework. Now we must lean how it feels to be a servant. Take a turn in the center of the circle and show the family what a servant is. Don't talk; just use your body to show us that you are a servant.
b. What is the difference between being a servant to someone and sharing in family work?
c. It seems that when you are a servant to someone in the family, you are teaching that person to take unfair advantage of the family, but when you are sharing in family work, you are learning to do your part.
d. What is the difference between a slave and a servant?

Exercise 4. Identifying Your Share

a. All of us can help with family work. Different people, because of their size and experience, can do different things for the family. What are some other things that limit what we can do to help? Some examples in include age, sex, special abilities, time away from home, health, and special interests.
b. Then there are things we need to think about in deciding who does what in the family work. In this exercise, describe three things you can do to help in the family work. Take a minute to think about it.
c. Who would like to go first in telling the family three things you can do as your share?

Exercise 5. Showing Love

a. There are many ways of showing love to family members without being a servant to them. You are each going to get a turn to express love to the family member sitting to your left. There is only one rule: You can't do anything that someone else has already done.
b. Everyone has to show a different way to say "I care for you."

Homework

a. Tthis week, we'd like you to play a game called Queen or King for a Day. Have you ever played that?
b. In this game, every family member gets a day off. The day you are queen or king, all of you have to do are the things that nobody else in the family can do for you. For example, (father's name) has to go to work, but he doesn't have to get the paper, empty the trash, turn the TV channel, get his own slippers. The servants in

the house can do those things for him. Who do you think the servants are the day one is the king?

c. The rest of you are the servants. All of you will get a chance to be queen or king and you will get even more chances to be a servant. You might want to make up a schedule for the week to see that everyone gets a turn to be queen or king.

Overindulgence

***ID*______________________________________*Date*________**

Exercise 1. Homework Discussion (Oversubmission)

a. How did your homework go this week?
b. How did you like being queen or king for a day?
c. How did you feel about being a servant?
d. How do you think you'd feel after a month of being a servant?
e. What did you learn from your homework?

Exercise 2. Definition and Extremes

a. What does it mean to be spoiled?
b. Would you agree that to be spoiled is to be given too much of something such as time, toys, clothes, or other things?
c. What happens to a person who is given too much?
d. Do we agree that a person who is given too much becomes unhappy? That person learns to expect more things all the time, without putting out any effort. How does the person feel whose family never gives him or her enough time or things?
e. That person may feel very mistreated and unloved. Please comment at will.

Exercise 3. Whining

a. Spoiled people tend to whine and complain a lot. Most of us complain some. Think back over the past week and think of a complaint you made or wanted to make. Take turns and make your complaint to your family—whine about it. Really feel sorry for yourself while you are whining. Think about it for a minute first.
b. Who would like to start?
c. How did you feel when you were whining and complaining?
d. How did you feel watching and hearing someone else whine and complain?

Exercise 4. Giving

a. To be happy, we must give as well as take. To know what to give someone, we must know what that person needs or likes. Have each family member make up a pretend present and have each tell why they think the recipient will like it.
b. Who would like to start?
c. When we are given everything we don't learn how to go after what we want. We learn to complain and make up excuses instead of acting. Please comment at will.

Exercise 5. Changing

a. Think of something you'd like to change and tell the family what it is. The thing you want to change may be in yourself, your family, or outside your family.

b. Now, list all the reasons you can't change what you want to change. Tell whether you think each reason is real or an excuse.
c. Anyone in the family who disagrees with you may say why, but we don't have time to argue about it now.

Exercise 6. Recognizing Your Abilities
a. Using your abilities is very satisfying.
b. Make up a short commercial or an ad for yourself that tells some of the things you do best. Take a few minutes to think of a commercial that really sells you.
c. Don't be afraid to brag; after all, it's a commercial. Whenever you are ready you can present your commercial.

Homework
During this week each of you should do a good deed for every member of the family. Remember to write down what you do for each family member so that we can talk about it next time.

Enjoying Bad Health

ID**______________________________________*****Date*****__________**

Exercise 1. Homework Discussion (Overindulgence)
a. Who will start us off by describing the good deed you did for each family member?
b. How did it feel to have a good deed done for you by a family member?
c. What did you learn from your homework?

Exercise 2. Definition and Extremes
a. Talk about your health. Have you ever been around someone who worries a lot about his or her health?
b. How do you think being sick a lot keeps people from enjoying life?
c. What would happen if we never thought about our health?
d. Then we need to think enough about our health to take care of ourselves. If we do not how are we going to take of loves ones who need us? Please comment at will

Exercise 3. Side Effects of Illness
a. Think about a time when you have been ill. What were some things you wanted to do but couldn't do because you were ill?
b. How did you feel when you couldn't do what you wanted?
c. What are some things you don't like to do that you got out of doing because you were ill?
d. How did you feel about that?

Exercise 4. Health Rules
a. Every family has some rules about health. For example, some families insist that everyone brush his or her teeth twice a day. What are some of the rules this family has about health? Try to get at least 5 to 10 rules.
b. Do you think any of these rules are unnecessary? Why? If the rules do seem unnecessary, maybe you should ask your family physician about it.

Exercise 5. Knowing Family Worries

a. You want you to get to know your family better. Each of you tell the family two things that you fear or worry about. The things that worry you don't have to be health; but if you do worry about your health, it's fine to say so.
b. Who will start?

Homework

For homework this week, find or make something up for the next session that shows how your health is most of the time.

Punitiveness

ID____***Date***________

Exercise 1. Homework Discussion (Hypochondriasis)

a. Let's set out everything you've brought to show your health. What does one of these say about someone's health? Would whoever brought this explain it? Follow this procedure until everyone has had a turn.
b. What did you learn from your homework?

Exercise 3. Definition and Extremes

a. What does it mean to punish someone?
b. Do you agree that to punish someone is to do something to that person so that he or she will see what was done wrong?
c. What happens to a person who is punished often?
d. Do you agree that a punished person begins to dislike the person who punishes him or her and also begins to feel like a person who is no good?
e. What happens to a person who is never punished?
f. Do you think that person may not learn that some things are wrong?

Exercise 4. Ways of Punishing

a. There are many ways to punish people. Let's see how many ways you can think of. Let's go around the circle and each of you tell us a way to punish. Who will start?
b. Are there any other ways that haven't been mentioned? If the family doesn't mention lecturing or not talking at all, ask: Can we punish by preaching or lecturing or by not talking at all?
c. Obviously, this family is aware of a good many ways to punish.

Exercise 5. Acting Out Punishment

a. Make up a very short story about something someone did that you could punish that person for. When you tell your story, the person on your left is to pretend that he or she is the one who did what you are describing. Then you are to punish that person, using one of the ways we've talked about. You may talk, just act, or do both; but if you decide to punish by hitting, just pretend to hit. You may stand or sit anywhere you like to do your acting. After each demonstration, the person being punished should answer the following question.
b. How did it feel to be punished? Do you think what you did deserved that kindof punishment?

c. Ask the person doing the punishing: Do you think (he/she) deserved that kind of punishment for what (he/she) did to you?

Exercise 6. Knowing Your Family Better

a. In this exercise, get to know your family better. Think of three words that describe you. There's one rule: You can't say anything that we can see for ourselves, such as that you are tall or blonde.
b. Every family member should perform this exercise.

Exercise 7. Patting Your Own Back

a. Everyone in a family likes something about himself or herself. Close your eyes, relax, and think of something you like about yourself.
b. Think of something you really like about yourself.
c. Now tell yourself what it is you like about yourself.
d. Keeping your eyes closed, lift your arm and pat yourself on the back.
e. Now open your eyes and tell how it felt to pat yourself on the back

Homework

For homework this week, practice that last exercise. Every night this week, when you go to bed, think of something you like about yourself or something you did that day that made you feel good about yourself. Then close your eyes, tell yourself about it, and pat yourself on the back.

Neglect

***ID*____*Date*__________**

Exercise 1. Homework Discussion (Punitiveness)

a. Did all of you practice patting yourselves on the back?
b. Was that hard or easy to do?
c. What did you learn from the homework?

Exercise 2. Definition and Extremes

a. What does it mean to be ignored?
b. Would you agree that to be ignored is to be overlooked?
c. What happens to the person who is very often overlooked?
d. Then the person who is often overlooked feels very lonely and unimportant. What happens to the person who is given too much attention?
e. Would you agree that the person who is given too much attention thinks he or she is more important than others and does not learn to consider others' feelings?

Exercise 3. Feeling Ignored

a. All of us feel ignored or overlooked at times. Take a minute to think of a time when you felt ignored or overlooked.
b. How did you feel when you were ignored? Let us go around the circle so that each of you can tell the family how you felt when you were overlooked. There are many reasons a person is not given attention. What are some times in a family when a person might get overlooked?

c. If the family gets stuck, offer an example: People may be busy with other things; a parent may be absent because of work, hospitalization, death, divorce, or separation; others may be preoccupied with thoughts, extensive social engagements, talking to others on the phone.
d. This family is certainly aware of a lot of things that might cause a person to feel overlooked. Allow each member to suggest additional examples of being ignored.

Exercise 4. Creating Overlooked Characters
a. Now, make up a short story about someone who feels very overlooked. Cinderella was overlooked in her family, wasn't she? See if you can think up a story about an imaginary person who has been overlooked. Take a few minutes to think.
b. Who will go first?

Exercise 5. Feeling Special
a. Everyone in this family is a very special person. Tell each family member what is special about him or her. Say: "(Name), something really special about you is…." Let us start with the youngest person.
b. How does it feel to be told one is special?

Homework
This week, try to spend some leisure time together, with every family member included. What you do is up to you. It can be anything from playing a game together to going out together.

Rejection

ID____________________________________***Date***________

Exercise 1. Homework Discussion (Neglect)
a. What did you do together as a family this week. What did you do?
b. What was special to each of you about the time the family spent together?
c. Sometimes, individual family members get so busy that there is no time for the family. We are glad you found time to play together this week.

Exercise 2. Definition and Extremes
a. What does it mean to be unwanted?
b. Do we agree that to be unwanted is to be put aside as unlikable?
c. What happens to a person who feels unwanted?
d. A person who is unwanted feels very lonely and unloved. What happens to a person who feels that everyone wants him or her all the time?
e. Would that person feel that he or she would like some time alone and think that there are too many demands?

Exercise 3. Feeling Unwanted
a. Most of us have felt unwanted at some time in our lives. Perhaps you were the last one chosen for the baseball team or did not receive an invitation to a party

you really wanted to go to. Think of a time when you felt unwanted either inside or outside the family.

b. After each story, ask: How did you feel when you thought you were unwanted?

Exercise 4. Showing We Care

a. All of us have ways of showing that we care about those we love. Tell each family member a way that you try to show your love for that person. It might be something you say or something you do.
b. If an example is needed, suggest that the mother might express her love by cooking someone's favorite food.

Exercise 5. Liking Yourself

a. Now we would like you to close your eyes and think of something someone has told you they like about you. It can be anything anybody has said that made you feel good about yourself. Think about it, keeping your eyes closed, and remember how you felt.
b. With your eyes still closed, put your arms around yourself and tell yourself you are lovable.
c. Ok, now open your eyes and smile. Now, we want you to picture yourself walking into a room where a party is going on. As you walk in, a group of people begin talking. Now close your eyes and remember how lovable you are. Put your arms around yourself and tell yourself again how lovable you are. Squeeze yourself lovingly.
d. Now, take turns telling us what those people are saying. When everyone has finished, tell the family to open their eyes.

Homework

This week, read the story of Snow White, Hansel and Gretel, or the ugly duckling. Read it together if possible; at least be sure that all of you read the same story. We will talk about the story next time.

Excessive Distance

ID ____ ***Date*** ________

Exercise 1. Distance Regulation

To keep the family together and protect it from change, three excessive roles can be played: *Pursuer*, *Distancer*, and *Regulator*. For instance, the Distancer may avoid emotional closeness but become a Pursuer sexually. An emotional Pursuer, by the same token, may become a sexual Distancer. The distance Regulator may play both roles, wanting intimates to come close, but when they do, they are put off or even rejected: "Come here I need your help…Go away you did not help me…."

1. Do you recognize these roles in your marriage or family?
2. If you do, which of these roles do you play best?
3. How do you play it?
4. Which of these roles do you play second best?
5. How do you play it?

6. Which of these roles do you play third best?
7. How do you play it?
8. What happens to you and to the rest of the family when you play these roles? Please explain in detail.
9. How do you set yourself up to play these roles?
10. Unless you like playing them and you get something out of playing them, how can you avoid setting yourself up to play them?

Homework

During the coming week, make an appointment with your partner or family members at least 24 h in advance to share and discuss your questions with your partner/family members. Make sure to keep written notes on the discussion. Bring these notes back to whoever is helping you with this or other workbooks.

Intimacy for Couples and Families

ID___________________________________**Date**___________

Love and Caring

Exercise 1. Love and Caring

a. What does love mean to you (couple or family)?
b. What does caring mean to you?

Exercise 2. You Only Hurt the Ones You Love

a. What does the title of this exercise mean to you?
b. How hurt have you been by those you love and love you?

Exercise 3. Establishing the Level of Hurt

a. Because you care for each other, there are still issues that have caused you (couple or family) a lot of hurt and pain.
b. Any denial of hurt and pain indicates a serious problem that must be discussed. Tell how an issue has hurt each of you.

Exercise 4. Recognizing Strength

a. It takes strength to ask for help. Weak people do not cry. Could you tell us how that statement applies to this family?
b. Strong people admit to being weak enough to ask for help. Please comment at will.

Exercise 5. Previous Attempts to Resolve the Issue

a. Please tell us about the ways you have tried to work on this issue in the past.
b. How have those measures worked out? Make certain that everyone discusses the successes and failures of earlier approaches.

Homework

During the coming week, start collecting in writing all the possible hurts you received from or have inflicted to those you love and who love you. At the end of the week, make an appointment 21 h ahead to share with each other all the hurts you have collected during the week. Keep written notes of what happened during this meeting and bring them to the next meeting.

Seeing the Good

ID__________________________________**Date**___________

Exercise 1. Checking on Homework (Hurts)

a. Did you meet to share your lists of hurts?
b. What happened?
c. How do you feel about sharing past hurts with each other?

Exercise 2. Definition

a. Talk about "seeing the good" and what it means to you as a couple or as family. What do you think it means to see the good in yourself and the other members of your family?
b. Discuss the similarities and differences in the proposed meanings.
c. Could you agree that seeing the good means playing up the positive side, the good side, of those we love?
d. When we love someone, we accept the bad things about them as things that are overshadowed by the good in them. What do you think of that?

Exercise 3. Interference

a. How do you show that you see the good in yourselves and in one another?
b. If someone has difficulty, ask: What is it about you that makes it hard for you to see the good in yourself and others?

Exercise 4. Practicing Good

a. Say something good about each other or other members of your family. Look each person in the face and tell that person about a good trait or quality he or she possesses.
b. How did it feel to tell the members of your family about the good in them?
c. How did it feel to be told good things about yourself?
d. Were you surprised to hear how much good there is in this couple/family?

Exercise 5. Both Sides of a Coin

a. Now, tell each other about a situation that has both good and bad aspects.
b. Is it better to work and think about mainly the good or the bad aspects of this situation?
c. Why?
d. Do you see any relationship between what you have told us and the old story about the optimist and the pessimist looking at the half-filled glass? Remember that the optimist said the glass was half-full, and the pessimist said it was half empty.
e. Which side do you want to take?

Exercise 6. Seeing Good Better

a. How could you do a better job of seeing the good in yourselves and one another?
b. The whole family should respond to and discuss each other's answers.

Homework
During the next week, make it a point to tell each member of your family something good that you recognize in that person.

Caring

ID__________________________________**Date**____________

Exercise 1. Discuss the Homework Assignment

a. What did you say good to each other?
b. How did it feel to receive and to give something good to those you love and who love you?

Exercise 2. Definition

a. What does *caring* mean to you? What does it mean to care for someone?
b. Discuss the similarities and differences in the proposed meanings.
c. Could we agree that to care is to understand the importance of one's self and the selves of one's family? If we care for someone, you see both yourself and that person as being important. What do you think about that?

Exercise 3. Showing Care

a. How do you show that you care for each other? Tell each other one way in which each person in the family shows you that he or she cares for you.
b. If a family member cannot think of a way, another person can remind him or her of possible responses.
c. If some family members show care in a destructive manner, what is each of your reactions to that way of showing care.

Exercise 4. Self-Care

a. Each of you in turn stand up and say: "I am a person, and I am important."
b. Then go up to each member of your family and say: "I care for you, and you are important to me."
c. How did it feel to tell your family that you care for them?
d. How did it feel to have others say that they care for you?

Exercise 5. Caring

a. Go to every member of your family and do something that shows that you care for that person. You might give that person a kiss, a hug, a handshake—anything that feels right to you.
b. Take detailed notes during this exercise.

Exercise 6. Caring Better

a. How could each of you do a better job of letting the other members of your family know that you care for them?
b. Keep in writing what has been said here.

Homework
During the next week, think of all the ways you care for and show your care for the members of your family. Every day tell each person that you care for him or her and do something to show it.

Sharing Hurt Feelings

ID____________________________________Date___________

Exercise 1. Discuss Homework Assignment (Caring)

a. Did you keep track in writing of what was said and done during the last meeting?
b. Do you care to share it with everybody?

Exercise 2. Definition

a. Let us talk about the "sharing of hurt feelings" and what it means to this family. What does it mean to share your hurt feelings with someone?
b. Could we agree that sharing of hurt feelings means telling the people you are close not only about your victories and happiness but also about your pain and defeats?
c. We share victories with anybody but our defeats belong to the family. What do you think of that idea?

Exercise 3. Sharing How?

a. How do you share your hurt feelings with one another? We would like each of you to tell us how you talk about your pains and defeats in this family.
b. Does it make you feel better to share your hurt feelings with the other members of the family?
c. If one or all family members report that they do not share hurt or that sharing hurt does not make them feel better, ask: What do you think it means that you do not share your hurt or that sharing your hurt does not make you feel better?

Exercise 4. Practicing

a. Tell each other something that is hurting you at this moment.
b. How did it feel to tell your family about your pains and defeats?
c. How did it feel to hear about your family's hurts?

Exercise 5. Responding to Sharing

a. Now, go to every member of your family, touch that person, and say "I am glad that you are willing to share your hurt with me. I want to know about your defeats and pains because I care about you and hope that I can do something to make things better for you."
b. How did you all feel about completing this exercise?

Exercise 6. Sharing Hurt Feelings Better

a. How could each of you do a better job of sharing your hurt with the members of your family?
b. How could this family better use the sharing of hurt to make each member, and the whole family, happier and stronger?

Homework

During the next week, think about how the members of this family share their hurts. Every day, tell each member of your family about something that hurts you. When someone tells you about his or her hurt, try to respond as you would want that person to respond to your hurt.

Forgiveness

ID________________________________Date__________

Exercise 1. Discuss the Homework Assignment (Hurt Feelings)

a. Did you do what you were asked to do at the end of last meeting?
b. What happened as a result?

Exercise 2. Definition

a. Let us talk about "forgiveness" and what it means to you. What does it mean to forgive someone?
b. Could we agree that forgiveness means not demanding that we and others be perfect? As human beings, you know, we really cannot be perfect.
c. Forgiveness also means not allowing the past to ruin the present. Just because someone may have goofed yesterday does not mean that that person will have to do wrong today. What do you think about that?

Exercise 3. Forgiving

a. When someone in this family has hurt someone else, how do you go about forgiving?
b. What do you think it means if you have difficulty forgiving?

Exercise 4. Practicing

a. If someone in this family has done something that is still hurting you, pretend to write that thing on a sheet of paper.
b. Look down at your imaginary paper and say: "It's crazy for me to have to carry this nonsense around with me all the time." Now throw the "paper" on the floor.
c. Will one of you now please pretend to set the pile of nonsense on fire.
d. It was not as big a fire as you thought it would be, was it?

Exercise 5. Practicing Some More

a. Go to each member of your family, touch that person, and say: "We are both human, so we cannot be perfect. But I am not going to let the past ruin the present. I forgive both of us."
b. How did it feel to be forgiven by the members of your family?
c. How did it feel to forgive yourself?
d. We do not have to forget to forgive. Can you learn from what has gone wrong in the past?

Exercise 6. Forgiving Better

a. How could each of you do a better job of forgiving?
b. If you cannot forgive yourself, you cannot forgive others. The best way to forgive oneself is to change one's behavior for the better.
c. How will you change for the better? Write it down in concrete and specific terms, make extra copies and share them with whoever is working with you on these exercises.

Homework

During the next week, every time you think of an instance when someone has hurt you in the past—this does not include ongoing conflict—write down what happened, tear the paper into little shreds, and flush it down the toilet.

Protectiveness

ID____________________________________**Date**____________

Exercise 1. Discuss the Homework Assignment (Forgiveness)

Exercise 2. Definition

a. What does "protection" mean to you? What does it mean to protect the members of your family?
b. Could you agree that protection means caring enough to defend yourself and the members of your family from attack: the protective person is willing to fight for self and for family. If you cannot protect yourself, how can you protect others in your family?

Exercise 3. Protecting How?

a. How do you protect yourselves and each other?
b. If one or more family members is not protective, ask: What do you think it means that you are unwilling to fight for yourself or your family?

Exercise 4. Protecting One Another

a. Now, think of the moment in your life when you felt the weakest and most helpless. In turn, go to the center of the room and stand there with your eyes closed. Continue to think of how you felt at that terrible moment. Make a circle around you with hands joined and get closer and closer to whoever is standing until one can feel the warmth of their bodies.
b. You start to feel safe and protected. You begin to feel less afraid and start to forget about that frightening moment in the past. When you are no longer thinking about the incident, open your eyes. Now, one should say: "You are now strong enough to go out on your own. But you can come back if things get too tough. We will protect and fight for you!"
c. How did it feel to be inside the circle?
d. How did it feel to be one of the protectors?

Exercise 5. Failures

a. Taking turns, tell about a time in your life when you failed in protecting yourself.
b. Discuss ways in which you could have protected yourself better.

Exercise 6. Better Protectiveness

a. How could you, in general, do a better job of protecting one another?
b. How could you, in particular, do a better job of protecting one another?

Homework

During the next week, think about how all of you protect yourselves and one another. Every day tell each member of the family about a concern or problem you have. When someone tells you about a problem, tell that person, in your own words, that you care enough to fight to make things better for him or her. Do what you can to help solve that person's problem or ease his or her concern.

Responsibility

***ID*____*Date*______**

Exercise 1. Discuss the Homework Assignment (Protectiveness)

a. How did this assignment workout for you?
b. Did it make any difference in your relationship with each other?

Exercise 2. Definitions

a. Today talk about "responsibility" and what it means to you. What does it mean to be responsible for yourself and, as members of the family, for your family?
b. Could we agree that being responsible means not blaming others for our own mistakes and unhappiness? It also means meeting our obligations, both financial and personal.
c. All the love and care in the world is useless if, for example, one here does not see that the rent is paid or that another does not cook any food. Feel free to comment at will.

Exercise 3. Showing Responsibility

a. How do you show that you are responsible? Each family member should describe at least one way in which he or she and another family member are responsible.
b. If someone has difficulty giving examples, ask the following question: "What is it about this couple/family makes it hard for you to be responsible?"

Exercise 4. Failures

a. Tell each of them about a time when you failed to take responsibility for yourself.
b. Now tell everybody how you could have handled the situation better.
c. How did the family feel about the better way of dealing with that situation?

Exercise 5. Assuming Responsibility

a. Stand up and face each other and say: "I am responsible for my own successes and happiness….just as I am responsible for my failures and unhappiness." Repeat this statement until the feeling is consistent with the message.

Exercise 6. Greater Responsibility

a. How could this couple/family, as a unit, be more responsible to itself?
b. What could you do to make this couple/family more successful and happier?

Homework

a. During the next week, think of something you should do in order to be more responsible for yourself. This should be something that will help make you more successful and happier. For example, you might take responsibility for straightening out your desk or closet so that you can find things more easily. Do not tell anyone what it is you are doing; no one else needs to know. The important thing is that you be responsible for yourself and to yourself.

Enjoyment

***ID*____________________________________*Date*_______**

Exercise 1. Discuss the Homework Assignment (Responsibility)

b. Did you carry out the homework assigned to you at the end of last meeting?
a. How did it workout?
b. How did you feel about it?

Exercise 2. Definition

a. Talk about "enjoyment" and what it means to you. What does it mean to enjoy yourself and for the family to enjoy itself?
b. Could we agree that enjoyment means looking at the good side of life? People who enjoy themselves are excited about life. They can laugh at themselves and experience pleasure without guilt.
c. What do you think of that description of enjoyment?

Exercise 3. Individual, Couple, or Family Enjoyment

a. How do you enjoy yourselves as

   i. An individual?
   ii. As a couple?
   iii. As a family?

b. How do you enjoy yourselves together? Do not accept an answer that includes the children. Each family member should name at least one way in which he or she individually experiences enjoyment and one way in which the couple or family enjoys itself.
c. If you have difficulty, think what it is about this family that makes it hard for you to enjoy yourselves.

Exercise 4. Seizing the Moment for Enjoyment

a. This exercise seems to have a 10-min blank spot. Why don't you spend that time doing something you enjoy? You may stay in the room you are in. Spend your 10 min together.
b. What did you do to enjoy yourselves?
c. Was it hard to think of some way the couple or the whole family could enjoy an unexpected 10 min together?
d. If the answer was yes, how do you feel about doing things on the spur of the moment?
e. How do you feel about doing nothing—can you enjoy it?

Exercise 5. The Right to Enjoy

a. In turn stand up face each other and say: "I am a person, not a working machine. I have the right to some enjoyment in life."
b. Specify what kind of enjoyment you think you have a right to.

Exercise 6. More Enjoyment

a. How could you as an:

   i. Individual?
   ii. Couple?
   iii. Family enjoy yourselves more?

b. Be realistic, concrete, and specific in how this enjoyment would come about.

Homework

During the coming week, plan an activity that you can enjoy as an individual, as a couple, and as a family. Then do it!

Intimacy Workbook Feedback Form

Now that you have completed this workbook, please respond to the following questions concerning the usefulness of its programmed intimacy practice exercises.

1. Using a scale of 1–7, rank the seven intimacy exercises according to their usefulness in improving/developing closeness with your partner or family. Rank the most useful task as "1." Rank the least useful task as "7"

Task	Rank
Love-caring...	____
Seeing the good...	____
Sharing Hurts...	____
Forgiveness...	____
Protectiveness..	____
Responsibility..	____
Enjoyment...	

2. How useful did you find the entire workbooks for improving/developing greater intimacy between you and your partner and between you and your family? Choose one of the following:
   a. Very useful
   b. Quite useful
   c. Somewhat useful
   d. Slightly useful
   e. Not useful at all

3. How would you rate this program's helpfulness for teaching couples and families to develop intimacy? Choose one of the following:
   a. Very helpful
   b. Quite helpful
   c. Somewhat helpful

d. Slightly helpful
e. Not helpful at all

4. How would you rate this program's usefulness in developing or improving your relationships in general? Choose one of the following:

   a. Very useful
   b. Quite useful
   c. Somewhat useful
   d. Slightly useful
   e. Not useful at all

5. How likely would you be to recommend this workbook to other couples of families you know? Choose one of the following:

   a. Very likely
   b. Quite likely
   c. Somewhat likely
   d. Slightly likely
   e. Not likely at all

6. Using your own words, what did you find useful about this workbook?
7. How could this workbook be improved

Single Parent Families

ID____________________________________**Date**_________

Exercise 1. The Meaning of Single Parenthood
The purpose of this exercise is to find out what it means to be a single parent.

a. What does it mean to you?
b. Ask the children: How does it feel to have only one parent in your home?

Exercise 2. The Outcome of the Loss
a. How does the loss of a wife/mother or husband/father change you?
b. How does the loss of a wife/mother or husband/father change your family?

Exercise 3. The Aftermath
a. What are some of the special problems that you as a family have had?
b. In you?
c. In your children?
d. In your relationships with your parents and in-laws?

Exercise 4. Disadvantages
a. What are the disadvantages of being a one-parent family?
b. What are the advantages of being a one-parent family?

Exercise 5. Resolving Feelings
a. Have there been times when you have blamed yourselves or each other for the loss of your wife/mother or husband and father?

b. How have you dealt with your feelings of anger, guilt, hurt?

Homework

a. Think more about your feelings about being a one-parent family so that you can tell us about them at our next meeting.

Handling New Responsibilities

ID______________________________________**Date**__________

Exercise 1. Checking on the Homework (One-Parent Family)

a. What feelings have you become aware of during the past week?
b. In yourself?
c. In your children?
d. In close relationships?

Exercise 2. Changing Roles

a. Think about all the things your wife/mother or husband and father used to do for you and your family.
b. Now that you have had some time to think, discuss those things with someone close to you.

Exercise 3. Taking On New Responsibilities

a. Talk about what you are doing to take care of these responsibilities.
b. List them in detail.

Exercise 4. Feelings of Resentment

a. Do you feel about being responsible for all these things?
b. Do you ever resent the fact that it is now your responsibility to handle the things that your former partner used to manage? Why or why not?

Exercise 5. Forming a Support Group

a. Do you ever feel that you have had to take on so many new responsibilities that it has interfered with other parts of your life?
b. If yes, how do you think you can better deal with your responsibilities? Is there any other person—a friend or a relative—you can turn to for help?

Homework

Before the next meeting, consider further how your new responsibilities have affected your life. If you feel overwhelmed by them, how might you handle them better?

Family Relationships

ID______________________________________**Date**__________

Exercise 1. Checking on the Homework

a. For your homework, you were to consider how your new responsibilities have changed your lives and how you might better deal with them.

b. What have you come up with?

Exercise 2. Working for Better Ways

a. Now that you are becoming aware of some of the negative ways you work as a family, we want you to discuss ways that might work better.
b. Think of ways you can improve your relationships with each other. Compromise may be necessary.

Exercise 3. Listening to Feelings

a. One way to improve your relationships is to know how to listen to feelings. We would like you to practice listening to feelings. Say how you feel right now or how you felt at some time during the past week. Have a child respond to the parent by finishing this sentence: "I hear you saying that you (feel/felt)…."
b. Now, are you, parent, satisfied with your child's response? Be sure that everyone has a turn and that each person expresses a feeling rather than a thought.

Homework

a. During the coming week, practice listening to each other's feelings. At least once a day, respond with "I hear you saying that you feel…" or "It sounds as though you feel…."
b. Also, at the end of each day, write down an instance in which you responded to someone's feelings and an instance in which someone responded to your feelings.
c. Keep track of these interchanges in writing because they will be discussed in the next meeting.

Outside Relationships

ID________________________________**Date**________

Exercise 1. Checking on Your Homework (Feelings)

a. For your homework, you practiced listening to each other's feelings. What was it like to respond this way?
b. What was the result of that homework on your relationships?

Exercise 2. Relating to Relatives

a. What kind of relationship does each of you have with your relatives?
b. Can you think of a way to improve your relationships with them?
c. Come up with a suggestion to help you work with your relatives better.

Exercise 3. Relating to Neighbors

a. How do you get along with neighbors? Can you come up with suggestions to make your relationships in the neighborhood more enjoyable?
b. How about acquaintances?

Exercise 4. Relating to the School

a. How do you get along with people in school
    i. The parent with teachers

ii. Children with teachers and classmates?

b. Can you think of ways to improve these relationships?

Homework
Think of ways of behaving—among yourselves and in your relationships with others—that can be helpful to each of you and the rest of your family. Write down your thoughts and bring them to the next meeting.

Positive Expression

ID__________________________________Date_________

Exercise 1. Checking on Your Homework (Behaving Helpfully)

a. For your homework, you were to think of ways of behaving that would improve your relationships.
b. What did you come up with?

Exercise 2. Practicing Expression

a. Think of some times when you have felt angry, upset, or frustrated with another member of your family. For example, perhaps you have disagreed with another member of the family but have been afraid or reluctant to say anything about it. Take a few minutes and write down two such situations.
b. Now describe one of the situations. As you do, speak directly to the family member involved. Try to avoid being critical or sarcastic. After each person has described one situation, each of you should describe the other situation he or she has written down.

Exercise 3. Pinpointing Feelings

a. Using the same situations, describe your feelings about those incidents. How do you feel when these incidents occur? Again, speak directly to the family member involved, without criticizing, blaming, or putting down.
b. How do you feel when you express your feelings this way?

Exercise 4. Proposing New Ways

a. One good way to express angry or frustrated feelings is to begin with a positive statement. For example, instead of saying "That was a dumb thing to do," it might be better to say "That might be true, but did you ever think of it this way?"
b. Now let us talk about a situation that might occur in your household: (Mother comes home, and the house is a mess. To the mother: Tell us how you would respond to this situation. Remember to begin with a positive statement.
c. Ask the children: Does this sound like a good way to express your feelings? If they answer no, what do you think would be a better way to handle this situation?

Exercise 5. Practicing Positive Ways

a. Another good way to handle anger or frustration is to think to yourself, "What is it that I am angry or frustrated about?" and then to express that simply and directly to the person with whom you are angry or frustrated.

b. Think of a situation in which you feel angry or frustrated with a member of the family and try to express your feeling simply and directly to that person using "I" feel etc.

Exercise 6. Being Kind to Each Other

a. Conclude this program by asking youself to consider some of the good things you do for each other.
b. Tell each other ten things that you do for your family or for a particular member of your family—working and making money, taking care of the house, being affectionate, and so on. Try to be concrete and specific.
c. Write the satisfactions on a list so that all of you can see the lists side by side. How do you feel about these lists?
d. Are you surprised that you do so many things for each other? Remember the items on these lists, and each time a family member does one of these things or does something else for you, let that person know that you appreciate it.

Homework

Consider further how your new responsibilities have affected your life. If you feel overwhelmed by them, how might you handle them better? If necessary, do ask for more help from professional who worked with you on this workbook.

Middle Years in the Family

***ID*____*Date*____________**

Exercise 1. Becoming Aware of Family Roles

a. Write the name of each family member across the top of this page. Under each name, write several words that describe that person's roles. For example, if your partner were on your sheet, you might write: (man/woman), (husband/wife), provider, chief cook and bottle washer, driver, etc.
b. Read what you wrote about yourself. Then, 1 ask each of you to read what you wrote about other family members. After each person has been described, ask: What similarities and differences do you see between your view of your roles and the other members' views of your roles?

Exercise 2. Defining Family Roles and Social Expectations

a. All of us watch TV and read books, newspapers, and magazines. We listen to friends, teachers, and business associates express opinions about what people "should" and "should not" be like. What messages do you get from "outside sources" about the way people are supposed to behave in the wife and mother roles?
b. In the husband and father roles?
c. In the daughter and sister roles?
d. In the son and brother roles? Now we want you to think of a family you have seen on TV. How is your family like this TV family in the way it expects family members to perform their roles? How is your family different from the TV family in its role expectations?

Exercise 3. Defining Family Roles and Family Expectations

a. Let us take another look at the way you as a family define your roles. I will call out a role, and you tell me the actions that this role player performs. For example, if I say "king," you might say "rules." Ready? Here we go. One family member call out the following, one at a time, allowing time for each family member to answer: mother, father, son, daughter, wife, husband, sister, brother. Keep the responses coming as quickly as possible.
b. When he/she said "mother" or "father" nobody said "diaper changer." Why is that? Let each answer. So this family is growing up. I wonder if we could agree that as time passes, the way your family defines its roles changes.
c. Can you think of some differences in the way you performed your family roles 5 years ago as compared with the way you perform them now?
d. How are family responsibilities divided now as compared with 5 years ago?

Exercise 4. Role Conflicts

a. Because each person has several roles to perform in a limited amount of time, we often find that performing one role conflicts with performing another. Think about all the roles the other members of this family perform and how you feel about how they perform their roles. Use this sentence as a guide to tell each person what you are satisfied with and what you are dissatisfied with. Look at each person, say his or her name, and say, "I appreciate—in your—role, and I am dissatisfied with—in your—role." For example, someone may say, "Dad, I appreciate the way you joke around with Mom in your husband role, and I am dissatisfied that you couldn't come to the school game in your father role." How did it feel to state your appreciations and dissatisfactions?
b. How did it feel to receive the family's appreciations and dissatisfactions? Now, we want you to think about yourself and your roles and express one satisfaction and one dissatisfaction with the way you perform your roles.

Exercise 5. Ranking Roles

a. Now that you have thought about the expectations for each of your roles and the conflicts you feel in trying to perform all of them, we want you to list your roles on this piece of paper and then put a star by the one you spend the most time on.
b. Now tell your family which role you starred. If you would like to make any changes in your role, tell your family what the changes are and why you would like them made.

Exercise 6. Responding to Role Changes

When one family member makes a change in the way he or she performs roles, other family members respond to those changes somehow. Each member will need the help and support of the others to make the changes that he or she wants to make in those roles. Think about the changes you want to make and what help you will need. Tell your family about your changes and ask for help by filling in the blanks of this sentence: "I would like to spend more time on my—role and less time on my—role, and I want you, (name a family member), to help me do this by (name a specific action)." Then we would like the person addressed to respond.

Understanding Life Positions in Adolescence

ID ____ ***Date*** ____________

Exercise 1. Drawing Yourself

Special materials: crayons or markers

a. To help everyone start thinking about parents' and teenagers' viewpoints, you first need to each get some paper and a crayon. Now, draw a picture of how you see yourself in your role as a parent or a teenager. The picture should say, "This is what it is like to be a parent in this family" or "This is what it is like to be a teenager in this family." Make your picture by yourself. Do not ask for help from someone else in the family and do not look at anybody else's picture. Take time to compare pictures in a few moments. Remember, this is not a test of artistic ability. Just draw your idea of what it is like to be a parent or a teenager in your family.
b. Now that you have finished, take turns explaining your picture. Who would like to start?
c. What did each of you like best about your picture?
d. What did each of you like least about your picture?

Exercise 2. Being a Parent

a. Now, your parents should think about being parents for a few minutes. What is the hardest thing about being a parent in this family?
b. What is the nicest thing about being a parent in this family?
c. What would you like your teenagers to know about being parents in this family right now?

Exercise 3. Being a Teenager

a. Think about being teenagers for a few minutes. What is the hardest thing about being a teenager in this family?
b. What is the nicest thing about being a teenager in this family?
c. What would you like your parents to know about being teenagers in this family?

Exercise 4. Parents, Too, Were Once Teenagers

a. Now that you have started to become aware of yourselves as parents or teenagers, do some things to help you understand a little more what it is like to be parents and teenagers in this family. Parents' should start thinking about your relationships with your own parents when you were teenagers. When you are ready, we would like you to share what you remember with your family. Who would like to start?

Exercise 5. Turnabout is Fair Play

a. Teenagers should change places with their parents. Pretend that you have changed roles with your parents and talk together about what it might be like if you were suddenly the parents in this family. What would be the hardest thing for you about becoming the parents in this family?
b. What would be the nicest thing for you about becoming parents in this family?

Exercise 6. Turnabout Again

a. Now, parents pretend that you have changed roles with your teenagers. Imagine that you are now the teenagers and they are your parents. Talk together about what it might be like if you were suddenly the teenagers. What would be the hardest thing for you about becoming teenagers in this family?
b. What would be the nicest thing for you about becoming teenagers in this family?

Exercise 7. Parents' Report Card

a. You teenagers think about your parents for a few minutes. What do you like most about your parents? Who would like to start? What do you think is the hardest thing for your parents to understand about you?
b. What would each of you like most to change in your relationship with your parents?

Exercise 8. Teenagers' Report Card

a. Now it would be helpful if you parents think about your teenagers for a few minutes. What do you like the most about your teenagers? What do you think is the hardest thing for your teenagers to understand about you?
b. What would each of you like most to change in your relationship with your teenagers?

Homework

As you think about what you have heard today, each of you should think of two things you might like to understand better about being parents and teenagers in this family. During the coming week, see if you can take the time to talk together about what you want to understand better.

Father In, Mother Out

ID____***Date***______________

Exercise 1. Life Positions

a. Place your chairs in a circle according to your ages. Keep some space between you and the next person. In this circle, each of you could be seen as representing a different stage in the life cycle because of your age and your life experiences. What does the space between you mean?
b. Would you agree that the space could mean that each of you is separate and has his or her own individual outlook on life?
c. What does the circle mean to you?
d. Would you agree that the circle could mean that each of you is similar in many ways because you share your lives as a family?

Exercise 2. Similarities and Differences in Life Positions

a. Where you are now sitting represents the present time in your life. Think for a few moments about a concern or something that is important to you about this time in your life. Then share that aloud with each other.
b. Beginning with oldest family member, look to the next youngest member and imagine a concern that you had when you were in that life position.

c. To youngest member of circle: Look back to a time when you were younger and think about a concern that you had then and tell your family about it.
d. Beginning with the youngest, look to the next oldest member and imagine a concern that you anticipate having when you are in this life position. The oldest person in the circle should look ahead to her/his own future and think of a concern that he/she anticipates.
e. Do you see any similarities between younger and older life positions?

Exercise 3. Inward and Outward

a. You may want to rearrange yourselves; the circle is not necessary for the remaining exercises. In this exercise, focus on a father's looking inward to the home, his wife, and family while a mother looks more outside the family, perhaps to new interests. This may be a time when a father has built most of his career and may be turning to the home and wanting to share more in the life of the family. This may be a time when a mother is free of many parenting and home-care responsibilities and may want to cultivate interests and talents outside the home. Do you see (father's name) moving inward?
b. What are some ways in which you see you father moving inward?
c. Do you see your mother moving outward?
d. What are some ways in which you see your mother moving outward?

Exercise 4. Independence of Children

a. This is also a time when children are beginning to move toward independence—perhaps going away to school, establishing their careers, and possibly marrying and establishing a home of their own. Do you see the children becoming more independent?
b. What are some ways in which you see the children becoming more independent?

Exercise 5. Dependence, Independence, and Interdependence,

a. What does it mean to this family to be dependent?
b. What does it mean to this family to be independent? Keep track of the most common answer to these questions. If dependence means (define as determined in discussion) and independence means (define as determined in discussion), what does interdependence mean to this family?
c. Would you agree that independence could mean that each of you takes responsibility for self and that dependence could mean that a person does not take responsibility for self?
d. Would you agree that interdependence could mean that people in a family relationship are sometimes separate and independent and sometimes have to lean on or depend on someone else, for example, as you did when you were children?
e. Would you agree that interdependence means sharing a close relationship and knowing when to be independent and when to be dependent?

Exercise 6. Bridging the Gap Between Present and Future

a. Begin with the present, as you are now in this family, then move into the future when you, (parents are again living together alone), and when you, the children are living away from home, perhaps at school or in your own homes.

b. Answer the following question three times: “Who are you now?” Begin each answer with “I am.” If task is not clear, say: You may answer with roles or descriptive words.
c. The following question is for the parents. “Who will I be when the children are no longer living in this home?” Begin your answers with “I will be.”
d. The following question is for the children. “Who will I be when I am no longer living in this home?” Begin each answer with “I will be.”
e. Would you agree that each of you is entering a different stage of the life cycle, yet all of you are similar because you are beginning anew?

Homework

For homework during this next week, think about some ways you can support one another as you move toward different life positions or in different directions.

Separating Teenagers from their Parents

ID____________________________________**Date**__________

Exercise 1. Separation as Rejection

a. Discuss the separation of parents and teenagers as telling something about how this family works or fails to work? What do you think about this?
b. Make sure that everyone answers, but do not let the discussion get out of hand.

Exercise 2. Desirable and Undesirable Separations

a. It looks as if we need to look at how this family allows its members to separate from each other.
b. How do you allow each of you to be an individual in his or her own right, that is, an individual with needs, rights, privileges, and responsibilities?

Exercise 3. Interdependence

a. It looks as though it is difficult for you to see yourselves as interdependent. Each of you seems to want rights and privileges but no responsibilities.
b. Each person should talk only about himself or herself.
c. Try to think of better ways (more constructive ways) of becoming individual adults. Let completing these practice exercises be one of the most constructive things you all have done.

Homework

Between now and next time, each of you should think what you can do to change things for the better in this family. Think about what you can do, not what someone else can do. Put it down in writing and bring your notes to the next meeting

Problems of the Parents

ID______________________________________***Date***______

Exercise 1. Checking on Homework

a. Discuss the homework and each family member write down what each one proposed to do to make things better.

b. Consider what you say a potential family contract.
c. If a family member is reluctant to commit himself or herself, realize that this means you want everybody in the family to change except yourself. In this way, one can defeat oneself and the family.

Exercise 2. Failing to Support Each Other

a. I wonder whether each of you has failed to support each other as partners and as parents.
b. Children can confront the parents on this issue.

Exercise 3. Going Into History

a. I wonder whether an inability to support each other as partners might impact your children.
b. How do you feel about your grandparents?

Exercise 4. Past Separations

a. The following questions are for the parents.
   i. Do you believe that each of you has been able to separate yourself as an individual adult from your own parents?
   ii. If each of you had trouble separating from your own parents, how hard will it be for your children to separate from you?
b. Let the children participate as much as they can.

Exercise 5. Approaching Middle Age

a. The following question is for the parents. How much might your inability to work together as partners and parents have to do with your reaching or approaching middle age?
b. What do children think about this issue?

Exercise 6. Guilt and Unexpressed Feelings

a. Now, to go back to your relationship with your children, is there any guilt or unexpressed feelings that you need to consider?
b. What do children think about this issue?

Exercise 7. Forgiveness

a. Can each of you forgive yourself and your parents for having goofed, for being imperfect, and therefore human? Unless you can forgive yourselves for being human, it will be very hard for you to accept yourselves and the rest of your family, especially your parents. If you cannot forgive yourself and your parents for mistakes, how can you expect your children to forgive you?
b. Open discussion for both parent and children

Homework

Between now and next time we meet, work on forgiving yourselves and accepting yourselves as first-rate human beings. Write down any thoughts you develop during this time and bring them along for next time we meet.

Binding Dependence

*ID*______________________________________*Date*______

Exercise 1. Discuss Homework

a. Have you been able to forgive yourself? Stay with this issue until a clear resolution is achieved for everybody.
b. In this and the next two practice exercises we are going to deal with how family members learn to become excessively dependent on each other or, on the other hand, learn to become excessively independent of each other.
c. Is there a middle solution to these extremes?

Exercise 2. The Meaning of Dependence

a. What does the word dependence mean to this family?
b. What does the word independence mean to this family?
c. What does the word interdependence mean to this family?

Exercise 3. Dealing with Dependence

a. How does this family deal with dependence?
b. Do you tend to spoil each other?
c. Do you ever say no to each other?
d. Who says yes to whom, when, and how?
e. How destructive is it for this family not to set any limits on each other?

Exercise 4. The Freedom to Be

a. Is everyone in this family allowed freedom of thought?
b. How much freedom is allowed to members of this family?
c. What kind of limits are allowed to limit freedom?

Exercise 5. Discriminating Feelings From Thinking and Acting

a. How much confusion and contradiction exists among what you feel, what you think, and how you act.
b. Practice "feeling" statements at will.
c. Practice "thinking" statements at will.
d. Practice "action" statements at will.

Exercise 6. Bribing and Blackmailing

a. How much control do you use on each other by playing on guilt, blackmailing or bribing each other?
b. Spoiling, unclear and contradictory limits, blackmail, and bribery are ways that can allow dependency in your family. What do you think?

Homework

During the coming week, think more about differentiating among pros and cons of dependence, independence, and interdependence. Write down whatever comes into your mind and bring your notes to the next meeting.

Expelling Dependence

***ID*____*Date*______**

Exercise 1. Checking on Homework

a. Did you take any notes? If yes, let us go over them in detail.
b. If no, let us discuss what we cover in the last workbook. What are your thoughts about dependence, independence, and interdependence?

Exercise 2. Depending on Each Other

a. Would allowing too much independence imply a denial or an unwilling-ness to recognize and accept some degree of dependence on each other?
b. Rewarding too much dependence would produce what long-term results?
c. Accepting interdependence would produce what long term-results?

Exercise 3. Accepting Responsibility

a. Do you think that you have been able to accept each other and your responsibilities to each other as parents and as children?
b. Has anybody in this family rejected responsibility for his or her behavior?
c. What is the long-term result of rejecting responsibility for one's actions?

Exercise 4. Neglecting Each Other

a. How much have you neglected each other?
b. Are you denying that any neglect has occurred?
c. How do the rest of you feel about the issue of neglect in your family?

Exercise 5. Rejecting Each Other

a. How much have you rejected each other?
b. Does anyone feel rejected by the rest of the family?
c. Why and how?

Exercise 6. Taking Independence for Granted

a. Do you think that anyone has been granted too much freedom and independence too soon?
b. Do you think that anyone has been granted too little freedom and independence too late?

Exercise 7. Learning to Be Loyal

a. Might there be a lack of loyalty or loyalty that is too weak in your family? Does anyone here feel loyal to anyone else in this family?
b. Think about loyalty. If you cannot be loyal to each other, how can you learn to be loyal to anyone else?

Exercise 8. Delegating Dependence

a. Let us talk about how most families use a combination of too much dependence and too much independence to keep children on a leash. Might this issue apply to your family? If yes, How?
b. If no, how?
c. If maybe, why?

Exercise 9. Clarifying Issues

a. Do you express clearly what you want from each other, or do you qualify what you say so that no issue is ever clear?
b. Can you state clearly what you want from each other?

Exercise 10. Children Tell the Truth

a. The following question is for the parents: "To what extent are your children responsible for saying and doing things that you as parents have been unable to say and do?"
b. How much of your children's behavior stems from your unmet goals or unfulfilled dreams and fantasies? One could wonder, then, whether your children's behavior could be understood as their having been sent on a mission to say and do the things you would have liked to do and say, either as an adolescent or as an adult.
c. Such a statement may sound farfetched at first blush but think about it as part of homework assignment.

Exercise 11. Acting Up to Distract

a. The following question is for the parents: "Might your children's behavior provide the excitements and thrills that you yourselves missed or are missing as partners, parents, and as individuals?"
b. Have the crises of middle-age impacted your children's behavior?

Exercise 12. Failures of the Marriage as Partnership

a. What does our children's behavior tell us about ourselves—as individuals, partners, and parents?
b. How much of your children's behavior stems from your desire to keep your marriage intact?
c. How much of your children's behavior stems from your inability to make things better for yourself as individuals and as a couple?

Homework

During the next week, become aware of the possibility that each of you is being used to fill the parts that are missing or incomplete in others. As long as you use each other, none can be free and separate from the rest of the family. Write down any thoughts that may come to you and bring your notes to the next meeting.

Liberation

ID ____ ***Date*** ______

Exercise 1. Checking on the Homework

a. Go over the homework assignment if done, otherwise ask for whatever thoughts may have been provoked by the last meeting.
b. Make sure everybody contributes to the discussion.

Exercise 2. Freedom and Responsibility

a. To be free of each other, we need to recognize our individual worth and importance. Are you convinced of your own worth and importance?

b. If anyone indicates low or negative self-worth, help that person to establish a better picture of himself or herself.
c. You might say one or more of the following to the family member with low self-worth:

   i. "If you do not think well of yourself, how do you expect others to?"
   ii. "No one can help you think well of yourself except you. If you do not, the whole family pays the price, as you have already seen."
   iii. "Not thinking well of yourself gives you tremendous control over your family. No one in this family can be free unless you are free of your poor feelings about yourself."

d. Ask for explanation for feelings of low-self-worth or importance.

Exercise 3. Good Things for Each Other

a. In spite of your problems, keep in mind the good things in your family relationship.
b. Talk about as many things as you can think of that you do for one another, such as working, taking care of the house or lawn, doing a certain favor at special times.
c. Stress whatever good there is in the family

Exercise 4. Confirming Statements

a. All family members take turns and confirm each statement saying, for example: Do you agree that (she/he) really does that for you?
b. Write the confirmed statement on a sheet of paper—the parent's statement in one column, the adolescent's in another.
c. If the family can come up with at least six or seven items in each column, skip the next exercise.
d. You do quite a few good, positive things for each other.
e. How do you feel about these lists?

Exercise 5. Being Good to Each Other

a. If the family has had a very difficult time with the last exercise or if they could not give examples of positive behavior toward each other. You may do more things for each other than those you have just stated; sometimes people need practice in recognizing their good deeds.
b. Would someone be doing something constructive for you if he or she went through your private belongings or put your clothes in a pile on the floor? This action is not considered a positive behavior.
c. Would someone be doing something positive for you if she or he prepared your dinner? Give more examples of positive behavior—not necessarily things you do, but things that would be considered good deeds?

Exercise 6. Practicing Constructiveness

a. Go through the exercise of making someone angry and being angry. Only this time, use the nondestructive way to express anger.

b. To express anger without insult or attack is not easy and generally goes against our habits. Why should we want to express anger this way? Is it because we would be much less likely to hurt those we love?
c. Let the family discuss the relationship between anger and hurt feeling.

Homework
All of you would have to work at mastering this new way of expressing yourselves. In the coming week, when angry situations arise, try to handle them nondestructively, even if you feel awkward or silly at first. When the storm has subsided, write down what happened and how it was handled so that it can be discussed next week. Are there any questions before we close?

Understanding Positions

ID____ ***Date***____________

Exercise 1. Checking on Homework
a. How did last week go?
b. Did you try to express your anger in nondestructive ways?
c. Check their homework from the preceding week and the week before if they were to repeat that assignment.
d. Deal with any problems by repeating the pertinent directions from this program. Today's exercise will be divided into two parts. We shall meet with you, (parents' names), and (co-helper's name) shall meet with you, (teenager's name).
e. If you are working alone, say: For the first half of the exercise, I would like to meet with you, (parents' names); then I would like to meet with you, (teenager's name), for the second half of the exercise. Is this agreeable to everyone?
f. If anyone objects, say: To help us work toward the goals of the workbook, it is in everyone's best interests that we work this way for today.

Exercise 2. (Parents): The Crises of Adolescence
a. As you know, adolescence can certainly be a time of stress and storm. At times it may seem to you that your teenager will do nothing except rebel against authority and convention. There is a consolation, though. Do you know what it is?
b. There is a method in (his/her) madness. (She/he) is trying to free (himself/herself) from childhood ties with you; establish new relationships with peers, and find (his/her) own identity.

Exercise 3. (Parents): Permissiveness and Over-Permissiveness
a. Can we distinguish the meaning between permissiveness and over-permissiveness. What do these words mean in your relationship with your teenager?
b. Could we agree that permissiveness is the acceptance of your teenager as a person with a right to (his/her) feelings and wishes and that over-permissiveness is allowing your teenager to express (his/her) feelings in ways that are undesirable and that go against your value system as parents?
c. Permissiveness can bring the confidence and the ability to express feelings appropriately; over-permissiveness brings anxiety and more and more demands for privileges that cannot be granted. How might this happen?

d. In summary, then, one way to look at the difference between permissiveness and over-permissiveness would be as a difference between, for example, accepting your teenager's restlessness and discontent and approving when (he/she) expresses those feelings in unpleasant ways. What would be an example of a way that you could tolerate unlikable behavior without approving it?

Exercise 4. (Parents): Setting Limits

a. Although your teenager may not acknowledge it, (he/she) needs your help but that help must be subtle. Continue to provide limits, guidelines, and values, even when your teenager protests. Of course, restrictions can be gradually lifted as (she/he) matures; but adolescents grumble as they may I sometimes feel a secret relief when parents add the weight of their authority to areas of uncertainty. What are your ideas along these lines?
b. As you become increasingly confident of your teenager, your silent love and (his/her) knowledge of your affection and respect will be (his/her) main supports. Does that seem reasonable to you?
c. Even if it seems that confidence and the ability to stand and wait are distant and difficult goals, you can begin to try some things right away.
First, allow your teenager (his/her) privacy. Resist all temptations to pry. This includes trying to be a pal. For respect to flourish, you must maintain enough distance between you and your offspring to provide privacy.
Second, respond to your child's moods and feelings genuinely and with empathy but not with over-concern and lecturing. Parents who want their teenagers to continue to express their feelings must ask questions and talk with them. Do you have any questions, suggestions, or ideas?

Exercise 5. (Teenager): Joining the Adolescent

a. What are some things you would like or ways that you would like your life to go that your parents are against or hesitant about? For example, wearing your hair a certain length or being able to have friends over at certain times.
b. How would you react if you could be taught how to get your parents to be more agreeably and to be more open to your requests and suggestions?

Exercise 6. (Teenager): Smiles and Thank Yous

a. When your mother does something extra special for you and you give her a big smile and a thank you, what does she do?
b. You might say your smile rewarded her and made it more likely that she would do something special for you again, right? What if you had turned away instead of smiling? She may be less likely to do the favor again.
c. Smiles and thank yous usually make people do more of things you want them to do. Other things you do also reward your parents. What are some of the rewards?
d. Can you recall all of the positive things mentioned several practice exercises ago?
e. It does not make a difference whether your parents are rational about certain issues—they are issues that matter to them. You can be treated more like you

want by rewarding your parent when they behave in ways that are pleasant to you and by not saying a word or expressing your discomfort (as you learned in the last practice exercise) when they are harsh. Do you have any questions?

Homework (Teenager)
Next time the discussion will be about appreciating the good things you do for each other. During this week, you might begin to test what you have discussed today. Any questions?

a. The giver knows that he or she appreciates it.
b. One way you can do this is by praise. What is praise?
c. Could we all agree that praise is a sincere, positive reaction to a person or an act and that praise is not the same thing as flattery, which is insincere and said for personal gain?
d. Why do some people feel anxious or embarrassed at receiving praise?
e. Would a certain type of praise make them feel that way?
f. Here are a few examples such as, "You are always so good," "You are a great poet," or "You are so smart." Praise that evaluates personality or character may be unpleasant. We may feel that we must deny it. On the other hand, praise that describes efforts, accomplishments, and feelings is helpful and safe. What are some examples of constructive praise? For example such as "Thank you so much for the card. It is so pretty and witty that I feel better already." "Your yard looks like a garden. It is a pleasure to look at it." "Thank you very much for the delicious dinner. It was super, Mom." Do you have any questions about using sincere descriptive praise for actions that merit praise?

Homework (Family)
For homework, do two things.

a. Write down ten nice things you have done for each other and how you showed your appreciation. If you praised the other person, write down the words you used. Any questions about that?
b. Write down all the conflicts that you have in this coming week. Try to reach a compromise; write that down, too. If you cannot compromise, do not fight about it; just write down the conflict.

Family Sexuality

ID____ ***Date***____________

Exercise 1. Definitions of Sex and Sexuality
a. Please tell what human sexuality means to you.
b. How does human sexuality differ from sex?
c. How are they similar?

Exercise 2. Life-Cycle Changes
a. As all of us know, biological and psychological changes occur at each stage of life. For instance, pubescence is generally thought to be a time of beginning

awareness of sexuality, whereas middle adulthood is thought to be a time of knowledge. What we would like you to do now is think about where you are in your life and what changes—biological and psychological—you are experiencing in your own sexuality. List these changes in a piece of paper or on the computer. Try to be as specific as you can because we are going to use these lists later. Take about 5 min to write as many changes as you can.

Exercise 3. Comparison of Changes

a. Now that you have made your lists of changes, we want you to move so that you are facing a family member of the same sex. For now, we are going to consider you and the person you face partners. Tell about the changes you are experiencing now.
b. Did you note any differences in your list and the list of your partner?
c. How about similarities?

Exercise 4. Intergenerational Comparisons

a. Now change places so that you are seated opposite the family member of your own age group. How do your lists compare?
b. Can you think of any other change?

Exercise 5. Intimacy

a. Interpersonal relationships may be one way of fulfilling our concepts of our own sexuality. What does an intimate relationship mean to you?
b. List things that you consider essential for an intimate relationship.
c. How do these lists compare?

Exercise 6. Role-Reversal Situations

a. As we have seen, there may be similarities and differences in our views regarding intimacy and our own sexuality, depending on our stage in the life cycle. Particularly at this stage in the family life cycle, differences may be accentuated and conflict may arise. Do you agree?
b. So that we may examine these differences, try to reverse your roles in the following situations.

   1. You, (male adolescent), and you, (female adolescent), are the parents, and your parents are now your children. You have given your son permission to take your new car out when he goes to his first school prom. He has had his driver's license for about a month. His date is with a girl you do not know. Discuss this situation with him.
   2. You, (names of adolescents), have given permission for your daughter to go out on her first single date. You do not know the boy, although your son says that he has a wild reputation and is a "real stud." Discuss this situation with her.

Exercise 7. Beginning Sexuality

a. As you remember from the first exercise, sexuality involves a number of aspects of the whole person, not just physical attributes. Discuss the beginning of teenage sexuality. This is a time when there may be some concerns about your body and about the role you will play as a sexual person. Think about your own awareness of your sexuality and your feelings and reactions to the following areas: body awareness, feelings of desire, masturbation, intercourse, birth control.

Note: This workbook is incomplete and a relevant addition should be obtained by any other workbook contained in this Appendix or in previous publications.

Marital and Parental Assertiveness

The purpose of this workbook is to increase marital and parental assertiveness.

Exercise 1. Conflict Fantasy

a. *You are going to use fantasy to help you learn more about yourselves. Please close your eyes and get comfortable. Become aware of yourself, your heartbeats, your feelings, and your physical comfort. You will begin your fantasy now. You are walking in a meadow: the sun is shining; it is warm but not too warm; you smell the flowers and feel the breeze in your face and everything is peaceful. Suddenly, you become aware of a wall in your way. It is a tall brick wall. You look to the right but see no end to the wall. You look to the left, and it appears equally endless. What will you do to get to the other side? Think quietly to yourself about what you would do.*
b. *Now turn to your partner and tell each other how you would cope with the wall. Make sure that you listen to each other with understanding; ask questions to make sure you understand exactly what your partner means; find out how your partner felt on first becoming aware of the wall. Let your partner know that you understand what he or she is saying.*

Exercise 2. Conflict

a. *Is there any similarity between the way you dealt with the wall and the way you handle conflict?*
b. *How do you usually handle conflict in your family?*
c. *What do you do when there are fights at the dinner table?*

Exercise 3. Who Am I?

a. *With the paper and pencil provided for you please for list ten answers to the question "Who am I?"*
b. *Now try to rank your answers in order of their importance to you and in terms of how much loss you would feel if this part of you were taken away.*

Homework

Practice listening to the members of your family this week and ask questions; check with them on the accuracy of their messages. One way to make sure you understand is to ask "Do you mean…?" Do this until you are sure you have heard the complete message and heard it accurately.

Communicating Feelings

***ID*____*Date*_______**

Exercise 1. Checking on Homework

a. How did the homework assignment work out?
b. Are there any questions?

Exercise 2. Feelings

a. Making feeling statements is a good way to communicate with family members. A feeling statement requires two things: first, that you be aware of your own feelings. Second, that you express your feelings in such a way that the other person can hear you. Name some feelings.
b. Make a list of the words suggested, then read the list and add any obvious omissions.

Exercise 3. Expressing Emotions

a. *We feel emotions—love, joy, fear, anger. We express emotions by smiling, laughing, yawning, and frowning. It is important to make sure our emotions, or our feelings, and our body messages say the same thing.*
b. *Call out some of the feelings on the list and ask group members to volunteer to act out-those emotions, without using words. Next, ask someone to act out a feeling and ask group members to guess what that feeling is.*

Exercise 4. "I" Messages

a. *Communicating your feelings in a congruent way means expressing yourself in "I" terms. It means taking responsibility for yourself rather than using generalities or blaming someone else for your thoughts.*
b. *Try to give your partner some "I" messages that you may not have shared with each other before.*

Exercise 5. Comparisons

a. *Expressing anger openly, just like expressing any feeling openly, brings better communication. Expressing hostility distances others and makes them feel they must defend themselves. You are to make a comparison about your partner that makes your partner look bad. For example, your partner's friend is a better cook. With each comparison, your partner will take one step back each time you compare (him/her) with the friend. Try to make at least three comparisons.*
b. *Can you feel how this distances you?*

Exercise 6. Hostility and "I Feel" Statements

a. *A hostile statement is a blaming or judging statement. You are to discuss which are the more direct statements in the following pairs of sentences:*
You are never on time.
I am angry with you for being late.
You make me feel so dumb or I feel foolish.
You drive like a speed demon or I am scared in the car with you.
You let me down or I feel rejected.

Exercise 7. Blaming

a. *Accusing and blaming results only in defending so communication is blocked.*
b. *What do you usually do when someone blames you?*

Homework

This coming week, pick at least three occasions to make "I" statements to tell your family how you feel when you talk with them about something important to you.

Asserting Yourself

***ID*______________________________________*Date*________**

Exercise 1. Making Requests

a. Sometimes you have to request a favor from someone or ask your family to do something for you. This may be something you hesitate to do.
b. Can you think of some examples of such requests? An example might be, "Will you watch the children while I go shopping?"
c. Write down as many reasonable requests you may make for something you need, like, or want.

Exercise 2. Saying No

a. Can you think of times you wanted to assert yourself but you did not?
b. Saying no to someone can be awfully hard, especially to someone close to you or someone you do not want to antagonize. Can you think of times when you agreed to do something so you would not hurt a member of your family and then felt angry with that person for putting you on the spot? Write down as many instances as you can.
c. How could you soften the blow of having to say "NO" to someone you love and who loves you? Write down as many instances you can think of.

Exercise 3. Righting a Wrong Situation

a. Sometimes you need to demand your rights as a person. For instance, you are in the checkout line of the grocery store, hurrying to get home to your family. You have one item in your hand. Suddenly a lady with a basketful of groceries cuts in line ahead of you. What do you do?
b. Sometimes we try to please others and ignore our own feelings and rights. Sometimes we blame or put down another person. Neither of these responses get us what we want. Do you ever find yourself doing this?
c. Asserting yourself not only gets you what you want; it helps you feel better about yourself. Does anyone have any comments or questions about that idea?

Exercise 4. Learning the Steps in Asserting Yourself

a. There are three steps to asserting yourselves:

   i. Understanding the other person
   ii. Giving a straight message
   iii. Making a definite request

The three steps are the following examples.

i. You let the other person know you understand when, for example, you say to your son, "I know you are enjoying that television program." Then present a straight message, along with your reason for the desired outcome.
ii. A straight message often begins with "but": "But I asked you to do the dishes before you turned on the TV."
iii. Then say exactly what you want to happen: "So I'll have to ask you to turn off the TV until the dishes are done."

Exercise 5. Role Playing
Role-play the following situations, using the three steps in Exercise 5.

a. You are in a restaurant, and the waitress brings you cold food. What would you do?
b. A friend stops by to visit you, but you are in a hurry to leave the house. What would you do?
c. You have been waiting for help in a store, and the clerk waits on someone who arrived after you did. What would you do?

Exercise 6. Straight Requests
a. If you want to assert yourself, it is important that you make a straight request for change. Couple or group members are to pair off and make eye contact with each other and their voices should be strong and that their nonverbal messages are consistent with their words. The listening partner will feed back what he or she sees and feels about the partner who is assertively requesting a change.
b. Make up as many requests as you can think of without expecting any answers from your partner in this exercise.

Homework
Try asserting yourself during the week. Practice in your family so that next week you can write down as many times you tried to assert yourself in the family and in public.

How does feeling more assertive work for you?

Fair Fighting for a Change

ID______________________________________***Date***_______

Exercise 1. Checking on the Homework
a. How did your assertiveness practice go during the week?
b. Do you have any questions or problems?

Have you ever thought of fighting as a chance for a clear talk? Fighting can serve a useful purpose. It can even help a relationship grow. Family members fight for better understanding, not a knockout. The objective of a good family fight is to exchange information about feelings and bring about change. Fair fighting means careful listening and the use of feedback.

Exercise 2. Timing—When and Where to Fight
a. How could you arrange to fight by appointment with members of your family?
b. The more deliberately a fighter gets his or her message together, the less likely it is that the fighter will be destructive. The fight for change should begin with

the aggressor's notice that he or she wants to fight. The aggressor might begin by saying "Please listen to me—I want to fight for a change." The invited partner can then accept or postpone the fight.

c. It is important, however, that information be current, so try to schedule a time as soon as possible. Try to follow a banking rule—the same-day clearance of checks. Now, we want you to plan ahead, pair off and practice asking for a fight.

Exercise 3. Before You Can Complain for a Fair Fight

a. Take the time to decide exactly what gripes you. Then decide what you want done about it.
b. Rehearse in your mind what you want to say and how you are going to say. Continue doing it until you are satisfied that what and how you are going to say it will not be destructive.

Exercise 4. How to Present Your Complaint

a. The form for presenting your complaint is descriptive: "What you do is. ….It's effect on me is…. When you do it, I feel…."
b. Be sure to explain how your partner's behavior affects you, hurts you, or angers you. This is the information that brings change.
c. Discuss the presenting of complaints and ask for a volunteer pair to role-play the presenting of a complaint. Couple or group members may help the volunteers with suggestions.

Exercise 5. Feedback

a. It is the complainer's responsibility to make sure the partner has heard the complaint and knows exactly what the aggressor means.
b. Feedback slows the fight and helps each partner get an accurate message.
c. Could the same pair that volunteered for the preceding exercise to role-play feedback on the complaint that was presented?

Exercise 6. Demand for Change

a. State clearly the behavior you want changed.
b. Then ask "How about it?" or "Will you do it?"
c. It is then up to your partner to accept or reject your request for change. Your partner must decide. "Do I want to do this? Can I do this?"
d. Discuss how comfortable they would be with this approach to fighting.

Exercise 7. How to End a Good Fight

a. There is really no end to fighting in a creative family—there are only pauses. Family members always need new information. When fighting is fair and constructive, there are no losses. Everybody should win. Fights end in rounds that are negotiated together. A fight ends when both fighters have said all they need to say on one specific issue.
b. Try to end the fight with some physical expression of good will. Couple or group members are encouraged to discuss fair fighting.

Homework

Pick a practice/pretend fight with a family member. Remember that what you want is new information about how your opponent feels. What you do not want are insults and hurt. Make sure to make an appointment at least 24 h ahead and not at the last minute.

How to Score a Good Fight

***ID*____*Date*__________**

Exercise 1. Checking on the Homework

a. How were the practice homework fights?
b. Couple or group members are to help each other if there are any problems.
c. Fair fighting means sticking to a single issue and keeping the fight in the "here and now."
d. There are several ways to do this.

Practice exercise in this workbook are designed to help you keep your fights constructive.

Is the fight based on a real issue, or is game playing involved?

a. Your couple or group will think of some examples of

   I. Authentic complaints
   II. Some phony complaints or
   III. Game-playing *maneuvers*

b. Discuss similarities and differences among authentic, phony, and game-playing complaints.

Exercise 2. Injury

a. It is important to keep the fight above the belt, so that, by keeping injuries above the belt the opponent can tolerate and absorb them which is ok.
b. The fighter who says something mean, hurtful, or intolerable to the opponent has hit below the belt.
c. How can you know the areas in which each member of your family is too vulnerable to be attacked?
   Can a family member call "foul" or "ouch"?
   Talk with your partner about your own personal belt line.

Exercise 3. Involvement

a. A good fight means plenty of give and take.
b. If one partner evades or denies, the fight and it becomes a one-way fight.
c. Ask your partner or group members for an example of a one-way fight.

Exercise 4. Responsibility

a. Each fighter must take responsibility for himself or herself.
b. A partner who blames someone else is dodging responsibility. For the group, how can a person "own" the responsibility for a fight when he or she is the non-aggressor?
c. Can you see the need for "I" statements?

Exercise 5. Humor

a. Find some appropriate humor in a fight.
b. This does not mean a put-down or sarcasm or ridicule.
c. Can you think of some examples of appropriate humor in a fight?

d. Think and write down as many possible humorous ways you can use to make a fight more human, less stressful, and acceptable.

Exercise 6. Communication

a. Is the complaint clear?
b. Is communication descriptive?
c. Is there feedback?
d. These are all important parts of a good fight. Discuss the questions together.

Exercise 7. Directness

a. A good fight is focused on the here and now. It is never fair to bring up the past. A fair fight is about current problems. It does not get displaced onto children or other people.
b. Who in the group can describe a "kitchen-sink" fight?

Exercise 8. Specificity

a. *It is important that complaints be limited to directly observable behavior.*
b. *Mind reading is not fair.*
c. *Role-play observable from mind-reading to demonstrate the difference.*

Homework

Pick another practice fight with a family member at a specific place and at a specific time. Include the strategies discussed in the last two practice exercises. The strategies include timing, presenting your complaint descriptively, getting feedback, and ending with goodwill. Try hard to make your fight constructive. Keep written notes of your fight.

How to Deal with Anger

ID______________________________________***Date***________

Exercise 1. Checking on Homework

a. *Begin by discussing homework: Does anyone have questions about constructive fighting?*
b. *Allow yourself time to report how fair fighting is working for you.*
c. *Couple or group members can help to reinforce one another.*

Today we are to look at some guidelines for dealing with someone who gets angry.

Exercise 2. Angry Feelings

a. *What happens to you when someone is angry with you?*
b. *How do you usually react?*
c. *How do you feel when you react?*

Exercise 3. Learning to Accept Angry Feelings as Expression of Hurt Feelings

a. *When someone is angry with you, it helps to listen, allowing that person to express his or her complaint. How can you let someone know that you hear the complaint?*

b. *Ask to role-play describing a complaint. Listen to the complaint and then let the aggressor know that he or she has heard the aggressor's message.*
c. If possible try to go below the anger and focus on how much hurt there is underneath the anger.

Exercise 4. Owning the Problem
a. *Another help in dealing with an angry person is to own the problem and express your desire to help solve it.*
b. *How would you feel if your partner listened to your gripe and then showed you that he or she would like to help you do something about it?*
c. *What could you say that would let your partner know that you would like to help?*

Exercise 5. Getting the Facts
a. *After you have allowed the angry person time to state his or her complaint, try to find out what can be done to keep this from happening again. How could you do this?*
b. *The objective of these guidelines is to help you learn to listen and hear what the angry person is saying, considering anger the smoke over the fire of hurt feelings.*

Exercise 6. Constructive Anger
a. *It is important for us to find out whether you are now more comfortable with feelings of assertiveness and aggression. Are there any comments or questions? Do you think you can now share your negative feelings more effectively with your family?*
b. *Do you think you can now use your anger constructively and fight fair with members of your family as well as outside your family?*

Note: There are numerous other workbooks about feelings: anger, sadness, and fear in many other publications (Hooper et al. 2014; L'Abate 2011a, c, 2013b, c, d).

Parental Effectiveness with Adolescents

***ID*____*Date*________**

Exercise 1. The Typical Ten
Listen to statements that you might hear from one of your children and then think of your typical response to such a statement. If the statement is not one that you usually hear, imagine one of your children saying it and try to imagine how you might answer. Write down your responses—we will discuss them later.

Read the following statements one at a time.

1. How come I have to empty the garbage all the time?
2. Sally never talks to me anymore. I see her in the halls, and she is like a walking iceberg.
3. School is the biggest waste of time. All you do is memorize a bunch of junk that never did anybody any good.
4. That little brat next door keeps kicking me in the shins. What a monster!

5. Tommy always gets to stay out late. How come I have to be in at 11, and he can stay out as late as he wants?
6. Will you get off my back?
7. Well, I did not make the basketball team for the third year in a row.
8. Linda has a date every Friday and Saturday night. I never get asked out.
9. I do not know what I want to do after high school. I am not even sure whether I should go to college or look for a job.
10. I have done this math problem three times, and I still cannot get it to come out right.

Exercise 2. Evaluating Answers

a. Now look at our answers and put an X next to the ones that are typical of the ways parents respond to their children. Did any of your answers give an order or tell the child to do something? If so, put an X next to it.
b. Would one of you give us an example—one you have written down or one that occurs to you now. Did any of your answers threaten or tell what consequences would occur if the child did something? If so, put an X next to it.
c. Can anyone give us an example?
d. Continue this format for the following questions.

    1. Did any of your answers tell the child what he or she should do or ought to do?
    2. Did you tell the child how to solve a problem or give the child advice or suggestions?
    3. Did you try to influence the child with logic or information?
    4. Did any of your answers express or imply a negative judgment of the child?
    5. Did any of your answers express or imply a positive judgment of the child?
    6. Did any of you call the child a name or shame the child?
    7. Did any of you tell the child why he or she was saying something? Did you play psychologist?
    8. Did any of you reassure or console the child, trying to make the feelings go away?
    9. Did any of you try to learn the reasons for the statement or try to get more information to help solve the problem?
    10. Did you try to distract the child from the problem?

Exercise 3. Hidden Messages

a. The answers you put an X beside are the typical ways that parents respond to their children. What hidden messages do responses like these send to the child?
b. If no one responds, what does that say about how the child feels or what the child is worth?
c. What is the result?

Exercise 4. Answers That Work

a. If these methods of answering our children do not work, what other way is there?
b. What are some of the answers that you did not mark with an X? Discuss them, being sure that they should not have been marked.

c. If they really should not be marked with an X, what makes them different?

Exercise 5. Who Owns the Problem?

a. In all examples presented earlier, the child had a problem. The child expressed a need or a desire for something. When your children have a problem, how do you feel?
b. Can we say that when our children have a need, we feel bad and we want to help them? Parents, too, have needs. Sometimes our children act in such a way that our needs are affected. Then we have a problem. It is important to be able to tell who has the problem so that we will know what to say. When parents have a problem, who needs to be helped?
c. Can we agree, then, that when the child has the problem, we want to help the child? When as parents we have the problem, we want to help ourselves.
d. Let us look at some problems and see if we can tell who owns the problem.

   1. Tom's hair is flowing over his shoulders. His father thinks it is disgusting and is concerned about the impression his son makes. Whose problem is it?

      I think we can say that it is the father's problem because he is the one who is bothered by the long hair and has the desire to change it.
   2. The television room is a mess, thanks to three active boys. Mother wants it cleaned up because a friend is coming over for a visit. Whose problem is it? I think we can say that it is Mother's problem because she is the one who needs to have it clean.
   3. Mary has delayed her homework until the last minute. Now she has only a half-hour to do it and asks her mother to help. Whose problem is it?I think we can say that it is Mary's problem because it is her homework and she is the one who needs to finish it.

You can see, from these examples, that the person who has the problem is the person who needs or desires change. Are there any questions about who owns the problem?

Homework

Your homework for next week has two parts. First, listen to yourself. Listen to how you typically respond to your children's problems. See what the results are. Second, when you have a conflict in your family, stop and ask yourself, "Whose problem is it?" Practice identifying who has the problem whenever a conflict arises. Bring in writing examples of a problem that belongs to you, the parent.

Learning to Listen

ID____***Date***_______

Exercise 1. Checking on the Homework

a. For your homework, you were asked to observe how you respond to your children. What did you learn from this?
b. You were asked to bring in a problem that you own. We will use those problems in our next practice exercise.

Exercise 2. Listening Intently

a. In this practice exercise, we are going to learn how to listen without interfering with what the other person is saying. First, find a partner whom you do not know.
b. Now, one of you tell your partner about the problem you had this week and why it was your problem. The partner should look away, look around the room, nod constantly in agreement—anything to indicate that he or she is not really hearing what you say. One talks, and the other does not listen. Are there any questions?
c. Ok, go ahead. Allow 2 to 3 min, reverse roles. Allow 2 to 3 min. Ok, stop. How did it feel to talk to someone who was not listening?
d. How did it feel to not listen to someone?
e. Now, let us repeat the exercise with the same partner, but this time, the person listening should sit still and look at the speaker's face while he or she is talking. Simply sit and listen to the other person, without nodding or looking away. Ok, go ahead. Allow 2 to 3 min, then reverse roles. Allow 2 to 3 min. Ok, how did you feel when you were talking to someone who was listening?
f. How did it feel to listen?

Exercise 3. Naming Feelings

a. This exercise is to remind us that we have many feelings. First, name a feeling. Be sure they name feelings rather than thoughts. Second, let us go around again and name some more feelings.
b. Can anyone add some more feelings?

Exercise 4. Listening to Feelings

a. Now practice listening to feelings.

    i. One should say how (he/she) feels right now or tell how (he/she) felt on a recent occasion.
    ii. Then the person next to (him/her) will respond, "I hear you saying that you (feel/felt)…" or "I guess you (feel/felt)…."
    iii. The speaker must be satisfied with the response before the listener can give a feeling of his or her own.

b. Continue with every member of the group. One person says how he or she feels, and the next person repeats what he or she heard the person say. Are there any questions?
c. Be sure that each of you gives a feeling rather than a thought and that the feeling is heard correctly.

Homework

For your homework, practice listening to your children's feelings. At least once a day, respond to one of your children with "I hear you saying that you feel…" or "It sounds as if you feel…" or some other statement to let your child know you understand how he or she feels. Keep a track of what was said in writing and be prepared to report the results next time.

"You" Messages Versus "I" Messages

*ID*____*Date*________

Exercise 1. Checking on the Homework

a. How did your children respond when you listened to their problems and feelings?
b. How did you feel about communicating with your children?

Exercise 2. Role-Playing

a. Teenager: Mad! I hate him! He's a creep and a rat! What was wrong with that one?
b. Did the parent's response match the extent of the teenager's feeling? What would a good response be?
   Teenager: What time will you be home from the party?
   Parent: You're concerned about our returning?
   Teenager: No, I just want to know when you'll be back.

c. How about this one?
d. Did the teenager need help with a problem, or did (he/she) just ask for information?
   Teenager: I got another C in English.
   Parent: You sound disappointed.
   Teenager: I guess I'm just stupid.
   Parent: Will you set the table, honey? Dinner's almost ready.

e. What went wrong here?
f. It takes time to listen to our children in this way. Is it worth the time it takes to help our children learn how to solve their own problems?

Exercise 3. How We Typically Handle Parents' Problems

a. Parents sometimes have problems. Parents need someone to listen to their problems. Let us look at some problems people have as parents and see how you would handle them. Write the words you would say in the following situation. Allow time for them to write their responses after you read each situation.

   1. You are talking to a friend. Your daughter keeps interrupting to ask for snacks and other things.
   2. You come home from work and find the family room in a terrible mess, with books and jackets everywhere.
   3. Your teenaged son leans way back in your 150-year-old chair.
   4. A glass of milk is sitting about an inch from the edge of the table.
   5. Your teenager's elbow is leaning on the table next to it.

b. Do you have any questions about who owns these problems?
c. All these situations are problems of the parent. Let us look at your responses to these situations. Did you respond with an order or a direct command? Put an X next to your answer if you did. Can anyone give an example of an order in one of these situations?
d. Did you respond with a threat? Put an X next to it. Can anyone give an example of a threat?

e. Did you respond by preaching or moralizing? Give yourself another X. How about an example? Did you respond with a suggestion or by offering a solution? Can someone give an example?
f. Did you answer by blaming or judging? How about an example?

Exercise 4. "I" Messages

a. All the responses we have talked about told your child what you thought he or she should do. How does that make the child feel?
b. Did any of you respond to a situation by simply stating your needs?
c. If you stated your needs, you probably began your response with "I" instead of "you." What is the difference between saying "I am disappointed" and saying "You disappoint me"?
d. Can we say that when we have a problem, we have the responsibility of owning it and the feelings that go with it?
e. When we have a problem and state our needs in that situation, we call these messages "I" messages. How do you think your children react to "I" messages?
f. Do you think your children would respect your needs if you stated them clearly?
g. Are you willing to try it and see?

Homework

For your homework, we are going to ask you to try sending "I" messages when you have a problem. First, be sure you own the problem. Then send an "I" message, stating your needs or feelings in the situation. Be prepared to tell the results next time by recording what happened in writing.

"I" Messages, Anger, and Conflict

ID___________________________________Date____________

Exercise 1. Discuss the Homework.

a. Did you practice I statements?
b. How did it go?

Exercise 2. Practice I Statements

a. For your *homework, you were asked to practice* sending "7" messages, and some of you ran into problems, so let us practice on a few more situations. Who will read the part of the teenager?
   Parent: I need to get dinner on the table, but it is covered with books.
   Teenager: So move them.
   Parent: I feel you are pretty careless about picking up your things.
   Teenager: So pick them up yourself.

b. What went wrong here?
c. Did the parent state her needs in the situation? What did she do when her words failed to get immediate results?
d. What was the result?
   Parent: You're an hour late. I expected you at midnight, and I'm really angry at you for being late.

Teenager: You could have gone to bed. I didn't ask you to wait up.
Parent: How could I sleep? You could at least have called.

e. What happened in this situation?
f. What feelings did the parent express?
g. What feelings did the parent fail to express?

Parent (calmly): It's three in the morning. You were supposed to be in by midnight. I was a little concerned about what had happened to you.

h. How is this situation different from the last one?
i. Did the parent's message match the feeling he or she probably had?

Parent: I am so angry with you that I could burst.

j. What is the effect of telling someone that you are angry at him or her?
k. How does it feel to be told that someone is angry at you?

Exercise 3. Anger As a Secondary Feeling

a. Anger is often the result of another feeling. For example, we may feel hurt and that makes us angry. Can you think of any other feelings that might go along with being angry? For the following examples, see if you can figure out what feeling is causing anger. Read the examples and then we will discuss them.

1. Your teenager said she would be home at midnight. It is 3:00 a.m. What feelings would cause anger in this situation?

b. We have already discussed an angry response in this situation. How would you answer if you wanted to express your other feelings? Can you think of a positive feeling that you might have rather than a negative one? They might feel relief.

2. Your spouse has forgotten your birthday. What feeling is causing anger in this situation?

c. How would you express your primary feeling?
d. What is the difference?

3. A teenager is picked up for possession of dope. He is your son. What feelings would you have, other than anger? Would you feel embarrassed? Hurt? Disappointed? Worried? Scared?

e. Can we always control our expression of anger when we feel it strongly?
f. What can we do after we express anger?
g. What would be the benefit of apologizing?
h. Could you then express the other feelings that you have?
i. How would that make the child feel?

Exercise 4. Conflict

a. What is conflict?
b. Is conflict healthy? Can it be healthy?
c. Who wins in the conflicts in your family? Who wins most of the time?

d. Who loses?
e. Is there an alternative to winning or losing?

Homework

For your homework, do observe how you handle conflicts in your family. Find an example of a conflict that needs to be resolved in your family, record it in writing and bring in next time we meet.

Conflict Resolution

ID________________________________Date___________

Exercise 1. Checking on the Homework

a. For your homework, you observed how conflicts were handled by your family. What did you learn from your observation?
b. Report about your specific examples of conflict situations.

Exercise 2. Win/Lose Conflict Solving

a. First, let us look at the examples. Who will read the part of the teenager?
   Teenager: If I'm not back by 11, don't wait up for me.
   Parent: I'd like you to be in by 11 o'clock.
   Teenager: It's a dance—nobody leaves a dance by 11.
   Parent: You will be in by 11. That's the rule, and we're sticking to it.
   Teenager: But all my friends will laugh if I have to—— Parent: No "buts." I'll see you at 11.
   Teenager: All right.
b. Who won this conflict? Who lost?
c. Who is controlling?
d. How do you think the parent felt afterward? How do you think the teenager felt?
e. Do you think the teenager will be in at eleven?
f. Do you think the teenager wants to be in at 11?
   Teenager: If I'm not back by 11, don't wait up for me.
   Parent: I'd like you to be in by 11.
   Teenager: It's a dance—nobody leaves a dance by 11.
   Parent: Our rule is 11.
   Teenager: But this is a special occasion.
   Parent: Oh, all right, but don't be too late.
g. Who won this conflict? Who lost?
h. Who is controlling?
i. How do you think the parent felt afterward?
j. How do you think the teenager felt?
k. Do you think the teenager will be in at 11?

Exercise 3. Setting Limits

a. It is a common belief that children want limits. Let us look at some of the ways we limit our children. Here are some examples. "You have to be in at 11"; "You may not associate with long-haired kids", "I cannot allow you to smoke pot." In setting limits this way, we exert our parental power over our children. How do teenagers react to parental power?

b. On the other hand, if we set no limits at all, we neglect our responsibility as parents. Is there an alternative?

Exercise 4. The No-Lose Method of Conflict Resolution

a. We need to learn a method of resolving conflicts in which nobody loses. Both win because the solution must be agreeable to both. The steps are as follows:

   i. A conflict of needs arises between parent and child.
   ii. Parent and child search for a solution.
   iii. Parent and child evaluate the possible solutions and choose a solution that is acceptable to both of them. Do you understand this method?

b. For your homework, you were asked to find an example of a conflict in your family. Let us see how we might solve some of these conflicts by the no-lose method.
c. Who has an example? Now role-play the conflict. Use the no-lose method.
d. Role-play as many conflicts as time allows.

Homework

For your homework, make a written list of problems or conflicts in your family. List as many things as you can think of about which you and your children disagree. You will not have to show your list to anyone but yourselves.

Conflict, Values, and Responsibility

ID________________________________**Date**____________

Exercise 1. Checking on the Homework

a. For your homework, you made a list of conflicts in your family. We will use this list in our first exercise. Put an X next to each area of disagreement in which you believe you could persuade your teenager that his or her behavior prevents you from meeting your needs.
b. What would be the value of resolving only those conflicts that you have marked with an X?
c. How many of the conflicts on your list are a question of values? Put a V beside the disagreements that are conflicts over values.
d. Can conflicts over values be resolved by the no-lose method?
e. What about conflicts that involve our children's health, such as smoking, drugs, reckless driving? Put an H next to the conflicts that involve their health.
f. Can you protect your children from these dangers?

Exercise 2. Why Use the No-Lose Method?

a. Let us review the no-lose method. A conflict arises; parent and child search for a solution; parent and child evaluate solutions and choose one that is acceptable to both of them. What part does active listening play in the no-lose method?

b. What is the benefit of listening to the needs of our children and being able to state our own needs clearly? Would a child who had a say in deciding on a solution be likely to carry it out?
c. When two people work on a solution, is the solution likely to be more or less creative?
d. What will be the effect on the child's long-term ability to solve his or her own problems? Is practice in thinking through problems valuable? What is the value of assuming the child will carry out the solution?
e. Would you say that "trust builds trust"? If your child does not carry out the solution, what can you do?
f. If necessary, say: You could send an "I" message. You could suggest that you start over. You could look for ways to help your child remember.

Exercise 3. Conflicts Between Children

a. Can the no-lose method be applied to conflicts between children?
b. Who owns the problem in a conflict between children? Would you agree that it is their problem?
c. What is the effect when parents move in to solve problems that do not belong to them?
d. Can we say that we deny our children the experience of learning how to resolve their problems?
e. Can children learn to resolve their own conflicts?

Exercise 4. Conflicts Between Adults

a. Can the no-lose method be applied to conflicts between adults?
b. How? Give examples of how it can be done.

Exercise 5. Responsibility

a. On your computer or on paper and with a pencil, draw a straight line about 6 in. long. At the end of the line on your left, put "adult 100% responsible for child." At the end of the line on your right, put "child 100% responsible for self." Now, we want you to put numbers indicating the ages of your children at appropriate places on the line. What is responsibility?
b. How can we teach responsibility?
c. What responsibilities do your children have?
d. Look back at your list of conflicts and see whether any of those conflicts could be resolved by giving the responsibility to your children.

Exercise 6. Expectations

a. Now, close your eyes and try to imagine your children as you would like them to be when they are adults.
b. What do you see them doing? What are they like?
c. You may open your eyes now. What did you see? What do you want for your children? Are your expectations realistic?
d. Do you think your children have expectations for themselves?
e. Whose expectations do you think they are more likely to meet? Do you think you have played a part in forming their expectations?
f. Why do you think it is difficult for parents to let their children grow up?

Homework

During the coming week, you need to record what happened among members of this family and use a family conference set at least 24 h ahead to discuss whatever issue has come up recently among yourselves. For guidelines about a family conference, search online.

Successful Aging

ID______________________________________**Date**____________

Exercise 1. Attitudes of Young People and Old People

a. You can work with your computer or with paper and a pencil. You are going to read several incomplete sentences. Each of you should complete each sentence twice, giving a different response each time. Write down the first things you think of, please do not spend a lot of time deciding what to write down. There are no right or wrong responses.
   Old people are…
   When people get old, they should….
   Young people are…
   When people are young, they should….
   If I were older, I would…
   As an older/younger person, I am….
   The typical picture of an older person is…
   The typical picture of a younger person is…
b. Allow yourself 4 to 6 min to complete this short exercise.
c. Take a turn to read aloud your responses to the sentences.
d. What do your responses say about how you view old people?
e. How do those of you who are older differ from the younger members in the way you feel about yourselves and each other?

Exercise 2. Adjusting to Old Age—Staying Active

a. One way that some people adjust to old age is to try to stay as active as they were during their middle years. They continue to be active in clubs and organizations and keep an interest in hobbies or find substitutes for them. Have you adjusted to old age in this way?
b. What are some of the pros and cons of dealing with old age in this way?

Exercise 3. Adjusting to Old Age—Disengagement

a. Another way that people can adjust to their old age is by gradually cutting down on how active they are—by dropping club memberships, seeing friends less often, and spending more time with their families or with hobbies. Does this describe you?
b. What are some of the pros and cons of this adjustment to aging?

Exercise 4. Adjusting to Old Age-Continuity

a. Another way that people adjust to old age combines the two ways that were already discussed. People who adjust in this way become less active physically and socially but keep to the same schedule that they always have, such as getting up and going to bed at the same time, maintaining their hobbies and interests, and staying interested in the kind of work they did. Have you adjusted to old age in this way?

b. What are some of the pros and cons about this way of growing old?

Exercise 5. Satisfaction in Old Age

a. How well have you adjusted to old age?
b. Are you satisfied with your life as an older person? What would you like to change or improve?
c. What can the family do to help you?

Exercise 6. Influence of Childhood Ideas

a. Can you remember what your ideas were of old people when you were children? What were they?
b. How do these childhood ideas about old people help or hinder your attempts to grow old successfully?

Homework

During the coming week, write down whatever ideas come into your head about how you are aging and how you plan to age successfully.

Recognition of Aging and Limitations

ID________________________________**Date**_________

Exercise 1. Awareness of Age

a. This first exercise is much like the one you did last time. Adults in the family are to complete the following sentence, writing down as many responses as you can think of in the next 5 min:

You know you are getting older when…

b. Read your responses aloud. Note your concerns about your diminished physical or mental abilities that are stated or implied in the responses of older members. What are some of the differences in how those of you of different generations see getting old?
c. What are some of the similarities?

Exercise 2. Feelings About Growing Old

a. What is it like for you to realize that you have lived most of your life?
b. What did you feel like when you first became aware that you were getting old?
c. In what ways do you feel different about getting older now?

Exercise 3. Dealing With Limits Imposed by Society

a. What are some of the ways our society makes people aware that they are growing old? Retirement is one way that our society increasingly limits the part the older person plays in our society. What experiences have you had with limits placed on you by society?

b. How can you best cope with those limits?

Exercise 4. Dealing with Physical Limitations

a. Have you felt a loss or a reduction of the physical strength or stamina or the mental sharpness of your younger years?
b. What is it like to experience this? Or if you have not had this experience, how might you feel when you do?
c. What can you do to delay or make up for loss of ability or skills?

Exercise 5. Dealing with Fragile Health

a. In addition to affecting our abilities, advancing age eventually affects our health. Has poor health been a problem for the older members of your family?
b. How does having had good health or poor health in the past affect a person's ability to adjust to poor health in old age?
c. What can the rest of the family do to help?

Exercise 6. Resisting Old Age

a. It is not an easy thing for anyone to adjust to old age.
b. What are some ways in which people resist old age or deny that they are getting older and more prone to health problems?

Homework

During the coming week, write down what you can do on the left side of a sheet and what you can no longer do on the right side.

Retirement and Redefining Physical and Social Life Space

ID____________________________________Date__________

Exercise 1. Checking on the Homework

a. Did you work on your two lists?
b. What can you still do?
c. What you can no longer do?

Exercise 2. Middle Age and Retirement

a. *In many ways the period between ages 45 and 55 is the time when a person is most socially active and influential. What experiences did you have between 45 and 55 that made it difficult for you to retire?*
b. *What about 56 to 65 years?*
c. *What about after 66 years?*

Exercise 3. Changing Life Space and Retirement

a. The image of retirement as an endless series of vacations is as unrealistic as the picture of the retiree and his wife secluding themselves in their home, refusing any and all visitors. Many couples, though, sell their houses and move into condominiums or apartments. Have you pulled back from the amount of physical space you once lived in?
b. Did you go through this transition? Was it an easy decision or one you made reluctantly?

Exercise 4. Adjusting to Less Physical Mobility

Decreased physical mobility is another fact of life for older people.

a. What does it mean to you not to be able to get around as easily or as quickly as you used to?
b. Do you depend on others to get around?
c. How does it feel now, knowing you were once very independent and you did not need to rely on others?
d. How does the rest the family feel about having an older person dependent on them?

Exercise 5. Adjusting to Lowered Social Influence

a. Sometimes the loss of influence and social activity in retirement makes an older person withdraw even further from society.
b. Have any of you experienced loneliness or isolation in retirement?
c. How can the family help?

Homework

During the coming week, look over the list of you can do and add what you can do to enjoy that you can do.

Finding Alternative Means of Need Satisfaction

ID___________________________________**Date**__________

Exercise 1. Checking on the Homework

a. Did you try to add how you can add some enjoyment to what you can do?
b. Can we add some suggestions of anybody else you know?

Exercise 2. Distinguishing Between Likes, Needs, and Wants

a. Each of you will please think for a minute about the differences among likes, needs, and wants.
b. Is what a person needs the same as what a person likes or wants?
c. Can you recognize the difference between your likes, needs, and wants?

Exercise 3. Listing Needs and Wants

a. Write down five likes that you have at this time of your life.
b. Write five needs that you have, and five things or qualities that you would like to have.
c. Write down five wants you would like to have available to you.
d. Take 2 to 3 min to complete this task. After you complete the task, you will have an opportunity to read your list. But, pay particular attention to overlapping likes, needs, and wants, especially among the older members.
e. Were you surprised by what was included in the lists?
f. What are the differences likes, needs and, wants of older family members and those of the younger ones?

Exercise 4. Effects of Aging on Likes, Needs, and Wants

a. How does the transition to old age affect what a person likes, needs, or wants?
b. Does the changes in old age make this distinction easier or harder for those of you who are older?

c. As you have grown older, have your likes become likes you needs, or your needs become more as your wants, or have your wants become your needs or your likes.

Exercise 5. Meeting the Need for Companionship

a. How does the older members of your family take care of needs for companionship and friendship?
b. How has old age affected your need for companionship?
c. How has old age changed the way you go about finding companionship?

Exercise 6. Learning to Enjoy Leisure

a. Some people who have worked hard most of their lives, especially those who have been self-employed, have difficulty adjusting to the leisure life that society permits older people. These people have difficulty accepting and enjoying leisure time. Have you had similar problems adjusting to retirement and old age?
b. What specific things can you do to fill the gap left by retirement and make better use of your leisure time?

Homework

During the coming week, use the list of needs that you made or make a new list of your needs and write down specific steps that you can take to meet them. Be as concrete and specific as you can.

Identifying New Criteria for Self-Evaluation

ID__________________________________Date__________

Exercise 1. Checking on your Homework

a. Have you completed your homework? If yes, what kind of steps are you going to take to meet them?
b. Can you think of additional steps to meet your needs?

Exercise 2. Valuing Yourself

a. *As you have done before, please write three responses to each of the following half-sentences:*
   - □ I feel good about myself when I…
   - □ My worth and importance as a person depend on…
   - □ My importance to others is based on…

b. Allow yourselves 2 to 3 min, then read your responses aloud.
c. Do you feel self-worth through productivity, doing activities.
d. Is there differences in the responses of middle-aged and older family members?
e. Are there differences between the older members and the middle-aged members of your family in the conditions under which you value yourselves? What are they?
f. What are the pros and cons of older people's evaluating themselves in the same way that younger people do?

Exercise 3. Importance of Physical Attractiveness

a. Most of us have, from an early age, been taught to be concerned about appearance and physical attractiveness. For men, this concern is often shown by the attention paid to strength, physique, or muscular development. For women in our society, this means concern about beauty and keeping a slim figure.
b. How do you as older people feel about your physical appearance?
c. How have you adjusted to changes in your body and physical appearance?
d. What does beauty and attractiveness mean to members of your family?
e. Are these terms the same or are they different?
f. Have your ideas about beauty and attractiveness changed as you have gotten older?

Exercise 4. Self-Worth as a Child

a. *What do you remember about the things that made you feel good about yourself, things that made you feel worthwhile as a child?*
b. *Were they things about your personality, things that you did or did not do, or things that you owned?*

Exercise 5. Self-Worth as an Adolescent

a. What do all of you remember about what made you feel good about yourself as a teenager?
b. What things made you respected, valued, or liked by others?

Exercise 6. Self-Worth as an Adult

a. What made you feel good about yourself as an adult, during your career and working life?
b. What things did you like and appreciate by others, or valued by society?
c. Were they things about your personality, things you did, skills you had, or the things you owned?

Exercise 7. Self-Worth in Old Age

a. *What will help the older members of your family feel good about themselves?*
b. *Is it fair or realistic for older people to evaluate themselves or be evaluated by society on the same basis that a younger person is evaluated?*
c. *What do all of you value in your older family members?*

Homework

During the coming week, continue thinking on your self-worth as a human being. Write down as many reasons to think well of yourself.

Reintegrating Values and Life Goals

ID____________________________________**Date**__________

Exercise 1. Checking on your homework

a. Did you do your homework?
b. How do you think of yourself now?

Exercise 2. Listing Your Life Goals and Values

a. Write down five goals in your life; five things that you have worked for or tried in whatever way to make a part of your life—past or present. Second, write down five values that you have now or have had in the past—principles that you believe in, that you try or have tried to live your life by.
b. Each one is read aloud what you have written?
c. How have your goals and values changed over the years? What events or experiences led to the change in your goals and values?

Exercise 3. Unmet Goals

a. Do you who are older have any "unfinished business" from your younger years or any goals that you had wanted to reach but did not by the time you retired or became ill?
b. How do you feel about not having reached these goals?
c. How realistic is it for you to continue to try to achieve them?

Exercise 4. Setting New Goals

a. What new goals can you, who are older, set for yourselves?
b. What strong points or abilities do you have now that you could use to achieve these goals?

Exercise 5. Changing Values

a. What values have remained unchanged from your younger years?
b. What values have developed since you retired or became aware that you were getting old?
c. How have the passing of time and the changes in growing old affected your values?

Exercise 6. Realistic and Unrealistic Values

a. What values do you have that are difficult to abide by because of the limitations of old age?
b. What kinds of problems can come up in trying to be true to unrealistic values?

Exercise 7. Respecting and Learning from the Elderly

a. What are some things that people can learn from the elderly in general and the older members of this family in particular?
b. What can society do or not do to make life more pleasant and comfortable for the elderly?
c. How can the older members of this family best cope with their situation until these changes come about?
d. How can other family members help?

Homework

During the coming week, try to put in writing some of the thoughts that have come about as a results of these exercises.

Widowhood

ID_______________________________Date________

This series of exercises can be used with widows/widowers of any age.

Exercise 1. Grief

a. Share as much of feelings of grief as you comfortably can.
b. Learn to understand them better if you share them with someone who loves you and who you love.

Exercise 2. Feelings About Death

a. Think about the moment when your spouse or partner died. Were you with him, or did you learn about it later?
b. How did you feel at that moment?

Exercise 3. Keying In or Blocking Out

a. Do you go through that moment again very often in your mind? How often?
b. Do you try to put that moment out of your mind? Why?

Exercise 4. Feelings—Here and Now

a. How do you feel now—right here—when you talk about that moment?
b. How did you feel in the past?
c. How do you think you are going to feel in the future?

Exercise 5. Grieving

a. Do you think that your family has allowed you to grieve?
b. Do you ever push tears away so that family members would not be impatient with you?
c. What about friends? Have they allowed you to grieve?
d. Do you feel as if they are impatient with your grief?

Exercise 6. Tea and Sympathy

a. Have you ever been annoyed with the expressions of sympathy that family and friends have given you?
b. What kinds of comments have annoyed you most?

Exercise 7. Support and Grief

a. Who do you think has best understood your grief?
b. In what way has this person understood your grief better than others have understood it?

Exercise 8. Loneliness

c. After the death of a spouse, loneliness can be especially painful. How does it effect you?
d. Trying to run away from those feelings is not only difficult but can also be more destructive than facing the painful feelings themselves. What do you think about this?

Exercise 9. Recognizing Loneliness

a. As so many things have to be taken care of after the death of a spouse, it is often quite some time before loneliness sets in. When were you first aware of loneliness?
b. What were the circumstances that led to your awareness of this feeling?
c. Can you describe how you felt?

Exercise 10. When I Feel Lonely

a. At what particular times do you feel most lonely?
b. What do you do about it?

Exercise 11. Avoiding Loneliness

a. Some widows/widoewers who are lonely attempt to deal with their loneliness by eating drinking, or smoking more than they normally do. Have you been doing any of these things?
b. Have any of these things helped?
c. In what way?
d. How long does the satisfaction from (eating/drinking/smoking) last?

Exercise 12. Getting Busy

a. People use other means of getting away from their loneliness, such as shopping, working, telephoning a friend, or going out to lunch, dinner, or a movie with someone. Have you done any of these things?
b. Have they helped?

Exercise 13. Overcoming

a. When you cannot do any of the things that we have mentioned, what do you do to overcome your loneliness?
b. Were those things successful?
c. How?

Exercise 14. Inner Resources

a. How can you use the resources within you to deal with your loneliness?
b. How can you help yourself?

Homework

During the coming week, write down your thoughts about "being alone" and "being lonely." How are they different and how do you plan to deal with each?

Finances

ID____________________________________**Date**____________

Exercise 1. Checking on the Homework

a. Did you work on your homework?
b. Was it useful?
c. How?

Exercise 2. Dealing with Finances

a. Whatever the circumstances, the money situation is there and must be dealt with.
b. Talk about some of the "panics" you may have had, as well as some of the errors and positive new decisions you may have made.

Exercise 3. Financial Awareness

a. When your spouse/partnet died, were you aware of how much or how little money you were going to have?
b. Did you feel financially secure or insecure?

Exercise 4. Benefits

a. Did you know about Social Security or Veteran's Administration benefits?
b. Did someone help you check on these, or did you do it alone?
c. Are these something that still has to be looked into?

Exercise 5. Financial Advice

a. Did anyone try to give you advice on what to do with your money?
b. Were you grateful for this advice, or did you resent it?
c. Did anyone try to get you to invest all your money in a speculative venture?
d. How did you handle that?

Exercise 6. Spendthrift or Miser

a. Perhaps after your spouse died, you had never had so much money at one time. Did you spend some of it recklessly because there was so much of it?
b. How did you feel about doing that?
c. How do you feel about it now?
d. Did you become concerned about money, becoming very frugal because you have to use this money for the rest of your life?
e. Are you still treating it that way?

Exercise 7. Lifestyle Changes

a. Have you had to make any changes in your life because of money? Are there things that you had that you can no longer have?
b. Are you angry about that? Are you perhaps angry with your husband for leaving you in that position?

Exercise 8. Decisions

a. Are there any positive decisions you have made about how you handle your money?
b. Responsibility for finances is scary, yet it can also give a feeling of independence and self-sufficiency. How do you feel about your responsibility and your independence?

Homework

During the coming week, work on putting your finances in order, including savings and bank accounts, available cash, and other liquid assets.

Children

ID______________________________________***Date***______

This week we are going to talk about children. Naturally, the death of their parent has affected them. This effect on them has, in turn, had an effect on you. Your relationship with your children is different now that they have only one parent. We are going to discuss some of the problems that may arise in that new relationship.

Exercise 1. Checking on the Homework?

a. Are your finances in order?
b. What did you do to put them in order?
c. Did you have help from reliable people?

Exercise 2. Children's Behavior

a. Have you noticed any changes in your children's behavior since their parent died?
b. What are they?

Exercise 3. Sudden or Slow Death and Children

a. If their parent had an extended illness and suffered a great deal, what effect do you think this had on them?
b. What effect do you think the suddenness of their father's death had on them?

Exercise 4. Sharing and Withholding

a. Do your children ever discuss their feelings about their parent's death with you?
b. How do you feel when they talk about their feelings? What do you think is the reason they do not talk about it?

Exercise 5. Listing Likes, Needs, and Wants

a. Write down five likes you have at this time of your life.
b. Write down needs that you have at this time of your life.
c. Write down five wants that you have, and five things or qualities that you would like to have.
   Take 5–6 min to complete this task, then have everyone read their lists aloud. Was anyone surprised by what was included in the lists?
d. What are the differences in older members of your family?
e. How does having had good health or poor health in the past affect a person's ability to adjust to poor health in old age?
f. What can the rest of the family do to help?

Exercise 6. Resisting Old Age

a. It is not an easy thing for anyone to adjust to old age. What are some ways in which people resist old age or deny that they are getting older and more prone to health problems?
b. Have you resisted old age or have you accepted it? Tell how you processed this transition.

Exercise 7. Retirement and Redefining Physical and Social Life Space

a. What are the demands and strains that growing old puts on?
b. Your physical mobility, on
c. Marital and family relationships, on
d. Social activity, and on
e. One's influence in general

Exercise 8. Middle Age and Retirement

a. In many ways the period between ages 45 and 55 is the time when a person is most socially active and influential. What experiences did you have between 45 and 55 that made it difficult for you to retire?
b. How about between 56 and 65 years?
c. How about between 66 and 75 years?
d. How about between 76 and beyond?

Exercise 9. Sharing or Shielding

a. Do you ever tell your children what your feelings are about their parent's death?
b. Are there times when you try to keep your feelings from them?
c. If yes, ask: Is it to protect them or what?

Exercise 10. Staying the Same

a. Do you attempt to keep things in your children's lives the way things were before their parent died?
b. How?
c. If things are not the same, why are you trying to keep them that way?

Exercise 11. Making Up the Loss

a. Have you sometimes spoiled your children since their parent died?
b. In what way?

Exercise 12. Resentments

a. Are there times you resent your children's dependence on you?
b. Have there been times that you have changed roles with your adult children?
c. Have they taken parent or adult responsibilities away from you?
d. Do you resent this? Although these changes may present problems in your relationship with your children, remember that the new relationship you create can be as rewarding or more rewarding than the old relationship.

Homework

During the coming week, write down any thoughts that come to your mind concerning what we covered in these exercises. Bring your notes with you for the next time we meet.

Remarriage, Dating, and Sex

ID____________________________________***Date***________

Exercise 1. Checking on the Homework

a. Did you do any writing about what we covered last time we met?
b. If you did, let us discuss it.

Exercise 2. Remarriage

a. Have you thought at all about remarriage? How soon after your husband's death did you start thinking about it?
b. Were your thoughts negative or positive?

Exercise 3. Then and Now

a. Are your thoughts about remarriage different from when you first started thinking about it?
b. How are they different?

Exercise 4. Dating

a. Have you thought about dating? What are your thoughts about it?
b. If you have dated, how did things go on your first date?
c. If you are still dating, what do you think now in comparison to what you thought when you first started to date?

Exercise 5. Whom to Date

a. If you do date, do you date only men/women who are marriageable?
b. If you do not date, would you, if you did date, date only men/women who are marriageable?
c. What are your reasons?

Exercise 6. Sexual Desires

a. Do you have a desire for sex?
b. When did you first become aware of this desire?
c. What were your thoughts about your desire for sex?
d. What do you think the reasons are that you have not thought about sex again?

Exercise 7. Sexual Attitudes

a. Whether or not you have had sex again, are your thoughts about sex different now than they were when you first thought about it?
b. What does sex mean to you?

Exercise 8. Loving Again

a. Do you think that you can love another person again?
b. What are your reasons?

Exercise 9. Building a New Life

a. After you become a widow(er), you have to build a new life. You are no longer married, so you no longer play that role. You must make changes in your personal, family, and social life, and you may have to build a new life outside your home. For many, it means returning to the working world. For some, it is not returning to but entering the working world for the first time. Let us cover some of the changes in building a new life.

Exercise 10. Changes

a. Can you think of some ways in which your life has changed since your husband's death?
b. Do you think these are good or bad changes? Why?
c. If bad, what do you think you could do to make them good?

Exercise 11. Family and Change

a. What are some of the ways that your life is different in relation to your immediate family?
b. Are these positive or negative changes?
c. If negative, how could you make some positive changes?
d. What about relationships with other relatives and in-laws?

Exercise 12. Friends and Change

a. Have you noticed a big change in your relationships with couples who were friends of you and your husband?
b. If yes: When did you first notice that change?
c. Why do you think these relationships have changed?
d. Does this change bother you?
e. Are you interested in continuing these relationships?
f. Why?

Exercise 13. New Friends

a. Have you formed any new relationships since you became a widow(er)?
b. If no: What do you think the reasons are that you have not formed any new relationships?
c. If yes: How did these new relationships come about?

Exercise 14. Beginning Again

a. Have you made any changes in your life outside your home, such as going to work or to school? If yes, what changes?
b. If no, what do you think the reasons are that you have not made any such changes?
c. Do you want to make such changes?
d. What are some ways to go about it?

This workbook is incomplete because there is no final exercise. Please use other final exercises from those included here.

LoveMaking: Sex and Sexuality

***ID*______________________________________*Date*______**

Before starting this series of exercises, it is important that participants borrow, rent, or purchase and see an X-rated or semipornographic movie. An informed consent form related to the nature of these exercises should be read and signed by both participants.

Exercise 1. Arousal

a. Did you find a movie to see?
b. If no X-rated movie was available, go on to let participants describe sexual encounters.
c. If an X-rated movie was seen, what did you think of the movie?
d. What parts did you find sexually arousing?
e. What (if anything) in the film turned you off?

f. Did you see anything you would be interested in trying yourselves?
g. Have you tried it?

Exercise 2. Self and Sexuality

a. Explain the difference among

    i. Sex
    ii. Sexuality
    iii. Sensuality
    iv. Lovemaking

b. Which one of these four words is most important to you?

Exercise 3. Pleasuring and Orgasm

a. Let us begin to deal with arousal. The two most common marital sex problems—premature ejaculation for men and delay (or the absence) of orgasm for women—are related to arousal. In most instances, these problems are not due to medical causes but due to poor arousal timing. Both of you need to think about what arouses your partner. Think of as many ways, things, and places as you can. One of you needs to tell all the things that arouse his or her partner. Record the list on computer or paper.
b. When your partner has finished, you do the same, that is, the husband (or male partner) should be telling the wife (female partner) what he thinks turns her on and vice versa.
c. All right, now that you have each given your list, tell your partner whether any things that arouse you were left off the list and whether you disagree with any part of the list.
d. Repeat the preceding procedure, but this time both of you should list what turns you off.

Exercise 4. Relaxing and Feeling

a. This is another relaxation exercise, but it will also help you get in touch with your feelings. This is also an exercise in giving and taking. Each of you will both give and take, so who wants to be the first giver? This is an exercise in body tapping. Stand behind your partner and begin to tap lightly with your fingertips on (his/her) head. Vary the pressure and cover the whole head and scalp (not the face yet). Feel the shapes, textures, lumps, and curves. Cover the whole head. When you are ready, move around to the face. Using the balls of your fingers, tap the face. Be gentler than with the head, especially around the eyes. Tap the entire face. Continue this procedure to the neck, shoulders, and back, explaining that these places should be tapped with the open fingers and palms. The back tapping should include the buttocks. Tap the chest and stomach in the same way. Keep the pace slow enough to be thorough but not boring. Remember to rest as needed. After the chest and stomach, have the tapper move to one arm and tap its entire length, hand, and fingers, varying the pressure as needed and steadying the arm with one hand while tapping with the other to keep the arm from flopping around.

b. After one arm has been tapped, compare your arms. How do they feel—their length, their temperature, their weight?
c. The tapper should proceed to the other arm. Compare the top half of your body with the lower half.
d. The tapper should do one leg, and compare the two, and finish with the other leg.
e. Allow a few moments to savor the feeling, then exchange roles and repeat the tapping exercise.

Homework

This week's homework assignment is in some ways similar to the exercise you just finished. On at least one night this week, lie together in bed, nude, and touch each other. Explore and caress each other's bodies except for your genitals and breasts. Do not talk while you are doing this. Take turns, a few minutes at a time, and caress your partner all over except, as I mentioned, the genitals and breasts. Express your feelings through your hands. Spend at least 30 min on this exercise. Afterward, talk about what you experienced with each other.

Good Timing

ID______________________________________***Date***________

Exercise 1. Checking on the Homework

a. How did the nonerotic, nonsexual caressing exercise go?
b. What did it feel like to explore your partner's body?
c. What did you "hear" from the nonverbal expression in your partner's hands?
d. What did you learn about yourself?
e. What did you learn about your partner?

Exercise 2. Getting Started

a. Do you make love spontaneously or by appointment?
b. Now about how you get started in your sexual activities. Who usually initiates lovemaking?
c. How much time do you spend on nonerotic, nongenital lovemaking?
d. How much time do you spend on genital lovemaking

Exercise 3. Specific Guidelines

a. Let us look at some ways to resolve the timing problem. Two exercises are important for prolonging male activity and facilitating orgasm in women. These exercises are the penis squeeze technique and the non-demand position for women.

   i. The squeeze technique first using illustrations to explain as follows. To perform this technique, take the position shown here, with you (the wife) sitting comfortably and you (husband) lying on your back. Using any manual or oral stimulation method you choose, stimulate his penis until it is erect and you (husband) feel the first signals of ejaculation. As soon as this happens, you (wife) take your thumb and two fingers and squeeze hard just below the ring (see picture of squeeze technique) with your thumb on the bottom side. Squeeze hard for a few seconds, until the urge to ejaculate subsides. If you squeeze soon enough and hard enough, the urge will go away, but not the erection. Repeat this procedure several times; your goal is a minimum of 10 min before ejaculation. Eventually (this may take several nights of working with the squeeze technique), the aim is to reach a point where the squeeze is not needed.

ii. The other part of this exercise is to increase your (wife) arousal level before you (husband) insert your penis so that both of you achieve satisfaction. Contrary to stories in romantic magazines, mutual orgasm is not the necessary or even the ultimate goal. Because of the timing discrepancy, it may be best if you (wife) reaches an orgasm, or almost reach it, before the penis is inserted. This avoids the timing problem. The non-demand position for female arousal is this. Using this position and what you (husband) learned about what turns your wife on and off, you (husband) will caress, massage, and stimulate your wife, arousing her as much as possible. You (wife) will guide him nonverbally toward or away from your special places. Accept her signals to increase or decrease pressure as she gives them.

Homework
On at least one night this week, take turns stimulating each other, (to wife) using the squeeze to prevent ejaculation, and (to husband) stimulate your wife to orgasm without intercourse. You may want to try other positions for stimulating your wife than the one shown in the picture. Obviously, oral stimulation is impossible in this position. This freedom of position goes for stimulating her only. In this assignment, the position and squeeze technique are essential to prolonging stimulation without orgasm. Remember, if you miss your timing on the squeeze play, continue until your wife reaches orgasm too, and then try again the next night. Do not get upset about mistakes. Keep on trying.

The Context of Love Making

ID____***Date***_______

Exercise 1. Checking on the Homework

a. Begin discussion of the homework assignment by asking the following questions. How did your homework assignment go?
b. Did you have any problems with the squeeze technique?
c. Did you experiment with various ways to excite you (wife) to orgasm? What were they?
d. What did you learn from this exercise?
e. Discuss Optional Exercises for Female Orgasm, including a vibrator.
f. Suggest these exercises if the husband's manipulations have not resulted in orgasm for the wife.

   i. Ask the wife whether she has ever achieved orgasm by masturbation. If so, suggest that she masturbate nearly to completion in her husband's presence, then instruct him in completing it. The couple may use the non-demand position or any other position they prefer.

ii. If the wife says she has not masturbated (or has not masturbated to orgasm), suggest that she try it alone, using any mood enhancers that arouse her. Suggest some, including erotic pictures or stories, if necessary. If this is successful, suggest the preceding exercise.

g. In stubborn cases, a mechanical massager can be used. This method has been demonstrated to be effective after fewer thanten applications.

Exercise 2. Positions and Lovemaking

a. At least indirectly, there was reference to oral-genital contact. By many state laws, this is one of the actions that, even between consenting adults in private, is illegal. At the other end of the spectrum is the view that any act between consenting adults that is not injurious is ok. Review various positions and sex acts. Which position does each of you prefer for making love?
b. Are there any other positions you like to use? What are they?
c. Are there any positions that really turn you off? What are they?
d. Are there any positions that you would like to try? Why not?

Exercise 3. Mood and Lovemaking

a. Aside from the techniques for sexual behavior, mood plays an important part in lovemaking. Let us look at some aspects of mood. Is there a special time for your lovemaking?
b. How rigid are you about the time? Have you tried different times?
c. What were the results?
d. What about place? Where do you have sex?
e. Have you tried other places?
f. Are some places better than others?
g. Why? Let us talk now about aphrodisiacs, mood enhancers. Do you know what an aphrodisiac is? An aphrodisiac is something that increases a person's sexual desire. Although there are no known, proven substances that are aphrodisiacs, some things make people feel sexier, more desirous of love making. Some examples are music, pictures, perfumes, incense, negligees, drinking, and combinations of these or other things. What works for each of you to improve your sexy mood?
h. Have you tried other things?
i. Are there things you would like to try but have not?
j. Why not?

Exercise 4. Making Each Step Count

a. Let us talk about how to handle the sequence of sex:

   i. Foreplay
   ii. Intercourse
   iii. Afterglow

b. Each is important to full sexual satisfaction. What does your foreplay usually consist of?

c. Can you think of any ways to improve it? We will deal more fully with intercourse later, so let us talk about *afterglow.* What does afterglow mean to you? After orgasm, both men and women pass through a stage of winding down, in which their sexual organs and physical beings return to their normal state. At the beginning of this period, men are unresponsive to any sexual stimulation, but women are responsive. This period can best be handled by cuddling until both of you are ready to either end the sexual encounter or start again.
d. What is your usual behavior immediately after orgasm? What does your after-climax behavior do for you?

Exercise 5. Sharing with Each Other
a. In this exercise, tell your partner, in explicit detail, how you would seduce and make love to him or her if you had complete responsibility and control.
b. Think of it as if you were writing the script, directing the action, and taking complete control of making love to your partner. Who wants to go first?

Homework
a. This homework assignment will move you one step closer to satisfactory intercourse. This position allows penetration with the least stimulation for the man. After stimulating each other as you did in the last homework assignment (using the squeeze two or three times), assume this position [female superior position]. You (wife) should lean over him at about a 45-degree angle, slide his penis in comfortably, and move back (do not sit down on his penis). Sit still in this position. Do not thrust, either of you. Concentrate on keeping the penis in your vagina. Remain motionless. If his urge to ejaculate builds, slide back, use the squeeze play, then reinsert. The goal for this position is a minimum of 10 min without ejaculation. You (wife) may finish this homework assignment by achieving orgasm.

Wrap-up

***ID*____________________________________*Date*______**

Exercise 1. Checking on homework
a. Discuss the homework assignment by asking the following questions. How did your homework go?
b. Were you able to reach the 10-min goal?
c. How did inserting the penis without ejaculation feel to each of you?
d. What did you learn from this?

Exercise 2. Postponements
a. Not only is timing important, as we have discussed, but frequency is also critical. Nearly 60 % of sexually active Americans have intercourse a minimum of once a week and that approximately 25 % have intercourse more than three times a week. This, of course, varies with the ages of the partners. Whatever is mutually agreeable to you is what is right for you.

b. The point of this exercise is to learn to handle refusals. We have already suggested one way to handle this. Specifically the proposal to make love should be met by asking whether it can be postponed to a more comfortable time.
c. Example: "*I would love to make love with you, but remember that I need to get up very early and I need a full night of sleep. Can we postpone it to tomorrow night?*"

Exercise 3. Interruptions

a. Discuss how to handle unexpected interruptions to lovemaking. In each of the following situations, assume you are making love and are finishing your foreplay when (i) the phone rings, (ii) the doorbell rings, (iii) your 3-year-old child knocks on your bedroom door.
b. Should you return to foreplay or proceed to intercourse?

Homework

Communicate long-time outcome to the professional who assigned you this workbook, either by phone, mail, or e-mail.

Physically Challenged Children

ID ____ ***Date*** __________

Exercise 1. Causes

a. What do you think are the causes of your child's handicap? Everyone has some idea whether the information is correct or incorrect. Where did you get your information?

4. Are you satisfied that you have the correct information?
5. If not: You can get correct information through: books, articles, or other sources of information.
6. When did you first learn that your child was handicapped?
7. How *did* you feel at that time?
8. Are you searching for help to understand why your child is handicap?

Exercise 2. Guilt

b. Many parents feel responsible for their child's handicap because of something they did or did not do.
c. Have you ever wondered why this happened to your child?
d. How would you answer these questions?

Exercise 3. Inadequacy

a. Did you or do you ever have feelings of inadequacy because your child is handicapped?
b. Do these feelings bother you? In what way?
c. How have you dealt with these feelings?
d. Are you satisfied with the way you have dealt with these feelings?
e. How might you handle them better?

Exercise 4. Responsibility

a. A previous exercise was about how it felt to have a handicapped child. Are there any questions or a comment about anything discussed then?
b. Let us discuss what it means to be responsible for the care of your handicapped child.
c. Do you believe that you understand fully your child's possibilities and limitations?

Exercise 5. Restrictions

a. What restrictions have you placed on your child within the family because of the handicap?
b. Why did you put these restrictions on (him/her)? Think first in terms of you child caring for (himself/herself).
c. Now answer the question in terms of what you expect of your child as a family member. Give the reasons for your answer.
d. Do you place restrictions on your child's activities and relationships outside the family?
e. If yes: What are your reasons for doing so?

Exercise 6. Resistance

a. Does your child agree with these restrictions? Which ones does your child go along with and which ones does (he/she) resist?
b. Self-care for example: What reasons does your child give for resisting or disagreeing with your restrictions?
c. What about in terms of family activities, what are the areas of agreement and on restrictions?
d. What reasons does your child give for resisting or disagreeing with the restrictions?
e. In activities and relationships outside the family, what are the areas of agreement and disagreement?

Exercise 7. Outside Activities

a. What outside activties would you like your child to do or to increase in terms of (his/her) self-care?
b. In what ways do you agree or disagree with your child?

Exercise 8. Inside Activities

a. What activities within the family would you like your child to do or to do more of?
b. What are the reasons your child gives for not doing them?
c. In what ways do you agree and in what ways do you disagree with your child?

Exercise 9. Relationship

a. What relationships outside the family would you like to see your child attempt?
b. What are the reasons (he/she) gives for not making these attempts?
c. In what ways do your agree and in what ways do you disagree with your child?

Exercise 10. Changes

a. If your child agrees to do more things in the areas we have been discussing, how would (his/her) relationship with you and others change?
b. Would these changes be good or bad? Why?
c. Are there any changes you would now like to work on?
d. How and when would you start?

Exercise 11. Necessary Changes

a. Have you made changes in your activities or lifestyle that you consider essential to your child's care and treatment?
b. How and when will you start?

Exercise 12. More Satisfaction

a. What would you like to do differently in caring for your child—something that would make your life more satisfing?
b. How could you go about doing this?

Homework

During the coming week, try one or more of the changes we have discussed. In our next meeting, the discussion will be about how the changes are working out.

Differentiation Between Handicap and Personality

ID ____ ***Date*** __________

Exercise 1. Personality

a. How would you describe your child's personality? How would (he/she) relate to you and others' life in general?
b. Why do you think your child is the way you describe (him/her)?

Exercise 2. Changes

a. What changes would you like to see in your child's personality?
b. How would you help your child accomplish this?

Exercise 3. Limitations

a. What are your child's limitations as you see them?
b. Does your child see (his/her) limitations as you see them?
c. In what ways are your child's perceptions of the limitation different from yours?
d. In what ways are (his/her) perception the same as yours?

Exercise 4. Assets

a. What are your child's assets as you see them?
b. Does your child acknowledge them?
c. Have you ever discussed yours child's assets with (him/her)?
d. If so, when did you do this and what was your child's reaction?

Exercise 5. Feelings

a. Can you express your true feelings about your child to (him/her)?
b. Do you believe that your child can tell you (his/her) true feelings about you?

c. Why do you say that? Have you and your child ever had an open exchange of feelings?
d. When was the last time you did this? What happened?

Exercise 6. Doing Things
a. Look at your relationship with your child in terms of doing things with (him/her). What do you enjoy doing with your child?
b. What things you do not enjoy doing with your child? Why?
c. What things does your child enjoy doing with you? Why?
d. Is there something your child does not enjoy doing with you? Why?
e. Which things do you do most often with your child?
f. Are these things enjoyable for both of you, for your child, for you, or for neither of you?

Exercise 7. Changing Relationships
a. Are there any changes you would like to make in your relationship with your child? What are they, and how would you go about making them?

The Challenged Child as a Family Member

***ID*______________________________________*Date*___________**

Exercise 1. Description
a. Describe your family.
b. What situations can you use to illustrate your description?
c. How do members of the family relate to each other? Do you like each other? Give some examples.
d. Is any family member left out of discussions or activities? Why does this happen?
e. Could this be changed? If so, how?

Exercise 2. Resentments
a. Does any family member resent another family member? Please give an example.
b. How is resentment related to hurt feelings?

Exercise 3. Communication
a. How does each of you communicate with the other members of the family? Do you communicate your feelings or simply ask for and give information?
b. Do some family members communicate better with one member than with another? Give examples.
c. Do you think this is good or bad?
d. Should it be changed? If so, in what ways?

Exercise 4. Positives
a. In what areas do you see positive things happening in your family?
b. What other areas could be more positive in your family?

Exercise 5. Negatives
a. In what areas do you see negative things happening in your family?
b. How strong are these negative things?
c. Can they be changed into positives?

Exercise 6. Improving Relationships

a. How would you change the ways you relate to each other and to the family as a whole?
b. What can you do to make these changes?

Homework

This week at home try the changes we have discussed today. We shall discuss these changes at the beginning of our next meeting.

The Outside World

ID**____** ***Date*****__________**

Exercise 1. Telling Others

a. Was it difficult to tell your friends and relatives that your child has a handicap? Give some examples of their reactions.
b. Did their attitudes bother you or hurt you?
c. In what ways?

Exercise 2. Others' Reactions

a. Did you notice any changes in how people treated you and your child in public?
b. Did this bother you? Does it still?

Exercise 3. Attending School

a. Having a handicapped child attend school can be a very frustrating experience. Was it for you, for your child, and for other members of the family?
b. How have you handled this?
c. Are you satisfied with the way you have handled school for your child? Would you like to change anything about it?

Exercise 4. Discomfort

a. When do you feel the most uneasy or most uncomfortable about the fact that you have a handicapped child?
b. Why?

Exercise 5. Differentness

Anything or anyone who is "different" somehow attracts other people's attention.

a. Have you ever found yourself staring at a handicapped person? What were your thoughts at the time?
b. Is it possible that others, not knowingly, do the same to you and your child?
c. Is there a person to whom you are or were so close that you could tell that person your true feelings about anything?
d. Has your relationship with that person changed since your child's handicap became known?
e. If so, in what ways? If not, why do you think your relationship has not changed?

Exercise 6. Criticism

a. Does anyone ever criticize you for the way you are rearing your child? What are their gripes and the reasons they give for them?

b. In what ways do you agree with them? In what ways do you disagree with them?
c. Does their criticism bother you? In what ways?

Exercise 7. Restrictions
a. Is there anything that you would like to do socially that you are not able to do?
b. What keeps you from doing this?
c. Is there an alternative or a way to get around these barriers?

Homework
This week, try to do something that you wanted to do but have put off for one reason or another.

Bringing It All Together

***ID*____*Date*__________

Exercise 1. Medical Care
a. Are you satisfied that your child is getting the best medical care possible? Give reasons for your answer. If not, what else do you think should be done?
b. Why isn't it being done?

Exercise 2. Education
a. Are you satisfied that your child is getting the best education possible?
b. If you are not satisfied, how do you think it should be changed?
c. Is there any way you can make that change?

Exercise 3. The Future
a. What do you think your child will be doing in 1, 5, 10, and 20 years?
b. What makes you think this?
c. Is this what you would like it to happen?
d. If it is not, what would you like to happen?
e. Is there anything you could do now to help make that happen?

Exercise 4. Institutional Help
a. What public or private agencies can you go to for advice or help in the care, treatment, and independent development of your child?
b. What services do they provide?
c. Where are they located?
d. Is there any charge? If so, how is it determined?

Exercise 5. Family Future
a. What do you see for your family 1, 5, 10, and 20 years from now?
b. What makes you think this?
c. Is this what you would like it to happen?
d. If it is not, what would you like to happen?

Exercise 6. Dreams and Realities
Is there anything you could do now to help that dream become a reality? We hope that you will carry out the ideas you have talked about in these exercises; the things that we have discussed might improve your life, the life of your child, and the lives of your family members.

The Golden Rule

***ID*____________________________________*Date*__________**

Exercise 1. Golden Rule

a. Have you ever heard of the Golden Rule? What does the Golden Rule mean to you?
b. How are the Golden Rule and the Law of Give and Take related to each other?
c. Do you agree that the Golden Rule means dealing with others the way we want them to deal with us? Please comment.
d. What happens when we fail to follow this rule in our dealings with others?
e. What happens to your relationship (marriage, family) when you fail to follow this rule?
f. What are the advantages of following the Golden Rule in your relationship?
g. What are the disadvantages?
h. What do you think would happen to your relationship if you were to commit yourself to follow the Golden Rule?
i. What do you think would happen to your relationship if both you and your partner (mate companion, parent, or child) failed to follow it?
j. How committed are you to follow this rule, and why?
k. List specific instances of when and where you failed to follow this rule and the outcome of that failure.
l. List specific instances of when and where you followed this rule and the outcome of having followed it.
m. Share your answers with your partner (family members) and discuss similarities and differences in your answers. What did you learn from this discussion?
n. In your own words, tell what you learnt from this exercise.

Catharsis

***ID*____________________________________*Date*__________**

Exercise 1. Getting Concerns Out Off Your Chests

a. You are encouraged to speak out, "getting concerns off their chests," suchyou're your feelings about each other and the problems in their marriage.
b. Remember to take notes.

Exercise 2. Reasons for Marrying

- Why did you get married?
- How do you feel about what your husband/wife just said?
- ***Exercise 3. Problems in the Marriage***

a. Only one spouse answer the following question. What problems are you having in your marriage?
b. The other spouse answer the following question. What do you think about what he/she just said? What do you think are the problems in your marriage?

c. Only the first spouse should answer the following question. Do you agree with what your husband/wife just said?

Exercise 4. How Problems Get Started

Alternating from one partner to the other ask the following questions

a. What do you think caused these problems?
b. How do you feel about what (*name*) just said? How do you think the problems got started?
c. How do you feel about that?
d. Do you want to work these problems out?

Exercise 5. The Good Things

- Today start to consider some good things: The things you do for each other.
- List ten things you do for your spouse—things like working and making money, things that you do to take care of the house, being affectionate, and so on.
- Alternate between the partners.
- Write the "satisfactions" on one sheet of paper so that both participants can see the lists side by side. List only the items that your spouse/partner confirms.
- How do you feel about these lists?

Exercise 6. Caring

- Are you surprised that you do so many things for each other?
- Why do you do these things for each other?
- Do you do these things because you care about each other?
- Do something during the next week and throughout these practice meetings. Each time your spouse does one of the things on the list or something else for you, let him or her know you appreciate it.
- Maybe you could both thank each other or say, "I know you do that because you care about me," or "We may have problems, but we do nice things for each other."
- It really is important to let people know you appreciate them. Please comment at will.

Exercise 6. Talking with Each Other

- How do couples talk with each other? What do you say when you disagree with each other about something, say, when or how to discipline the children or where to go for an evening out?
- You should each outline how he or she would handle such a situation. Wouldn't it be better if you added a positive statement to each negative statement you make to each other?
- For example, instead of saying "That was a dumb thing to say," wouldn't it be better to say, "That may be true, but have you ever thought of it this way? "

Exercise 7. Disagreements

a. Now think of a recent negative statement or disagreement you expressed to your spouse. Tell what you said at that time.
b. Now make the statement again, but this time rephrase it positively or add a positive statement to it. Do not dwell on the reasons for the negative statements.

We are not interested in why you made the negative statement. We only want to know what was said and how it could have been said more positively.

c. Work until your spouse is happy with the restatement. Go through several examples, both of past disagreements and of those that might arise in the future.

Homework

From now on, each time you have a negative statement to make to your spouse, either rephrase it positively or add a positive statement to it. You may find it helpful to pause a moment to think about what you are going to say. Do not respond to a completely negative statement. Ask your partner to rephrase it more positively. Do you have any questions about that? Make sure you keep running notes of what happened. We will discuss them on our next meeting.

New Satisfactions

***ID*____*Date*______**

Exercise 1. Checking on the Homework

a. How did things go last week?
b. Did you thank your spouse/partner for the things you do for each other?
c. Did you state things more positively?

Exercise 2. Adding Satisfactions

- Today you are going to try to think of new, additional satisfactions you can give each other. Attempt to come up with a list of ten items for each of you.
- Start with five areas in which you have been having the most difficulty. Let us make the first five new things you can do for each other come from these five areas. Feel free to make suggestions to each other.
- Alternate between each other in taking items. What nice things will you do for your spouse that you are not doing now? Write the satisfactions on one sheet of paper so that both of you can see the two lists side by side.
- Be as objective and specific as possible. For example, "I'll dry the dishes each evening" is more objective and specific than "I'll help around the house." Be realistic; outlandish promises will surely be broken.
- As each new satisfaction is stated, the spouse who is not speaking needs to answer the following question. Is that something you would like? List only the items with which the spouse agrees.
- We are not interested in past problems. We want to know about new things you are going to do for each other in the future.
- When the lists are complete, decide is it fair? Do you think the items on the two lists are equally good and will require an equal amount of effort?
- Look for inequality in the lists and correct it by modifying specific items.

Exercise 3. Doing New Things

- Now that you have agreed on ten new satisfactions to be performed by each of you, it is time to put all this into writing. You have made a list of the ten things you are currently doing for your spouse/partner. Add that to the list of ten satisfactions you agreed on today.

- You should formally agree to provide these satisfactions to each other by signing these lists. The penalty for not holding up your end of the bargain is that your spouse will stop doing the things on his or her list for 1 day.
- But remind each other of the penalty before you resort to it. You both need to sign it and keep copies. Keep the lists where both of you have access to them. If there are any disagreements about whether or not you are holding up your end of the bargain, try to reach a compromise.

Homework

During the coming week, discuss the areas in which you show weakness and try to come up with compromises and new ways of doing things that will make both of you happier in these areas. But do not argue about it: If you cannot agree quickly on a better way of doing something, go on to something else. Keep running notes of what happened and bring them to the next meeting.

Compromise

***ID*____*Date*________**

Exercise 1. Checking on the Homework

a. How did last week go?
b. Did you give each other the new and the old satisfactions?
c. It may be necessary to renegotiate items on your lists.
d. Did you come up with any new ways of doing things in any areas?

Exercise 2. Pinpointing Conflict Areas

a. Now tell each other a specific area in which you seem to be having the most difficulty. Give an example of a conflict in that area.
b. Write the conflict on a sheet of paper. Draw three vertical lines beneath the conflict.
c. Answer the following question separately. How do you want things to work in this area?
d. One of you write a brief answer on the left side of the paper and the other write a response on the right side of the sheet. Now look at the page.
e. Here we have a conflict in what each of you wants in this area. Obviously, both of you cannot have your own way.
f. So we are going to have to try to come up with a compromise. Any ideas about how this conflict could be handled so that both of you would be happy?
g. If this question causes too much fighting, switch to another conflict in this area where you have already gotten over your anger.
h. When you do decide on a compromise, write it down in the middle of the page, between your wishes as originally stated.
i. Now let us see if this is going to be a workable compromise. For the next week, please handle this conflict this way.

Exercise 3. Continued Pinpointing

a. Repeat the procedure in the preceding exercise with a conflict in the area of next greatest unhappiness. You might arrive at a compromise if you looked at things from both points of view. Also, you may already gotten your strong feelings about this conflict out of the way.

b. You cannot solve problems when you feel too strongly about something, such as when you are too mad or too excited. When that is over, try to work toward a compromise. Do you understand how?

Exercise 4. Responsibility.

a. You are responsible for doing things to make your marriage better. We cannot give you a happy marriage. And spouse alone cannot make your marriage happy. You must both, as individuals and as a couple, be responsible for making changes and improvements in yourselves so that your marriage can continue to grow.
b. When conflicts come up in the future, try using this procedure to resolve them after you have worked through your feelings. Remember that compromises are a way for you to show each other that both of you are important.

Homework

During the next week, keep praising your spouse for the nice things you do for each other. During the next week, continue to acknowledge the nice things you do for each other, state disagreements positively, do for each other the good things that you have agreed to do, live up to your contracts, use the compromise procedure, and abide by the results. Do keep written running notes of what happened because we will need to look at them the next time we meet.

Summing Up

***ID*____________________________________*Date*_________**

Exercise 1. Checking on the Homework

a. Did you do your homework?
b. Did you keep written running notes?
c. Why do you think you need to keep running written notes?
d. What happens if your do not keep those notes?

Exercise 2. Keeping Commitments

a. Now let us check on how you are coming along with the things you have agreed to do. Are you acknowledging the nice things you do for each other?
b. Are you continuing to state disagreements more positively?
c. Are you continuing to do the additional nice things for your spouse that you agreed to do?
d. Are you living up to your contracts?
e. Have you abided by the compromises you reached in our past meetings?
f. Are you using the compromise procedure to settle disagreements at home?

Exercise 3. Reciprocity

a. Have you figured out the basic goal of this workbook. What do you think? Want a hint? The key word is reciprocity. Have you ever heard of the Golden Rule? What is it? to reciprocity.

b. The basic goal of this workbook has been to learn to make fair and even arrangements with each other. You do something positive for your spouse/partner, and your spouse does something positive for you. Things work out only when we are fair with ourselves and with each other.
c. What do you think?

Exercise 4. Collecting Feedback

a. What do you think we have accomplished working together? How do you feel about that?
b. From now on you will have to deal with your marriage and problems by youselves. Let us see how this is going to work out. Talk about ways to improve your marriage. If they begin to talk about past problems or hurt feelings, say: We are not here to talk about the ways you have been defeating yourselves. Talk about ways to make things better. When the first conflict arises, say: When you come to conflicts or areas where you think improvements are needed, try using the techniques we have been working on here to make things better. There are many other practice exercises you may need if you want further help.

References

Abrahams, S. (2013). Three generations under one roof. *AARP Bulletin, 54*(3), 16–20.

Abramowitz, J. S., Deacon, B. J., & Whiteside, S. P. H. (2012). *Exposure therapy for anxiety: Principles and practices*. New York: Guilford.

Alexander, J., & Barton, C. (1995). Family therapy research. In R. H. Mikesell, D. D. Lusterman, & S. H. McDaniel (Eds.), *Integrating family therapy: Handbook of family psychology and systems theory* (pp. 199–215). Washington, DC: American Psychological Association.

Alexander, J. F., & Robbins, M.S. (2010). Functional family therapy: A phase based and multicomponent approach to change. In R. C. Murrihy, A. D. Kidman, & T.H. Ollendick (Eds.), *Handbook of clinical assessment and treatment of conduct problems in youth* (pp. 245–272). New York: Springer.

Alexander, J. F., Waldron, H. B., Robbins, M. S., & Neeb, A. A. (2013). *Functional family therapy for adolescent behavior problems*. Washington, DC: American Psychological Association.

American Psychiatric Association. (2004). *Diagnostic and statistical manual for mental disorders*. Washington, DC: American Psychiatric Association.

American Psychological Association. (2013). Guidelines for psychological practice in health care delivery systems. *American Psychologist, 68*, 1–6.

American Psychological Association. (2013). Guidelines for psychological evaluations in child protection matters. *American Psychologist, 68*, 20–31.

American Psychological Association. (2013). Specialty guidelines for forensic psychology. *American Psychologist, 68*, 7–19.

American Psychological Association. (2014). Guidelines for prevention in psychology. *American Psychologist, 69*, 285–296.

American Telemedicine Association (2013). *A lexicon of assessment and outcome measures for telemental health*. No address available.

Amodio, D. M. (2014). Dual experiences, multiple processes: Looking beyond dualities for mechanisms of the mind. In J. W. Sherman, B. Gawronski, & Y. Trope (Eds.), *Dual-process theories of the social mind* (pp. 560–577). New York: Guilford.

Anchin, J., Magnavita, J., & Sobelman, S. (2012). Inaugural editorial statement. *Journal of Unified Psychotherapy and Clinical Science, 1*(1), 1.

Angier, N. (26 November 2013). The changing American family. *New York Times Review-Science.*

Angyal, A. (1941). *Foundations for a science of personality*. Cambridge: Harvard University Press.

Antonopoulou, E. (2004). Humor theory and translation research: Proper names in humorous discourse. *Humor: International Journal of Humor Research, 17*(3), 219–255.

Back, M., Baumert, A., Denissen, J., Hartung, F., Penke, L., Schmukle, S., Schönbrodt, F., Schröder-Abé, M., Vollmann, M., Wagner, J., & Wrzus, C. (2011). PERSOC: A unified framework for understanding the dynamic interplay of personality and social relationships. *European Journal of Personality, 25*(2), 90–107. doi:10.1002/per.811.

Bakan, D. (1966). *The duality of human existence: Isolation and communion in Western man.* Boston: Beacon.

Bakan, D. (1968). *Disease, pain, and sacrifice: Toward a psychology of suffering*. Boston: Beacon.

Bargh, J. A., & McKenna, K. Y. A. (2004). The Internet and social life. *Annual Review of Psychology, 55,* 573–580.

Barlow, D. H., & Carl, J. R. (2011). The future of clinical psychology: Promises, perspectives, and predictions. In D. H. Barlow (Ed.), *The Oxford handbook of clinical psychology* (pp. 891–911). New York: Oxford University Press.

Barnett, J. E., & Shale, A. J. (2012). The integration of complementary and alternative medicine (CAM) into the practice of psychology: A vision for the future. *Professional Psychology: Research and Practice, 43,* 576–585.

Bateson, G., Jackson, D. D., Haley, J., & Weakland, J. (1956). Toward a theory of schizophrenia. *Behavioral Science, 1,* 251–264.

Baumeister, R. F., & Bargh, J. A. (2014). Conscious and unconscious: Toward an integrative understanding of human mental life and action. In J. W. Sherman, B. Gawronski, & Y. Trope (Eds.), *Dual-process theories of the social mind* (pp. 35–49). New York: Guilford.

Becvar, D. S. (2003). Eras of epistemology: A survey of family therapy thinking and theorizing. In T. L. Sexton, G. R. Weeks, & M. S. Robbins (Eds.), *Handbook of family therapy* (pp. 3–20). New York: Brunner/Rutledge.

Belar, C. D. (2012). Reflections on the future: Psychology as a health profession. *Professional Psychology: Research and Practice, 43*(6), 545–550. http://psycnet.apa.org/journals/pro/43/6/545/.

Bentson, V. L., Acock, A. C., Allen, K. R., Dilworth-Anderson, P., & Klein, D. M. (Eds.). (2005). *Sourcebook of family theory & research*. Thousand Oaks: Sage.

Berntson, G. G., & Cacioppo, J. T. (2012). Reductionism. In L. L'Abate (Ed.), *Paradigms in theory construction* (pp. 365–374). New York: Springer-Science.

Bickman, L., Nurcombe, B., Townsend, C., Belle, M., Schut, J., & Karver, M. (1999). *Consumer measurement systems in child and adolescence mental health.* Canberra: Department of Health and Family Services.

Bickman, L., Kelley, S. D., Breda, C., de Andrade, A. R., & Riemer, M. (2011). Effects of routine feedback to clinicians on mental health outcomes of youths: Results of a randomized trial. *Psychiatric Services, 62,* 1423–1429.

Bickman, L., Kelley, S. D., & Athay, M. (2012). The technology of measurement feedback systems. *Couple and Family Psychology: Research and Practice, 1,* 274–284. doi:10.1037/a0031022.

Bleasdale, F. A. (1987). Concreteness-dependent associative priming: Separate lexical organization for concrete and abstract words. *Journal of Experimental Psychology: Learning, Memory, and Cognition, 13*(4), 582–594.

Bloom, B. D. (1985). A factor analysis of self-report measures of family functioning. *Family Process, 24,* 225–239.

Bloom, S. L. (2013). The sanctuary model. In J. D. Ford & C. A. Courtois (Eds.), *Treating complex traumatic stress disorders in children and adolescents: Scientific foundations and therapeutic models* (pp. 277–293). New York: Guilford.

Bobbitt, B. L., Cate, R. A., Beardsley, S. D., Azocar, F., & McCulloch, J. (2012). Quality improvement and outcomes in the future of professional psychology: Opportunities and challenges. *Professional Psychology: Research and Practice, 43*(6), 551–559. http://psycnet.apa.org/journals/pro/43/6/551/.

Boswell, J., Sharpless, B. A., Greenberg, L. S., Heatherington, L., Huppert, J. D., Barber, J. P., Goldfried, M. R., & Castonguay, L. G. (2011). Schools of psychotherapy and the beginning of a scientific approach. In D. H. Barlow (Ed.), *The Oxford handbook of clinical psychology* (pp. 98–127). New York: Oxford University Press.

Boyd-Franklin, N., Cleek, E. N., Wofsy, M., & Mundy, B. (2013). *Therapy in the real world: Effective treatments for challenging problems*. New York: Guildford.

Bray, J. H. (1993). Families in demographic perspective: Implications for family counseling. *Family Journal, 1,* 94–96.

Bray, J. H., Harvey, D. M., & Williamson, D. S. (1987). Intergenerational family relationships: An evaluation of theory and evaluation. *Psychotherapy, 24,* 516–528.

Brown, N. J. L., Sokal, A. D., & Friedman, H. L. (2014). The persistence of wishful thinking: Response to "Updated thinking on positivity ratios." *American Psychologist,* in press.

Bucci, W., Creelman, M. L., & Severino, S. K. (1991). The effects of menstrual cycle hormones on dreams. *Dreaming, 1*(4), 263–276.

Bundlr (2 January 2014). The changing face of psychology: Science. <theguardian.com>.

Bying-Hall, J, (1995). Creating a secure family base: Some implications of attachment theory for family therapy. *Family Process, 34,* 45–58.

Canli, T. (Ed.). (2006). *Biology of personality and individual differences*. New York: Guilford.

Caprara, G. V., & Cervone, D. (2000). *Personality: Determinants, dynamics, and potentials*. New York: Cambridge University Press.

Carlson, C. I., Ross, S. G., & Stark, K. H. (2012). Bridging systemic research and practice: Evidence-based case study methods in couple and family psychology. *Couple and Family Psychology: Research and Practice, 1,* 48–64.

Carroll, K. M. (2013). Treatment integrity and dissemination: Rethinking fidelity via the stage model. *Clinical Psychology: Science and Practice, 20,* 99–106.

Cassady, J., & Shaver, P. R. (Eds.). (1999). *Handbook of attachment: Theory, research, and clinical implications*. New York: Guilford.

Ceccarelli, G. (Ed.). (1996). *La specificita' psicologica: Dai fondamenti teorici all 'intervento (Psychological specificity: From theoretical foundations to inter-ventions)*. Florence: Angelo Pontecorboli.

Chambliss, D. L., & Holon, S. D. (1998). Defining empirically supported therapies. *Journal of Consulting and Mental Health, 66,* 7–18.

Ci, C. (2009). The impact of the abstractness-concreteness of an ad copy on consumers' responses to a product: The moderating role of consumers' regulatory foci and types of product attribute. *Dissertation Abstracts International Section A, 69*(9–A), 3373.

Cigoli, V., & Scabini, E. (2012). The systemic paradigm: The intersubjective narrative approach versus the relational-generational one. In L. L'Abate (Ed.), *Paradigms in theory construction* (pp. 217–234). New York: Springer-Science.

Cohen, L. L., La Greca, A. M., Blount, R.L., Kazak, A. E., Holmbeck, G. N., & Lemaneck, K. L. (2008). Introduction to the special issue: Evidence-based assessment in pediatric psychology. *Journal of Pediatric Psychology, 33,* 911–915.

Colesso, W. (2012a). Alexithymia dimensions in addiction. In M. Cusinato & L. L'Abate (Eds.), *Advances in relational competence theory: With special attention to alexithymia* (pp. 281–298). New York: Nova Science.

Colesso, W. (2012b). Alexithymia dimensions in aging. In M. Cusinato & L. L'Abate (Eds.), *Advances in relational competence theory: With special attention to alexithymia* (pp. 233–242). New York: Nova Science.

Colesso, W. (2012c). Produced and spontaneous emergent interactionism. In L. L'Abate (Ed.), *Paradigms in theory construction* (pp. 375–396). New York: Springer-Science.

Colesso, W. (2012d). The continuum of likeness scales: A proposal for evaluating self-identity differentiation. In M. Cusinato & L. L'Abate (Eds.), *Advances in relational competence theory: With special attention to alexithymia* (pp. 139–160). New York: Nova Science.

Colesso, W. (2012e). Updating the RC-Ecomap research: A multi-model, theory-derived instrument. In M. Cusinato & L. L'Abate (Eds.), *Advances in relational competence theory: With special attention to alexithymia* (pp. 161–184). New York: Nova Science.

Colesso, W., & Scilletta, C. (2009). La relazione scuola-famiglia nella prospettiva dei genitori usando un modello di competenza relazionale. [The relationship between school and family in the perspective of parents using a model of relational competence theory]. *Rivista di Studi Familiari, 1,* 53–72.

Colesso, W., & L'Abate, L. (2011). Relational creativity: A redundant construct and a teachable competence? In A. M. Columbus (Ed.), *Advances in psychology research,* (Vol. 83, pp. 79–97). New York: Nova Science.

Colesso, W., & Garrido, M. F. (2012). Advances in RC-Ecomap research: Administrations of its validity and reliability. In M. Cusinato & L. L'Abate (Eds.), *Advances in relational competence theory: With special attention to alexithymia* (pp. 185–209). New York: Nova Science.

Colesso, W., Cusinato, M., & L'Abate, L. (2013). Self-identity differentiation: A supermodel expanded into two other models. In E. L. Anderson & S. Thomas (Eds.), *Socialization: Theories, processes, and impact* (pp. 79–100). New York: Nova Science.

Corcoran, K., & Fisher, J. (2013). *Measures for clinical practice and research. Volumes 1 and 2.* New York: Oxford University Press.

Corr, P. J., & Matthews, G. (Eds.). (2009). *Personality psychology*. New York: Cambridge University Press.

Cusinato, M. (2012a). Comparing two versions of the Relational Answers Questionnaire. In M. Cusinato & L. L'Abate (Eds.), *Advances in relational competence theory: With special attention to alexithymia* (pp. 93–112). New York: Nova Science.

Cusinato, M. (2012b). Existentialism. In L. L'Abate (Ed.), *Paradigms in theory construction* (pp. 317–339). New York: Springer-Science.

Cusinato, M. (2012c). Self-presentation strategies: A new version. In M. Cusinato & L. L'Abate (Eds.), *Advances in relational competence theory: With special attention to alexithymia* (pp. 113–128). New York: Nova Science.

Cusinato, M. (2012d). Understanding alexithymia through an information processing model. In M. Cusinato & L. L'Abate (Eds.), *Advances in relational competence theory: With special attention to alexithymia* (pp. 61–78). New York: Nova Science.

Cusinato, M., & Colesso, W. (2007). Creazione e validazione di un modello di atteggia-menti childfree. [Creation and validation of a childfree attitude model]. *Rivista di Studi Familiari, 12,* 82–96.

Cusinato, M., & Colesso, W. (2008). Validation of the continuum of likeness in intimate relationships. In L. L'Abate (Ed.), *Toward a science of clinical psychology: Laboratory evaluations and interventions* (pp. 335–352). New York: Nova Science.

Cusinato, M., & L'Abate, L. (1994). A spiral model of intimacy. In S. M. Johnson & Greenberg (Eds.), *The heart of the matter: Perspectives on emotion in marital therapy,* (pp. 108–123). New York: Brunner/Mazel.

Cusinato, M., & L'Abate, L. (2005a). The dyadic relationships test: Creation and validation of a model-derived, visual-verbal instrument to evaluate couple relationships. Part I. *American Journal of Family Therapy, 33,* 195–206.

Cusinato, M., & L'Abate, L. (2005b). The dyadic relationships test: Creation and validation of a model-derived, visual-verbal instrument to evaluate couple relationships. Part II. *American Journal of Family Therapy, 33,* 379–394.

Cusinato, M., & L'Abate, L. (2008a). Likeness: A hidden ingredient in family therapy. *American Journal of Family Therapy, 36,* 116–125.

Cusinato, M., & L'Abate, L. (2008b). Selfhood: A hidden ingredient in family therapy. *Journal of Family Psychotherapy, 19,* 320–329.

Cusinato, M., & L'Abate, L. (2012a). *Advances in relational competence theory: With special attention to alexithymia*. New York: Nova Science.
Cusinato, M., & L'Abate, L. (2012b). Implications of research on alexithymia for relational competence theory. In M. Cusinato & L. L'Abate (Eds.), *Advances in relational competence theory: With special attention to alexithymia* (pp. 299–307). New York: Nova Science.
Cusinato, M., & L'Abate, L. (Eds.). (2012c). Unexpressed and expressed hurts: Two different trajectories for similar feelings. In M. Cusinato & L. L'Abate (Eds.), *Advances in relational competence theory: With special attention to alexithymia* (pp. 221–229). New York: Nova Science.
Cusinato, M., Aceti, G., & L'Abate, L. (1997). Condivisione del dolore e di intimitÃ di coppia [Sharing hurts in intimate couples]. *Famiglia, Interdisciplinarietà, Ricerca, 2,* 131–150.
Custer, R., & Aarts, H. (2014). Conscious and unconscious goal pursuit. Similar functions, different processes? In J. W. Sherman, B. Gawronski, & Y. Trope (Eds.), *Dual-process theories of the social mind* (pp. 386–399). New York: Guilford.
Czerwińska, M. (1978). A psychological analysis of vocational decisions by young people: A developmental approach. *Psychologia Wychowawcza, 21*(4), 385–396.
Datchi, C. C., & Sexton, T. L. (2013). Can family therapy have an effect on adult criminal conduct? Initial evaluation of functional family therapy. *Couple and Family Psychology: Research and Practice, 2,* 278–293.
Dattilio, F. M., & Epstein, N. B. (2003). Cognitive-behavioral couple and family therapy. In T. L. Sexton, G. R. Weeks, & M. S. Robbins (Eds.), *Handbook of family therapy* (pp. 147–176). New York: Brunner/Rutledge.
De Giacomo, P., L'Abate, L., Pennebaker, J. W., & Rumbaugh, D. (2010). Amplifications and application of Pennebeker's analogic to digital model in health promotion, prevention, and psychotherapy. *Clinical Psychology and Psychotherapy, 17,* 355–362.
De Giacomo, P., Mich, L., Santamaria, C., Sweeney, L. G., & De Giacomo, A. (2012). Information processing. In L. L'Abate (Ed.), *Paradigms in theory construction* (pp. 341–364). New York: Springer-Science.
DeRosa, R. R., & Rathus, J. H. (2013). Dialectical behavior therapy with adolescents. In D. Ford & C. A. Courtois (Eds.), *Treating complex traumatic stress disorders in children and adolescents: Scientific foundations and therapeutic models* (pp. 225–247). New York: Guilford.
DiMatteo, M. R. (2013). Enhancing patient adherence to treatment. In G. P. Koocher, J. C. Norcross, & B. A. Greene (Eds.), *Psychologist's desk reference* (3rd ed., pp. 182–185). New York: Oxford University Press.
Dimeff, L. A., Paves, A. P., Skutch, J. M., & Woodcock, E. A. (2011).Shifting paradigms in clinical psychology: How innovative technologies are shaping treatment delivery. In D. H. Barlow (Ed.), *The Oxford handbook of clinical psychology* (pp. 618–648). New York: Oxford University Press.
Egan, T. (2000, April). Referential activity, signification, and the question of meaning: An interdisciplinary approach to the interweave of linguistics with psychoanalysis. *Dissertation Abstracts International, 60*(10–B), 5223.
Emery, F. E. (Ed.). (1969). *Systems thinking*. Baltimore: Penguin.
Emery, R. E., Shim, H. J., & Horn, E. (2012). Examining divorce consequences and policies and the question: Is marriage more than a piece of paper? In L. Campbell & T. J. Loving (Eds.), *Interdisciplinary research on close relationships: The case for integration* (pp. 227–250). Washington, DC: American Psychological Association.
Feibleman, J., & Friend, J. W. (1945). The structure and function of organization. *Philosophical Review, 54,* 19–44.
Fiedler, K., & Hutter, M. (2014). The limits of automaticity. In J. W. Sherman, B. Gawronski, & Y. Trope (Eds.), *Dual-process theories of the social mind* (pp. 497–513). New York: Guilford.
Fischer, L. (1982). Transactional theories but individual assessment: A frequent discrepancy in family research. *Family Process, 21,* 313–320.
Foa, U., & Foa, E. (1974). *Societal structures of the mind*. Springfield: C. C. Thomas.
Ford, J. D., & Courtois, C. A. (Eds.). (2013). *Treating complex traumatic stress disorders in children and adolescents: Scientific foundations and therapeutic models*. New York: Guilford.

Ford, J. D., Blaustein, M. E., Hahib, M., & Kagan, R. (2013). Developmental trauma therapy models. In J. D. Ford & C. A. Courtois (Eds.), *Treating complex traumatic stress disorders in children and adolescents: Scientific foundations and therapeutic models* (pp. 261–276). New York: Guilford.

Forster, J., & Liberman, N. (2014). Beyond control versus automaticity: Psychological processes driving postsuppressional rebound. In J. W. Sherman, B. Gawronski, & Y. Trope (Eds.), *Dual-process theories of the social mind* (pp. 439–453). New York: Guilford.

Foxx, R. M. (2013). The maintenance of behavior change: The case for long-term follow-up. *American Psychologist, 68,* 728–736.

Fryling, M. J., & Hayes, L. I. (2012). Interbehaviorism. In L. L'Abate (Ed.), *Paradigms in theory construction* (pp. 187–206). New York: Springer-Science.

Fujita, K., Trope, Y., Cunningham, W. A., & Liberman, N. (2014). What is control? A conceptual analysis. In J. W. Sherman, B. Gawronski, & Y. Trope (Eds.), *Dual-process theories of the social mind* (pp. 50–65). New York: Guilford.

Gallego, M. J., & Emmelkamp, P. M. G. (2012). Effectiveness of internet psychological treatments in mental health disorders. In L. L'Abate & D. A. Kaiser (Eds.), *Handbook of technology in psychology, psychiatry, and neurology: Theory, research, and practice* (pp. 395–422). New York: Nova Science.

Gallo, K. P., & Barlow, D. H. (2012). Factors involved in clinician adoption and non-adoption of evidence-based interventions in mental health. *Clinical Psychology: Science and Practice, 19,* 93–106.

Garland, A., Schoenwald, S. K. (2013). Use of effective and efficient quality controls methods to implement psychosocial interventions. *Clinical Psychology: Science and Practice, 20,* 33–43.

Gaudiano, B. A. (29 September 2013). Psychotherapy's image problem. *The New York Times.*

Gawronski, B., Sherman, J. W., & Trope, Y. (2014). Two of what? A conceptual analysis of dual process theories. In J. W. Sherman, B. Gawronski, & Y. Trope (Eds.), *Dual-process theories of the social mind* (pp. 3–19). New York: Guilford.

Geisinger, K. F. (Ed.). (2013). *APA handbook of testing and assessment in psychology.* Washington, DC: American Psychological Association.

Gerhand, S., & Barry, C. (2000). When does a deep dyslexic make a semantic error? The roles of age-of-acquisition, concreteness, and frequency. *Brain and Language, 74*(1), 26–47.

Gianesini, G. (2012). Alexithymia dimensions and emotionally perceived parenting styles. In M. Cusinato & L. L'Abate (Eds.), *Advances in relational competence theory: With special attention to alexithymia* (pp. 243–268). New York: Nova Science.

Gibb, H., & Wales, R. (1990). Metaphor or simile: Psychological determinants of the differential use of each sentence form. *Metaphor & Symbolic Activity, 5*(4), 199–213.

Goertz, G. (2009). Point of departure: Intension and extension. In D. Collier & J. Gerring (Eds.), *Concepts and methods in social science: The tradition of Giovanni Sartori* (pp. 181–202). New York: Rutledge.

Goldstein, N. E. S., Kemp, K. A., Leff, S. S., & Lochmanm J. E. (2012). Guidelines for adapting manualized interventions for new target populations: A step-wise approach using anger management as a model. *Clinical Psychology: Science and Practice, 19*(4), 385–401.

Guerra, C., & Capitelli, M. (2009). Success and limits of reductionism: Case studies in chemistry. In L. L'Abate, P. De Giacomo, M. Capitelli, & S. Longo (Eds.), *Science, mind and creativity: The Bari Symposium* (pp. 61–88). New York: Nova Science.

Guiter-Mazer, I. (1997). Predictors of treatment outcome in severely mentally ill inpatients. *Dissertation Abstracts International, 57*(12–B), 7726.

Harkness, A. R. (2007). Personality traits are essential for a complete clinical science. In S. O. Lilienfeld & W. T. Donohue (Eds.), *The great ideas of clinical science: 17 principles that every mental health professional should understand* (pp. 263–29). New York: Routledge.

Harter, S., Waters, P. I., Pettitt, L. M., Whitesell, J. K., Kofkin, J., & Jordan, J. (1997). Autonomy and connectedness as dimensions of relationship styles in men and women. *Journal of Social and Personal Relationships, 14,* 147–164.

Harwood, T. M., & L'Abate, L. (2010). *Self-help in mental health: A critical review*. New York: Springer-Science.

Hassin, R. R., & Sklar, A. Y. (2014). The human unconscious: A functional perspective. In J. W. Sherman, B. Gawronski, & Y. Trope (Eds.), *Dual-process theories of the social mind* (pp. 299–313). New York: Guilford.

Haugvik, M. (2012). Structured parallel therapy with parents in time-limited psycho-therapy with children experiencing difficult family situations. *Clinical Child Psychology and Psychiatry, 18,* 504–518.

Hegi, K. E., & Bergner, R. M. (2010). What is love? An empirically based essentialist account. *Journal of Social and Personal Relationships, 27,* 620–636.

Hertlein, K. M., & Blumer, L. C. (2014). *The couple and family technology framework: Intimate relationships in a digital age*. New York: Routledge.

Hetherington, L., Messer, S. B., Angus, L., Strauman, T. J., Friedlander, M. L., & Kolden, G. G. (2012). The narrowing of theoretical orientation in clinical psychology doctoral training. *Clinical Psychology: Science and Practice, 19,* 364–374.

Higgins, E. T. (2014). Promotion and prevention: How 'O' can create dual motivational forces. In J. W. Sherman, B. Gawronski, & Y. Trope (Eds.), *Dual-process theories of the social mind* (pp. 423–435). New York: Guilford.

Hillix, W. A., & L'Abate, L. (2012). The role of paradigms in science and theory construction. In L. L'Abate (Ed.), *Paradigms in theory construction* (pp. 3–18). New York: Springer-Science

Hillix, W. A., Rumbaugh, D. M., & Savage-Rumbaugh, E. S. (2012). The emergence of reason, intelligence, and language in humans and animals. In L. L'Abate (Ed.), *Paradigms in theory construction* (pp. 397–420). New York: Springer-Science.

Hoagood, K. E. (2013). Don't mourn: Organize. Revising mental health services research for healthcare quality improvement. *Clinical Psychology: Science and Practice, 20,* 120–126.

Hofferth, S. L., & Casper, L. M. (Eds.). (2007). *Handbook of measurement issues in family research*. Mahwah: Erlbaum.

Hogan, T. P. (2013). Locating information about psychological tests and measures. In G. P. Koocher, J. C., Norcross, & B. A. Greene (Eds.), *Psychologist's desk reference* (3rd ed., pp. 145–147). New York: Oxford University Press.

Hogan, R., Johnson, J., & Briggs, S. (Eds). (1997). *Handbook of personality psychology*. San Diego: Academic.

Hogue, A., Ozechowski, T. J., & Robbins, M. S. (2013). Making fidelity an intramural game: Localizing quality assurance procedure to promote sustainability of evidence-based practices in usual care. *Clinical Psychology: Science and Practice, 20,* 60–77.

Holcomb, P. J., Kounios, J., Anderson, J. E., & West, W. (1999). Dual-coding, context-availability, and concreteness effects in sentence comprehension: An electro-physiological investigation. *Journal of Experimental Psychology: Learning, Memory, and Cognition, 25*(3), 721–742.

Hooper, L. M., L'Abate, L., Sweeney, L. G., Gianesini, G., & Jankowski, P. J. (2014). *Models of psychopathology; Generational processes and relational roles*. New York: Springer-Science.

Hunsley, J., & Mash, E. J. (2011). Evidence-based assessment. In D. H. Barlow (Ed.), *The Oxford handbook of clinical psychology* (pp. 76–97). New York: Oxford University Press.

John, O. P., Robins, R. W., & Pervin, L. A. (Eds.). (2008). *Handbook of personality: Theory and research*. New York: Guilford.

Johnsen, J. A. K., Vambheim, S. M., & Wangberg, S. C. (2014). Language of motivation and emotion in an internet support group for smoking cessation: Exploratory use of automated content analysis to measure regulatory focus. *Psychology Research and Behavior Management, 7,* 19–29.

Johnson, R. E. (1974). Abstractive processes in the remembering of prose. *Journal of Educational Psychology, 66*(5), 772–779.

Johnson, J. H. (2012). The changing landscape of clinical psychology. *Clinical Psychology: Science and Practice, 19,* 17–20.

Joint Task Force for the Development of Telepsychology Guidelines for Psychologists (2013). Guidelines for the practice of telepsychology. *American Psychologist, 68,* 791–800.

Jongsma, A. E., Jr. (2013). Recommended homework during psychotherapy with couples and individuals. In G. P. Koocher, J. C. Norcross, & B. A. Greene (Eds.), *Psychologist's desk reference* (3rd ed., pp. 508–517), New York: Oxford University Press.

Jordan, K., & L'Abate, L. (1995). Programmed writing and therapy with symbiotically enmeshed patients. *American Journal of Psychotherapy, 49,* 225–236.

Jurist, E. L. (2013). Commentary on Norcross and Karpiak's "Clinical psychologists in the 2010s: 50 years of the APA division of clinical psychology". *Clinical Psychology: Science and Practice, 20,* 221–223.

Karlin, B. E., & Cross, G. (2013). From the laboratory to the therapy room: National dissemination and implementation of evidence-based psychotherapies in the U.S. Department of Veterans Affairs Health Care System. *American Psychologist, 69,* 19–33.

Kazantzis, N., & L'Abate, L. (Eds.). (2007). *Handbook of homework assignments in psychotherapy: Research, practice, and prevention.* New York: Springer-Science.

Kazantzis, N., Deane, F. P., & Ronan, K. R., & L'Abate, L. (Eds.). (2005). *Using homework assignments in cognitive behavior therapy.* New York: Routledge.

Kazdin, A. E. (2008). Evidence-based treatment and practice: New opportunities to bridge clinical research and practice, enhance the knowledge base, and improve patient care. *American Psychologist, 63,* 146–159.

Kazdin, A.E. (2013). Behavior modification in applied settings (7th ed.). Long Grove: Waveland.

Kazdin, A. E., & Rabbitt, S. M. (2013). Novel models for delivering mental health services and reducing the burden of mental illness. *Clinical Psychological Science, 1,* 170–191.

Kendall, P. C., & Comer, J. S. (2011). Research methods in clinical psychology. In D. H. Barlow (Ed.), *The Oxford handbook of clinical psychology* (pp. 52–75). New York: Oxford University Press.

Kennedy, J. A. (1992). *Fundamentals of psychiatric treatment planning.* Washington, DC: American Psychiatric Association.

Kerig, P. K., & Alexander, J. F. (2012). Family matters: Integrating trauma treatment into functional family therapy for delinquent youth. Special issue on trauma and juvenile delinquency: New directions in interventions. *Journal of Child and Adolescent Trauma, 5,* 205–223.

Klatzkin, A., Lieberman, A. F., & Van Horn, P. (2013). Child-parent psychotherapy and historical trauma. In J. D. Ford, & C. A. Courtois (Eds.), *Treating complex traumatic stress disorders in children and adolescents: Scientific foundations and therapeutic models* (pp. 295–313). New York: Guilford.

Klauer, K. C. (2014). Random-walk and diffusion models. In J. W. Sherman, B. Gawronski, & Y. Trope (Eds.), *Dual-process theories of the social mind* (pp. 139–152). New York: Guilford.

Klein, S. B. (2012). The self and the brain. *Social Cognition, 30,* 474–518.

Klein, S. B. (2014a). Dual process models of trait judgments of self and others. In J. W. Sherman, B. Gawronski, & Y. Trope (Eds.), *Dual-process theories of the social mind* (pp. 264–278). New York: Guilford.

Klein, S. B. (2014b). Sameness and the self: Philosophical and psychological considerations. *Frontiers in Psychology, 5,* 1–15.

Klein, S. B. (2014c). What can recent replication failures tell us about the theoretical commitment of psychology? *Theory & Psychology, 24,* 326–338.

Kliethermes, M., Nannery, R. W., Cohen, J. A., & Mannarino, A. P. (2013) Trauma-focused cognitive-behavioral therapy. In J. D. Ford & C. A. Courtois (Eds.), *Treating complex traumatic stress disorders in children and adolescents: Scientific foundations and therapeutic models* (pp. 184–201). New York: Guilford.

Kluger, J. (22 April 2013). Too old to be a dad? *Time*, pp. 38–43.

Koerner, A., Hood, H. K., & Antony, M. M. (2011). Interviewing and case formulation. In D. H. Barlow (Ed.), *The Oxford handbook of clinical psychology* (pp. 225–253). New York: Oxford University Press.

Korzybski, A. (1949). *Science and sanity: An introduction to non-Aristotelian systems and general semantics.* Lakeville: The International Non-Aristotelian Library Publishing House.

Kuhn, T. S. (1970). *The structure of scientific revolutions.* Chicago: University of Chicago Press.

L'Abate, L. (1976). *Understanding and helping the individual in the family*. New York: Grune & Stratton.

L'Abate, L. (1977). *Enrichment: Structured interventions with couples, families, and groups*. Washington, DC: University Press of America.

L'Abate, L. (1983). *Family psychology: Theory, therapy, and training*. Washington, DC: University Press of America.

L'Abate, L. (Ed.). (1985). *Handbook of family psychology and therapy. Volumes I & II*. Pacific Grove: Brooks/Cole.

L'Abate, L. (1986). *Systematic family therapy*. New York: Brunner/Mazel.

L'Abate, L. (1987). *Family psychology II: Theory, therapy, enrichment, and training* (pp. 1–289). Washington, DC: University Press of America.

L'Abate, L. (1990). *Building family competence: Primary and secondary prevention strategies*. Newbury Park: Sage.

L'Abate, L. (1991). The use of writing in psychotherapy. *American Journal of Psychotherapy, 45*, 87–98.

L'Abate, L. (1992). *Programmed writing: A self-administered approach for interventions with individuals, couples, and families*. Pacific Grove: Brooks/Cole.

L'Abate, L. (1994). *A theory of personality development*. New York: Wiley.

L'Abate, L. (1996). Workbooks for better living. www.mentalhealthhelp.com.

L'Abate, L. (1997a). Distance writing and computer-assisted training. In S. R. Sauber (Ed.), *Managed mental health care: Major diagnostic and treatment approaches* (pp. 133–163). Bristol: Brunner/Mazel.

L'Abate, L. (1997b). *The self in the family: Toward a classification of personality, criminality, and psychopathology*. New York: Wiley.

L'Abate, L. (1999). Taking the bull by the horns: Beyond talk in psychological inter-ventions. *The Family Journal: Counseling and Therapy for Couples and Families, 7*, 206–220.

L'Abate, L. (Ed.). (2001a). *Distance writing and computer-assisted interventions in psychiatry and mental health*. Westport: Ablex.

L'Abate, L. (2001b). Hugging, holding, huddling, and cuddling (3HC): A task prescription in couples and family therapy. *The Journal of Clinical Activities, Assignments, & Handouts in Psychotherapy Practice, 1*, 5–18.

L'Abate, L. (2002). *Beyond psychotherapy: Programmed writing and structured computer-assisted interventions*. Westport: Ablex.

L'Abate, L. (2003). *Family psychology III: Theory building, theory testing, and psychological interventions*. Lanham: University Press of America.

L'Abate, L. (2004a). *A guide to self-help workbooks for clinicians and researchers*. Binghamton: Haworth.

L'Abate, L. (2004b). La lenta scomparsa della famiglia: Chi prendera' il suo posto? (The slow disappearance of the family: Who will replace it?). *Saggi: Child Development & Disabilities, 30*, 23–34.

L'Abate, L. (2004c). Systematically written homework assignments: The case for homework based treatment. In L. L'Abate (Ed.), *Using workbooks in mental health: Resources in prevention, psychotherapy, and rehabilitation for clinicians and researchers* (pp. 65–102). Binghamton: Haworth.

L'Abate, L. (2004d). The role of workbooks in the delivery of mental health services in prevention, psychotherapy and rehabilitation, In L. L'Abate (Ed.). *Using workbooks in mental health: Resources in prevention, psychotherapy, and rehabilitation for clinicians and researchers* (pp. 3–64). Binghamton: Haworth.

L'Abate, L. (Ed.). (2004e). *Using workbooks in mental health: Resources in prevention, psychotherapy, and rehabilitation for clinicians and researchers*. Binghamton: Haworth.

L'Abate, L. (2005). *Personality in intimate relationships: Socialization and psycho-pathology*. New York: Springer-Science.

L'Abate, L. (2006). Toward a relational theory for psychiatric classification. *American Journal of Family Therapy, 34*, 1–15.

L'Abate, L. (2007a). A completely preposterous proposal: The dictionary as an initial vehicle of change in the family. *The Family Psychologist, 23,* 39–42.
L'Abate, L. (2007b). Introduction: Section IV. Writing. In L. L'Abate (Ed.), *Low-cost approaches to promote physical and mental health: Theory, research, and practice* (pp. 219–266). New York: Springer-Science.
L'Abate, L. (Ed.). (2007c). *Low-cost approaches to promote physical and mental health: Theory, research, and practice.* New York: Springer-Science.
L'Abate, L. (2008a). A proposal for including distance writing in couple therapy. *Journal of Couple & Relationship Therapy, 7,* 337–362.
L'Abate, L. (Ed.). (2008b). *Toward a science of clinical psychology: Laboratory evaluations and interventions.* New York: Nova Science.
L'Abate, L. (2008c). Working at a distance from participants: Writing and nonverbal media. In L. L'Abate (Ed.), *Toward a science of clinical psychology: Laboratory evaluations and interventions* (pp. 355–383). New York: Nova Science.
L'Abate, L. (2009a). A bibliography of secondary references for relational competence theory. In L. L'Abate, P. De Giacomo, M. Capitelli, & S. Longo (Eds.), *Science, mind, and creativity: The Bari Symposium* (pp. 175–196). New York: Nova Science.
L'Abate, L. (2009b). An historical and systematic perspective about distance writing and wellness. In J. F. Evans (Ed.), *Wellness & writing connections: Writing for better physical, mental, and spiritual health* (pp. 53–74). Enumclaw: Idyll Arbor, Inc.
L'Abate, L. (2009c). A theory-derived structured interview for intimate relationships. *The Family Psychologist, 25,* 12–14.
L'Abate, L. (2009d). Hurt feelings: The last taboo for researchers and clinicians? In L. Vangelisti (Ed.), *Feeling hurt in close relationships* (pp. 479–497), New York: Cambridge University Press.
L'Abate, L. (2009e). In search of a relational theory. *American Psychologist, 64,* 776–788.
L'Abate, L. (2009f). Paradigms, theories, and models: Two hierarchical frameworks. In L. L'Abate, P. De Giacomo, M. Capitelli, & S. Longo (Eds.), *Mind, science, and creativity: The Bari symposium* (pp. 107–156). New York: Nova Science.
L'Abate, L. (2009g). Resilienza: un construtto alla ricerca di una teoria (Resilience: A construct in search of a theory). *Rivista di Studi Familiari: FIR, Famiglia, Interdisciplinarita', Ricerca, 9,* 7–26.
L'Abate, L., (2009h). The drama triangle: An attempt to resurrect a neglected pathogenic model in family therapy theory and practice. *American Journal of Family Therapy, 37,* 1–11.
L'Abate, L. (2009i). *The Praeger handbook of play across the life cycle: Fun from infancy to old age.* Westport: Praeger.
L'Abate, L. (2011a). *Hurt feelings: Theory, research, and applications in intimate relationships.* New York: Cambridge University Press.
L'Abate, L. (2011b). Psychotherapy consists of homework assignments: A radical iconoclastic conviction. In H. Rosenthal (Ed.), *Favorite counseling and therapy homework techniques: Classic anniversary edition* (pp. 219–229). New York: Routledge.
L'Abate, L. (2011c). *Sourcebook of interactive practice exercises in mental health.* New York: Springer-Science.
L'Abate, L. (2011d). *The seven sources of pleasure in life: Making way for the upside in the midst of modern demands.* Santa Barbara: ABC–CLIO.
L'Abate, L. (2012a). A hierarchical framework for relational competence theory. In M. Cusinato & L. L'Abate (Eds.), *Advances in relational competence theory: With special attention to alexithymia* (pp. 13–48). New York: Nova Science.
L'Abate, L. (2012b). Couple and family assessment: Current and future prospects. In L. Sperry (Ed.), *Assessment of couples and families: Contemporary and cutting-edge strategies* (2nd ed., pp. 309–328). New York: Routledge.
L'Abate, L. (2012c). Essentialism. In L. L'Abate (Ed.), *Paradigms in theory construction* (pp. 421–436). New York: Springer-Science.

L'Abate, L. (2012d). Materialism. In L. L'Abate (Ed.), *Paradigms in theory construction* (pp. 257–271). New York: Springer-Science.

L'Abate, L. (2012e). Of paradigms, theories, and models: The relevance of a conceptual hierarchical structure for communication science. In R. Luppicini (Ed.), *Handbook of research in psychotechnology* (pp. 84–104). Hershey: IGI Global.

L'Abate, L. (Ed.). (2012f). *Paradigms in theory construction*. New York: Springer-Science.

L'Abate, L. (2012g). Technological practices in the neuroscience. In L. L'Abate & D. A. Kaiser (Eds.), *Handbook of technology in psychology, psychiatry, and neurology: Theory, research, and practice* (pp. 3–18). New York: Nova Science.

L'Abate, L. (2012h). Workbooks: Programmed interactive practice exercises. In L. L'Abate & D. A. Kaiser (Eds.), *Handbook of technology in psychology, psychiatry, and neurology: Theory, research, and practice* (pp. 375–394). New York: Nova Science.

L'Abate, L. (2013a). *Beyond a systems paradigm: Emerging constructs in family and personality psychology*. New York: Springer-Science.

L'Abate, L. (2013b). *Clinical psychology and psychotherapy as a science: An iconoclastic perspective*. New York: Springer-Science.

L'Abate, L. (2013c). Recommended online computer-assisted treatments. In G. P. Koocher, J. C. Norcross, & B. A. Greene (Eds.), *Psychologists' desk reference* (3rd ed. pp. 521–528). New York: Oxford University Press.

L'Abate, L. (Ed.). (2013d). *Research on pre-para-post-therapeutic approaches in mental health: Prevention, promotion, psychotherapy, and rehabilitation*. New York: Nova Science.

L'Abate, L. (Ed.). (in press). *Research on online/offline interventions in mental health: A critical review*. New York: Nova Science.

L'Abate, L., & Colondier, G. (1987). The emperor has no clothes! Long live the emperor! A critique of family systems thinking and a reductionistic proposal. *American Journal of Family Therapy, 15,* 19–33.

L'Abate, L., & McHenry, S. (1983). *Handbook of marital interventions*. New York: Grune & Stratton.

L'Abate, L., & Rupp, G. (1981). *Enrichment: Skill training for family life*. Washington, DC: University Press of America.

L'Abate, L., & Cusinato, M. (2007). Linking theory with practice: Theory-derived interventions in prevention and family therapy. *The Family Journal: Counseling and Psychotherapy with Couples and Families, 15,* 318–327.

L'Abate, L., & De Giacomo, P. (2003). *Improving intimate relationships: Integration of theoretical models with preventions and psychotherapy applications*. Westport: Praeger.

L'Abate, L., & Goldstein, D. (2007). Workbooks to promote mental health and life-long learning. In L. L'Abate (Ed.), *Low-cost interventions to promote physical and mental health: Theory, research and practice* (pp. 285–302). New York: Springer.

L'Abate, L., & Kaiser, D. A. (Eds.). (2012). *Handbook of technology in psychology, psychiatry, and neurology: Theory, research, and practice*. New York: Nova Science.

L'Abate, L., & Kern, R. (2002). Workbooks: Tools for the expressive writing paradigm. In S. J. Lepore & J. M. Smyth (Eds.), *The writing cure: How expressive writing promotes health and well-being* (pp. 239–255). Washington, DC: American Psychological Association.

L'Abate, L., & Platzman, K. (1991) Programmed writing (PW) in therapy and prevention with families. *American Journal of Family Therapy, 19,* 1–10.

L'Abate, L., & Sweeney, L. G. (Eds.). (2011). *Research on writing approaches in mental health*. Leiden: Brill.

L'Abate, L., & Weinstein, S. E. (1987). *Structured enrichment programs for couples and families*. New York: Brunner/Mazel.

L'Abate, L., & Young, L. (1987). *Casebook of structured enrichment programs for couples and families*. New York: Brunner/Mazel.

L'Abate, L., & Sweeney, L. G. (2012). Criteria and processes in paradigm selection. In L. L'Abate (Ed.), *Paradigms in theory selection* (pp. 437–447). New York: Springer-Science.

L'Abate, L., Boyce, J., Fraizer, L. M., & Russ, D. (1992). Programmed writing: Research in progress. *Comprehensive Mental Health Care, 2,* 45–62.
L'Abate, L., Odell, M., Shelling, G., Young, K. S., & Hewitt, D. H. (1994). The skills of the marriage and family therapist in straddling multicultural issues. *American Journal of Family Therapy, 22,* 145–154.
L'Abate, L., L'Abate, B. L., & Maino, E. (2005). A review of 25 years of part-time professional practice: Workbooks and length of psychotherapy. *American Journal of Family Therapy, 33,* 19–31.
L'Abate, L., Capitelli, M., De Giacomo, P., & Longo, S. (Eds.). (2009). *Science and creativity: The Bari symposium*. New York: Nova Science.
L'Abate, L., Cusinato, M., Maino, E., Colesso, W., Scilletta, C. (2010). *Relational competence theory: Research and mental health applications*. New York: Springer-Science.
L'Abate, L., van Eigen A., & Rigamonti, S. (2011). Relational and cross-cultural perspectives on non-violent externalizing personality disordered women: Introduction to research. *American Journal of Family Therapy, 39,* 325–347.
Lacewing, M. (2014). Psychodynamic psychotherapy: Insight, and therapeutic action. *Clinical Psychology: Science and Practice, 21,* 154–171.
Landsverk, J. (2013). Reflections on treatment integrity in a dissemination and imple-mentation framework. *Clinical Psychology: Science and Practice. 20,* 114–119.
Lanier, J. (2013). *Who owns the future?* New York: Simon & Schuster.
Lanktree, C., & Briere, J. (2013). Integrating treatment of complex trauma. In J. D. Ford & C. A. Courtois (Eds.), *Treating complex traumatic stress disorders in children and adolescents: Scientific foundations and therapeutic models* (pp. 143–160). New York: Guilford.
Leary, T. (1957). *Interpersonal diagnosis of personality*. New York: Ronald.
Lebow, J. L. (2006). *Research for the psychotherapist: From science to practice*. New York: Routledge.
Lei, H., Nahum-Shani, I., Lynch, K., Oslin, D., & Murphy, S. A. (2012). A "SMART" design for building individualized treatment sequences. *Annual Review of Clinical Psychology, 8,* 21–48.
Levine, C. (1994). AIDS and the changing concept of the family. In R. Bor & J. Elford (Eds.), *The family and HIV* (pp. 3–22). London: Cassell.
Lewis, M. (2014). *The rise of consciousness and the development of emotional life*. New York: Guilford.
Liddle, H. A., Santisteban, D. A., Levant, R. F., & Bray, J. H. (Eds.). (2002). *Family psychology: Science-based interventions*. Washington, DC: American Psychological Association.
Lilienfeld, S. O. (2010). Public skepticism of psychology: Why many people perceive the study of human behavior unscientific. *American Psychologist, 67,* 111–129.
Lilienfeld, S. O. (2012). Further sources of our field's embattled public reputation. *American Psychologist, 67,* 808–809.
Littrell, M. A., & Littrell, J. M. (1983). Counselor dress cues: Evaluations by American Indians and Caucasians. *Journal of Cross-Cultural Psychology, 14*(1), 109–121.
Lockhart, R. S., & Martin, J. E. (1969). Adjective order and the recall of adjective-noun triples. *Journal of Verbal Learning & Verbal Behavior, 8*(2), 272–275.
Loughlin, S. M., & Alexander, P. A. (2012). Explicating and exemplifying empirical and cognitivist paradigms in the study of human behavior. In L. L'Abate (Ed.), *Paradigms in theory constructions* (pp. 273–295). New York: Springer.
Luscombe, B. (2013). The end of alimony: The American divorce is undergoing its biggest change in decades. Call it the revenge of the second wives. *Time, 181*(20), 44–49.
Magnavita, J. J. (2012a). Advancing clinical science using system theory as a framework for expanding family psychology with unified psychotherapy. *Couple and Family Psychology: Research and Practice, 1,* 3–13.
Magnavita, J. J. (2012b). Reflections on personality systematic and a unified clinical science. In L. L'Abate (Ed.), *Paradigms in theory construction* (pp. 207–213). New York: Springer.
Maheu, M. M., & Gordon, B. (2000). Psychotherapy on the Internet: Legal, ethical and practice issues. *Professional Psychology: Research and Practice, 31*(5), 484–489.

Maheu, M. M., Herman, A., & Kinn, J. T. (2013). *Empirical validation for smartphones and mobile device apps*. Presented at a symposium for the Annual Convention of the American Psychological Association, Honolulu. Hawaii, August 4.

Maino, E. (2012a). Alexithymia dimensions as parenting challenges. In M. Cusinato & L. L'Abate (Eds.), *Advances in relational competence theory: With special attention to alexithymia* (pp. 281–298). New York: Nova Science.

Maino, E. (2012b). Relational competence and alexithymia: How are they related? In M. Cusinato & L. L'Abate (Eds.), *Advances in relational competence theory: With special attention to alexithymia* (pp. 79–92). New York: Nova Science.

Marks, I. M., & Cavanah, K. (2009). Computer-aided psychological treatments: Evolving issues. *Annual Review of Clinical Psychology, 5,* 121–141.

Marks, I. M., Cavanah, L., & Gega, L. (2007). *Hands-on help: Computer-aided psycho-therapy*. New York: Psychology.

Masheck, D. J., & Aron, A. (Eds.). (2004). *Handbook of closeness and intimacy*. Mahwah: Erlbaum.

Masterman, M. (1970). The nature of a paradigm. In I. Lakatos & A. Musgrave (Eds.), *Criticism and the growth of knowledge* (pp. 59–90). New York: Cambridge University Press.

McAdams, D. P. (1988). Personal needs and personal relationships. In S. Duck (Ed.), *Handbook of personal relationships: Theory research and intervention* (pp. 7–21). New York: Wiley.

McGrath, R. E., & Postal, K. (2013). Answers to the most important questions about health care reform. *New Jersey Psychologist, Spring Issue*, 25–30.

McLeod, B. D., Southam-Gray, M. A., Tully, C. B., Rodriguez, A., & Smith, M. M. (2013). Making a case for treatment integrity as a psychosocial treatment quality indicator for youth mental health. *Clinical Psychology: Science and Practice, 20,* 14–32.

Mellins, C. A., Ehrhardt, A. A., Newman, L., & Conard, M. (1996). Selective kin: Defining the care-givers and families of children with HIV disease. In L. Sweet Jemmott & A. O'Leary (Eds.), *Women and AIDS: Coping and care* (pp. 123–149). New York: Plenum.

Mikulincer, M., & Shaver, P. R. (2007). Attachment in adulthood: Structure, dynamics, and change. New York: Guilford.

Miller, G. (2012). The smart-phone psychology manifesto. *Perspectives on Psychological Science, 7,* 221–237.

Miller, A. (2013). Can this marriage be saved? *Monitor on Psychology, 44*(5), 42–47.

Millon, T., Blaney, P., & Davis, R. D. (Eds.). (1999). *Oxford textbook of psychopathology*. New York: Oxford University Press.

Mirsalimi, H. (2014). The art of psychotherapy and the artificial artist/empiricist distinction. *Personal Communication*, March 15, 2014.

Mitchell, B. A. (2006). *The boomerang age: Transition to adulthood in families*. New Brunswick: Transaction.

Mitchell, C. W. (2013). Reducing resistance in psychotherapy. In G. P. Koocher, J. C. Norcross, & B. A. Greene (Eds.), *Psychologist's desk reference* (3rd ed., pp. 258–262). New York: Oxford University Press.

Mogoaşe, C., Brăilean, A., & David, D. (2013). Can concreteness training alone reduce depressive symptoms? A randomized pilot study using an internet-delivered protocol. *Cognitive Therapy and Research, 37*(4), 704–712.

Moors, A. (2014). Examining the mapping problem in dual-process models. In J. W. Sherman, B. Gawronski, & Y. Trope (Eds.), *Dual-process theories of the social mind* (pp. 20–34). New York: Guilford.

Morozov, E. (2013). *To save everything, click here: The folly of technological solutionism*. New York: Public Affairs.

Moskowitz, G. B. (2014). The implicit volition model: The unconscious nature of goal pursuit. In J. W. Sherman, B. Gawronski, & Y. Trope (Eds.), *Dual-process theories of the social mind* (pp. 400–422). New York: Guilford.

Mussweiler, T. (2014). Same or different? How similarity versus dissimilarity focus shapes social information processing. In J. W. Sherman, B. Gawronski, & Y. Trope (Eds.), *Dual-process theories of the social mind* (pp. 328–339). New York: Guilford.

Navalta, C. P., Brown, A. D., Nisewaner, A., Ellis, B. H., & Saxe, G. N. (2013). Trauma systems therapy. In J. D. Ford & C. A. Courtois, (Eds.), *Treating complex traumatic stress disorders in children and adolescents: Scientific foundations and therapeutic models* (pp. 329–347). New York: Guilford.

Nelson, A. P., & O'Connor, M. (2013). Adult neuropsychological assessment. In G. P. Koocher, J. C., Norcross, & B. A. Greene (Eds.), *Psychologist's desk reference* (3rd ed., pp. 95–99). New York: Oxford University Press.

Nikowitz, S. (2001). Narratives of tension events and psychotherapy outcome: A microanalysis of statements on post-session questionnaires given by therapists and patients in brief relational therapy. *Dissertation Abstracts International, 61*(7-B), 3854.

Norcross, J. C. (Ed.). (2011a). *Psychotherapy relationships that work: Evidence-based responsiveness*. New York: Oxford University Press.

Norcross, J. C. (2011b). Purposes, processes, and products of the task force on empirically supported therapy relationships. *Psychotherapy, 38*(4), 345–356.

Norcross, J. C. (2014). Tailoring psychotherapy to the individual client: Treatment adaptations that work. Invited talk to the 28th International Congress of Applied Psychology, Paris, France, June 15th.

Norcross, J. C., & Karpiak, C. P., (2012). Clinical psychologists in the 2010s: 50 years of the APA Division of Clinical Psychology. *Clinical Psychology: Science & Practice, 19,* 1–12.

Norcross, J. C., & Wampold, B. E. (2011). What works for whom: Tailoring psychotherapy to the person. *Journal of Clinical Psychology: In Session, 67,* 127–132.

Norcross, J. C., Koocher, G. P., & Garofalo, A. (2006). Discredited psychological treatments: A Delphi poll. *Professional Psychology: Research and Practice, 37,* 515–522.

Norcross, J. C., Koocher, G. P., Fala, N. C., & Wexler, H. K. (2010). What does not work? Expert consensus on discredited treatments in the addictions. *Journal of Addiction Medicine, 4*(3), 174–180.

Nordal, K. C. (2013). Putting your practice assessment to work: The Medicare Physician Quality Reporting System: What psychologists need to know now. Washington, DC: *APAPO Supplement to the Monitor on Psychology*.

O'Donohue, W. T. (2013). *Mental health and the philosophy of science*. New York: Springer-Science.

O'Donohue, W. T., & Draper, C. (2011). *Stepped-care and e-health: Practical applications to behavior disorders*. New York: Springer-Science.

Olson, G. R., & Olson, J. S. (2003). Human-computer interactions: Psychological aspects of the human use of computing. *Annual Review of Psychology, 54,* 491–516.

Olson, M. R. (1991). Supportive growth experiences of beginning teachers. *Alberta Journal of Educational Research, 37*(1), 19–30.

Overton, W. F. (2012). Evolving scientific paradigms: Retrospective and prospective. In L. L'Abate (Ed.), *Paradigms in theory construction* (pp. 31–67). New York: Springer-Science.

Paivio, A. (1966). Latency of verbal associations and imagery to noun stimuli as a function of abstractness and generality. *Canadian Journal of Psychology/Revue Canadienne De Psychologie, 20*(4), 378–387.

Paivio, A. (1967). Paired-associate learning and free recall of nouns as a function of concreteness, specificity, imagery, and meaningfulness. *Psychological Reports, 20*(1), 239–245.

Paivio, A. (1968). A factor-analytic study of word attributes and verbal learning. *Journal of Verbal Learning & Verbal Behavior, 7*(1), 41–49.

Pappachan, P. P., & Ziefle, M. M. (2008). Cultural influences on the comprehensibility of icons in mobile-computer interaction. *Behaviour & Information Technology, 27*(4), 331–337.

Patterson, T., & Sexton, T. (2013). Bridging conceptual frameworks: A systemic heurstic for understanding family diversity. *Couple and Family Psychology: Research and Practice, 2,* 237–245.

Patterson, J. E., Miller, R. B., Carnes, S., & Wilson, S. (2004). Evidence-based practice for marriage and family therapists. *Journal of Marital and Family Therapy, 30,* 183–195.

Payne, B. K., & Cameron, C. D. (2014). Dual-process theory from a process-dissociation perspective. In J. W. Sherman, B. Gawronski, & Y. Trope (Eds.), *Dual-process theories of the social mind* (pp. 107–120). New York: Guilford.

Pennebaker, J. W. (1997). Writing about emotional experiences as a therapeutic process. *Psychological Science, 8,* 162–166.
Pequegnat, W., & Bray, J. H. (1997). Families and HIV/AIDS: Introduction to the special section. *Journal of Family Psychology, 11,* 3–10.
Pequegnat, W., & Bray, J. H. (2012). HIV/STD prevention interventions for couples and families: A review and introduction to the special issue. *Couples and Family Psychology Research and Practice, 2,* 79–93.
Pequegnat, W., Bauman, L. J., Bray, J. H., DiClemente, R., et al. (2001). Measurement of the role of families in prevention and adaptation to HIV/AIDS. *AIDS and Behavior, 5,* 1–19.
Perry, B. D., & Dobson, C. L. (2013). The neurosequential model of therapeutics. In J. D. Ford & C. A. Courtois (Eds.), *Treating complex traumatic stress disorders in children and adolescents: Scientific foundations and therapeutic models* (pp. 249–260). New York: Guilford.
Pfeifer, R., & Scheier, C. (1999). *Understanding intelligence.* Cambridge: MIT Press.
Pidgeon, V. (1985). Children's concepts of illness: Implications for health teaching. *Maternal-Child Nursing Journal, 14*(1), 23–35.
Pilkonis, P. A., Choi, S. W., Reise, S. P., et al. (2011). Item banks for measuring emotional distress from the patient-reported outcomes measurement information system (PROMIS®): depression, anxiety, and anger. *Assessment, 18*(3), 263–283.
Pinsof, W. M., & Lebow, J. L. (Eds.). (2005). *Family psychology: The art of the science.* New York: Oxford University Press.
Pinsof, W. M., Goldsmith, J. Z., & Latta, T. A. (2012). Information technology and feedback research can bridge the scientist-practitioner gap: A couple therapy example. *Couple and Family Psychology: Research and Practice, 1,* 253–273.
Prager, K. J. (1995). *The psychology of intimacy.* New York: Guilford.
Proudfoot, J. (2012). The future is in our hands: The role of mobile phones in the prevention and management of mental disorders. *Australian & New Zealand Journal of Psychiatry, 47,* 111–113.
Quinn, W. H., & Davidson, B. (1984). Prevalence of family therapy models: A research note. *Journal of Marital and Family Therapy, 10,* 393–398.
Rapaport, A. (1969). *Operational philosophy.* Chicago: International Society for General Semantics.
Regan, J., Daleiden, E. L., & Chorpita, B. F. (2013). Integrity in mental health systems: An expanded framework for managing uncertainty in clinical care. *Clinical Psychology: Science and Practice, 20,* 78–98.
Riegler, A. (2012). Constructivism. In L. L'Abate (Ed.), *Paradigms in theory construction* (pp. 235–256). New York: Springer.
Rezensky, R. H. (2013). Quality education in professional psychology: Flowers blooming, Flexner, and the future. *American Psychologist, 68,* 703–716.
Ryback, D. (2012). Humanism and behaviorism. In L. L'Abate (Ed.), *Paradigms in theory construction* (pp. 235–256). New York: Springer.
Rychlak, J. F. (1968). *A philosophy of science for personality theory.* Boston: Houghton-Mifflin.
Sajatovic, M., & Ramirez, L. F. (2001). *Rating scales in mental health.* Hudson: Lexi-Comp Inc.
Salzberg, P. M. (1976). On the generality of encoding specificity. *Journal of Experimental Psychology: Human Learning and Memory, 2*(5), 586–596.
Sartori, G. (2009a). Concept misinformation in comparative politics. In D. Collier & J. Gerring (Eds.), *Concepts and methods in social science: The tradition of Giovanni Sartori* (pp. 13–43). New York: Routledge.
Sartori, G. (2009b). Guidelines for concept analysis. In D. Collier & J. Gerring (Eds.), *Concepts and methods in social science: The tradition of Giovanni Sartori* (pp. 97–159). New York: Routledge.
Scharff, J. S., & Scharff, D. E. (2003). Object relations and psychodynamic approaches to couple and family therapy. In T. L. Sexton, G. R. Weeks, & M. S. Robbins (Eds.), *Handbook of family therapy* (pp. 59–82). New York: Brunner/Routledge.

Schmidt, E., & Cohen, D. (2013). *The new digital age: Reshaping the future of people, nations, and business*. New York: Knopf.

Schwanenflugel, P. J. (1991). Why are abstract concepts hard to understand? In P. J. Schwanenflugel (Ed.), *The psychology of word meanings* (pp. 223–250). Hillsdale: Erlbaum.

Schwanenflugel, P. J., & Shoben, E. J. (1983). Differential context effects in the comprehension of abstract and concrete verbal materials. *Journal of Experimental Psychology: Learning, Memory, and Cognition, 9*(1), 82–102.

Schwanenflugel, P. J., & Stowe, R. W. (1989). Context availability and the processing of abstract and concrete words in sentences. *Reading Research Quarterly, 24*(1), 114.

Schwanenflugel, P. J., Harnishfeger, K. K., & Stowe, R. W. (1988). Context availability and lexical decisions for abstract and concrete words. *Journal of Memory and Language, 27*(5), 499–520.

Seginer, R. (1988). Adolescents' orientation toward the future: Sex role differentiation in a sociocultural context. *Sex Roles, 18*(11–12), 739–757.

Seginer, R., & Halabi, H. (1991). Cross-cultural variations of adolescents' future orientation: The case of Israeli Druze versus Israeli Arab and Jewish male. *Journal of Cross-Cultural Psychology, 22*(2), 224–237.

Semin, G. R., Garrido, M. V., & Farias, A. R. (2014). How many processes does it take to ground a concept? In J. W. Sherman, B. Gawronski, & Y. Trope (Eds.), *Dual-process theories of the social mind* (pp. 542–559). New York: Guilford.

Sexton, T. L., Patterson, T., & Datchi, C. C. (2012). Technological innovations of systematic measurement and clinical feedback: A virtual loop into the future of couple and family psychology. *Couple and Family Psychology: Research and Practice, 1,* 285–293.

Shiffman, S., Stone, A. A., & Hufford, M. R. (2008). Ecological momentary assessment. *Annual Review of Clinical Psychology, 4,* 1–32.

Shirk, S. R., & Peterson, E. (2013). Gaps, bridges, and the bumpy road to improving clinic-based therapy for youth. *Clinical Psychology: Science and Practice, 20,* 107–113.

Silverstein, M., & Giarrusso, S. (Eds.). (2013). *Kinship and cohort in an aging society*. Baltimore: Johns Hopkins University Press.

Simons, A. D., & Rozek, D. C. (2013). Wanted: Reliable and valid measures for the science of cognitive behavioral therapy dissemination and implementation. *Mental Health: Science and Practice, 20,* 181–194.

Simons, A. D., Rozek, D. C., & Serrano, J. L. (2013). Wanted: Reliable and valid measures for the science of cognitive behavioral therapy dissemination and implementation. *Clinical Psychology: Science and Practice, 20,* 181–194.

Slaikeu, K. A., Tulkin, S. R., & Speer, D. C. (1975). Process and outcome in the evaluation of telephone counseling referrals. *Journal of Consulting and Clinical Psychology, 43*(5), 700–707.

Sloman, S. (2014). Two systems of reasoning. In J. W. Sherman, B. Gawronski, & Y. Trope (Eds.), *Dual-process theories of the social mind* (pp. 69–79). New York: Guilford.

Smyth, J. M., & L'Abate, L. (2001). A meta-analytic evaluation of workbook effecti-veness in physical and mental health. In L. L'Abate (Ed.), *Distance writing and computer-assisted interventions in psychiatry and mental heath* (pp. 77–90). Westport: Ablex.

Sommerville, J. A., Upshaw, M. B., & Loucks, J. (2012). The nature of action representation in infancy. *Advances in Child Development and Behavior, 43,* 351–387.

Southam-Gerow, M. A., & McLeod, B. D. (2013). Advances in applying treatment integrity. Research for dissemination and implementation science: Introduction to special issue. *Clinical Psychology: Science and practice, 20,* 1–13.

Sperry, L. (Ed.). (2012). *Assessment of couples and families: Contemporary and cutting-edge strategies* (2nd ed.). New York: Routledge.

Spiegel, J. (1971). *Transactions: The interplay between individual, family, and society*. New York: Science House.

Spreen, O., & Schultz, R. W. (1966). Parameters of abstraction, meaningfulness and pronunciability for 329 nouns. *Journal of Verbal Learning & Verbal Behavior, 5*(5), 459–468.

Spring, B., & Neville, K. (2011). Evidence-based practice in clinical psychology. In D. H. Barlow (Ed.), *The Oxford handbook of clinical psychology* (pp. 128–150). New York: Oxford University Press.

Stanton, M., & Welsh, R. (2012). Systemic thinking in couple and family psychology: Research and practice. *Couple and Family Psychology: Research and Practice, 1,* 14–30.

Stanovich, K. E., West, R. F., & Toplak, M. (2014). Rationality, intelligence, and the defining features of Type 1 and Type 2 processing. In J. W. Sherman, B. Gawronski, & Y. Trope (Eds.), *Dual-process theories of the social mind* (pp. 80–91). New York: Guilford.

Strack, F., & Deutsch, R. (2014). The reflective-impulsive model. In J. W. Sherman, B. Gawronski, & Y. Trope (Eds.), *Dual-process theories of the social mind* (pp. 92–104). New York: Guilford.

Strecher, V. (2007). Internet methods for delivering behavioral and health-related interventions (eHealth). *Annual Review of Clinical Psychology, 3,* 53–76.

Tee, J., & Kazantzis, N. (2011). Collaborative empiricism in cognitive therapy: A definition and theory for the relationship construct. *Clinical Psychology: Science & Practice, 18,* 47–61.

Teo, T. (2012). Psychology is still a problematic science and the public knows it. *American Psychologist, 67,* 807–808.

Tompkins, M. A. (2013). Improving completion of therapeutic homework. In G. P. Koocher, J. C. Norcross, & B. A. Greene (Eds.), *Psychologist's desk reference* (3rd ed., pp. 246–251). New York: Oxford University Press.

Tracey, T. J. G., Wampold, B. E., Lichtenberg, J. W., & Goodyear, R. K. (2014). Expertise in psychotherapy: An elusive goal? *American Psychologist, 69,* 218–229.

Tryon, W. W. (2012). Emergence vs. reductionism. *American Psychologist, 67,* 806–87.

Tulving, E., & Thomson, D. M. (1973). Encoding specificity and retrieval processes in episodic memory. *Psychological Review, 80*(5), 352–373.

Urquiza, A. J., & Timmer, S. (2013). Parent-child interaction therapy. In J. D. Ford & C. A. Courtois (Eds.), *Treating complex traumatic stress disorders in children and adolescents: Scientific foundations and therapeutic models* (pp. 315–328). New York: Guilford.

van Dam, W. O., Rueschemeyer, S., & Bekkering, H. (2010). How specifically are action verbs represented in the neural motor system: An fMRI study. *Neuroimage, 53*(4), 1318–1325.

Van Emmerik, A. A. P., Reijntjes, A., & Kamphuis (2013). Writing therapy for post-traumatic stress: A meta-analysis. *Psychotherapy and Psychosomatics, 82,* 82–88.

VandenBos, G. R. (Ed.). (2007). *APA dictionary of psychology*. Washington, DC: American Psychological Association.

VandenBos, G. R., Meidenbauer, E., & Frank-McNeil, J. (Eds.). (2014). *Psychotherapy theories and techniques: A reader*. Washington, DC: American Psychological Association.

von Bertalanffy, L. (1950). The theory of open systems in physics and biology. *Science, 111,* 23–29.

von Bertalanffy, L. (1968). *General systems theory*. New York: Braziller.

Waldron, H. B., & Brody, J. (2010). Functional family therapy for adolescent substance use disorders. In J. Weisz & A. Kazdin (Eds.), *Evidence-based psychotherapies for children and adolescents* (2nd ed., pp. 401–415). New York: Guilford.

Wampold, B. E. (2001). *The great psychology debate: Models, methods, and findings*. Mahwah: Erlbaum.

Weeks, G. R., & L'Abate, L. (1982). *Paradoxical psychotherapy: Theory and practice with individuals, couples, and families*. New York: Brunner/Mazel.

Weiner, I. B. (2012). Education and training in clinical psychology: Correcting some mistaken beliefs. *Clinical Psychology: Science and Practice, 19,* 13–16.

Wesselmann D., & Shapiro, F. (2013). Eye-movement desensitization and reprocessing. In J. D. Ford & C. A. Courtois (Eds.), *Treating complex traumatic stress disorders in children and adolescents: Scientific foundations and therapeutic models* (pp. 203–223). New York: Guilford.

Whipple, J. L., & Lambert, M. J. (2011). Outcome measures for practice. *Annual Review of Clinical Psychology, 7,* 87–112.

Whitehead, A. N. (1936). *The concept of nature*. Cambridge: Cambridge University Press.

Wieland, S., & Silberg, J. (2013). Dissociation-focused therapy. In J. D. Ford & C. A. Courtois (Eds.), *Treating complex traumatic stress disorders in children and adolescents: Scientific foundations and therapeutic models* (pp. 162–183). New York: Guilford.

Williams, L., Edwards, T. M., Patterson, J. E., & Chamow, L. (2011). *Essential assessment skills for couple and family therapists*. New York: Guilford.

Woods, B. L. (2012). Biopsychosocial. In L. L'Abate (Ed.), *Paradigms in theory construction* (pp. 169–186). New York: Springer.

Yapko, M. D. (1988). *When living hurts: Directives for treating depression*. New York: Brunner/Mazel.

Yapko, M. D. (1994). *Suggestions of abuse: True and false memories of childhood sexual trauma*. New York: Simon & Schuster.

Yapko, M. D. (1997). *Breaking the patterns of depression*. New York: Random House Doubleday.

Yapko, M. D. (1999a). *Breaking the patterns of depression*. New York: Broadway.

Yapko, M. D. (1999b). *Hand-me-down blues: How to stop depression from spreading in families*. New York: San Martin's Griffin.

Yapko, M. D. (2009). *Depression is contagious: How the most common mood disorder is spreading around the world and how to stop it*. New York: Free Press.

Yapko, M. (2013). Workshop: Global or over-general thinking and mental health: The therapeutic merits of concreteness and specificity. Workshop 12, The Evolution of Psychotherapy, Anheim, CA. December 13.

Yarmey, A., & O'Neill, B. J. (1969). S-R and R-S paired-associate learning as a function of concreteness, imagery, specificity, and association value. *Journal of Psychology: Interdisciplinary and Applied, 71*(1), 95–109.

References

Williams, L., Edwards, T. M., Patterson, J. E., & Chamow, L. (2011). *Essential assessment skills for couple and family therapists*. New York: Guilford.

Index

L. L'Abate, *Concreteness and Specificity in Clinical Psychology*,
DOI 10.1007/978-3-319-13284-6

MIX
Papier aus verantwortungsvollen Quellen
Paper from responsible sources
FSC® C105338

If you have any concerns about our products,
you can contact us on
ProductSafety@springernature.com

In case Publisher is established outside the EU,
the EU authorized representative is:
Springer Nature Customer Service Center GmbH
Europaplatz 3, 69115 Heidelberg, Germany

Printed by Libri Plureos GmbH
in Hamburg, Germany